RACE TO HAWAII

THE 1927 DOLE AIR DERBY AND
THE THRILLING FIRST FLIGHTS THAT
OPENED THE PACIFIC

JASON RYAN

CHICAGO
REVIEW
PRESS

Copyright © 2018 by Jason Ryan
All rights reserved
Published by Chicago Review Press Incorporated
814 North Franklin Street
Chicago, Illinois 60610
ISBN 978-0-912777-25-2

Library of Congress Cataloging-in-Publication Data

Names: Ryan, Jason (Journalist), author.
Title: Race to Hawaii : the 1927 Dole Air Derby and the thrilling first flights
  that opened the Pacific / Jason Ryan.
Description: Chicago, Illinois : Chicago Review Press Incorporated, [2018] |
  Includes bibliographical references.
Identifiers: LCCN 2017057554 (print) | LCCN 2017058376 (ebook) | ISBN
  9780912777269 (adobe pdf) | ISBN 9780912777276 (epub) | ISBN 9780912777283
  (kindle) | ISBN 9780912777252 (cloth)
Subjects: LCSH: Transpacific flights—History—20th century. | Dole Air Race
  (1927) | Aeronautics—Hawaii—History—20th century. | Airplane
  racing—United States—History—20th century.
Classification: LCC TL531 (ebook) | LCC TL531 .R93 2018 (print) | DDC
  629.1309164/3—dc23
LC record available at https://lccn.loc.gov/2017057554

Typesetting: Nord Compo

Map illustrator: Chris Erichsen

Printed in the United States of America
5 4 3 2 1

For Iris and LouLou, my adventure girls.

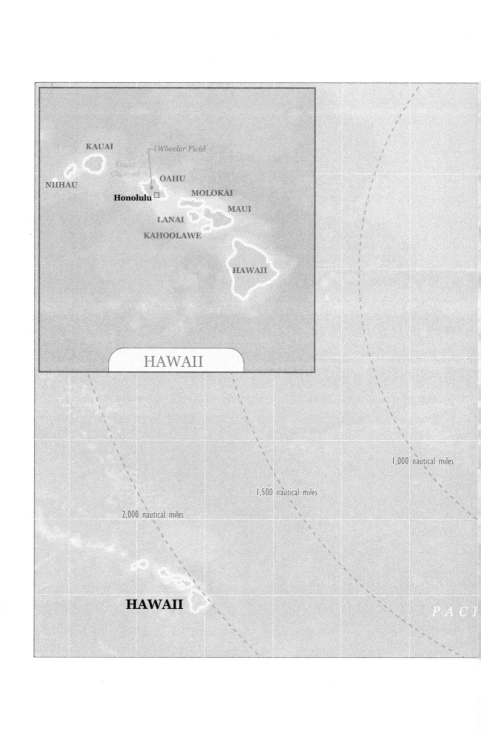

KAUAI |Wheeler Field

Kauai Channel OAHU

NIIHAU MOLOKAI

Honolulu □ MAUI

LANAI

KAHOOLAWE

HAWAII

HAWAII

1,000 nautical miles

1,500 nautical miles

2,000 nautical miles

HAWAII

PACI

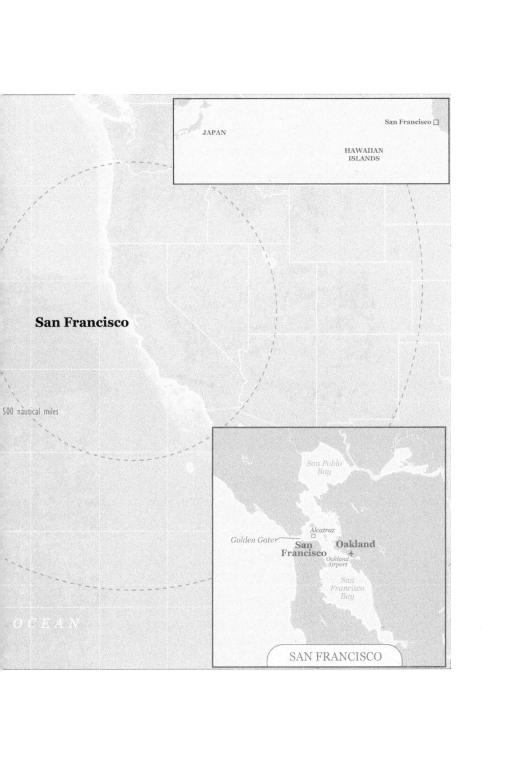

CONTENTS

AUTHOR'S NOTE

IT IS ONE OF the most isolated places on earth, surrounded in every direction by a thousand miles of deep, blue ocean. Hawaii is so small, and so remote, that the island chain escaped much of the world's notice until 1778, when a two-ship expedition led by English explorer Captain James Cook encountered the island of Kauai during a voyage across the Pacific Ocean. Cook and his Royal Navy crews aboard HMS *Resolution* and *Discovery* were on their way to search for the Northwest Passage, a sea channel through the Arctic that connected the Pacific and Atlantic Oceans. But before finding any frigid shortcut, Cook stumbled upon unknown tropics.

Cook, who would be killed by Hawaiians during a return trip to the islands a year later, was hardly the first to sail to Hawaii. Polynesian voyagers from the Marquesas Islands are believed to have settled parts of the Hawaiian Islands as early as AD 300 when they crossed the ocean in dug-out canoes. Then, about AD 1000, a larger wave of settlers sailed to Hawaii from Tahiti, expertly navigating their long journey by taking cues from the waves, sun, and stars. These were astounding, weeks-long journeys, with Tahitians sailing more than 2,500 miles across open water, battling adverse currents, winds, and storms, before reaching the Hawaiian Islands—mere pinpoints in the Pacific. After this amazing migration, few, if any, other foreigners are believed to have reached the shores of Hawaii until Cook arrived.

The Hawaiian archipelago is hardly minuscule, yet it can be challenging to find. Hawaii stretches 1,500 miles and contains approximately 137 islands, but the majority of these islands are tiny, and this tally includes numerous reefs, shoals, atolls, and large, craggy rocks. The most massive landforms exist at the southern tip of the archipelago, where eight major islands—Hawaii, Kahoolawe, Kauai, Lanai, Maui, Molokai, Niihau, and Oahu—constitute nearly all of Hawaii's landmass and are the only places ever populated by humans. But even these mountainous islands—which all lie within a three-hundred-mile stretch of the archipelago—are rendered puny when viewed within the entirety of the surrounding Pacific Ocean, which covers a third of the planet.

After Cook's visits to Hawaii, it wasn't long before other European sailors stopped at the islands for trade and respite. Within a few decades, American missionaries arrived to settle Hawaii, slowly wresting control and ownership of the islands away from native rulers. In 1900, seven years after white residents of Honolulu deposed the Hawaiian monarch, Hawaii officially became a US territory. More American visitors and settlers began arriving to the formerly isolated nation, with wealthy travelers able to cruise to the islands aboard swift ships powered by steam. A steam liner voyage from California to Hawaii took as little as a week at the beginning of the twentieth century, a far cry from the grueling, uncertain trips earlier travelers had undertaken by sail that dragged on for weeks or months. Still, even with a speedy steamship, Hawaii loomed far from any shore, out of reach of all but the most ambitious or affluent adventurers. To get a taste of Hawaii around the turn of the twentieth century, most people had to read the tantalizing accounts of popular writers like Jack London, Robert Louis Stevenson, or Mark Twain, each of whom spent months on the islands after long ocean voyages.

The airplane promised a way to hasten island travel, to deliver people to Hawaii within a day's time. Since its invention in 1903, the airplane had begun upending the world's transportation networks. Whether flying cross-country, over mountains, above a great lake, between metropolises, or even to one of the world's polar ice caps, there were few places an airplane could not travel. But the lone exception, the one place airplanes could not overtake all other types of transportation, were the world's oceans. There is nothing on earth so vast and empty as its oceans, and for many years no plane could carry enough fuel to cross one.

I made my first trip to Hawaii in the spring of 2013, flying aboard a jet from Seattle to Honolulu as part of a research trip for a previous book about Hawaiian gangsters. I recall few significant memories of the flight, which I suppose I should consider a good thing. Like many modern fliers, I have an expectation (a hope, really) that I will land safely at my destination. Hence, my most memorable flights tend to be the ones where I momentarily feared for my life, when I've fretted over severe turbulence, poor weather, a windy approach, or any other unpleasantness while airborne.

Not only was my flight to Hawaii safe, one might say it was also boring. Routine. Commonplace. I was one of about eight million people to fly to Hawaii that year. The only details that I can pull from my memory are of reading an airline magazine article about the wiliwili tree, one of Hawaii's many exotic plants, and of moving to a window seat toward the end of the flight so I could spy Oahu before we landed. I've always enjoyed seeing new landscapes from the vantage point of an airplane window, and it was no different in the case of Oahu. I switched my airplane seat because I was eager to see the Paradise of the Pacific as soon as possible, to confirm with my own senses Hawaii's vaunted beauty, even if from a bird's-eye view. Staring down at the volcanic cone of Diamond Head at the southern tip of Oahu, the islands did indeed seem gorgeous. I was eager to plant my feet on Hawaiian soil.

For some others who flew to Hawaii, the sight of any of the major islands did not inspire wonder so much as relief. Once upon a time, flying to Hawaii was not routine or commonplace, and certainly not boring. When aviators attempted the first flights to Hawaii in the 1920s, the Hawaiian Islands were not just a destination but salvation. After taking off from California and flying for twenty-six hours straight, pilots low on both fuel and stamina were desperate to land.

I didn't reflect on the pioneering flights to Hawaii during my own six-hour hop to Honolulu from Seattle. I had never enjoyed a particular fascination with aviation, even as a boy, generally considering the airplane as a means to an end. I had also come to more or less dislike flying as an adult, what with the aggravations of tightened security, cramped seats, and other aviation-related hassles that seem to have proliferated in the last few decades I've been alive. Maybe I've just gotten grumpier as I've aged; in any case, when the flight is over, I walk briskly off the Jetway.

About two years ago, I found myself with a few hours to spare one afternoon in Washington, DC, where I had just arrived by train to Union Station. I decided to walk to the Capitol and then on to the nearby Smithsonian National Air and Space Museum, which contained a new exhibit that intrigued me: *Hawaii by Air*. It had been years since my visit to Hawaii, but the Aloha State held a special place in my heart. En route to the exhibit, I looked forward to learning more about Pan American Airways' Clipper ships, the giant seaplanes of the 1930s that provided luxurious in-flight accommodations. Given that modern airlines had suspended basic meal and snack service in recent years, I found it hard to believe people once flew to Hawaii on a plane containing individual sleeping quarters and a dining room featuring white linen, silver, and china.

But while walking through the museum, I soon focused on another part of the exhibit: details of the precarious, pioneering flights to Hawaii. The Smithsonian exhibit made me consider that the initial flights to Hawaii were nearly as magnificent as the earliest ocean voyages to the islands. Polynesian voyagers and American aviators alike braved the big, blue ocean in fragile vehicles in search of mere specks of land among the sprawling Pacific. The aviators, of course, enjoyed many technological advantages unavailable to ancient Polynesian explorers. But the science of aviation was so new, and aviation equipment so unreliable, that the first fliers to Hawaii were forced to rely on some of the same time-tested navigational techniques the Polynesians used to locate Hawaii.

In the following pages, I chronicle the pioneering flights to Hawaii, which all occurred in 1925 and 1927. Though few people today know of them, the daring trips were front-page news at the time, often mentioned in the same breath as Charles Lindbergh's solo nonstop flight across the Atlantic Ocean in May 1927—a much-heralded feat that made the twenty-five-year-old American airmail pilot a worldwide celebrity. The flights to Hawaii embody the exhilaration associated with the golden age of aviation, the period between world wars when a burgeoning aviation industry featured boundless energy and innovation, fearless pilots, and bold, and sometimes impractical, airplane designs. The sky was the limit.

Planes could fly and land almost anywhere during this golden age, as few regulations existed to govern pilots and their flight paths, and airports were often nothing more than fields outside of towns. Planes were accessible to the public, able to be touched and closely inspected, and not isolated on runways and tucked away behind fences and other security perimeters. Many of the era's planes featured open cockpits, allowing the aviators to feel the wind rip through their hair. Flight during the golden age of aviation was visceral, truly akin to what a bird experiences, and nothing like the common experience of air travel today, in which passengers are crammed into planes, generally secluded from the natural environment surrounding them, and harried by travel regulations and security procedures.

Just as a handful of noteworthy islands compose Hawaii, a handful of noteworthy airplane flights compose this book. I tell the story of the pioneering flights to Hawaii in three parts. First is a tale of incredible resourcefulness and endurance, when the US Navy made the first attempt to fly to Hawaii in three flying boats. Next comes a flight by the US Army, whose careful planning, superior equipment, and flying professionalism stood in stark contrast to the hasty preparations made by a rival, civilian pilot determined to take off at the same time and race the military to Hawaii. Finally, the book closes with an account of the Dole Air Race, when pilots and navigators in eight civilian airplanes took off in succession, each aiming to reach Hawaii first and collect a large cash prize. This chaotic competition, pitting attractive and affable aviators against each other in a mad dash to a tropical paradise, thrilled and saddened the country.

All these airplanes departed from San Francisco Bay on a 2,400-mile flight path—essentially the same distance the Tahitians traveled centuries earlier—but not every plane reached Hawaii. When these gutsy fliers embarked across the Pacific, they confronted a seascape that offered nothing but mile after mile of rippling waves, loneliness, and thick fog. Beyond monotony and poor visibility, these pilots also contended with drowsiness, fatigue, vertigo, hunger, and nervousness, not to mention the failure of compasses, engines, and other crucial equipment.

Some aviators who set forth for Hawaii won great public acclaim; others suffered violent deaths. The pioneering fliers to Hawaii—an eclectic lot that included military men, barnstormers, a Hollywood stunt pilot, a Wall Street bond salesman, and a schoolteacher—provide a vivid glimpse of the exuberance and optimism present in the Roaring Twenties. Though their personalities and flying proficiencies varied, these aviators were bonded by their common destination and the knowledge that no matter how thorough their preparations, the flight to Hawaii was filled with tremendous risk.

People have recognized the danger of taking to the air for ages, a hazard perhaps best illustrated by the ancient Greek myth of Icarus, whose homemade wings of wax and feathers melted when he ignored his father's caution and dared fly too close to the sun, sending him plunging to the sea. The first brave souls flying to Hawaii possibly felt their plight was eerily similar to that of Icarus. The aviators' flight plans required them to fly away from California, into a setting sun, on wooden wings wrapped in fabric, while assorted cynics warned of the dangers of the trip. Still these pilots and crew fueled up their planes, pointed them west, and courageously took off above the Pacific. In a day's time they expected to see Hawaii, or else wave after wave after wave.

PART I

THE NAVY'S
PN-9 NO. 1

SAN FRANCISCO SEEMED A ghost town. The city's office buildings were empty, its shops devoid of customers and clerks. Almost anyone attending to business the Monday morning of August 31, 1925, was doing so hurriedly, eager to join neighbors along the waterfront or on rooftops across the city. Few people were willing to miss the spectacle of a lifetime: the takeoff of two navy flying boats en route to the faraway paradise of Hawaii.

Thrilled by the prospect of air travel across the massive Pacific, residents waited eagerly for the aircraft to begin their daring journey. Straining their eyes across the bay, the crowd watched to see at any moment the seaplanes slowly lift from the water and turn west toward new horizons. Every vantage point had been claimed. Spectators and automobiles blackened the slopes of Telegraph Hill along the eastern, bay side of the San Francisco peninsula. At the western end of the city, atop Sutro Heights overlooking the Pacific Ocean and Golden Gate, it was much of the same. In between, through the Presidio, along every wharf and cove, atop a long seawall and throughout the Marina District, people crowded together to catch a glimpse of the flying boats.

Across the Golden Gate the crowds proved just as thick. The entire population of Marin County was said to have gathered on the hills above Lime Point, as well as quite a few people who drove in from nearby Sonoma Valley. Closest to the action was the audience on the bay itself, those lucky enough to squeeze onto assorted watercraft that stalked and circled the floating planes. The navy and coast guard patrolled the bay furiously to keep the curious a safe distance

1

from the transpacific fliers, with Eagle boats, sub chasers, and cutters shooing away anyone who ventured too close.

The excitement felt across San Francisco and its outskirts penetrated the pair of aircraft bobbing in the bay. The flying boats were more or less airplanes devoid of landing gear and whose fuselages could float. When the first of these machines was towed into San Francisco Bay in preparation for takeoff, chief machinist's mate Skiles Pope compared it to "leading a racehorse out on the track." His fellow crewman aboard the flying boat, aviation machinist's mate William M. Bowlin, was similarly moved by the hoopla concerning the historic journey and the potential consequences, both good and bad, of such a bold flight. That morning, after years of military service, the twenty-six-year-old finally mailed home to Indiana his government-provided life insurance policy.

Less impressed by the hubbub was Commander John Rodgers. On the eve of the biggest flight of his career, the forty-four-year-old career navy officer was conspicuously silent and determined. While other officers joked and smiled all morning, Rodgers was taciturn, especially with the many journalists hounding the two navy flying crews. Any talking, the old salt knew, should come later, after he and his fellow officers and sailors accomplished their mission and reached the Hawaiian capital, Honolulu, on the island of Oahu. Then he'd be more than happy to boast about becoming the first men to fly an airplane to Hawaii. Until then, there remained much work to do. The pride of the navy was at stake, and the world was watching.

The airplane had been invented just twenty-one years earlier, when brothers Wilbur and Orville Wright launched an aircraft of their own design and manufacture from the sand dunes of Kitty Hawk, North Carolina, on December 17, 1903. The brothers' longest flight that day lasted just 59 seconds and traversed 852 feet, but it signaled a new dawn of aviation and inspired countless adventurers. In the next two decades bold pilots blazed air routes across the globe, flying clear across the English Channel, the continental United States, the Mediterranean Sea, and the Atlantic Ocean. By 1925, however, no one had tried to cross the Pacific. That would change this afternoon.

Rodgers spent the morning preparing his aircraft for takeoff, adjusting the flying boat based on observations made during a final test flight the day before. He took stock of the weather, leaning out from a hatch atop the plane and gazing toward downtown San Francisco, just a few miles away. The conditions were ideal for takeoff, with light wind, calm water, and, mercifully, no fog.

Navy ships cruising the Pacific radioed reports of good weather, too. These reports, however, did not particularly encourage Rodgers. Should the weather be too calm, he knew, his plane would not fully benefit from the typical trade winds that blew across the ocean. The navy was counting on a favorable tailwind to help carry their aircraft across the water. Weather experts assured the fliers they'd encounter the trade winds soon after leaving the California coast.

As morning stretched into early afternoon, the navy fliers ate an early dinner on board their aircraft—the last decent meal they'd receive before reaching Honolulu. They read a telegram from Washington, DC, learning secretary of the navy Curtis Wilbur wished them "every success." The fliers then received a distinguished guest, Rear Admiral William A. Moffett, chief of the navy's Bureau of Aeronautics. Arriving by motorboat, the rear admiral wished the men luck and handed Rodgers two commemorative letters for overseas delivery to Hawaii.

Nicknamed the "Air Admiral" for his strong support of military aviation, Moffett had just arrived to San Francisco via steamship from Hawaii. While on the islands, Moffett had inspected the navy's air station at Pearl Harbor and taken a tour of Oahu by air. Before leaving, Moffett promised residents in Honolulu that regular airmail and air passenger service would soon be established between Hawaii and coastal California. This revolution in the skies, he said, would begin with the navy's pioneering flights across the Pacific. "The proposed airplane flight from San Francisco to Honolulu this month is the most important event in naval aviation since the World War," proclaimed Moffett. "The flight means much to Honolulu, as well as the mainland, in peacetime as well as in war. We know it can be done—and if the planes fail in this effort—another attempt will be made very soon." Not only planes but also airships. Moffett informed the Honolulu crowd that the navy planned to have one of its dirigibles float over the Pacific to Honolulu within two months.

Part of Moffett's confidence stemmed from the fact that a navy flying boat had been the first aircraft to cross the Atlantic Ocean six years earlier. During that mission, Lieutenant Commander Albert Read and a crew of five piloted the NC-4 across the ocean in hopscotch fashion. Leaving New York City on May 8, 1919, the flying boat took nineteen days to cross the Atlantic, making essential stops for repairs and fuel in Massachusetts, Nova Scotia, Newfoundland, and the Azores before finally reaching Lisbon, Portugal, then continuing on to England. Navy ships were stationed at intervals along the overseas route to provide rescue and repair services in the event of an emergency ocean landing or crash.

Despite the protracted nature of the trip, the flight was a milestone for aviation. But in a sign of how quickly this new industry was evolving, the navy's accomplishment was eclipsed weeks later. On June 14, 1919, British aviators John Alcock and Arthur Whitten Brown crossed the Atlantic Ocean by traveling nonstop in a small Vickers Vimy biplane from Newfoundland to Ireland. Though their flight was not perfect—Alcock and Brown crash-landed in an Irish bog soon after crossing over terra firma—the men did fly from North America to Europe without any stops or detours. The world rejoiced at Alcock and Brown's triumph, and King George V knighted the men, who both survived their crash landing.

Five years later, in 1924, it was the US Army's turn to crow, as two of its pontoon-fitted biplanes made the first successful flights around the world. Starting in Seattle, four Douglas World Cruisers operated by the Army Air Service headed west to Alaska, then Asia, then the Middle East and Europe before crossing the Atlantic and traversing the United States. The trip took a total of 175 days and covered more than twenty-seven thousand miles across twenty-one countries. It also featured about fifty-seven stops for repairs, refueling, and rest. But no matter the many stops, or the fact that two of the army planes did not finish the mission, the flights were a major coup for the United States, who bested the rest of the world and earned the distinction of being the first country to have a plane circle the globe.

Now the US Navy was plotting to steal back the glory, eager to one-up the army and cross the Pacific, or, to be precise, half the Pacific. Unlike the aforementioned aviators, who skirted open water in favor of routes that hugged coasts and minimized the distance spent flying across channels, the navy did not plan for its flying boats to touch down again until reaching Oahu. In other words, while the army's round-the-world flights were broken into dozens of legs, or hops, that averaged 483 miles, the navy was attempting to make a single nonstop leap over open ocean. And though the navy and newspapermen were fond of calling this flight the "Hawaiian Hop," their alliterative phrasing understated the rigors of the air voyage.

The navy had been planning its West Coast–Hawaii Flight for at least three years, though it was still uncertain whether to have its flying boats depart from bays outside San Diego or San Francisco. While San Francisco was closer to Hawaii by two hundred miles, some navy experts argued that winds were generally more favorable if traveling from San Diego, which could result in a shorter flight despite the longer distance. To make the best decision, Commander Rodgers decided to scout both locations in the final weeks before his flight. First he surveyed San Diego, where he and other navy fliers had arrived in late summer to outfit their planes and train for the transpacific flight. Then Rodgers flew north to San Francisco, where he and his crew were given a warm reception and invitations to many parties. Local officials lobbied him incessantly, eager to secure San Francisco as the hop-off point. Rodgers didn't mind the attention. "Upon our arrival, much to our surprise, we were met by the mayor of the city and the public-spirited citizens of San Francisco . . . a brigade of newspaper men and photographers," he wrote. "This turnout showed me for the first time the amount of interest that was being taken in the flight by the people of the United States."

Polite as Rodgers was listening to these boosters, their flattery did not sway the commander as he assessed the merits of each city and considered the needs of his aircraft. Flying boats required long stretches of water to take off, especially if loaded heavily with fuel and emergency equipment, as they certainly would be on this long-distance flight. It helps if this stretch of water is shallow, as this would "form a firmer roadbed so to speak" and more quickly enable lift, explained Rodgers. It also helps to take off while running with the tide but into the wind. Rodgers discovered that all these conditions could be met on San Pablo Bay, the northern part of San Francisco Bay. Dismissing fears of fog near the Golden Gate as overblown and "bugaboo," Rodgers recommended to his navy superiors that the flights should leave from San Francisco. The navy concurred.

Three navy flying boats were originally slated to attempt the Hawaiian Hop, each of them twin-engine biplanes. One, PB-1, was made in Seattle by the ten-year-old aircraft manufacturer Boeing (*P* standing for *Patrol*, *B* for *Boeing*). The other two planes were nearly identical flying boats named PN-9 No. 1 and PN-9 No. 3, each produced at the Naval Aircraft Factory in Philadelphia (*P* for *Patrol*, *N* for *Navy*). Pilots and crews from the navy's aircraft squadron scouting fleet were chosen to make the flight. This included Rodgers, who was named flight unit commander, in charge of all three airplanes from his position in the flagship, PN-9 No. 1.

The PN-9 was the navy's most modern version of the flying boat, valued for its reliable performance. In May 1925, three months before the navy planned to take off for Hawaii, navy pilots set an endurance record for this type of flying boat by flying PN-9 No. 1 for more than twenty-eight hours above Philadelphia before landing as the aircraft's fuel supply neared exhaustion. The flight was certainly a testament to the plane's capabilities, though the distance traveled while circling Philadelphia for twenty-eight hours was just barely enough to reach Hawaii from California, so long as pilots encountered no headwind.

The PN-9 was big, heavy, and relatively slow, capable of cruising at an average speed of seventy miles per hour. Its metal fuselage stretched forty-nine feet from nose to tail and was melded to a wide, all-metal boat hull that made the craft buoyant. This was the first navy flying boat to replace a wooden hull with metal. Specifically, the PN-9 hull was made of duralumin, an aluminum-copper alloy that was stronger and lighter than wood. The use of such aluminum sheathing would soon become commonplace in aircraft manufacturing.

Atop the PN-9 were affixed two sets of seemingly oversized wings that measured close to seventy feet long and nine feet wide. Each was made of wooden ribs covered in fabric and painted with aircraft dope. Under each end of the bottom wing was a pontoon to help stabilize the flying boat in the water.

Weighing twenty thousand pounds fully loaded, the sturdy, supersized flying boat was deemed a "leviathan of air and sea" by one newsreel. To lift the seaplane into the air, the navy installed two 500-horsepower Packard engines between the upper and lower wings, each with a wooden propeller measuring thirteen feet in diameter. While much of the flying boat's exterior was aluminum and gray in appearance, the tops of both PN-9s' wings were painted yellow to help searchers find the aircraft in case of an ocean landing. The flagship of the West Coast–Hawaii Flight, PN-9 No. 1 also had a bright yellow bow. All in all, said Rodgers, the PN-9 was "the best flying boat ever gotten out."

The three navy flying boats were originally expected in San Francisco on August 22, 1925, one week before the historic flight was to commence. None arrived as scheduled. The PN-9s remained in San Diego suffering mechanical issues, including radiators that vibrated excessively. Rodgers, his crew, and a slew of navy mechanics had been laboring furiously for weeks to prepare the planes. Administrative tasks and training needs so overwhelmed Rodgers and his crew that the commander persuaded his superior, Captain Stanford E. Moses, to come and help provide relief.

"The whole outfit was working like trojans both day and night," wrote Rodgers. "Sheaves of radios were sent and received. Mail was sky high, filled with matters of importance and tons of letters from curio collectors desiring that they be carried to Hawaii in the seaplanes."

After a short delay, the mechanical problems were fixed and the PN-9s departed north from San Diego. An oil leak in PN-9 No. 1, however, soon forced that plane down in Los Angeles for additional repairs. PN-9 No. 3 flew successfully to the army's Crissy Field in San Francisco, which featured seaplane facilities along the bay, right at the foot of the cliffs of the Presidio. Meanwhile, the PB-1 made by Boeing experienced troubles of its own traveling to San Francisco and was forced to make an emergency landing soon after taking off from Seattle. On account of ongoing mechanical problems, the new airplane was in danger of being scratched from the mission.

These mechanical mishaps inspired little worry among the navy, despite occurring on the eve of a flight during which there would be no place to put down for repairs save the ocean. Beyond its faith in its mechanics to make the required fixes before takeoff, the navy's bullishness stemmed from its plan to station ships every two hundred miles along the flight route, as it had done similarly six years earlier when sending the first flying boat across the Atlantic. These dozen or so guard vessels, strung out across half the Pacific, would serve as navigational guideposts for the aviators, provide continuous radio communication to the plane crews, and, if needed, render aid to any downed plane, whether its crew was in need of fuel, spare parts, or rescue. While the guard vessels could not help guarantee a nonstop flight would indeed be made to Hawaii, the ships did significantly insure against any loss of life in the attempt.

But so long as the navy fliers encountered friendly winds, Rodgers and his fellow aviators did not plan to rendezvous with any of these ships. Still, during a briefing a day before the transpacific flight, the commander acknowledged the chance of falling short should the weather not cooperate. So long as the navy planes encountered an offshore tailwind, said Rodgers, their fuel supplies would last all the way to Hawaii. But if the planes were forced to buck a headwind instead, he could offer no similar guarantee.

Even though the navy intended for its planes to land in Pearl Harbor alongside Oahu, the mission's 2,400-mile flight path, or base course, traced southwest from San Francisco to the island of Maui, one hundred miles south of Oahu and the midpoint of the chain of major Hawaiian Islands. It was a sound strategy to aim for the center of Hawaii, as even a relatively small navigation error could doom the transpacific flight. Shifting winds, severe storms, inattention, miscalculations by the navigator—there were any number of reasons a plane might deviate from its course. If this navigational error was greater than three degrees from the start of the course, a plane's crew would not even spy Hawaii's distant shores, and instead obliviously pass to the north or south of the islands, where there is nothing but the open, sloshing ocean—an ocean that would coldly receive the plane when the aircraft exhausted its fuel.

The flying crews wanted to avoid an ocean landing, especially on the vast Pacific. The Pacific is the world's largest ocean, its nearly sixty-four million square miles accounting for approximately half the world's surface water. It stretches from pole to pole and is larger than all of the land on earth combined. The Pacific is the deepest of the world's oceans and contains the deepest point on earth, the Mariana Trench, which plunges nearly seven miles beneath the waves. As countless mariners have discovered over the course of human history, it is easy to become lost within the Pacific.

The ocean's name is a misnomer. The immense body of water is in fact frequently violent and impossible to pacify. Each summer it spawns typhoons that batter Asia. Three-quarters of the world's volcanoes lie in a rough semicircle around the Pacific, including those whose cones extend above the surface to form the Hawaiian Islands. The bulk of the world's seismic activity—about 90 percent of the earthquakes on earth—occur within this underwater Ring of Fire.

Yet so long as the planes spotted each guard ship in succession, navy planners believed, the Pacific could be crossed in relative safety. The planes would be charting their own course for Hawaii, too, relying primarily on dead reckoning, which is an estimation of location based on the planes' speed and direction. To confirm their position, the fliers planned to also navigate by the stars and use radio bearings transmitted from guard vessels.

The airplane crews expected to encounter a guard vessel every two hours, with the navy ships under order to produce heavy smoke in their engine rooms when planes were scheduled to pass overhead during daytime. For ships that would be passed at night, the navy instructed their crews to shine a searchlight into the sky or fire rockets into the air. After all three navy planes had passed, a guard vessel was expected to steam at high speed after them in case of emergency, at least until the planes reached the next station. The navy was confident the three flying boats would travel in a pack, within sight of each other the entire journey.

The command of the Pacific fleet put forth great effort and much communication to establish this naval lifeline to Hawaii. Still, at least one commander, W. R. Van Auken of the aircraft tender USS *Aroostook*, had reservations about the plan. In a memo to Moses, the land-based commander of the flight project, Van Auken sketched a number of possible emergency scenarios, asking in each case if his ship should attempt to rescue a downed plane or stay put to aid the incoming planes that remained in the air. These concerns, Van Auken said, were prompted by the difficult circumstances encountered during previous searches at sea for downed airplanes.

"During the past year while the *Aroostook* has been tending planes on the West Coast and in Hawaii, there have been many instances of poor or no radio communication from planes, inaccurate navigation position given or completely unforeseen casualties, in which fortunately there were no lives lost," Van Auken wrote on July 25, 1925. "Considering the possible situations which may arise in this long flight . . . the Commanding Officer feels a great responsibility which the *Aroostook* bears as the aviation ship and lane guard tender at the western end of the Hawaii flight."

Three days later Moses responded somewhat dismissively to Van Auken's concerns. In a reply addressed to Van Auken and each of the other commanders of the guard vessels, Moses indicated that proper attention to previous orders would answer most of Van Auken's queries. "No reason exists why planes and plane guard ships cannot navigate accurately," wrote Moses. "Careful compliance in all instructions is essential."

Indeed, Rodgers was dependent on thousands of his fellow officers and sailors to help make the flights a success. Rodgers trusted mechanics to put the planes in top working order, weather analysts to make reliable forecasts and predictions regarding wind currents and precipitation across the Pacific, technicians to fine-tune the plane's radio and navigation equipment, sailors to man posts on each guard vessel across the Pacific, officers to implement the extensive planning for the flight, and also navy physicians, who encouraged the crew to drink water and, in case of drowsiness or cramping, to rub themselves vigorously. Most of all, Rodgers relied on the crew of four accompanying him to Hawaii within PN-9 No. 1.

Each member of the crew was tasked with critical work aboard the flying boat. For Pope, a thirty-year-old Tennessean, and Bowlin, an amiable youngster from Indiana, engine maintenance occupied their time. The chief machinist and his mate were charged with monitoring and maintaining the two power plants propelling the plane across the Pacific, as well as the flying boat's fuel supply. These chores demanded close attention, as Pope and Bowlin were expected to continually adjust the source of the engines' fuel supply, strategically switching between the ten fuel tanks located within the plane to keep an even trim.

Pope and Bowlin were also qualified pilots, able to relieve the plane's chief pilot, Lieutenant Byron J. Connell. The thirty-one-year-old from Pennsylvania had studied engineering in college before joining the navy and becoming an aviator. After serving in the Panama Canal Zone as a flight squadron commander, the navy sent him back to school for training in aeronautical engineering at the Massachusetts Institute of Technology. Soon after graduation in 1924, the navy tapped Connell to serve as second in command aboard PN-9 No. 1.

Rounding out the crew was chief radio operator Otis Gilbert Stantz, another twenty-six-year-old Hoosier and, married with two children, the only family man of the bunch. Formerly a radio instructor within the navy's aviation ground school, Stantz manned the radio sets aboard PN-9 No. 1, responsible for communicating with the guard vessels bobbing on the ocean below. Rodgers was proud of his crew, observing that none of the men had to be persuaded to attempt the dangerous trip. In fact, Rodgers noted, pilots during this early era of aviation had to constantly be dissuaded from attempting dangerous stunts. While a certain degree of recklessness was necessary for a pilot—how else to muster the courage to attempt the first parachute jump, loop through the sky, fly over huge bodies of water, or, indeed, to step into a fragile flying machine at all and take to the air—aviation was not well served by the needless deaths of accomplished and promising young aviators. Rodgers, perhaps reflecting on his own experience as a sometimes reckless amateur flier, lamented the difficulty of urging restraint to young pilots whose instincts and ambitions goaded them to continually fly higher, farther, and faster. "The chief concern and hardest duty of the seniors in the service is to hold young men and make them comply with safety precautions, which are carefully edited and widely published throughout the aviation service," said the veteran navy officer.

From the perspective of the navy brass, there was no one better suited to lead the pioneering adventure to Hawaii than Commander John Rodgers. His name alone spoke volumes. As long as there had been a US Navy, there had been a John Rodgers prominently among its ranks. The tradition began in 1798, during the formal establishment of the US Department of the Navy, when President John Adams appointed Rodgers's great-grandfather and namesake, John Rodgers, a second lieutenant aboard the frigate *Constellation*. It was the beginning of a brilliant career for Rodgers, who became one of the navy's great officers and patriarch of one of the navy's most impressive families. During his naval service, Rodgers fought Barbary pirates, commanded the New York flotilla, and became a national hero during the War of 1812, where he continued to fight in one battle despite a cannon fracturing his leg. "He was to me the complete impersonation of my ideal of the perfect naval commander," US senator Thomas Hart Benton of Missouri wrote of Rodgers.

When not at sea, Rodgers was partial to spending time at Sion Hill, a family estate situated upon a crest of rolling pastureland, overlooking the town of Havre de Grace, Maryland, and the mouth of the Susquehanna River, where it flowed into Chesapeake Bay. Sion Hill began construction in 1797 as a boys' academy, but in 1806, when Rodgers came to own the property through marriage, the two-story brick building with commanding views was transformed into a home. Sion Hill would remain in the Rodgers family for at least two centuries.

It was at Sion Hill that the next John Rodgers was born in 1812. This John Rodgers followed directly in his father's footsteps, serving at age sixteen aboard *Constellation* as he began a fifty-four-year career in the navy that culminated with the rank of rear admiral. In the decades to come, he surveyed much of the world, fought in the Second Seminole War, and captured the ironclad Confederate warship *Atlanta* during the US Civil War. President Abraham Lincoln recognized Rodgers's "gallantry . . . zeal and bravery" in 1863 by gifting him a silver service that was placed at Sion Hill.

The next John Rodgers, born in 1848, was a nephew of the rear admiral, as well as a grandson of another naval hero, Commodore Matthew Perry, who championed the use of steamships in the navy and who famously established diplomatic relations with Japan in the 1850s through a series of gunboat expeditions to the isolationist island nation. Perry's older brother, Oliver Hazard Perry, was also a stalwart of the navy, lionized as the "Hero of Lake Erie" for his defeat of a British naval squadron during the War of 1812, in which Perry fought with a battle flag that implored, "Don't Give Up the Ship." "We have met the enemy," Perry famously wrote after the Battle of Lake Erie, "and they are ours."

The John Augustus Rodgers partly descended from the Perry family also became a rear admiral in the US Navy, just as four other Rodgers men had since 1900. And it was his son, also John Rodgers, born January 15, 1881, in Washington, DC, who further burnished the naval legacies of the Rodgers and Perry families through his military exploits. Unlike his illustrious forebears, however, the latest John Rodgers's most notable successes occurred above the ocean in a plane, not atop the water in a ship.

Naval aviator John Rodgers's career began in 1898, when he served aboard the cruiser *Columbia* in the Caribbean Sea during the short-lived Spanish-American War. A year later, upon the appointment of President William McKinley, John Rodgers entered the US Naval Academy, where he played football. He graduated four years later in 1903—the same year Wilbur and Orville Wright successfully made the first powered flight in an airplane at Kitty Hawk. Rodgers distinguished himself quickly upon reentering active duty as an officer. As Commander H. Osterhaus of the cruiser *Cincinnati* wrote in a 1905 personnel report, "Midshipman Rodgers gives promise of becoming a most excellent officer. He is zealous and ambitious, always ready for any duty. . . . Of his character I cannot speak too highly."

Rodgers and his family suffered tragedy a few years later when Rodgers's younger brother Alexander went missing in 1910 while hiking through Alaska. John and his father both traveled fruitlessly to Alaska in search of the twenty-one-year-old. Alexander's disappearance, however, did not discourage Rodgers from seeking adventure just as bold and dangerous.

Rodgers began his own romance with the phenomenon of flight in 1911 when he experimented with man-carrying observation kites aboard the armored cruiser USS *Pennsylvania*. In one test Lieutenant Rodgers attached himself to a string of a dozen or so high-flying kites and rose more than four hundred feet into the air, and possibly as high as one thousand feet. As *Pennsylvania* steamed ahead at twelve knots and sailors on deck tightly gripped the kite tether, Rodgers floated high above the stern as part of a "human kite tail," taking photographs and signaling his observations to the crew below.

Commander John Rodgers, circa 1920, member of a storied American military family. For much of the history of the US Navy, there had been a John Rodgers prominently among its officer ranks. *NH 75882, courtesy of Naval History and Heritage Command*

Despite an eagerness to attempt high-flying stunts, Rodgers did not fit the typical mold of the wild-eyed, excited, and outlandish daredevil. The thrills he experienced affected him subtly, as he was slow-spoken and seldom smiled, though he was neither unintelligent nor humorless. In portraits he appears serene and confident. Writers have observed the strong aspects of his features, describing a hawk-like nose, constantly pursed lips, and iron jaw. Rodgers was blue-eyed and sandy-haired, possessing a tall, thin figure.

His flight by kite was not the only aerial highlight aboard the *Pennsylvania* at that time. Two weeks earlier, Rodgers and his fellow crew facilitated the first landing of a plane on a ship when Eugene Ely, whose body was wrapped in bicycle inner tubes and whose head was encased in a football helmet, landed a Curtiss biplane on the deck of the *Pennsylvania* as the cruiser lay anchored in San Francisco Bay.

But the best was yet to come for Rodgers, who six months later in Dayton, Ohio, learned from members of the Wright Company how to fly an airplane. During this training Rodgers called on the company's cofounder, and inventor of the airplane, Orville Wright. The young naval officer was sufficiently impressed by the one-time bicycle maker, discovering him to be a "considerable surprise."

"He showed none of the earmarks of a bicycle repair man," said Rodgers. "On the contrary, he appeared to be exactly what he is, a well-educated engineer, unassuming but self-reliant, caring more for his own opinion of himself than for the opinion of others on that subject."

Rodgers dined with Orville at the modest Wright family home, joined by Orville's father and sister, though brother Wilbur was away in Europe. He found the entire Wright clan enchanting and intelligent, later expressing great admiration for the brothers' accomplishments: "Young America . . . will do well to consider the character of the Wright brothers. These men sought to reach a definite objective. They set about it quietly and independently, relying upon themselves alone. Their unparalleled success affected them not at all, and after receiving the plaudits of the world, they went home, took off their coats and returned quietly to their work where they had left off."

After becoming acquainted with Orville Wright and training to become a pilot in Dayton, Rodgers was named Naval Aviator No. 2. There was just one problem with his new position: the navy had no plane for him to fly. A few flying machines, however, were on order from the Wrights and rival airplane maker Glenn Curtiss. When a Wright biplane did arrive later that year, Rodgers flew the aircraft from the Naval Academy in Annapolis, Maryland, to the nation's capital, circling the Washington Monument a few times before landing near the White House. On another celebrated outing, he flew to Sion Hill in Maryland, surprising his parents and remaining brother, Robert.

About this same time, Rodgers took a leave of absence from the navy to barnstorm across the country with his partially deaf cousin, Calbraith "Cal" Perry Rodgers, whom he had persuaded to also take flying lessons from Orville Wright. Believing the navy might frown on him taking to the air out of uniform, John grounded himself and served as his cousin's mechanic as they entertained crowds with an airplane. He also helped plan his cousin's attempt to fly the plane *Vin Fiz* across the country in a bid to win the Hearst Prize for the first transcontinental flight.

True to its grape soft drink–inspired name, *Vin Fiz* fizzled, suffering five major crashes, many hard landings, and plenty of mechanical problems after heading west from New York in September of 1911. John followed his heavily bandaged cousin by train, helping him rebuild the plane time and time again as Cal made seventy stops in his quest to reach the West Coast. Finally, after forty-nine days, and to great public acclaim, *Vin Fiz* reached the coast of California, though Cal Rodgers was nineteen days too late to claim a prize from newspaper publisher William Randolph Hearst. In any case, Cal Rodgers would not have enjoyed the money for long; he died four months later after flying into a flock of birds and crashing into the ocean off Long Beach, California.

Cal Rodgers's flying death was not atypical. Just months before, Ely perished, too, during a plane crash at an air show in Georgia. The famous pilot was one of ninety-nine people to die in air accidents in 1911. Months earlier he seemed to anticipate his death, telling the *Des Moines Register* he had no plans to retire from flying. "I guess I will be like the rest of them," said Ely, "keep at it until I am killed."

John Rodgers apparently had his own troubles keeping aircraft in one piece. Though extremely passionate about flying airplanes, he was not entirely proficient, with one fellow officer remarking that Rodgers "never showed good flying sense." Within a year the navy removed Rodgers as a flight instructor at the Naval Academy and transferred him back to sea duty as commander of the gunboat USS *Yankton*. Rodgers may also have been transferred because he married Ethel Greiner in 1911. Apparently the navy was fearful that the new Mrs. Rodgers might soon become a widow if her husband kept flying.

Nonetheless, in 1912 Rodgers had another close call in an airplane while flying over San Diego Bay in California. After experiencing mechanical problems, he had steered the plane back toward shore, flying just above the waves. Before reaching land, his plane dropped suddenly toward the water. He cut himself loose from the plane and bailed over its side, just in the nick of time. The plane crashed into the shallow bay and buried itself into the submerged sand below. "The only fact that saved him was the depth of the water which broke the force of his fall," said one witness. "His machine was wrecked, and had he remained in his seat he would have been dragged down and drowned."

During World War I, Rodgers served aboard subs and on mine duty in the North Sea, earning the Distinguished Service Medal before becoming executive officer, or second in command, of the battleship USS *Nevada*. Yet by 1922 Rodgers was enmeshed again in aviation, placed in command of Naval Air Station Pearl Harbor in Hawaii, where he made frequent flights during both day and night. During this command he developed a deep fondness for the islands and made many friends. Among these friends was the Vaughan family, which included the young beauty Jean Vaughan, whose older brother was a navy officer who had died in a 1920 plane crash in Panama. Rodgers served as godfather to one of Jean Vaughan's nephews.

At every assignment, John Rodgers lived up to the expectations of his famous name. Those who served under him reserved the highest praise for the officer. "Tell you this," said Pope aboard PN-9 No. 1, "there never was a better commander than John Rodgers."

By 1925, after Rodgers's subsequent command of the aircraft tender USS *Wright*, as well as a divorce, he was selected to lead the navy's West Coast–Hawaii flight. Now gazing across San Pablo Bay toward San Francisco from within PN-9 No. 1, Rodgers was eager to return to Hawaii. After shaking hands with Moffett from the bow of the seaplane and bidding the rear admiral goodbye, he and his crew made a failed attempt at takeoff, plowing across the bay, and into a headwind, for nearly two miles without taking to the air. The massive load of fuel aboard made it difficult to become airborne.

As the crew of PN-9 No. 1 prepared for another attempt, their sister ship, PN-9 No. 3, made its own run across the flats of the bay, charging along the shore until lifting off the water and ascending slowly into the sky. The flagship then readied for a second try, with Rodgers ordering all crew save he and Connell, the pilot, toward the rear of PN-9 No. 1 in order to redistribute some of the weight of the heavy, fuel-laden flying boat. Also placed aft were the many loose five-gallon gasoline cans for extra fuel.

Sitting in the pilot's cockpit beside Rodgers at 2:45 that afternoon, Connell fretted about the sudden absence of a headwind. *I'll break this thing, sink it, or I'll get off*, Connell thought.

The lieutenant then opened the engine throttles and began another dash across the bay. Leaving Connell to the controls, Rodgers headed aft, positioning himself between the engines, hoping this final redistribution of weight might make the critical difference in getting airborne.

Sheltered from wind by surrounding hills, the flying boat roared across the water at a brisk clip. The plane was a bit lighter now, as the crew had not refueled since the first takeoff attempt. Slowly, after running four miles, the flying boat lifted from the water, only to return a moment later, hopping atop the surface of the bay like a skimmed stone. Then, finally . . . takeoff! At 2:52 in the afternoon, PN-9 No. 1 joined its sister ship in the air. Left behind was the Boeing plane, still suffering from mechanical difficulties.

Among the thousands of people witnessing the event from the shorelines surrounding the bays was James Rolph, mayor of San Francisco, who described the successive takeoffs in a letter sent to his political counterpart

Commander John Rodgers (center) and his crew waving from atop the fuselage of navy flying boat PN-9 No. 1 before their takeoff for Hawaii from San Pablo Bay outside San Francisco on August 31, 1925. Rodgers is standing in the two-person pilot's cockpit, though he most often occupied the darkly painted navigator's cockpit at the front of the plane during his journey to Hawaii. *Courtesy of the Hawaii Department of Transportation Airports*

in Honolulu. "Running parallel with the shore for a mile or more," he wrote, "they rose as gracefully as two birds."

Rolph watched as these two birds, clad in cloth and metal with whirling propellers, floated low in the sky, barely clearing ship masts on account of all the gasoline they carried. Six other navy planes followed close behind, escorting PN-9 Nos. 1 and 3 across San Pablo Bay, then San Francisco Bay, and past Alcatraz Island, home to an imposing US military prison. Army planes from Crissy Field were in the air, too, dipping their wings in salute to the potential transpacific fliers

With the city of San Francisco to the left and Marin County to the right, the flying boats then passed through the famous Golden Gate, which had yet to be bridged. Here the bay narrowed before giving way to the vast Pacific. As the flying boats left the continent behind, appearing as "mere silver butterflies against a golden screen," according to one observer, their crews set course for Hawaii. The army and navy escort planes peeled away, bidding farewell, or aloha, to the intrepid crews aboard PN-9 Nos. 1 and 3.

Within a few hours, Rodgers and the crew of PN-9 No. 1 radioed a message to Wallace Rider Farrington, the territorial governor of Hawaii: "SEE YOU TOMORROW."

When a ship came to port in old Hawaii, half the town turned out to greet it. In the early twentieth century a steamer arriving to Hawaii promised the delivery of not only visitors but also mail, newspapers, and packages. Hundreds of residents gathered along the Honolulu waterfront to cheer the arrival of a new ship, among them many lei sellers eager to place their floral wares around the necks of tourists.

As Albert Pierce Taylor wrote of the festive scene in *Under Hawaiian Skies*:

> The boat came up to the dock. The Hawaiian Band was always there and played it in. Everybody on the wharf wanted to show hospitality to every traveler aboard the ship. Strangers they might have been all their lives, these travelers from Akron or St. Louis, or Council Bluffs, or London, or New York, to the people on the dock, but that didn't matter. Often a stranger found himself in a hack with a couple of Honolulans, might have been men, and might have been young women, it didn't

matter—on the way to the Royal Hawaiian hotel. And how the hotel leaped into life after a somnolent seven days or two weeks. From the dock the Honolulans flowed into the hotel, and many into the cool basement barroom for Scotch and soda, and other things, too, and that night the band gave a concert in the bandstand in front of the hotel and the new people danced with "old friends" of a few hours, all Honolulans. The navy officers came up from their ships moored in old "naval Row" and spent a pleasant evening, and plans were made by all for picnics and horseback rides, or bathing parties out at Long Branch or Sans Souci or the Inn, and dinner parties on home lanais or aboard the warships. Oh, they were real days, were those old days.

If that was the reception given a mere steamship, the celebration of the first airplane to reach Hawaii promised to be magnificent. Honolulu residents eagerly awaited the navy planes and the promise of quick transpacific travel. It would be exhilarating to spy a few specks in the sky and watch as they loomed larger and larger, slowly coming in for historic landings.

Though the crews aboard the navy planes were expected to be the first to fly to Hawaii, they would not be the first to fly above Hawaii. That distinction belonged to J. C. "Bud" Mars, who shipped the airplane *Honolulu Skylark* to Oahu in 1910, took off from a polo field, and then soared above Moanalua Valley. Below, gathered on the hillsides, thousands of residents watched as Mars climbed as high as 1,500 feet in his Curtiss biplane. To Mars's frustration, few of these residents paid for the privilege of seeing him fly, prompting him to deride them as "deadheads" and "pikers."

After performing for three days in Hawaii and making little money, Mars packed his biplane aboard another ship to continue his flying tour in Asia. He became the first man to fly in Korea, the Philippines, and other Asian countries, delighting crowds wherever he traveled. "I suppose we met with our greatest response in Japan," he said, "although there doesn't seem to be a spot on the globe where people don't go plain crazy over aviation."

In 1913 the first passenger flight occurred in Hawaii. In 1917 the first army air unit was stationed on the islands. A year later, an army aviator accomplished the first inter-island flight, flying between Oahu and Molokai. But if airplanes were old news in Hawaii by 1925, transpacific flight was another story. The "entire city" of Honolulu stood ready to welcome the navy planes with a barrage of leis, whistles, and flags, claimed one news report. Honolulu's chamber of commerce erected a bulletin board along an exterior wall of the Hawaiian Trust Company's downtown building, charting the progress of the planes as learned through radio reports. Residents crammed onto sidewalks and atop a nearby fence, eager to read the updates. A block away, displayed in a café window within the Alexander Young Hotel, sat a cake in the shape of an airplane. One word was written across the sugary, frosted flying machine: "Welcome."

Honolulu officials planned to host a community luncheon the next day atop the hotel's rooftop garden to honor the eagerly awaited aviators. Hawaii's governor and Honolulu's mayor planned to attend, as well as at least one admiral and one general. Fancy watches would be awarded to the first fliers to conquer the Pacific. Before that, however, there'd be a reception at Ford Island in Pearl Harbor, with the Daughters of Hawaii on hand to place leis around the aviators' necks. Those heading to Pearl Harbor to greet the aviators were encouraged to get on the road early, as heavy traffic was expected. Even though the navy crews would be flying through the night to reach Hawaii, Honolulu's residents did not plan to let them sleep upon arrival. They were counting on them to join the party.

The bustle in the air in Honolulu was not attributable to airplanes alone. Many changes were occurring in Hawaii, which had been annexed into the United States in 1898, five years after the overthrow of the Hawaiian monarchy by a group of wealthy white planters and businessmen. In the ensuing decades, white elites continued to control the Hawaii Territory, especially the owners and directors of the largest sugar companies on the islands, an informal group of corporations known as the Big Five, who would come to own a majority of the land in Hawaii and control much of its industry.

Beyond these powerful sugarcane processors, who relied heavily on immigrant labor from Asia, other agricultural entities also loomed large in Hawaii, including the Hawaiian Pineapple Company, known as HAPCO. Created in 1901 by James Dole, two decades later the company was supplying 75 percent of the world's pineapples. To meet all this demand, Dole's firm bought the entire island of Lanai and transformed it into a plantation, earning Lanai the nickname "Pineapple Island." Dole and other planters created national advertising campaigns to peddle their produce, spreading the message of Hawaii's tropical delights far and wide. As a 1915 Association of Hawaiian Pineapple Packers advertisement boasted in mainland American newspapers: "Ready to serve, delicious and economical. The tender, flavory slices are packed in their own rich syrup. Everyone likes Hawaiian Canned Pineapple."

At the same time, Hawaii's profile was growing abroad thanks to early movies filmed in the Paradise of the Pacific and through the exploits of the famed Hawaiian surfer and Olympic athlete Duke Kahanamoku. The result of all this cultural exportation was a tourism boom. Fancy hotels were being built upon Waikiki Beach and surrounding wetlands were drained in order to prime ocean-side acreage for development. Boosters in Honolulu wanted to share island delights with as many people as possible, and the airplane promised a faster way to deliver customers.

Across the city, spirits were high as residents awaited the navy flying boats. Factoring in the two-and-a-half-hour time difference between Hawaii and California, Commander Rodgers, his crew, and those aboard the sister ship were expected to arrive at Pearl Harbor about 2:00 PM on August 31, 1925. Once the PN-9s were within sight, factory and steamer whistles would be unleashed en masse, telling all of Oahu that the planes' arrival was imminent.

After leaving the California coast behind, Commander John Rodgers confirmed his plane was steering a correct course for the Farallon Islands, a cluster of small, craggy islands thirty miles west of the Golden Gate. This would be the only landmark he and his fellow aviators would encounter before reaching Hawaii. The navy fliers spotted the Farallon Islands about a half hour after leaving San Francisco, cruising above the rocks at a mere three hundred feet. The heavy fuel load aboard PN-9 No. 1 would not allow the flying boat to soar any higher.

Having successfully fulfilled this first leg of the journey, Rodgers next anticipated seeing the first of the dozen or so guard vessels, the destroyer USS *William Jones*, in approximately two hours. Now that they were airborne, he and the crew on board PN-9 No. 1 again rearranged the loose fuel cans to obtain perfect trim, eventually emptying them, one by one, into the main fuel tank as the engines burned through gasoline. After tossing the empty cans overboard to make space, the crew spread themselves about the plane, each taking his position and settling in for the long flight.

Since taking off, copilot Lieutenant Byron Connell remained at the controls in the pilot's cockpit, occasionally relieved for short spells by crewmates. Beside Connell was a copilot's seat, usually occupied by either Chief Skiles Pope or mate William Bowlin. The copilot's seat featured its own set of controls, including a wheel, yoke, and rudder bar. Engine controls were located between the pilot seats, to be shared, and an instrument panel spread before the aviators, containing air speed meters, steering compasses, and gauges that measured oil pressure, water temperature, and engine revolutions. Also pasted inside the pilot's cockpit was a note stating the RPM, or revolutions per minute, to be maintained each hour in order to most efficiently operate the engines and conserve precious fuel.

Compasses installed about the plane made sure the crew knew exactly which direction PN-9 No. 1 was flying. Acting as navigator was Rodgers himself. The navigation cockpit sat in the bow, just forward of the pilot's cockpit. Inside were two compasses, a chart board, indicators of speed and altitude, and a chronometer to measure time. At the rear of the cockpit on wooden shelves sat a pair of sextants, instruments long valued by mariners, that enable a navigator to determine his whereabouts by taking measurements of the position of the sun or stars compared to the horizon. To make such observations, Rodgers poked his head up through an open hatch into the plane's cold slipstream, much like a prairie dog, and gazed outside the aircraft.

One of the most important things for Rodgers to measure was drift, or to what degree the wind was pushing the airplane off course. Drift indicators were placed to the fore and aft of the navigator's hatch—a series of simple marks and mounts on the top of the fuselage that helped the navigator measure the speed and direction of the wind. By focusing on a smoke bomb tossed to the sea, or by staring at the smokestack of a ship just passed, the navigator could measure how severely and in which direction the wind was blowing the airplane away from a stationary plume of smoke, as measured by the series of marks extending away from the center of the plane.

Since wind can change course and speed frequently, Rodgers made regular drift observations and then relayed these readings to the pilot, who adjusted course accordingly. The ships Rodgers and his crew encountered in the guard line then verified their route. As extra help, PN-9 No. 1 requested radio bearings from the nearest ship every fifteen minutes or so. Only as a last resort was

Rodgers planning to use the sextants to navigate, a time-consuming process that required precision and the reference of mathematical tables.

Both flying boats passed the first guard vessel, *William Jones*, as expected in the early evening, with Rodgers and crew passing five miles north of the destroyer. As Rodgers charted course and Connell stayed put in the pilot's cockpit, the three other crew members toiled about the plane, operating the radio and monitoring the engine and fuel supply. Conditions were cramped, despite the large size of PN-9 No. 1's fuselage. Ten or so massive fuel tanks filled with 1,181 gallons of gasoline occupied much of the plane's interior. Another ninety-seven-gallon tank was installed in the top wing. A fourteen-inch-wide passageway ran between the interior tanks. The passageway was not only narrow but also low, requiring the crew, especially mechanics Pope and Bowlin, to keep heads ducked when traversing the plane.

Behind all the fuel tanks, tucked against the tail of PN-9 No. 1, was the radio cockpit. This was the province of chief radio operator Stantz, who not only received and transmitted messages to ships and shore but also relayed messages, and other information, to his crewmates within the plane, where the engine noise was deafening. One of the flying boat's internal communication networks involved a blinker system of flashing lights to pass messages between the radioman, pilot, and navigator. Another was a mechanical system featuring a hollow tube fastened to a wire strung from the tip to tail of the plane, allowing messages to be dropped in the tube and propelled up and down the line. The crew also communicated by hand signals and through handwritten notes.

To send and receive information outside the plane, Stantz used separate pieces of radio equipment. Messages arrived to his ears via a battery-powered receiving set. The antenna for this set measured four hundred feet long and, after being unspooled after takeoff, trailed behind the flying boat like the train on a bride's wedding dress. Originally the crews had tied a lead weight to the end of the antenna, to prevent it flapping wildly. Yet this caused the antenna to hang low beneath the plane, and prevented flying at low altitudes. So the navy men improvised, something they'd come to do often on this flight, and affixed to the end of the antenna a conical sleeve, which acted like a windsock. This maneuver prevented flapping and allowed the antenna to still trail the plane, though not as closely to the ground.

On the transmission side, messages coded by Stantz entered the airwaves via a sending set powered by a wind-driven generator on the outside of the plane. In an effort to save weight, PN-9 No. 1 did not carry an auxiliary, battery-powered sending set.

Sometime after passing *William Jones*, Stantz left his radio momentarily to grab an orange and some coffee from the stash of rations carried for the flight. Returning to the set, he radioed his fellow sailors on sea and land to inquire about PN-9 No. 3, which he had not heard transmit any recent messages. Despite assurances from navy leadership that the planes attempting to cross the Pacific would maintain visual contact their entire flights, the crew of PN-9 No. 1 had lost sight of their sister ship soon after takeoff.

"SAY HAVE YOU GOT ANY DOPE ON 93D SHE LEFT FRISCO BEFORE WE DID HAVENT BEEN HEARD FROM SINCE ABOUT 1530," radioed Stantz.

An answer came two minutes later. It was not good news.

"YES JONES AND MCCAWLEY SEARCHING FOR #3," said the reply, referencing two navy destroyers sent to the rescue.

After watching PN-9 No. 1 begin its first takeoff attempt on San Pablo Bay, Lieutenant Allen P. Snody patiently waited two full minutes before opening the throttle on his own plane. His flying boat picked up speed quickly, skimming across the flats at seventy-five miles per hour. But like its sister ship up ahead, PN-9 No. 3 was struggling to become airborne. While gently steering the flying boat left to avoid running ashore, Snody ordered two of his crew to move to the rear of the plane with as many tin cans of gasoline as they could carry. Once this weight shifted aft, the plane's nose lifted and PN-9 No. 3 rose into the air.

On account of all the fuel aboard, the plane stayed low as it approached the Golden Gate. So low that it had to turn sharply to avoid a collision with a steamer in the ship channel. Disaster avoided, at least for now, Snody turned over the controls to his copilot, Lieutenant Arthur Gavin, and settled into the navigation cockpit in the bow.

To the crew's dismay, the plane was vibrating in strange fashion. Snody surmised that a propeller tip had been damaged when it continually chopped through waves during the plane's extended takeoff. In any case, the shaking did not seem to affect flight performance, and there would be no replacing or repairing the propeller until they landed in Hawaii and shut off their engines.

PN-9 No. 3 passed the guard vessel *William Jones* at about 6:00 PM, five miles south of the destroyer. The weather had so far been ideal, reported Snody, save for the wind, which shifted direction and velocity constantly. In the first two hundred miles of the flight, Snody ordered seven course corrections for the flying boat on account of the erratic wind.

Peering out of the navigator's hatch, he analyzed the movement of clouds overhead. He observed the wind to be stronger at higher altitudes and instructed Gavin to ascend as the plane's weight allowed. By nighttime the crew planned to be flying above the clouds, avoiding anticipated rainsqualls and taking advantage of fiercer gusts.

When PN-9 No. 3 was 250 miles off the California coast, the crew spotted their sister ship in the air five miles to the north. PN-9 No. 1 was flying low, too. At dusk, Snody and his crew lost sight of Commander John Rodgers's plane.

About the same time, a crewman aboard PN-9 No. 3 inspected the port engine, discovering a small oil leak. With one hundred gallons of oil aboard in reserve, Snody did not consider the leak a significant problem. A half hour later, as he relaxed in the navigator's cockpit, preparing to fly through the night, a flashlight shone in his face. Something was very wrong, his crew told him.

Glancing at an oil pressure gauge, Snody could see the needle had gone to zero! The plane would have to land immediately or risk the engine exploding and sending shrapnel through the fuselage. Rushing to the pilot's cockpit, Snody hopped in the copilot's seat and seized the controls from Gavin.

To make a successful emergency sea landing, navy protocol called for Snody to turn into the wind and begin a long glide. As the plane slowly descended, the radioman was to broadcast their position repeatedly while the long, trailing antenna was reeled in. The longer the plane stayed in the air to broadcast emergency messages, the better.

With an engine on the verge of exploding, Snody would need to forgo the leisurely glide. The pilot made a hard, 120-degree right-hand turn into the wind and quickly dropped the plane to just twenty-five feet over the water, the radio antenna drooping into the sea. Thanks to a nearly full moon and underwing lights, he could see that the seas below were rough, featuring irregular ten-foot waves. He hesitated to land the plane parallel to the water, fearful it would fall flatly against the waves, turn over, and crash. Actually, Snody didn't want to land the plane at all on the rough sea since a few tons of fuel remained aboard.

But having no other choice, he throttled down as low as possible while still continuing a glide. He pulled back on his stick, pointing the plane's nose upward fifty degrees and dropping the tail. Maintaining this angle, he lowered the flying boat into the sea, where it settled nicely on one wave before slamming into another. The impact of the second wave bounced the flying boat thirty feet back into the air, and also knocked it off a horizontal plane. Worried that a wing tip could now dip into the ocean and flip the aircraft, Snody increased engine power to level PN-9 No. 3 and then once again dropped it into the drink. Upon landing on the sea, five waves pounded the plane before a sixth washed over it entirely. Emerging from the drenching, the flying boat bobbed comfortably on the ocean. Snody's deft landing was later praised by the navy as a "feat of airmanship which should be recognized as a remarkably fine piece of work."

Now consigned to the sea, the astonished aviators could hardly believe their plane was intact and no one was injured. Yet the crew recognized they were not out of danger, especially if the flying boat had been compromised. As Snody later wrote, "After each member of the crew had relieved himself of a few general remarks, a rapid survey of the hull was made to learn the extent of the damage."

To the crew's relief, the plane was still watertight, though its hull had bent inward. Struts near the tail had broken away, an oil line was severed, and two gas tanks had been ripped from their moorings, spilling fuel in the plane. Perhaps most astounding was the condition of the remaining fuel tanks. Previously square in form, the tanks were warped into cylinders upon the crash landing, such was the force with which the flying boat landed. It was a wonder the crew had not been crushed or incinerated.

"Down we went and the strain upon the plane was terrific," Snody later wrote. "The tanks flattened out but they did not burst, nor did a single stanchion of the plane give way. I never saw a stronger machine in my life."

Based on their position midway between the destroyers *William Jones* and *McCawley*, Snody and his crew knew it would be hours before the nearest guard vessel came to their rescue. The aviators drained the spilled gasoline from the plane and taxied slowly in the dark with their functioning engine, attempting to stay along the base course between San Francisco and Hawaii and ensure their rescue. Snody then established a watch in the pilot's cockpit while the remainder of the crew tried to get some sleep.

Midnight passed and a new day started. At 1:00 AM a spotlight shone in the distance—it belonged to *William Jones*. The crew of PN-9 No. 3 fired white flares into the sky from a Very pistol. The destroyer acknowledged the plane in return by blinking its searchlight. Within two hours the flying boat was harnessed and enjoying a tow back to San Francisco, away from Hawaii.

Spirits were high on board PN-9 No. 1 as it blazed steadily across the Pacific. Lieutenant Byron Connell remained at the controls and Commander John Rodgers in the navigation cockpit as the plane finished the first third of its journey, with none of the crew reporting feelings of drowsiness. After midnight, just before *William Jones* rendezvoused with the downed PN-9 No. 3, radio-man Otis Stantz began transmitting messages from the air. One of his first communications was addressed to Mayor Rolph of San Francisco, who had watched the flying boats depart his city ten hours earlier. "THE COMMANDER FLIGHT . . . OFFICERS AND CREW OF THE PN9 SEAPLANE WISHES TO THANK THE CITIZENS OF SAN FRANCISCO FOR THEIR HOSPITALITY KINDEST INTEREST AND COOPERATION IN THE WEST COAST HAWAIIAN FLIGHT," Stantz radioed at 12:35 AM.

Five minutes later, he sent word to be passed on south to San Diego, where the navy flight crews and assorted ships had trained for the transpacific flight: "THE NEXT ONE GOES TO THE MAYOR OF SAN DIEGO . . . IT IS THE SAME WORDING EXCEPT CHANGE FRISCO TO DAGO." Two minutes later, Stantz gave an update on the crew: "EVERYTHING OK FEELING FINE ALL OF US."

The crew sustained themselves by consuming portions of their rations, each man receiving a supply of eight ham sandwiches, five oranges, four quarts of water, half a pint of soup, a pickle, chocolate milk tablets, three pints of coffee, some cream, and ten cubes of sugar. In case of emergency, three pounds of hard tack and six pounds of canned beef were available, too—a food supply projected to last the crew three days. These emergency rations were rather light, but the crew was keen on reducing the plane's weight and confident they'd quickly be rescued by a ship should they have to ditch at sea.

Also available, should the fliers be interested, was a thermos bottle of poi, a soupy, traditional Hawaiian food made from taro root. The poi was given to Rodgers by friends just before he departed from San Francisco. Perhaps his buddies thought the crew might want to acclimate themselves to island cuisine before their arrival, which the crew felt was all but assured. Sitting beside Connell in the pilot cockpit, chief machinist's mate Skiles Pope wrote a note to the lieutenant that said they'd be sure to see Oahu if they could just fly safely through the night.

Rodgers and his crew maneuvered about their plane in uniform, with woolen socks and underwear underneath to protect them from any chill they might encounter, especially if they flew at higher altitudes. Summer flying suits were worn above it all, along with their helmets, goggles, and, if necessary, leather flying jackets. At nighttime, the crew attached flashlights to their helmets, which were powered by dry-cell batteries tucked into their pockets. The headlamps supplemented the small lights they had installed above every instrument dial in the plane. The instrument lighting was a small but critical innovation. Other aviators had learned the hard way that, unless illuminated, the dials on the cockpit dash were impossible to read when darkness came. Much of the progress in early aviation occurred this way, with pilots learning from others' mistakes and inexperience.

Because of cloud cover, moonlight was limited, though enough penetrated the clouds to allow Connell to discern a horizon from his pilot's seat. Absent a horizon, it becomes difficult for pilots to maintain a level course, especially if they're at all sleepy. Even a slight bank of the airplane can gradually lead to a tailspin. At low altitudes, even the most talented of pilots might not have enough time to right the plane. Connell was flying at a mere five hundred feet, halfway between the ocean and the clouds, "giving the impression we were flying through a big dark cavern," said Rodgers. If Connell flew any higher, the sea and horizon became blurred together and were lost in darkness.

These conditions demanded vigilance from the pilot, and Connell slowly grew tired, each hour that passed feeling especially long to the young flier, in part because of monotony, in part because the plane lacked a tailwind. His back also ached from absorbing the vibrations of the plane, which reverberated through his aluminum pilot's seat and felt cushion. Around midnight he passed off the controls to Pope and sought to fortify himself with one of the ham sandwiches. Not just any ham sandwiches, either, but specially prepared ham sandwiches that navy doctors claimed would provide maximum nourishment. Connell could hardly swallow the meal. *When I tried my first I decided that science was all right in its place, but couldn't make tough, dry meat tender and appetizing,* Connell thought as he labored to chew the ham.

Meanwhile, to Rodgers's satisfaction, PN-9 No. 1 stayed on course as it crossed the Pacific, encountering each guard vessel as expected every two hundred miles, successively spying the searchlights of the destroyers USS *McCawley,* USS *Corry,* USS *Meyer,* and USS *Doyen.* Still, he was careful to double-check every bit of progress. Standing in the navigation cockpit and watching the compass needle, he would suddenly tug on a line that he had laid throughout the plane and tied to some of his crew's feet. The tug indicated his compass was on course, and also that the yoked crewmen should compare this bearing with the compasses located further aft. "He did this quite a few times," said chief mechanic Pope. "I wondered if he was anxious about the compass checking or was jerking the line to see if we were asleep."

Since smoke bombs would disappear into the darkness, Rodgers tossed a float light into the ocean after passing each of the guard vessels during the night. The commander watched to see how sharply the wind-buffeted plane veered away from the fallen float light, which remained more or less stationary atop the rolling waves. His observations throughout the night revealed the wind pushed the plane south a near-constant three degrees. This was easily compensated for by steering the flying boat back north. But what couldn't be compensated for was the lack of a tailwind, which weather experts had predicted would be encountered halfway through the trip. Without a brisk tailwind, it was unlikely the plane could reach Hawaii on their dwindling gasoline supply.

Beyond struggling against disadvantageous winds, PN-9 No. 1 was suffering a problem with its port engine, whose exhaust burned yellow instead of blue. The yellow flame indicated the engine was not running efficiently, and Rodgers's crew noted the plane was consuming an extra six gallons of fuel each hour. No matter how the crew adjusted the mixture of fuel and oil, the port engine would not produce the desired blue flame. What's more, PN-9 No. 1 used fifty gallons of fuel during their failed takeoff attempt on San Pablo Bay, when the flying boat plowed through water for miles.

Still, the plane hummed along happily. Soon after daybreak it passed guard vessel USS *Langley,* the navy's first aircraft carrier, ten miles to the south. Roughly two hours later, it passed USS *Reno* fifteen miles to the north, again spotting the guard vessel without difficulty. The looming gasoline shortage, however, preoccupied the crew. All five navy fliers were crushed by the prospect of having to interrupt the flight to refuel. As Pope observed, Connell in particular could hardly hide his disgust. "Every time I looked at him he was watching the gas tank, on his face the sourest, most down-hearted look I ever saw on a man's face," said Pope. "I was sure when he caught my eye that I must have looked the same to him. We both were shaking our heads. I think we felt like pulling the plane straight up and letting her crash in."

Desperate to remedy the shortage and determined to ascertain there were no leaks, Pope checked the fuel line connections as soon as Bowlin relieved him in the copilot's seat. Discovering a bit of fuel in the bilge below one tank, he took a sponge and mopped up whatever moisture he found. Then he squeezed the sponge dry within the main tank, enabling a bit more flying time. No matter these efforts, the fuel supply was running dangerously low. His efforts exhausted, he joined Stantz in the radio cockpit, where they enjoyed breakfast, chowing down on an orange and coffee apiece.

After passing *Reno*, Rodgers gave notice via Stantz's radio messages that PN-9 No. 1 planned to make a sea landing beside the airplane tender USS *Aroostook*, a guard vessel stationed four hundred miles away. The flying boat crew calculated they would have plenty of fuel to reach the ship, with an estimated forty minutes of flying time to spare, though certainly not enough to travel the additional four hundred miles or so of ocean that separated *Aroostook* from Hawaii. It was a disappointing decision for Rodgers to make, given that he and his crew would not complete a nonstop flight to the islands despite years of preparation by the navy. Yet he had no choice—the fuel supply was insufficient. He resolved to finish the journey after refueling, anticipating PN-9 No. 1's arrival in Hawaii just a few hours later than expected. Already the plane was two hours behind schedule.

Each of the navy guard vessels in place along the route from San Francisco to Hawaii carried 250 gallons of fuel and 25 gallons of oil as emergency reserves for the flying boats. As an aircraft tender, *Aroostook* carried even more, with at least that much fuel and oil for all three navy planes originally involved with the transpacific flight. The ship also carried a small seaplane atop its deck, which could be hoisted and lowered to the water, where it would then take off for reconnaissance or emergency rescue missions.

After landing on the sea in the vicinity of *Aroostook*, Rodgers planned to tie PN-9 No. 1 alongside the aircraft tender, receive a fuel line, and refill his tanks. Meanwhile, crews aboard the ship and flying boat would attempt to calm the sea by dispensing oil onto the ocean, creating a smooth, heavy slick that the plane could use as a runway, albeit a slimy one. Beyond directly dumping oil into the sea, the navy had also devised a plan to hang large canvas bags of oil from assorted parts of the seaplane, which would allow a slow and steady drip of oil through the porous fabric onto the seawater surrounding the plane.

But *Aroostook* remained hundreds of miles away. As the flying boat passed the destroyer USS *Farragut* sometime after noon on September 1, 1925, Stantz continued to transmit messages reporting the plane's low fuel supply and the likelihood of a sea landing. Should the wind hold steady, Rodgers and his crew expected to reach *Aroostook*, next in line among the guard vessels, in two and a half hours. "HAVE ONLY ABOUT THREE HUNDRED GALLONS LEFT HAD TO BUCK A HEAD WIND FOR SEVERAL HOURS YESTERDAY DON'T BELIEVE IT POSSIBLE TO MAKE IT NOW WITHOUT GASSING," said one message.

Rodgers and his crew could rest assured that, so far on this journey, PN-9 No. 1 had encountered every navy ship positioned along the base course between San Francisco and Hawaii, easily sighting each ship's fuming smokestacks or bright searchlights as they passed overhead a few miles to the north or south. Yet while those ships served as validation of the flying boat's route, the crew knew *Aroostook* loomed as much more than a milestone for PN-9 No. 1. A refueling rendezvous with the aircraft tender was crucial for finishing the flight.

Eager to keep close to the base course, Rodgers ordered a ten-degree course correction to the south. Stantz kept sending radio messages of their progress to keep the navy alert. "GETTING INTERESTING; JUST A LITTLE GAS LEFT IN GRAVITY TANK. OUT NOW WRESTLING TO GET AS FAR NMK IF POSSIBLE," he wrote, using a code to refer to *Aroostook*.

It was now midafternoon on September 1, 1925, and nearly twenty-four hours since departing San Francisco. Thirty minutes after passing *Farragut*, PN-9 No. 1 received radio bearings from *Aroostook* that placed the ship to the north of their position. Rodgers had essentially ignored the bearings sent from each guard vessel the entire flight, relying instead on dead reckoning because of the bearings' potential inaccuracies, especially when more than fifty miles away from a ship. Yet as PN-9 No. 1 neared *Aroostook*, the bearings Stantz received every few minutes consistently indicated the ship was north of the base course. Therefore Rodgers ordered a course recorrection of ten degrees to the north.

Whatever misgivings the commander had about relying on the radio bearings were outweighed by the urgent need to locate the ship, which to his alarm had yet to be spotted. Rodgers reasoned that *Aroostook* must for some reason be cruising to the north of the base course, and at this juncture it was critical to find the ship, not stay on course. He could take some comfort from the fact that *Aroostook* had performed superbly during training exercises for the West Coast–Hawaii Flight. It was the ship's commander, W. R. Van Auken, who had previously posited so many different types of emergency situations in correspondence among officers involved with the flight, asking for his superior's guidance in how to respond to each one. What's more, Van Auken, a close friend to Rodgers and his classmate at the Naval Academy, had written personally to his pal before takeoff, informing him that he was making a special effort to be prepared for any circumstance. Indeed, Van Auken had requested his ship be stationed toward the end of the line of guard vessels, anticipating that the flight would become most challenging as it neared its conclusion, when fuel was low and fatigue was strong.

As the flying boat turned slightly north, communications increased between PN-9 No. 1 and *Aroostook*, with Stantz flustered by the ship's slowness in responding. The seas were rough and no ship was in sight; only a rainsquall sat dead ahead. Rodgers hoped *Aroostook* was cloaked behind it. Taking no chances, Stantz kept sending radio messages to the fleet, advising them of the plane's imminent depletion of fuel. "PLANE VERY LOW ON GASOLINE AND DOUBT ABILITY TO REACH DESTINATION. KEEP CAREFUL LOOKOUT," he wrote.

With Bowlin at the controls, the flying boat pressed forward into the storm, desperate to find the ship. Visibility became limited, and the crew could see nothing but water, in the form of either waves or the driving rain that pelted PN-9 No. 1.

"ARE YOU MAKING SMOKE AND FLASHING LIGHTS?" Stantz radioed at 3:50 PM.

"YES," replied *Aroostook*. "YES PLENTY SMOKE."

The crew of PN-9 No. 1 looked below at the menacing waves and wondered about the wisdom of flying until the gas ran out and the engines ceased.

"WE WILL CRACK UP IF WE HAVE TO LAND IN THIS ROUGH SEA WITHOUT MOTIVE POWER," radioed Stantz.

A minute later, Stantz asked for another bearing. An hour had passed since he had asked if *Aroostook* was producing smoke, but the fliers could discern nothing on the horizon. He then made inquiries about the weather surrounding *Aroostook*: "ARE YOU IN THE RAIN? AROOSTOOK IS IT RAINING WHERE YOU ARE?"

"NO," came the reply.

"IT IS RAINING HERE," said the exasperated radioman.

The flying boat soon emerged from the squall and clear visibility was restored. Yet to Rodgers and his crew's disappointment, *Aroostook* was nowhere to be found. Only endless-seeming ocean spread out before them in every direction. Pope stood in the engineer's cockpit between the engines and gazed at the sea. With the fuel tanks in the fuselage "dry as a powder house," the chief machinist's mate had a reprieve from duty and an excuse to daydream. Staring at the endless waves, Pope irrationally wished he would suddenly spy Diamond Head, the famous volcano that sits at the end of Waikiki Beach in Honolulu. The Hawaiian landmark did not appear. Instead Pope only witnessed the whizzing of the messenger tube as Rodgers and Stantz repeatedly flung it fore and aft. The commander and radioman were in constant and urgent communication from their respective perches in the navigator and radio cockpits. "The messages were flying back and forth so fast I thought the carrier wire would get hot," said Pope, who soon scrambled back to the radio cockpit, not desiring to be potentially crushed by the massive engines and fuel tanks during a rough landing.

Ten tense minutes passed before Stantz once more asked *Aroostook* about the weather. Receiving no response, he asked again. About 4:15 PM, Rodgers began writing a message for Stantz to transmit that detailed the plane's whereabouts.

Suddenly the gas gave out and the plane's fuel-starved engines stopped in midflight eight hundred feet above the waves. A sea landing imminent, Connell quickly seized the controls from Bowlin and spiraled into the wind while the rest of the crew braced themselves against parts of the plane. As PN-9 No. 1 entered a powerless glide toward the heaving sea, no effort was made to reel in the long antenna trailing behind. Tucked in the radio cockpit at the rear of the plane, Stantz frantically sent out a final message:

"LANDING, LANDING, PLEASE SEND DESTROYER, LANDING."

Earlier that morning in Honolulu, eyes stared upward at the skies that extended across the sea, looking to catch a first glimpse of the flying boat carrying Commander John Rodgers and his crew. Some hopeful observers had stayed awake through the previous night, updating PN-9 No. 1's progress on the blackboard hanging along an exterior wall of the Hawaiian Trust Company building. Radio reports indicated the aircraft had last passed USS *Farragut* and was en route to *Aroostook*, the second-to-last guard vessel along the air route from San Francisco. But as time passed, no more updates trickled in and no flying boat floated across the sky.

About lunchtime the residents of Hawaii received shocking news: the plane had run out of fuel and landed in the ocean, away from navy ships. The *Honolulu Advertiser* published a noontime extra, proclaiming, "The Flight Is Doomed."

The navy wasn't so grim. It regarded the forced landing as a mere hiccup. Rodgers's superior, Captain Stanford E. Moses, predicted Rodgers's survival and even suggested, inexplicably, that he had somehow perhaps already reached Hawaii. "Rodgers knows what he is up against. His plane could land on the rough sea and still survive without difficulty as she is very seaworthy," said Moses. "She might have landed on or near one of the small islands."

Rear Admiral William A. Moffett, who had personally bid farewell to Rodgers and his crew one day earlier on San Pablo Bay, echoed Moses's confidence, himself predicting the plane would soon refuel and resume its flight to Hawaii. Moffett expressed no concern for the missing aviators and maintained that the navy would indeed make a nonstop flight to Hawaii, perhaps within the week, as the Boeing flying boat, PB-1, was scheduled to finally depart San Francisco. "We'll try again Thursday with another and if that doesn't go through we'll try again. We'll keep on trying until we get through," said Moffett.

PN-9 No. 1 was still missing the next day, despite every available navy ship, boat, seaplane, and sub in the vicinity of Hawaii searching for it. The ships searched a large circle of ocean measuring more than two hundred miles in circumference—the navy's best guess for where the lost seaplane might be. After analyzing radio reports and ocean currents, the navy narrowed the search area. Still, the ocean to be scoured was vast, and there was no guarantee the plane was within these limits, or even floating atop the water at all. Nonetheless, guard vessels and other navy watercraft rushed across the Pacific to help locate PN-9 No. 1. Navy leaders expected to locate the missing aviators, especially since the flying boat was able to attempt a sea landing with empty fuel tanks.

"We are not worried yet by the failure to find Commander John Rodgers," said Moffett. "He should have landed light. If PN-9 No. 3 could make it safely, loaded almost to the utmost with fuel, it is reasonable to think that the other plane could make a landing easily."

Another, unidentified navy officer seconded the air admiral's faith in Rodgers, claiming, "If anybody can do it, John Rodgers can."

Newspapermen in Hawaii were quicker to abandon hope, finding that the plight of Rodgers and his crew made for good copy. In the absence of factual information on their whereabouts, the *Honolulu Advertiser* substituted dramatic language and paraphrased radio communications in its writing:

> Shadows, grim and ghostly—rode with Commander John Rodgers and his crew—shadows of death perhaps, spectres stalking the skies and hovering above the seas. A world in suspense hopes this may not be so. A gallant commander, and his gallant comrades, may have gone down into the depths—to their last resting place. Tragedy may have ended an epochal event—instead of triumph. Sensing a disastrous finish, the commander's last message seemed to forecast his own doom. "We are gone," he said, "if we land in these seas without motors."

The editorial continued to state that the names of Rodgers and his crew "will be emblazoned on the tablets of enduring fame—and the world will never forget them."

Commander John Rodgers was not yet ready to have his name etched into the annals of history. He and his crew were alive and well, floating nicely in the middle of the Pacific Ocean. Thanks to Lieutenant Byron Connell's maneuvers at the controls, PN-9 No. 1 alighted gently atop the waves after running out of fuel, coming to a soft stop without skipping across the sea. Chief machinist's mate Skiles Pope said Connell's delicate touch at the controls saved them from becoming "shark feed." Rodgers deemed it a "perfect landing," especially since Connell was forced to plop the flying boat down in rough seas and light winds without working engines. Moreover, Connell was exhausted, having piloted the plane himself for much of the last twenty-five hours, his eyes flitting constantly between the horizon and compasses in order to stay on course.

It was late afternoon when the seaplane made its emergency landing. Rodgers and his crew said nothing as the craft settled onto the ocean and then rocked in the waves. Radio operator Otis Stantz confessed he was madder than a wet hen, and his crewmates felt about the same—too disgusted to even speak. The fliers' disappointment was so pronounced it obliterated any appreciation for the fact they had all survived the forced landing without injury.

Here we had worked night and day for three months to make a nonstop flight and had failed, Connell thought angrily.

As they awaited the arrival of *Aroostook*, the crew made a quick check of the aircraft, which was intact. The fliers could imagine no reason they would not continue flying to Hawaii after being refueled by the ship. To help *Aroostook* spot them, and to receive radio messages since the three-hundred-foot copper antenna that trailed the plane was now submerged, the crew launched a radio kite, lofting an antenna up into the air. Then the crew broke for lunch, where Stantz enjoyed more coffee and oranges. Their adrenaline spent and their stomachs at least half full, fatigue finally caught up with the fliers, none of whom had slept since waking up in San Francisco a day and a half earlier. The bulk of the crew laid down for a nap, hopeful for a few winks of sleep before *Aroostook* found them.

There were no prime spots to bed down. Climbing out of the pilot's cockpit and atop the aircraft, between the upper and lower wings, Connell fell asleep in open air on top of the hull. Then Rodgers silently came outside from the navigator's cockpit and lay down atop the hull, too. Pope pitied the disappointed expression that covered Rodgers's face. He grabbed a life preserver and handed it to the crestfallen commander. "Captain, here's a little softer pillow than that metal," said Pope, uttering his first words since the sea landing. Then Pope, who adored and revered Rodgers as much as the rest of the crew, protectively tethered the commander to a strut, as the seaplane was rolling violently atop the waves, saying, "Captain, you'd better put a line around you. You might slip over."

"A good idea," said Rodgers, who soon fell into a deep sleep.

Below, within the fuselage, Stantz was snoozing in the radio cockpit. The radioman had hardly glanced outside after landing, instead he tumbled off his stool onto the metal floor decking above the bilges. There he wrapped his body around fuel tanks and went to sleep, putting a seat cushion under his head, which remained wrapped in a helmet. Pope shook Stantz awake and urged him to go topside, explaining the gas fumes in the bilge would sicken him. But Stantz, already feeling seasick, would not budge.

Pope and machinist's mate William Bowlin stayed awake while the others slept. Only a half hour lapsed before they witnessed the radio kite founder in light winds and nosedive into the sea, destroying itself. *It's better you took that dive than we*, Pope thought.

In a few hours Stantz awoke and more items dropped into the sea: the half-digested oranges and coffee the radioman vomited out of his stomach.

"A great day for the fishes," remarked Pope.

Connell kept his appetite, at least at first. Upon waking from his nap the pilot again tried to swallow a ham sandwich. The meat tasted just as funky— "strong enough to knock one down." The lieutenant tossed it into the bilge without a second thought.

Bowlin had a similar reaction to the supposedly scientifically enhanced ham, eating a few bites of sandwich before tossing the remnants overboard, much to his commander's dissatisfaction. "You'd better be saving that," Rodgers admonished his crew. "You might need it later on."

The crew smoked cigarettes freely as darkness descended on the ocean. They remained confident they would soon spot the lights of *Aroostook* or another refueling ship. Bowlin and Pope took their turns to sleep, waking up around midnight. Refreshed and less downtrodden, the fliers talked openly of their disappointment of having to land at sea and disrupt the nonstop flight. Rodgers was unbothered and assured his crew redemption was in store. "It's all right," he intoned. "We will do it again."

Still no ship was in sight. Its absence began to wear on Pope, who had assumed a night watch after midnight while the others slept. Alone in the pilot's cockpit, dark thoughts crept into his mind, so grim they "never could be put on paper." Only when he slept again later that night were these fears purged.

Stantz struggled through his night watch as well. Searchlights would appear to him on the horizon only to be revealed as stars—or his imagination—when he rubbed his eyes and cleared his vision. Eager to refill his stomach, he looked for more oranges. Finding none, he contented himself with a cup of coffee and dreamed of a feast waiting for them in Honolulu.

The next morning, September 2, 1925, or day two at sea, the men woke with revived spirits. Stantz began immediately to string the spare antenna around the plane, insulating the copper wire with waxed cord to prevent contact against the fuselage. Connell and Bowlin helped their seasick crewman stretch the antenna along the wings and fuselage, teasing their fellow sailor for looking so "peaked under the gills."

The new antenna allowed the crew to receive radio messages from ships hundreds of miles away. The crew heard everything now, including weather reports, news stories, updates on the movement of navy ships searching nearby, and, most frustratingly, messages directed specifically to PN-9 No. 1. Rodgers and his crew could only listen helplessly, unable to reply to these radio transmissions since the generator powering their radio transmitter was driven by airflow. If the plane was not flying, the crew could not obtain the power needed to send messages to guide the navy to their plane.

"It was a queer sensation," Rodgers observed, "listening to those hunting for us and being unable to communicate with them."

Or as radioman Stantz, who cried tears of anger as he attempted to broadcast messages, understated, "We were listening all the time to what was being said about us. We were only sorry we couldn't answer back."

To the crew's disappointment, they overheard how the navy was concentrating their search approximately sixty miles to the south of the plane's position, having overestimated how swiftly the flying boat would drift toward Hawaii. Though this distance certainly meant refueling would be delayed, the fliers did not despair and remained confident they would eventually resume their flight. After all, the possibility of a forced sea landing was carefully considered during the navy's planning of the West Coast–Hawaii Flight. They expected a destroyer on the horizon soon.

"How'd you happen to pick out such a deserted section of the Pacific to land on," Pope kidded Connell.

The lieutenant would not be baited. "They will find us," he replied. "If the navy ships don't, some merchant ship will, for we are right in the shipping lane."

As the men foraged the plane for breakfast, they discovered Rodgers's poi had spoiled overnight. Their bread has started to grow mold, too, leaving the crew to enjoy water and water alone for their morning meal. Hoping to salvage the repulsive and moldy ham sandwiches, Connell spread the bread and meat along a wing to roast in the sun.

The crew was chatty, having shed the glum moods that overwhelmed them the day before. The seas were calm in the morning, prompting Connell to daydream of PN-9 No. 1 soon receiving fuel and lifting easily off the water, back on track for Honolulu. As the day progressed and the sea became rougher, they noticed waves lapping at the tips of the lower wing and sometimes spilling over it. Wary of the wing becoming damaged, the men stripped fabric away from the tip and edges, revealing the wood framing underneath, which the waves could filter through without danger. They were careful to leave the bulk of the fabric in place, unwilling to forfeit use of the wing when they took off again.

With little to do but wait, the men lounged about the flying boat, with Stantz still trying to shake his seasickness. Rodgers quipped that their predicament was enviable, as some people paid large amounts of money to cruise about the ocean in yachts half as plush. The hours passed fairly comfortably, with cigarettes in sufficient supply, before darkness came again. During the evening the crew was startled to attention by a radio message from *Aroostook*: "IF YOU SEE AROOSTOOK NEAR YOU, FIRE STAR SHELL OR SHOW LIGHT. WE THOUGHT WE SAW A FLARE AHEAD."

The fliers had not sent a flare aloft, but the plane's anchor light was aglow on the top wing—perhaps that's what *Aroostook* had spied. With high hopes Connell shot a flare into the sky, yet nothing further followed on the radio. Nonetheless, the crew prepared to sleep with the hope that they'd wake to the sight of a ship. As some men laid down their heads, others assumed a night watch. Rodgers used a sextant to take a sighting in the sky and reestablish their position. He estimated the flying boat bobbed 450 miles from Hawaii.

Throughout the night heavy waves washed across the remaining fabric of the plane's lower wing. Anyone awake listened to the disconcerting noise of spars cracking, buckling under the weight of the water. A broken wing would be devastating, with no chance of making repairs at sea to fly on toward Hawaii. It could also be fatal, compromising the flying boat and leaving it at the mercy of the waves, which would inevitably pound the seaplane apart.

Whatever uneasy sleep the crew was experiencing ended abruptly the next morning when the lookout, Bowlin, excitedly announced the sighting of a ship. "I see smoke ahead!" the youngster shouted.

The crew sprang to action. The ship appeared to be a steamer, which disappointed the crew since the commercial ship would be unable to refuel the flying boat. But at least, they reasoned, the steamer could radio the nearby navy ships and broadcast PN-9 No. 1's exact position. While Stantz headed to the radio cockpit and donned headphones to receive messages, Connell and Bowlin climbed onto the top wing and attempted to signal the ship cruising just a few miles away. Connell waved a piece of fabric attached to a stick so vigorously that he exhausted himself and was barely able to climb down. Bowlin fired flare after flare into the sky until Rodgers urged him to show some restraint. Yet the steamer plied on, oblivious to Bowlin's flares and Connell's flailing.

The crew was in shock. How could they have gone unnoticed? Eventually they reasoned that the steamer's crew must have been blinded. PN-9 No. 1 had the bad fortune of bobbing directly between the steamer and the rising sun.

The near miss flustered them. It was now apparent that no refueling rendezvous was guaranteed. The fliers took stock of their rations. They had eaten heartily on their daylong flight, leaving just six remaining sandwiches, seven quarts of water, and two quarts of cold coffee to share among five men. Also on board, if necessary, were the emergency supplies of corned beef and hardtack, a long-lasting biscuit common to ships voyaging across the ocean. To conserve water, Rodgers had each man write his name on his canteen and then took the two extras for safekeeping.

The day passed and no other ships appeared on the horizon. Watching the seas turn rough and pound their seaplane, the crew was obliged to cut large swaths of fabric away from the lower wing, allowing the waves to wash cleanly through the ribbed frame. This action, taken reluctantly, increased the seaplane's stability atop the waves but also dashed any hope that PN-9 No. 1 would again take to the sky to finish the journey. Yet the navy men would not be denied the sunny shores of Hawaii. Grabbing hold of the fabric torn from the lower wing, the crew rigged sails between the upper and lower wings of the biplane. If PN-9 No. 1 could not fly their craft to Hawaii, decided Rodgers, then he and his crew would sail it, taking advantage of trade winds that led to the islands. They set off, slowly but steadily, on a southwest course.

As night fell over Hawaii on September 2, 1925, sailors and soldiers kept lookout along island coasts, watching for emergency flares in the dark sky. Nearby destroyers, having scoured the sea all day for the missing aviators, turned off their engines to conserve fuel, content to drift until daybreak, when the search would resume. Eighteen other destroyers from the Pacific fleet kept their engines running through the night and steamed toward Hawaii as reinforcements, ending far-flung maneuvers near Samoa, more than 2,500 miles away. The guard vessel USS *Langley* was nearing Hawaii, too, after cruising toward the islands from its position along the base course. Atop the aircraft carrier's deck were plenty of planes that could be launched to bolster the rescue efforts. As all these vessels slowly converged around Hawaii, the navy appeared to be holding true to its promise to "search every drop of water."

The next day, September 3, 1925, brought fresh despair to the navy and its already beleaguered flight program. While on a publicity tour across the Midwest, the airship *Shenandoah* crashed in Ohio during a storm, killing fourteen of its crew. Then two Hawaii-based navy planes crash-landed into the sea while looking for Rodgers and his crew. No one was injured during these sea ditches, and the pilots were rescued, but secretary of the navy Curtis Wilbur, a lawyer, dared not risk increased liability from aircraft. He quickly canceled the flight of the still-delayed PB-1, acknowledging his decision to end the Hawaiian Hop was unpopular with the navy fliers that served under him.

Among those aviators was Lieutenant Commander James Strong, in charge of the Boeing plane, who claimed he would forfeit his right leg to fly to Hawaii. He wrote to Moses, the flight project commander, in hopes Wilbur would change his mind:

> In spite of the recent unfortunate and regrettable mishap to aviation, the attempt to span the Pacific should be given more impetus and support than ever before. It is up to the Navy to put this flight across and I feel that a discontinuation of effort now will set aviation back a full year. I feel confident that the PB-1 can make a non-stop flight from San Francisco to Honolulu. The plane is now ready, waiting for favorable weather and authority to leave.

Strong's appeal was unsuccessful. His complaint was mild, too, compared to the vitriol spouted by army colonel William Mitchell, former assistant chief of the Army Air Service. For years Mitchell had castigated American military leadership for decisions regarding air power, criticizing the top brass for continuing to invest in ground and sea power rather than exploit the potential of the airplane. To Mitchell's dismay, the American military reduced its commitment to aviation following World War I, its leaders unable, or unwilling, to recognize the advantages a superior air force would bring to the battlefield.

Following the downed flying boats in the Pacific and the crash of the *Shenandoah*—operations Mitchell denigrated as "a parade of our navy"—the outspoken colonel went on the offensive with renewed vigor, no matter the fact he still wore an army uniform. While his caustic commentary resonated with the media and many civilians, military leaders were appalled by his charges. "These accidents are the direct result of incompetency, criminal negligence, and almost treasonable administration of the national defense by the war and navy departments," said Mitchell. Aviation policy, he continued, is made by senior officers who "know nothing about flying, and the lives of the airmen have been used merely as pawns in their hands."

In case his criticism was unclear, the colonel launched into a full tirade:

> The airmen themselves are bluffed and bulldozed so they dare not tell the truth, knowing full well that they will be deprived of their future careers and sent to most out-of-the-way places on the pretext that their telling the truth deprived them of all chances of advancement, unless they subscribe to the dictates of their non-flying bureaucratic superiors. The conduct of the war and navy departments has been so disgusting the last few years as to make any self-sacrificing officer ashamed of the cloth he wears.

Mitchell then targeted the planning of the navy's West Coast–Hawaii flight specifically, dismissing the attempt as "propaganda, and not real service," with little justification for the journey:

> Even if it had been made successfully to Honolulu it would have meant little, either commercially or strategically, compared with what a flight to Europe or to Asia would have demonstrated. . . . Three airplanes were built to participate in it. These showed nothing novel in design and were not tried for this kind of work. One never got away from the Pacific Coast. One flew miles out and was forced to land in the water. One was lost on account of being out of gasoline somewhere on the high seas. . . . Patrol vessels were stationed every 200 miles, a distance entirely too far apart. The whole Pacific fleet should have been employed there instead of joy-riding around the Antipodes. . . . Why, if they expected to run short of fuel, as indeed they might, they made no arrangement

for refueling the airplane while aloft, and why was a crew of five carried when the weight of one or two could have replaced additional fuel?

As a final broadside, he blamed the deaths of many American military aviators directly on the armed services, saying, "The bodies of former companions and buddies moulder under the soil of America, Asia, Europe, and Africa. Yes, many were sent there directly by official stupidity. We all make mistakes, but criminal mistakes are made by the armies and the navies whenever they have been allowed to handle aeronautics and show their incompetency."

Mitchell was soon court-martialed for insubordination. In Hawaii the search for Rodgers and his crew continued, with the navy publicly maintaining hope the aviators would be found alive.

"CHEER UP JOHN. WE WILL GET YOU YET," *Aroostook* radioed from sea.

The voice of Commander John Rodgers boomed unexpectedly throughout the plane the morning of September 4, 1925.

"Good morning, stranger," shouted Rodgers, startling his crew.

The others aboard PN-9 No. 1 were confused. It was their fourth day stranded at sea. They had not seen another soul since they left San Francisco five days earlier.

"Who is it?" Chief Skiles Pope asked his commander.

"There are a couple of nice little playmates over there for you," Rodgers responded. "Some tiger sharks."

The navy could not find Rodgers and his crew, but a school of sharks had more luck. A dozen intrepid sand sharks, which can grow to ten feet in length and weigh more than four hundred pounds, had followed the plane for days, arriving soon after the emergency sea landing. Hour after hour, Rodgers and his fellow aviators watched as twelve dark fins trailed menacingly behind them. Alone, famished, and without fuel atop the rolling Pacific, the aviators could have done without these grim, sharp-toothed traveling companions. Rodgers stared this danger in the face each morning by leaning down toward the water and greeting the sharks. "Not today, mister, not today," he said as dorsal fins cut through the water in front of him.

Eventually a battery of barracuda began to tag along. Then, this morning, the pair of tiger sharks joined the hunt, the newcomers conspicuously larger than the sand sharks. These two—"big black fellows" according to aviation machinist's mate William M. Bowlin—measured about fourteen feet in length. The fearsome creatures were "always waiting," said Bowlin, "I guess for a choice bit of human flesh."

Lieutenant Byron Connell was grateful for the metal hull that separated him from the assorted beasts below. "You'll wait a long time before you gain anything from following this craft!" he thought to shout to the sharks.

The crew, desperately low on food and water, might have hoped to eat one of the sharks, or even barracuda, except that they carried no fishing line or tackle aboard the seaplane. So instead they made do with their meager and unappetizing supplies, swallowing what they could. "Have a piece of toast," Connell said with a smile, repeatedly offering his crewmates the sunbaked, formerly moldy bread that he had stuck on a wing. With some satisfaction, the lieutenant noticed that the ham he had also cooked had been disappearing little by little into men's stomachs.

When these foods were gone, the fliers turned to the crackers and canned corned beef, or corn willy as it was known among sailors. The beef was repulsive without water, even to near-starving men. Rodgers, in fact, refused to eat the corn willy a second time without adequate water. "It is like running a motor without gasoline and oil," said the commander. Connell ignored Rodgers's warning about the corned beef and paid a steep price the next day. It was another great day for the fishes.

Meanwhile, the crew stalked the plane for scraps of food that had been discarded days earlier. Once radioman Otis Stantz prowled with a flashlight, in search of an orange peel he could ingest. Pope, too, was thankful to find a rind. "You don't know how good orange peeling is when you have nothing else," he said.

Another day Rodgers reached beneath the floorboards, into the bilge, and retrieved a piece of sandwich crust as big as his thumb. He showed off his find before devouring it with gusto. "It was tough, pretty tough . . . to see that gallant officer, our commander, John Rodgers, scanning the bilge waters of the PN-9 No. 1 for crumbs that might have dropped from our sandwiches," said Pope.

If Rodgers's scavenging disheartened Pope, it at least invigorated the commander. With similar zeal Rodgers called his crew's attention to a "beautiful fish" that jumped into his navigator's cockpit that evening, apparently attracted by the light he had been shining across the navigator's table. The crew watched as he tenderly stroked the small flying fish, which was no bigger than a minnow, and offered to share his catch. Then the commander placed the fish in his mouth and swallowed. Sometimes, Rodgers observed, it is the cheapest things that become the most valuable.

His starved, dehydrated, and demoralized crew agreed wholeheartedly with their leader. "This remark was fully realized as we lapped water from the wing fabric or retrieved bits of orange peel and bread crust from the scum of the bilges," said Bowlin.

Also contained in the bilge was the thermos of soured poi that Rodgers had discarded. It had continued to ferment there until one day the thermos exploded with a mighty boom, giving the crew a good laugh.

In an effort to obtain more food, the men fashioned crude fishing lures from torn fabric and metal wire. They placed lights by the door of the radio cockpit, hoping another finned friend might hop on board at night. Yet neither the lures nor the lights helped the crew catch any more fish.

More encouraging than the food and water supply were some of the radio reports Stantz received, keeping constant vigil over the radio. When he received radio bearings from another ship, he passed them along immediately so the flying boat could be steered in that direction. Yet the plane had significant limitations as a sailing craft, preventing any rendezvous. It could not be steered more than five degrees from the wind, or else waves would pummel the pontoons beneath each wing, risking their breakage and, in turn, the plane's seaworthiness. When the seas became rough, the sails had to be hauled down in order to preserve stability.

The flying boat would also not travel much faster than two or three knots, a snail's pace that also contributed to its inability to catch any nearby navy ships. Still, slowly but surely, Rodgers and his crew coaxed PN-9 No. 1 toward Hawaii, determined to reach their destination, not by drifting but by sailing—a distinction that mattered very much to the proud navy men.

The crew was further encouraged by *Aroostook*'s radio message of support. After promising Rodgers, "WE WILL GET YOU YET," the ship urged the flying boat crew to "USE STARS AND TAP ON HULL, SUBMARINES WILL HEAR YOU ON OSCILLATORS. USE RADIO RECEIVER AS TRANSMITTER." They took this advice seriously. At one point Pope and Bowlin pounded so furiously on the hull of the flying boat that they woke Stantz from a slumber.

"Go easy on that hammer, you'll knock a hole in the bottom!" Stantz shouted upon his rude awakening. Yet the radioman was just as overzealous. When he grew restless during his solitary night watches, Stantz would scour the flying boat for the hammer and let loose a few whacks against the hull. Though he knew, thanks to radio messages, that no subs were in the vicinity, it still reassured him to bang about the plane. As evidence of the crew's enthusiasm, the hammer's handle soon broke apart.

When he wasn't beating up PN-9 No. 1, Stantz attempted to operate the radio transmitter, ever hopeful of being able to send messages to the navy ships searching nearby waters. He cannibalized PN-9 No. 1's engine parts in an attempt to power the transmitter, substituting a spark coil in place of the useless wind-driven radio generator. When that didn't work, he and his fellow crew removed the flywheel starter from the starboard engine and attempted to attach it to the radio transmitter generator by using hoses and clamps. After initially demonstrating promise, the makeshift device fell to pieces when spun at high speeds. Stantz then improvised once more, swapping out even more parts to construct a transmitter that delivered huge shocks to the crew when they inadvertently brushed against a wire. "I don't think there's much doubt about that thing puttin' out," said Rodgers after receiving a severe spark and shock to his neck.

The makeshift radio transmitter enabled Stantz to broadcast very weak radio messages. To the crew's disappointment, no ships were close enough to receive the messages. Despite the lack of success, Stantz's attempts buoyed the crew's spirits. "We managed to keep our hopes alive by believing that Stantz would get his set in sending order," said Pope. "We can't give him too much credit for the way in which he worked night and day on the set of his."

The crew also toiled to operate a gasoline-powered still that Rodgers carried on board at the insistence of his elderly mother. Since the tanks were bone dry, the crew burned bits of wood and fabric torn from the wings for fuel, eventually distilling a quart of seawater after five hours' manipulation. It was painstaking work for a low yield. "At this rate we would have to burn up the whole plane to make enough water to be of any value," said Connell.

For all their efforts and innovations, the fliers found themselves in the same predicament—stranded at sea without adequate food or water. The men had reduced their water consumption to a few swallows a day before having to cut back further, allowing themselves only the occasional chance to simply moisten their mouths with a few drops. It was hot within the plane, exacerbating their thirst. Escape to the wings or to the top of the hull provided some relief, but also invited the blast of the sun on their shirtless skin. The merciless rays caused them severe sunburn. And still, the horizon and skies stayed disappointingly empty of ships, hour after hour, as the sun marched up and down the sky.

By September 6, 1925, day six at sea, the crew was out of food, nearly out of water, and becoming extremely weak. Their thirst was so severe that they hardly noticed they were starving. Desperate for hydration, the men used torn sheets of wing fabric to try to catch water delivered by brief rainsqualls. Since one side of the fabric was coated with airplane dope and aluminum paint, they elected to collect rainwater on the other side, which featured unadulterated fabric. Yet the fabric absorbed the rainwater completely, forcing the men to desperately press their tongues against it to gain tiny bits of moisture. They also licked the hull to collect droplets accumulated on the sheet metal. The moisture hardly quenched their thirst, but it was at least something. During the next storm, the fliers vowed, they would attempt to collect the rainwater on the painted side of the fabric.

Unwilling to wait for that squall, they next drained water from engine radiators. It was undrinkable, laced with a chemical compound called Liquid X, used to seal small leaks. The crew strained the radiator water through mesh, a chamois, and wing fabric, but could not filter out the toxic Liquid X. It was maddening to be surrounded by water and to have it in good supply on the plane but not be able to drink a drop, all of it polluted by salt, aluminum, or poisonous radiator compound.

The men thought of their loved ones back home. Young Bowlin, otherwise unflappable, wondered aloud if his grandmother, who had raised the orphaned boy, was aware of the crew's plight. He hoped not, fearing for her health. Stantz became downhearted after digging through the spare parts box one day and encountering a picture of his "kiddies." He began dwelling on the search efforts and wondering why no navy vessels had come to the rescue.

Thanks to Stantz's radio work and Rodgers's navigational plotting, the crew knew the location of every searching ship. So long as they sailed toward the islands, Rodgers reasoned, they would eventually encounter one of the navy ships plying the waters around Hawaii. His plan was sound so long as the navy continued the search. Yet during day seven at sea, this plan was thrown into jeopardy, as Stantz heard radio chatter indicating the search might be suspended. To the crew's dismay, radio messages indicated a number of fellow naval aviators and officers—including all twenty-one pilots aboard the aircraft carrier *Langley*—had given up all hope of finding the missing plane.

Publicly the navy expressed great confidence that Commander John Rodgers and his crew would be found. Privately, however, some officers wondered whether the plane was truly afloat. They surmised instead that PN-9 No. 1 crashed and sank immediately, especially if the pilot's vision was limited by heavy rain, which could have obscured the ocean and led to a hard landing atop the waves. "It's too bad but we had better check Commander John and his crew off the list," said one unnamed officer at the Naval Air Station at Pearl Harbor.

Since the plane's emergency landing, a number of false sightings of the flying boat had occurred, as well as the appearance of possible clues to the flight's fate. On a beach on the Big Island, two kapok life jackets washed ashore—the type worn by naval aviators. Reconnaissance planes observed a suspicious vessel off Kauai, but upon closer inspection discovered it was an abandoned sampan, the flat-bottomed fishing boat favored by Asian immigrant fishermen. Navy lookouts glimpsed flashes of light that might have been emergency flares but were revealed to actually be torches on other sampans. With so many small fishing vessels plying the waters off Hawaii, the local Japanese fishermen's association offered to help search for PN-9 No. 1. The navy politely declined the offer, explaining enough navy vessels were already involved.

Some of those navy ships were beginning to run out of fuel, they had been searching for so long. They returned to Pearl Harbor to gas up, compare notes between officers, and then return to sea to search some more. As Saturday, September 5, 1925, approached, four days since anyone heard from PN-9 No. 1, the destroyers steaming from Samoa began nearing Hawaii, as did aircraft carrier USS *Langley*, cruising to the islands from the opposite direction. The squadron commander offered a reward to the first sailor to spot the missing plane. Some skippers on individual destroyers upped the ante, offering their own incentives to keep their crew alert. By the time all these ships arrived, there would be at least twenty-six destroyers searching seventy thousand square miles of ocean near Hawaii. Additionally, thirty-four planes would take to the sky, keeping an eye out over 12,500 square miles, while submarines cruised the ocean surface, including a line of nine subs spread across Kauai Channel between Oahu and Kauai. As one skipper said, "We'll be here all right, even if we have to rig awnings for sail and dole out water with a medicine dropper."

Yet those destroyers might arrive too late, as more and more navy officers began to lose hope that the flying boat would be found. A naval aviator aboard *Langley* hypothesized that PN-9 No. 1 sunk within a half hour of landing on the waves. Then Rodgers's superior officer, Captain Stanford Moses, asked other aviators on the aircraft carrier their thoughts on the matter. They replied via radio: "TWENTY-ONE AVIATORS ON THE LANGLEY CONCUR THE PLANE HAD SUNK AND THE SEARCH SHOULD BE DISCONTINUED."

Moses soon shared the same opinion. "We have virtually given up hope of rescuing the crew," he said publicly. "We now have eleven destroyers fueling at Honolulu for the purpose of engaging in a final survey of the waters where the PN-9 No. 1 came down. We have done all that could be done."

Day in and day out, the searches turned up nothing. Still, the navy continued the effort, no matter the hopelessness some of its officers expressed. Strange things occur at sea, old salts maintained, and a rescue was still possible. "Don't you think for a moment those fellows are in bad," said Lieutenant William McDade of the aircraft tender USS *Gannet*. "When we find them, they will be sitting on top of the plane or on some barren island perhaps, and the first thing they will say will be, 'Hello, boys, glad to see you!'" Yet nearly a week had passed since the navy fliers had started their journey. With each passing day, it seemed less likely a miracle would prevail.

As the chamber of commerce in Honolulu solicited money to build the first airport in Hawaii, there were calls to name it in honor, or memory, of Commander John Rodgers. As Hawaii's territorial governor Wallace Rider Farrington wrote in a message to the navy three days after the aviators went missing, "Whatever their fate, they have upheld the best traditions of the great pioneers of our country, the men who drive ahead and are not afraid."

By day seven the canteens were dry and empty, just like the plane's fuel tanks, just like the mouths and stomachs of the crew of flying boat PN-9 No. 1. The navy fliers hoped desperately for rain. Without it they might not live to reach Hawaii's shores, which Rodgers knew loomed only 150 miles away. For days he had dutifully tracked their progress, using his sextant a few times each day and night to ascertain the plane's location.

Their proximity to Hawaii was only a small consolation. Weaker by the day, Rodgers and his crew struggled to man the flying boat's controls without falling asleep. They gave up trying to construct a radio transmitter. Mostly the men lay prostrate about the boat. If they did move, they crawled.

Each crewman had lost at least ten pounds since leaving San Francisco. Not only gaunt, parched, and famished, they were also burned and blistered from sun exposure. It seemed no relief—from thirst, from hunger, from the sun—would be provided by the navy, where a considerable contingent of the crew's fellow fliers firmly believed they had dropped deep down into Davy Jones's locker. The lost fliers were still smarting from that incorrect verdict, astonished that other naval aviators had given up any hope of their survival. "It made us damned mad," said Stantz. "But what could we do?"

That night Rodgers's navigation was confirmed: they could see searchlights from the army's Schofield Barracks on Oahu in the distance. Save the sharks, barracudas, and Rodgers's minnow, it was the first sign of life the navy men had seen in days. They were ecstatic. Steering in the pilot's cockpit, Pope asked Rodgers how close they were to land. "Only about a hundred miles," Rodgers replied matter-of-factly.

Though this distance was farther than Pope had imagined, the searchlights were beacons of hope for the lost crew. The next morning, Pope imagined, they'd begin their sail into Pearl Harbor, their journey nearly complete. But he underestimated the significant challenge of reaching shore. It was one thing to see land from their makeshift sailing vessel; it was another to actually get there.

According to Rodgers's projections, PN-9 No. 1 would soon sail along the northern shore of Oahu before entering Kauai Channel—the seventy-two-mile-wide stretch of water that separates Oahu and Kauai, two of Hawaii's northernmost islands. Because the crew could only steer a minimal amount off the wind using their improvised sail, they risked passing in between the islands without the ability to reach either of them. With an island tantalizingly close on each side, they would be powerless to make a sufficient break for either shore.

Fearful of being swept beyond the islands into a vast expanse of empty ocean, Lieutenant Connell mustered the strength, and ingenuity, necessary to rip long metal floorboards from the fuselage and fashion them into leeboards to help improve steering. By lashing three floorboards together and plunging them deep under the boat, perpendicular to the fuselage and wings, Connell effectively created twenty square feet of keel underwater. This allowed PN-9 No. 1 to now turn fifteen degrees from the wind and maneuver with much more flexibility. Connell's crewmates praised his brilliance before Rodgers teased him for not thinking of the idea any earlier. The crew brightened as they tested their new steering system during day eight at sea.

Yet the next day, even with this improvised keel, it seemed impossible to reach Oahu, which now appeared clearly in the distance. Shifting winds carried the flying boat swiftly into Kauai Channel and Rodgers expressed doubt that PN-9 No. 1 could turn sharply enough to make their original destination. The island of Kauai, he said, might be their last and only chance. The crew discussed their predicament as they sailed along, each man voicing his thoughts on the wisest course of action. With Oahu in plain sight and Kauai still beyond the horizon, some predictably favored steering hard toward Pearl Harbor. Rodgers didn't believe the turn could be made. Finally, the commander called a halt to the debate. "Well, that is enough," he declared. "We are going to go to Kauai. That is final."

The decision did not suit Pope, whose long face made clear his disappointment. He exchanged "funny looks" with Rodgers as the commander tried to explain his rationale. Pope wasn't buying it. "I don't know much about navigation, but what I can't yet see is why Rodgers sailed the plane to Kauai, 100 miles away, when Oahu was only 50 miles from us," said the aviation mechanic. "I could not reconcile myself to leaving what we could see for what we couldn't see." His crewmates eventually teased him about his despondency.

"Pope kept looking back at Oahu as if he was losing his last friend and all hope was gone," said Connell.

Rodgers, on the other hand, was steadfast in his decision. If they had to sail to Kauai, he said, so be it: "It was the best island anyway." "I've had some pleasant experiences on the Garden Isle, boys, and I know they'll show us a good time if we drift in there," said the unflappable commander.

A fierce storm soon washed away Pope's frustration, at least temporarily, offering rain showers to the parched sailors, who had last tasted water a day or so earlier, when they desperately drank from Rodgers's canteen, which he had carefully conserved and shared. The rainwater was truly a gift from heaven, and this time the crew collected the precipitation on the painted side of the torn wing fabric and then strained their liquid bounty through their shirts in an attempt to filter out aluminum paint. The cotton filter only helped so much, as the paint and dope-laden water tasted horrible. It was, said the crew, the most "slippery" water they ever drank. Yet fifteen minutes after ingesting the tainted rainwater, all five men were revitalized, their lives prolonged.

The boost in energy helped offset new setbacks and the accompanying drop in morale. The crew spied two airplanes heading directly for them, but then watched despairingly as the potential rescuers turned away, apparently oblivious to the flying boat beneath them. Days earlier, the minesweeper USS *Pelican* had done the same thing, just like the commercial steamer had done at the beginning of PN-9 No. 1's sea journey. The men could not stand having their hopes of rescue dashed again and again. "Fate seemed certainly against us," said one crewman. "Three times we thought we were sighted only to see them put about. Believe me that was tough."

For nine days the crew had sailed alone in a seaplane they had fashioned into a sailboat. They were without food and water, without fuel, and increasingly without hope. Their fellow aviators' loss of confidence had stung; the flying boat crew worried that the search would be called off any minute, with the navy abandoning Kauai Channel just as they were passing between the islands. And now airplanes, oblivious to the stranded sailors below, teased the men from above. Only the sharks could seem to lay eyes on the missing fliers.

"That, I think, was when our hopes sank to their lowest ebb," said the crewman. "It was too much and I for one was ready to call the shark up and say, 'Come and get me any time you're ready, big boy!'"

But as spirits flagged and sharks stalked, Rodgers displayed a cheerful demeanor alongside an iron will. "Hell, boys, we might be worse off than this," he told his disheartened crew, grinning. "Why I once knew a man who was adrift for fifteen days with nothing but a log under him!" The commander's good spirits and constant jokes helped stave off desperation. Rodgers—or "Navigatin' John"—had expertly navigated PN-9 No. 1 since the plane hit the water, giving his men great confidence in his leadership. He had successfully sailed a flying boat to the tiny Hawaiian Islands using primitive, yet time-tested, marine technology. The crew considered themselves exceedingly fortunate to have such an able and inspiring leader—a "bundle of pluck and courage," as Pope called him. "That means everything to the crew when it suffers the hard luck we had," he said. "There is a satisfaction in knowing that you have a superior officer who takes whatever the fates have in store and never flinches. Captain John Rodgers is the kind of officer that men would do anything for."

Preparing for landfall on Kauai, the crew kept awake that night until the lights of Oahu faded away. The moon was now waning, half of it visible. The darkness did not ease Pope's anxiety, no matter the faith he placed in Rodgers: "We knew our fate depended on the next day. We decided that if we missed Kauai we were lost, because no ships would search that side of the island."

When Connell attempted to relieve Pope from his watch in the pilot's cockpit late at night, Pope urged the lieutenant to go back to bed. "I knew I could not sleep, even if I tried, until we had sighted Kauai," said Pope.

On the morning of September 10, 1925, or day ten at sea, Kauai supposedly loomed in the distance. The crew had hoped to see the island at daybreak but instead were greeted by rainsqualls that limited visibility and made them nervous. By 9:00 AM the bad weather finally lifted, revealing the island at an incredibly close distance. Renowned for its beauty, Kauai was especially alluring to five starved sailors who had been stuck at sea for ten days. "There was Kauai sitting majestically in plain view," said Connell. "It was a wonderful sight." His crewmates were overjoyed, too, suddenly moving about the ship as if they were in perfect health. The men cheered their commander, crediting him for saving their lives. Rodgers just smiled in return.

Yet as the flying boat sailed close to Kauai, it was Rodgers who became nervous. He knew from experience that reefs around the island made it dangerous to reach shore. And as a student of naval history, he recalled the saga of sailors aboard *Saginaw*, a side-wheel navy ship that wrecked on a reef near the Kure Atoll in the middle of the Pacific in 1870, stranding ninety-three men on a small island. To obtain help, five men volunteered to sail a twenty-two-foot boat to the main islands of Hawaii, more than a thousand miles away. One month later, after exhausting their food supply and losing their oars, the crew of five spotted Kauai. But as they approached the island, their boat was tossed across the reefs. Four of the men drowned while a lone survivor was able to swim to shore, where he gave news of the shipwreck. Hawaii's king, Kamehameha V, quickly dispatched a ship to rescue the castaways that remained on Kure Atoll, all of whom were still alive.

As Rodgers spotted Kauai's "frowning cliffs," he fretted about sailing PN-9 No. 1 over these same reefs into one of the island's harbors. He and his men were so weak, he knew they could not hope to swim to safety should they be tossed into the sea. Fearing a court martial, he also didn't want to carelessly lose one of the navy's few flying boats. The navy motto expressed on his ancestor Oliver Hazard Perry's battle flag—"Don't Give Up the Ship!"—undoubtedly echoed through his head. "After sailing the plane 450 miles," Rodgers said, "I did not wish to be wrecked when landing."

Approaching Kauai's eastern shore, the men burned rags in a bucket, making smoke signals that would hopefully be seen on land. A crewman once again stood atop the upper wing, waving a stick with fabric attached, hoping to draw attention. By midafternoon they remained about fifteen miles off the coast. Rodgers was wary of trying to make a landing through the reefs with darkness looming. They decided to wait for morning before sailing into port. What was one more day of being missing?

The irony of the situation did not evade the commander. "We were confronted by a situation of trying to prevent ourselves from reaching the land that had been the objective of our days and nights of constant effort," said Rodgers, ordering the construction and deployment of an improvised sea anchor made of engine batteries and wire so that the flying boat might slow its progress.

Just then, about 2:40 PM during the missing fliers' tenth day at sea, the navy submarine R-4 appeared behind them. The sub's crew initially surmised they may have found the missing seaplane, but reconsidered when they noticed men moving atop its fuselage and wings. Anyone stranded at sea for nine days, they reasoned, would not be moving so spritely aboard the plane. They steamed ahead at full speed to get a better look.

The flying boat crew spotted the sub heading for them. The men of PN-9 No. 1 spoke not a word, though at least one admitted to mouthing a silent prayer of thanks. As the sub approached, it requested identification via semaphore: "WHAT PLANE IS THAT?"

"PN-9 NO. 1 FROM SAN FRANCISCO," the flying boat signaled back.

The sub moved closer, within thirty feet, to where the sub and plane crews could hear each other shout.

"Do you want to come aboard?" asked R-4's commander, Donald R. Osborn.

"No!" the flying boat crew responded with determination, explaining they were heading for port, either at Ahukini or Nawiliwili on Kauai's eastern shore.

"Stand by in case we miss the harbor," said Rodgers, who insisted he and his crew finish the journey.

Osborn stewed over Rodgers's refusal, unwilling to let the missing naval aviators endanger themselves further after miraculously being found alive. The sub commander wondered if Rodgers and his men were in their right minds. He was prepared to physically remove the men from the plane should they refuse a tow from the submarine.

"I'LL TOW YOU TO NAWILIWILI," said Osborn.

"All right, but give us some food, cigarettes, and matches. We have been five days on one canteen water," Rodgers relented, acknowledging the danger of drowning should PN-9 No. 1 go it alone over the reefs. "Let them tow us in," he told his crew. "Any ship takes a pilot going into harbor."

After water and bags of bread, sausage, canned peaches, and pears came aboard, the crew shouted another request to the submarine: "Give us some more of those peaches!" And then as his men greedily guzzled fresh water, Rodgers paused to offer a joke, suggesting they put aluminum paint in the water to make it taste natural.

The flying boat was towed to shore with some difficulty but finally reached Kauai late at night and was anchored. As the crew transferred into a small craft to take them to the beach, a large mullet jumped inside the rowboat. Stantz lifted the slippery fish up in his arms and laughed. "Big boy, if you had only done that two days ago you would not have lasted long," said the radioman.

Rodgers was the last man to leave PN-9 No. 1, stepping onto the rowboat and then Kauai as scores of residents cheered him and his crew, the locals having gathered at the beach as the news of their survival spread. As the fliers were shown to a cottage at a nearby hotel in Lihue, Rodgers began making plans for the next day, dead set on completing his journey, and not abandoning ship. "I'm going to ride that plane in when it is towed to Oahu," he insisted. Alternatively, he said he would instead repair PN-9 No. 1 in Kauai and then fly it to Honolulu himself. The onlookers could hardly believe what they were hearing.

"Another of his determinations we'll have to dissuade him from," said a fellow navy officer.

Doctors ordered the excited commander to bed, filling him and his crew with sleeping potions to facilitate their sleep. Still, Rodgers resisted. "I don't want to go to bed," he said after emerging from a hot bath. "I want to stay up and enjoy life."

The radio message from submarine R-4 was plainly written, with no hint of emotion. Yet upon reaching USS *California*, the flagship of the Pacific fleet, a wave of celebration washed over the battleship. After *California* relayed the note to shore, good cheer spread across Honolulu, the rest of Hawaii, and after that the world. "PLANE PN-9-1 LOCATED BY R-4 15 MILES NORTHEAST OF NAWILIWILI. PERSONNEL SAFE. AM TOWING THE SAME TO NAWILIWILI."

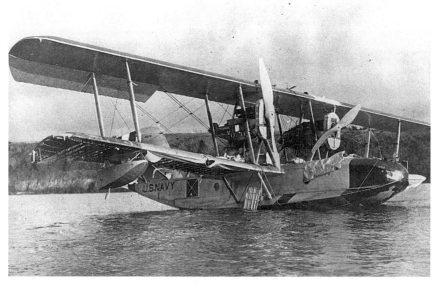

The navy's PN-9 No. 1 anchored in Kauai's Nawiliwili Harbor after its eleven-day flight and voyage across the Pacific Ocean ended in September 1925. Wooden ribs can be seen on the underside of the bottom wing, where fabric was removed to create a makeshift sail. An improvised keel made from metal floorboards dangles into the water alongside the starboard side of the flying boat's hull, beneath its lower wing. *Courtesy of the Hawaii Department of Transportation Airports*

Hardly anyone could believe the news: Commander John Rodgers and crew were safe after being missing for nearly ten days. It was astonishing: after flying for over twenty-five hours across nearly 1,900 miles of ocean and exhausting their fuel supply, Rodgers and his crew landed their flying boat atop the rolling ocean, affixed a sail between its wings, and sailed another 450 miles or so to reach the shore of Kauai.

"Up to the wardroom—all about and through the intricate and numerous passages of the vessel the message was whispered. It reached the decks—it reached up the ship's conning house. It reached every nook and cranny of the leviathan of steel. . . . Rodgers has been found. He's alive. He's safe," said one news report.

Once the news reached the quarters of Admiral S. S. Robinson, he ordered all navy ships back to port, the search now over and a tremendous success. Praise was soon heaped on the resourceful aviators and their fellow sailors. As journalist Charles Edward Hogue wrote:

> The indomitable spirit of the American Navy was never more strikingly exemplified than during the past nine days and nights while Commander John Rodgers and his companions on the US seaplane PN-9 No. 1 were adrift at sea. Landsmen wavered between hope and despair during those days: old salts shook their head dubiously, and shorestaying officialdom feared the worst. But the Navy itself held fast: surrender is a word missing from its vocabulary.

The saga of Commander Rodgers and his crew, wrote Hogue, was a "dramatic story of a nation's grief and a world's sympathy over an episode that threatened tragedy but—seldom found outside fiction—has ended happily."

In Honolulu there was pandemonium as news of the rescue spread across the city. Steamers clanged their bells and tied down their whistles, sending shrill—and sustained—sounds up and down the waterfront. Telephones rang nonstop. Dinner parties were canceled. People poured into cars across Oahu and cruised downtown, only to find the streets of Honolulu overrun with "thousands of persons shouting, shrieking, yelling . . . as the news of the rescue spread like a forest fire before a gale," reported the *Honolulu Advertiser*.

The *Advertiser* itself was nearly delirious, assigning its entire staff to cover the story. The paper soon printed three extra editions, each of which the crowds quickly snatched up, with people riding by on trolleys, holding up newsprint to share headlines like "When the Old Burg Went Mad" and "Whole City Goes Wild When Astounding News of Rescue Is Confirmed." One man grabbed an entire stack of papers, tossed a newsboy a dollar, and danced down the sidewalk, dishing copies to whomever he passed. Once the crowds were done shrieking, they sang a hymn together, *"Praise God from whom all blessings flow."* One Honolulu resident became upset as a friend relayed the happy news to her. "Wait! Don't tell me any more. I'm crying. I can't talk," said the woman, who claimed to be a friend to Rodgers.

Almost no one, it seemed, was absent from the celebration. Even if the *Advertiser* indulged in hyperbole, the scene seemed nothing short of electric, with the flight, and plight, of the crew of PN-9 No. 1 serving as an inspiring and redemptive tale that touched hearts across the islands. "As the truth of the report was realized the first awed silence was broken and the city literally went wild. Telephone wires hummed, children—and their elders—dashed from house to house crying the good news. Women wept tears of joy, children shouted with laughter, and staid men tossed dignity to the winds and capered with delight," the paper wrote. "Honolulu gasped in amaze. It couldn't be. But it was. Rodgers and his fellow flyers have lived to tell the tale."

An editorial continued to summarize the hysteria:

> Few messages in all history have been so vibrant with glad tidings. Few messages in all history have sent such a thrill of joy to so many millions of people upon the face of the earth! . . . Story of stories—for the world believed them dead. Surprise of all surprises—for the last fading gleam of hope had gone aglimmering! Joy of all joys—for hope kindled again—sparkled—flared—and flamed into reality. Verily a miracle of old! Verily the dead come to life.

At the café within the Alexander Young Hotel, the cake in the shape of the flying boat still stood in the window display. It was now quite stale, but still displayed its message of "Welcome." Elsewhere in Honolulu, a couple ushered a newborn into the world. Their son's name, they decided, would be Rodgers Martin Rofino, in honor of the death-defying naval commander.

The navy, if not quite as effusive as the residents of Honolulu, was just as proud of its men. "We are delighted," said navy secretary Curtis Wilbur. "We are very happy the men are safe."

The navy and Associated Press rushed to reach the fliers' families with the good news. In most cases, the journalists were quicker to the punch. When the press reached Rodgers's brother Robert, a correspondent read him dispatches about the rescue. On the other end was extended silence. Finally, Robert Rodgers spoke up. "Will you please read that again?" he asked, before wondering aloud if the news was indeed true.

In Jackson, Tennessee, Chief Skiles Pope's sister came undone when she received news of her brother's rescue. Passing the telephone to a friend, she explained through sobs that she had given up hope of ever seeing her brother alive again.

In Richmond, Indiana, it was more of the same, with the aunt of aviation machinist's mate William M. Bowlin proclaiming, "Oh thank God my prayers have been answered!"

Perhaps sweetest of all was the reaction of chief radio operator Otis Stantz's family, who lived in Terre Haute, Indiana. His wife, described as being plucky and tough during the ten days PN-9 No. 1 was missing, was overcome with joy upon learning her husband was alive. Though Stantz's wife was speechless, the couple's son managed to get a few words out. "Oh!" said an excited Otis Jr. "They've found my daddy!"

And in Los Angeles, the young Jean Vaughan, formerly of Hawaii— "tall, slender, blond and blue-eyed" according to one of the journalists who ambushed her—was questioned aggressively about her relationship to the flying boat commander. Reporters had been told Vaughan and Rodgers were engaged to be married, though Vaughan refused to comment on this rumor. "I shouldn't talk about it; I just shouldn't. I don't want to appear in this light of thrusting myself into the glory that properly belongs to Commander Rodgers," said the flustered twenty-year-old, explaining Rodgers was an old family friend. "Now please can't you just forget this story?"

A reporter did not believe Vaughan was totally forthcoming about her feelings for Rodgers. "Whether the beautiful Los Angeles girl spent sleepless hours during the long search for the lost PN-9 No. 1 or not, this much is certain," wrote the correspondent. "She appeared very happy tonight through all her embarrassment."

After an unpleasant ten days at sea, the naval aviators formerly aboard PN-9 No. 1 slept in relative luxury in a cottage at the Lihue Hotel, provided by its proprietor, Kauai sheriff William Henry Rice. The next morning the crew received breakfast as well as plenty of cigarettes and cigars, courtesy of the Kauai Chamber of Commerce. Additionally, a state senator loaned the aviators his car and Sheriff Rice's wife gave them leis. Yet the fliers seemed more interested in returning to sleep than touring the island in flower necklaces.

As the crew breakfasted, reporters and photographers waited outside the hotel cottage, eager to interview the men and snap a picture before they shaved. Impatient for news, the journalists begged hotel waiters for news tips as the staff shuffled about, asking how the aviators appeared and what stories they were sharing inside the cottage. When the reporters did finally speak to the navy men, they were surprised to learn the aviators were uninterested in rehashing portions of the journey or speculating how close they may have been to rescue. "Mathematical problems involving position didn't interest them half so much as thoughts of food and rest," wrote *Honolulu Advertiser* correspondent Ray Coll Jr.

Despite a good night's rest, the men appeared haggard, each sporting ten days of stubble on their scorched, sunburned faces. If one did not know they had been stranded at sea for ten days, one might mistake them as hoboes.

Doctors continued to examine them, proclaiming them to be in good health, but exhausted. Commander John Rodgers, they noticed, was especially fatigued. "That's easily explained," one of Rodgers's crew told reporters. "He stood every watch; he wouldn't sleep. There's a MAN for you."

Praise for the commander continued to pour from the lips of Rodgers's charges. "He kidded us through," they explained. "Not once did he lose heart. Doleful messages we received failed to make any impression on him. He joked about them and the surprise in store for the folks ashore when we should finally turn up safe and sound."

The crew of PN-9 No. 1 soon after arriving to Kauai, before the navy men were allowed a full shave and scrub. The aviators suffered from extreme sunburn, hunger, and thirst while sailing their flying boat to Hawaii after running out of gas. (From left to right) William H. Bowlin, machinist's mate; Lieutenant Byron J. Connell; Commander John Rodgers; Skiles R. Pope, chief machinist's mate; Otis G. Stantz, chief radio operator. *Courtesy of the Hawaii Department of Transportation Airports*

When Rodgers was able, he returned the compliments, proud to report his crew was "always cheerful and worked with as much energy as if getting full rations every day. . . . As a matter of fact," he said, "it appears from what we heard after our arrival that we were the least concerned people in the world."

With all the questions being shouted their way, the crew had only one in return: Did the Boeing plane eventually take off and make a successful nonstop flight to Hawaii?

No, they were told. A nonstop flight to the Hawaiian Islands had yet to be accomplished, by the navy or anyone else. Rodgers and his crew soon volunteered that they would try again, and this time be successful.

Hours later, the aviators boarded USS *MacDonough*, which had arrived from Oahu loaded with doctors and nurses. As the destroyer returned to Pearl Harbor with the men aboard, Rodgers dictated an account of his journey to be broadcast publicly from the ship's radio room. He delivered this account haltingly, his tired mind struggling to recall basic words and ideas. At one point, when he deemed the flight a failure, other officers listening to his story rebuked him. Nonsense, they countered, the flight of PN-9 No. 1 was in fact one of the greatest tales in the history of flight. Rodgers's journey to Hawaii by air and sea was nothing less than epic.

As *MacDonough* neared Oahu, a crowd gathered at Pier 1010 at the navy yard within Pearl Harbor to welcome the flying boat's crew. Behind the crowd a rainbow arced over the steep, green Koolau Mountains, and as dusk approached people craned their necks to try to catch a glimpse of Rodgers aboard the looming destroyer. With the ship nearly to the dock, surrounding vessels let loose their whistles and sirens blared. Then church bells in Honolulu were rung so vigorously that the bells of St. Andrew's Cathedral and St. Clement's Church cracked. Rodgers and his crew waved from the ship's bridge as the crowd shouted to the men, which added to the din.

"How are you old boy?" sailors called up to the commander, who was smoking a cigar through a close-lipped smile.

"Three cheers for John Rodgers and his crew!" another sailor shouted, to which the crowd responded heartily, with Admiral John McDonald, commandant of the Fourteenth Naval District, joining in the celebration.

As the sun dipped below the horizon just before *MacDonough* came to rest, the battleship *Nevada* shone a bright spotlight on the pier. Additionally, flares were lit, making the illumination even more intense as the ship was secured. Into this incredible spotlight strode Rodgers, dazed and blinking hard against the glare. The hero, dressed in khaki uniform and cap, appeared somber and sea-worn. His eyes looked heavy and his body lean. Yet he remained smiling.

The admiral greeted him, as did Hawaii's territorial governor, Wallace Farrington, and Farrington's wife, who placed even more leis around each aviator's neck. Rodgers thanked the crew of *MacDonough* for their hospitality before turning to the crowd assembled on the pier. "Good evening, governor. I have some mail here for you people," he said, pulling from his coat a package of letters that had been entrusted to him before he departed San Francisco. The crowd could see his mouth twitching from exhaustion. The commander spoke with marked tenderness, and his hand was conspicuously bandaged, having been broken the night before when helping anchor his flying boat off the beach on Kauai. Delivering the letters, he ignored the shouts—"Oh, John . . . John!"—that came frequently from the crowd.

Noticing the aviators' fatigue, navy officers and civic leaders escorted the five men to waiting cars. Though tired, all seemed in good spirits, save Skiles Pope, who slumped into an automobile seat and tried to ignore the hoopla. Meanwhile, William Bowlin was lapping up the attention, basking in the hero treatment and happily sharing stories of his adventure. "Feel fine," said the twenty-six-year-old. "Never felt better in my life."

As the small motorcade moved away from the pier, Bowlin called to a friend in the crowd: "They're going to shove us in the hospital for the night— they sure do keep an eye on us—but I'm going to town tomorrow!"

Rodgers and his crew remained in the spotlight, at least figuratively speaking, for the next two weeks. In Honolulu they were feted continuously after coming ashore, including being made guests of honor during an impromptu thanksgiving organized at the Hawaiian capitol. Governor Farrington said he wanted to give the navy crew a "real Hawaiian aloha." More than five thousand residents turned up to cheer the aviators during the thanksgiving, with the crowd becoming so unruly that police struggled to keep order. Bands played loudly, fireworks screamed into the air, and, as Rodgers and his crew pulled up in cars, whistles, sirens, and horns blasted. A near stampede occurred, forcing the police to shove the crowd backward.

Rodgers, gamely embracing all the attention, addressed the excited audience before him. "Now, let me correct an erroneous impression. We were not drifting. We were sailing," said the hero. "We were making the great speed of two knots an hour—and we knew that, sooner or later, we would make port. And we were about to make port when somebody came along and found us. Of course we did not arrive in Hawaii according to previously well laid plans, but everybody now seems satisfied, so I guess it's all right," continued Rodgers, who exited the event as the band launched into a rendition of the "Star-Spangled Banner."

Days later the fliers were honored during a luncheon atop the roof garden of the Alexander Young Hotel, where they were presented watches, yet more leis, and basketfuls of gold and red hibiscus flowers. Local girls sang songs about Kauai, and a pair of eighty-year-old women danced a hula. Addressing a crowd of six hundred people, Governor Farrington paid the navy men tribute, while also teasing them a bit. "This is not a land of cowards—because cowards have never reached here—but a land built up by brave pioneers and the sons who followed in their footsteps. That land welcomes you," he said. "You sent me a radiogram the afternoon you sailed. It said: 'See you tomorrow.' That tomorrow was a long time arriving—but it was a great day when it did arrive."

And then, that same afternoon, before leaving Hawaii the next day for San Francisco, Rodgers and his crew met another crowd at the governor's official residence, Washington Place, to say goodbye and shake hands with 1,500 people. Rodgers remained cheerful in the face of so many cameras and audiences. When speaking to journalists, he expressed amusement over all the attention: "You newspaper men are all right. I'll give you credit. You are on the job—and I like a fellow who is on the job. You made a good job of consigning me to the deep—and then made a fine job of it when you resurrected me."

"How does it feel to be 'dead'?" a reporter asked.

"Wonderful sensation," he replied. "One advantage of being dead, you soon learn what the world thinks of you." Rodgers then gently addressed some of the cynics associated with his disappearance and rescue:

> While we were out there sailing along, we often heard how our plane had dropped to the bottom of the ocean. We heard condolences— and we heard bitter words tossed about. We heard suggestions as to how the accident could have been prevented. We heard very clearly expressed explanations how we plunged downward the moment we landed. So we decided that those who had not seen us go down knew more about it than we did—and we resigned ourselves to the inevi- table—for the time being. Having no way to answer back, we didn't answer back. We just came back.

Arriving in San Francisco a week or so later, he and his men were hon- ored in grand fashion again, this time by being placed at the head of a parade and military procession that marched up Market Street to city hall, where they were feted by the mayor and other California dignitaries and politicians. The men repeated their stories for the crowd, and civic and military lead- ers again paid them tribute. Mayor James Rolph lauded Rodgers as a man without nerves.

"But I have nerves," responded Rodgers, "and every one of them is tingling at this wonderful reception. . . . There is nothing in the world like San Francisco hospitality."

More gifts were bestowed upon the heroes. Rodgers received a silver service he could place at home at Sion Hill, a companion set to pair with the service President Abraham Lincoln gifted his ancestor—the second John Rodgers of navy fame—more than sixty years ago. Connell received a silver service, too, while each enlisted member of the crew received a diamond ring engraved with his name, depictions of flying boats, and the words "endurance and heroism" on the gold band. All men had originally been offered cash prizes, which they declined out of modesty, not expecting San Francisco residents would insist they accept some kind of reward. "Golden Gate, gee, it was good to pass through again," said Pope of his return to the mainland. "And now it's golden rings. You can't beat San Francisco."

After that reception and another in Oakland, Rodgers was called to Washington, where he and Connell were due to testify during hearings on air safety in the military. He had also been named assistant chief of the navy's Bureau of Aeronautics, a sizable promotion almost without precedent in the navy. From this post he could champion his philosophy regarding aviation and his belief that risk-taking was a necessary part of its progress. "Aviation is a hazardous calling . . . if you advance in it," said Rodgers. "If you stand still, fly around in circles in the same plane, it is safe. But advance, go out . . . in all kinds of weather or attempt new distances, and it's dangerous."

"If there are swivel chair men in Washington who are afraid of taking the planes out of the hangar," he continued, "we will never benefit by aviation in this generation."

Within two months the restless officer asked the navy for a transfer from Washington to sea duty, but was refused. In time he was relieved of his position and tasked with further study of overseas flight, including the planning of a second attempt to fly nonstop to Hawaii.

And so it was nearly a year later that a mechanic and Rodgers, still unmarried, took off from Anacostia Field in Washington, DC, for a flight north to the Philadelphia Naval Shipyard. There Rodgers planned to inspect PN-10s, the navy's latest version of a flying boat. Connell was due to join him.

Piloting a small biplane toward the shipyard, Rodgers began to glide in for a landing late in the afternoon on August 27, 1926. When the plane descended to a height of about one hundred feet, it suddenly lurched into the Delaware River, which flowed past the navy base just one hundred yards away. Navy personnel ran, and then swam, to the accident site just offshore. There they found Rodgers and the mechanic alive but severely injured, trapped inside the aircraft with their heads barely above water. The rescuers worked in water up to their necks for the next hour, attempting to free the men from their harnesses and the severely crumpled aircraft.

Rodgers sat in a pool of water within the cockpit, the smashed engine pressed tight against his chest. His ribs were crushed and likely pressing upon his organs. One leg was split open, clearly broken in two places. "Go easy, boys, I'm caught somewhere," he said in a low, labored voice.

Despite much pulling and twisting, rescuers could not free Rodgers from the plane with their bare hands. Eventually a barge with tools arrived to the crash site. With wrenches and saws in hand, rescuers, including Connell, slowly removed Rodgers, all while medical personnel administered stimulants to keep him awake. Despite the rescuers' efforts, the commander faded in and out of consciousness, pleading with the men to handle him gently. The color drained from his face and he suffered tremendous pain. He requested that his mother be called to him, but it was too late. An ambulance brought Rodgers to the nearby naval hospital, where he died from shock and internal bleeding.

Four days later Rodgers's body arrived at Arlington National Cemetery following a viewing at Sion Hill. A carriage pulled by six horses delivered the commander to his grave beneath four stately oaks, all while a navy band played Frederic Chopin's "Funeral March." Exactly one year after taking off into the sky for Hawaii, Rodgers was placed beneath the ground in Virginia, buried with full honors. With the fearless naval aviator tucked tight within his grave, it remained for another brave flier to make the first full Hawaiian Hop.

PART II

THE ARMY'S
BIRD OF PARADISE

IT WAS NEWS HEARD around the world. On May 20, 1927, Charles Lindbergh took off from Long Island, New York, and began a perilous flight across the cold Atlantic Ocean. For more than thirty-three hours Lindbergh was alone in his small single-engine plane, *Spirit of St. Louis,* unable to catch a wink of sleep as he steered through the morning, afternoon, and night. The next day the exhausted flier crossed into France and made a beeline for Paris, knowing that his final destination—Le Bourget Airport—was a few miles northeast of the city.

As he approached in darkness late at night, Lindbergh was confused by thousands of lights concentrated on the ground below, mistakenly believing he was headed toward an industrial complex. He soon realized the lights were car headlamps—lots of them. More than 150,000 people had come to the airport to greet the pilot and give him a hero's welcome. Upon landing on solid ground, Lindbergh found he could not travel much farther. "I start[ed] to taxi toward the hangars," he said, "but the entire field ahead [was] covered with running figures!"

Frenchmen mobbed the plane, pulled Lindbergh out of the cockpit, and made him airborne once again, throwing the hero upward onto their hands and shoulders. Lindbergh had just completed the first solo nonstop flight across an ocean, and the crowd knew that his 3,600-mile triumph heralded the beginning of routine intercontinental air travel.

Not that it had been easy: Lindbergh had endured a tortuous day and a half crossing the Atlantic, relegated to a wicker chair placed before an instrument panel. The panel, upon which he penciled tally marks after the passing of each hour, was devoid of many instruments, including a fuel gauge. Lindbergh deemed such an instrument superfluous—either he had enough fuel to make it or he didn't. A gauge would only give him early warning, so why carry the extra weight?

He applied the same rationale to other aviation equipment, reasoning a parachute and radio held little utility and therefore should stay off his airplane. To save even more weight, he cut the bottoms and tops off his maps and even forbade a decorative layer of veneer from being applied to the plywood instrument panel. His rations were minimal as well, with the pilot allowing himself a mere five sandwiches, or one for roughly every seven hours of flight.

Adding to Lindbergh's discomfort was the fact that he could not see directly out the front of his airplane. The great distance he was attempting to travel required large fuel tanks, which he installed directly behind the engine, and in front of the tiny cockpit, in order to spare himself from a precarious position within the fuselage. "You'd be like the filling in a sandwich—your knees against the firewall, your back against the gasoline," he explained. Yet such an arrangement blocked his view out the front windshield, meaning that whenever he wanted to see ahead, he had to briefly turn the plane to the right or left and glance out a side window. Alternatively, he could stare forward through a custom-made periscope, which certainly would have contributed to the feeling that he, essentially flying blind within a capsule, was piloting a submarine as much as an airplane. But perhaps Lindbergh should not have been surprised to find himself packed tight inside a container of metal and paper wrapping— *Spirit of St. Louis*'s manufacturer, Ryan Airlines, leased its factory space within a San Diego fish cannery.

These hardships, as well as trouble with fog, icing, storms, and sleepiness, were all but forgotten upon Lindbergh's arrival in Paris and his anointment as a worldwide hero. While other aviators had flown across the Atlantic in assorted fashion during the last eight years, no pilot had made the crossing alone and with such panache. Lindbergh, it was noted, executed his New York–to–Paris flight plan perfectly.

By 1927 nearly one hundred people had already made the Atlantic crossing by air, the bulk of them within two rigid airships that floated to the United States from Scotland and Germany. Six others had been aboard US Navy flying boat NC-4, which hopscotched across the Atlantic in 1919, as well as four crew aboard the two US Army planes that slowly flew around the world in 1924 on a trip featuring more than fifty stops. In 1919 British aviators John Alcock and Arthur Whitten Brown made perhaps the most notable crossing of the Atlantic by flying nonstop from Newfoundland to Ireland, though the relatively short ocean route they chose between the two islands was of limited practical value. In January 1926 a Spanish Army crew that included pilot Ramón Franco, brother to the future Spanish leader Francisco Franco, flew from the Spanish coast to Brazil in a flying boat, making a handful of stops. Portuguese aviators made their own transatlantic flight by flying boat in March 1927, also flying to Brazil in multiple legs.

Yet Lindbergh's solo nonstop flight between two world metropolises was almost beyond comparison. The twenty-five-year-old airmail pilot, the son of a late congressman from Minnesota, crossed the Atlantic with little help, relying on his own common sense and pluck as well as financial support from a small group of businessmen from St. Louis, Missouri. The flight allowed him to claim a $25,000 cash prize offered by New York hotelier Raymond Orteig, a French expatriate keen on promoting air travel between the United States and his homeland.

Lindbergh was not alone in seeking to fly between New York and Paris. His vaunted competitors for the Orteig prize included the World War I French flying aces René Fonck and Charles Nungesser, flying separately, and American competitors that included Richard Byrd, who in 1926 won great acclaim for his purported, but unproven, North Pole exploration by airplane. All these rivals favored using small crews of aviators aboard expensive, multiengine airplanes. Aiming to avoid the infighting and mishaps that came to plague these rival teams, Lindbergh favored a simpler approach; using one pilot to fly a small plane with one engine.

Critics deemed such an approach reckless, a surefire recipe for disaster on such a long journey. Lindbergh, or the "Flyin' Fool" as one newspaper labeled him, was not considered a serious contender to cross the Atlantic. But the truth was the ambitious young pilot had identified a huge advantage in choosing to rely only on himself and his single-engine plane. Lindbergh was nimbler and beholden to no one, free from the conventional wisdom that a flight across the Atlantic required tremendous resources. To his mind, a flight across the Atlantic Ocean could be no worse than the nighttime airmail routes he flew through the Midwest during winter. "New York to Paris—it sounds like a dream. And yet—if one could carry fuel enough . . . if the engine didn't stop . . . if one just held to the right course long enough, one should arrive in Europe," he later wrote of his reasoning.

When the hotelier Orteig originally offered his cash prize for a nonstop flight between New York and Paris in 1919, there were no takers. Few, if any, planes made at the time could carry enough fuel to fly that distance. Such a journey seemed outright preposterous to much of the public. When Lord Northcliffe, publisher of London's *Daily Mail*, offered a similar cash award in 1913 to the first pilot to fly nonstop between the British Isles and the United States, competing newspapers mocked him, offering prizes for the first people to fly to the moon, Mars, and Venus.

By the time Orteig renewed his contest in 1925, the aviation world had changed. Planes were lighter, faster, and more fuel efficient—so much so that a young pilot like Lindbergh could turn the dream of flying across the Atlantic into reality. Lindbergh's accomplishment earned him many honors: the French president awarded him the Legion of Honour; US president Calvin Coolidge bestowed upon him the Distinguished Flying Cross; *Time* magazine named him Man of the Year; and New York City threw the hero a ticker-tape parade upon his homecoming.

All the hoopla indicated one thing: a new era in flight had begun. As Lindbergh said, "The pioneering is over, but the perfecting is yet to be done."

Among those particularly excited by Charles Lindbergh's flight was the Hawaiian pineapple tycoon James Dole. He read reports of the ocean crossing while visiting San Francisco, a city 2,400 miles and half an ocean away from his home and business on the island of Oahu. Hawaii's "Pineapple King" had hardly digested the news when he received a telegram from newspapermen back home. Like people the world over, *Honolulu Star-Bulletin* editors Riley Allen and Joe Farrington were awestruck by Lindbergh's stunning feat. Inspired by the Orteig prize, the editors asked Dole to sponsor his own reward for the first person to pilot a plane from the mainland to Hawaii. If Lindbergh could cross the Atlantic, the editors wondered, why couldn't another intrepid aviator, or Lindbergh himself, fly halfway across the Pacific? As a portion of the editors' choppy telegram to Dole stated:

IN VIEW LINDBERGHS ATLANTIC FLIGHT PACIFIC REMAINS ONE GREAT
AREA FOR CONQUEST AVIATION STOP SITUATION THIS MOMENT RIPE
SOMEONE OFFER SUITABLE PRIZE NONSTOP FLIGHT HAWAII . . . WE
BELIEVE YOU MAN TO DO THIS STOP PRIZE SHOULD BE KNOWN DOLE
PRIZE STOP THIS WILL PUT YOUR NAME EVERY NEWSPAPER IN WORLD
BESIDES GREAT CREDIT TERRITORY PINEAPPLE INDUSTRY . . . AWAIT
ANXIOUSLY FAVORABLE REPLY . . . NOT PUBLISHING ANYTHING UNTIL
HEARING FROM YOU.

The proposition intrigued Dole. He knew the establishment of regular air travel could help Hawaii emerge from its isolation. In the early 1920s, just eight thousand people visited the islands each year. Dole and other civic leaders knew there was room for plenty more guests.

Dole himself first traveled to Hawaii in 1899 after graduating from Harvard University with an agriculture degree. By steaming to Hawaii, the twenty-two-year-old was following in the footsteps of some of his ancestors. Early in the nineteenth century a number of Protestant missionaries endured miserable, five-month ocean voyages from Boston to settle in Hawaii.

The Protestant settlers were mostly successful in their aims, shaping Hawaiian society by introducing their own religion and written language. The white settlers gained influence with Hawaiian rulers and eventually toppled the monarchy in 1893 when Queen Liliuokalani relinquished her throne in the face of an armed revolt. Sanford Dole, a cousin to James Dole's father, was named president of the Republic of Hawaii the next year and governed the islands until their annexation into the United States four years later.

As boys, Sanford Dole of Honolulu and his far-flung cousin Charles Dole in New England had mailed packages to each other, trading island staples like sea shells, coral, and lava for New England delicacies of cracked butternuts and maple sugar. Charles grew up to graduate summa cum laude from Harvard and then became an outspoken and well-liked progressive minister in Massachusetts. On September 27, 1877, his wife, Fannie, gave birth to their firstborn, James Drummond Dole.

The Doles spent much of each year living just outside Boston, where Charles Dole was the minister of the First Congregational Church of Jamaica Plain. In summers the family moved to a home in Southwest Harbor, Maine, buoyed financially by an inheritance Fannie Dole received. Young James was mesmerized by this "lovely play ground" by the sea, where he wrote that one could find "a lake between nearly every pair of mountains and a trout brook running into nearly every lake." Others felt just as passionate about the area, with some of the country's richest families, including the Morgans, Rockefellers, and Vanderbilts, purchasing grand summer homes on other parts of Maine's Mount Desert Island.

Fannie gardened and painted in Maine while her three children sailed, untying their boats from a dock just a short walk down from their hillside home. In Maine, James Dole discovered he had a green thumb just like his mother, sowing corn and beans in the garden. Yet when it came to schoolwork, he displayed much less passion and natural talent. "Jim did not specially shine as a scholar, but we were never worried over this," wrote his father. "The processes of his mind were straightforward and he possessed good common sense."

At Harvard, Dole earned a single A in his classes—for a half course in botany his freshman year. As he continued his studies, he enrolled within the Bussey Institution at Harvard, which taught agriculture and horticulture. Beyond farming basics, Dole absorbed lessons he'd find particularly useful in the coming years, such as instruction on how to preserve meats and vegetables and strategies for using machinery to efficiently process large amounts of crops.

Upon graduation from Harvard, he decided, rather unconventionally, to become a farmer in Hawaii. With his parents' encouragement, he sold his sailboat in Maine and departed for the islands, carrying $1,500, five letters of introduction, a book on bookkeeping, and a pair of pruning shears. The young Yankee imagined paradise awaited in the tropics. "I got the notion that life in Hawaii was just one long, sweet song," he later wrote. "I had the idea that after two or three years of reasonable effort expended on cheap government land, I would be able to spend the rest of my life in a hammock, smoking cigars rolled from tobacco grown on my own place, and generally enjoying a languorous life of ease and plenty."

When James Dole arrived to Oahu in November 1899, he moved into the Honolulu home of his uncle Sanford and aunt Anna. Charles Dole had maintained his pen pal relationship with Sanford since their childhoods, remaining intimate enough with the president of the Republic of Hawaii to feel comfortable expressing his opposition to his cousin's usurpation of the Hawaiian monarchy. James's farming career started slowly, in part due to the disruption caused by a large quarantine in Honolulu to prevent the spread of the bubonic plague, which had been discovered in the city's Chinatown. Dole spent much time at the beach his first few months in Hawaii. He also read Shakespeare, wrote a few travel articles, and trimmed his uncle's kiawe trees for a dollar a day, putting his shears to good use. It seemed an easy transition for the young man, who benefited from the social connections and prominence of his relative. When friends in New England wrote to Dole, they were instructed to send mail to:

> Mr. James D. Dole
> Honolulu, Hawaiian Islands
> c/o President Dole

During the summer of 1900 Dole bought sixty-one acres in Wahiawa, twenty-five miles northwest of Honolulu, which at that time could be reached by a five-hour journey by horse and buggy or cart. The property, covered with wild grass and guava bushes, afforded views of the ocean in two directions. Gorgeous green mountains and rolling fields surrounded his acreage. No buildings existed on the property, so Dole lived with the neighbors as he cleared and planted the land.

In time Dole built and lived in his own barn in Wahiawa, sharing the quarters with a horse named Withers who had a cracked hoof. After a while Dole moved from the barn to a one-room shack. A hen came into his home every morning to lay an egg on a shelf. Dole enjoyed his foray into farming, no matter the hard labor, long hours, and little pay. His father, ever the mentor, cautioned his son to take hardship in stride and not become overwhelmed. "Don't take the business too seriously, laugh every day, use your philosophy and see that it becomes a religion for your comfort and uplift. A man needs a bit of quieting thought every day, that he may do his work more effectively," Charles wrote in 1903. "It is quite as necessary as food in order to keep his nerves from jarring."

Dole planted a plethora of crops in his first years as a farmer—star fruit, coffee, cashews, watermelons, potatoes—but only one was particularly profitable: pineapple. Hawaiians knew this food as *hala kahiki*, or "foreign fruit." Though pineapple has become strongly associated with Hawaii, it is not indigenous to the islands. Rather, pineapples are native to South America, originally coming from Paraguay and Brazil before spreading across the world.

The market for fresh pineapple was limited, especially in isolated and sparsely populated Hawaii. Yet the market for canned pineapple, Dole surmised, could likely be much, much larger. By canning and preserving pineapples, Dole knew he could sell the fruit the entire year and ship it to any part of the world. The young entrepreneur soon raised money from investors in Hawaii and New England, purchased machinery, and in 1901 incorporated the Hawaiian Pineapple Company, or HAPCO.

Dole was not the only farmer in Hawaii who grew pineapples for export. Yet the young man from New England quickly outdistanced his competitors through his shrewd leadership of HAPCO. Eager to grow the company in a hurry, he established business partnerships that facilitated product distribution and helped begin the construction of a cannery on Oahu. In 1907 Dole relocated the cannery from Wahiawa to Honolulu's waterfront, right beside a can factory and railroad line. Logistically speaking, this was a magnificent improvement. Now the HAPCO cannery could receive fresh pineapple on railroad cars that rolled in from the Wahiawa fields and place the fruit in cans obtained from the factory next door.

Now that Dole could efficiently ship canned pineapple to the mainland, he needed a robust market for his exotic fruit. He persuaded other Hawaiian planters to invest with him in a national marketing campaign for pineapple. The campaign's many ads in magazines and newspapers featured smooth slogans that promised the superiority of pineapples grown on the islands.

"Don't ask for pineapple alone, insist on HAWAIIAN pineapple," read one ad.

Said another, "Hawaiian pineapple is no more like other canned pineapple than a Baldwin apple is like a raw turnip."

Many pineapple advertisements included recipes, which were useful for potential consumers entirely unfamiliar with the fruit. Dole's own grandmother thought the pineapple was some type of hard apple. For customers like her there was the following type of ad: "It Cuts with a Spoon—Like a Peach."

On November 16, 1916, Americans celebrated Hawaiian Pineapple Day. James A. Dunbar and Alfredo Perez composed lyrics and music, respectively, for the holiday's "Pineapple Rag." As the song bragged:

> Talk about your Boston beans or hoe-cake from the South,
> Or chicken à la Maryland that melts in your mouth,
> There's nothing in creation or that's in the eating line

That can compare in flavor to the "apple of the pine."
This pineapple, this pineapple, it's got me going right,
I call for it at breakfast and cry for it at night,
And every minute in between if you would win my smiles
Give me a juicy pineapple from the fair Hawaiian Isles.

Beyond boosting HAPCO's marketing, Dole sought to improve the company's canneries. In 1911 he hired the mechanical draftsman Henry Gabriel Ginaca to create a new machine for processing pineapples. The existing machinery was dangerous, sometimes cutting employees' fingers as well as pineapples. It was also inefficient, requiring much additional processing work by hand. It took Ginaca two years, and two failed prototypes, before he invented a machine that could process thirty-five pineapples a minute—a tremendous improvement that would soon increase to the rate of one hundred pineapples a minute. The Ginaca machine—which automatically chopped off the top and bottom of a pineapple, cored and skinned the fruit, and then sliced what was left—proved a major boon for business.

HAPCO's fortunes soared thanks to all these innovations, and Dole became a rich man. By 1922 or so, he bought a large house on Green Street in Honolulu that sat on five acres along the slopes of Punchbowl volcano. Dole employed gardeners and other staff on the property, ensuring that he, his wife Belle, and their five children would always have orchids blooming in the greenhouse, canaries singing in the aviary, and fresh milk squeezed from the estate's dairy cows. His third child and oldest daughter, Betty, recalled pleasant days on Green Street: "When I was growing up, father was called 'The Pineapple King' and I had all the advantages of growing up as a pineapple princess. I lived in a big beautiful house with a cook, a downstairs maid, an upstairs maid, a chauffeur, and four yardmen. I had the best of medical and dental care, travelled twice to Europe, and went to private schools."

The home featured oak parquet floors, a parlor containing a piano and phonograph, a library, and a porch with a Ping-Pong table and wicker furniture. Belle and the children slept on the second floor while James slept in a round room on the third floor that afforded views of downtown Honolulu and the Pacific Ocean. In time he would also purchase a home on Kahala Beach near Diamond Head and build a shed on Kailua Beach, where his family could shower and enjoy the comforts of a restroom. During summers the family moved to Dole's original farm in Wahiawa, where he had erected a prefabricated cedar house beside his old one-room shack.

Dole had little time to fully enjoy these properties. He worked long hours, usually arriving home just in time to dine with his family. Many weekends were devoted to HAPCO, as were extended trips around the world. In 1921, for example, he traveled to Mexico, the Philippines, Fiji, Malaya, and Australia to search for new areas to plant pineapple. None of these lands, he decided, could compare to Hawaii.

For years HAPCO had leased agricultural fields on Oahu and Maui to supplement the pineapple harvests from their own plantations. But always, Dole felt, the company could use more land to grow more fruit. In 1922 he attempted to solve this problem in a big way, negotiating the purchase of the Hawaiian island of Lanai, just sixty or so miles southeast of Oahu, close to Maui. For $1.1 million, HAPCO received eighty-nine thousand dry and dusty acres, a quarter of which was suitable for cultivation. "We bought Lanai to get room to grow in," said Dole.

In previous decades herds of cattle and other livestock that grazed across ranches had denuded much of Lanai's vegetation. As a result the island dried up, eroded, and became covered in cacti. To grow pineapples efficiently on the island, Dole constructed a costly reservoir and pipe system to deliver water from the rainy east side of the island to the dry, western portion. He constructed the town of Lanai City to house the immigrants he lured to work in HAPCO's new fields. The Pineapple King also planted trees, paved roads, and dredged and blasted a twenty-seven-foot harbor out of rock. In celebration of these accomplishments, HAPCO chartered a steamship on January 30, 1926, to deliver 140 dignitaries and guests to Lanai, including Hawaii's governor. These guests were chauffeured across the island in Ford automobiles and served a gourmet buffet.

By 1927, a quarter century after Dole founded his pineapple company, HAPCO was the leading pineapple producer in Hawaii, processing one hundred thousand tons of pineapple a year and controlling a third of the canned pineapple market, supposedly selling pineapple in nearly every grocery store in the United States. The company's pineapple fields had grown from Dole's original sixty-one acres in Wahiawa to forty-thousand acres, half of which was on Lanai. HAPCO operated a massive cannery that operated night shifts to fulfill demand and was capable of producing half a million cans of pineapple a day. These cans were then branded under a variety of different labels, from Paradise Island to HAPCO's Best to Pacific Gems and more.

Thanks to Dole's and other growers' efforts, pineapple was one of the largest industries in Hawaii, second only to sugar. HAPCO's workforce was no longer limited to James Dole and Withers the lame horse, but included 2,750 permanent workers and 4,250 seasonal employees. Many of these workers were Asian immigrants who labored in the pineapple fields and cannery, performing exhausting and monotonous jobs. In the newly constructed plantation village of Lanai City, Asian and Hawaiian workers lived in segregated housing that contained no indoor plumbing, electricity, or gas.

Despite these conditions, which mirrored the hardships of immigrants who harvested and processed Hawaii's vast sugarcane fields, Dole otherwise sought to treat his workers well, at least in his own mind, promising a "square deal to every employee." HAPCO operated an employee cafeteria and children's nursery at its cannery, sent medical nurses to make rounds through the plantation villages, and built recreational ball fields for employees and their families to use. The company paid annual bonuses based on a worker's longevity at HAPCO and offered employees the chance to buy stock and receive a pension. "I have been particularly interested in trying to organize our business in such a way that every employee, so far as possible, may feel that his interest is that of the company and vice versa," said Dole.

Dole's leadership of HAPCO earned him celebrity status in Hawaii, with the press reporting on his comings and goings from the mainland. When his oldest son, Dick, eloped in Las Vegas, the sudden nuptials made front-page news for days. HAPCO's board valued Dole so much that it paid him $50,000 a year beginning in 1925 and insured his life for $1 million. When a competitor sought to purchase HAPCO in the late 1920s, the company was valued at $46.7 million. But Dole was not interested in selling. The new pineapple fields being planted on Lanai would potentially double the company's production, and Dole, whose own name was just starting to be stamped onto pineapple can lids in an effort to better brand the fruit, had no plans for stepping away from the helm.

It was during this period of bullishness and expansion that Dole received a telegram from the editors at the *Honolulu Star-Bulletin* requesting that he capitalize on the worldwide excitement concerning Lindbergh's Atlantic crossing. The Pineapple King wasted little time accepting their suggestion, deciding that it was in both HAPCO's and Hawaii's best interests to sponsor an air contest to the Hawaiian Islands. It was obvious that air travel was changing the world, and he did not want Hawaii to be left behind. On May 24, 1927, three days after Lindbergh's flight to Paris, Dole telegrammed the *Star-Bulletin* editors from San Francisco to confirm he would sponsor a prize to encourage the first overseas flights to Hawaii:

> JAMES D. DOLE ... BELIEVING THAT LINDBERGHS EXTRAORDINARY FEAT IN CROSSING THE ATLANTIC IS THE FORERUNNER OF EVENTUAL TRANSPACIFIC AIR TRANSPORTATION OFFERS TWENTY FIVE THOUSAND DOLLARS TO FIRST FLYER AND TEN THOUSAND TO SECOND FLYER TO CROSS FROM NORTH AMERICAN CONTINENT TO HONOLULU IN NON STOP FLIGHT.

As the editors predicted, aviators far and wide heard Dole's announcement. For every pilot who admired Lindbergh's gumption, here was a chance for similar flying glory and a fat paycheck. Amateur pilots across the country scrambled to find a plane to take across the Pacific to Hawaii.

The next day, communicating by telegram to Honolulu's rival daily newspaper, the *Advertiser*, Dole elaborated on his hopes for the contest, stating that air travel meant Honolulu residents could receive visitors and mail much more quickly, leaving the islands far less isolated. Such progress should not come at the expense of safety, however. "NO PRECAUTION CAN BE TOO GREAT TO SATISFY ALL WHO ARE SINCERELY INTERESTED IN THE PERMANENT DEVELOPMENT OF AVIATION," telegrammed Dole, who offered to personally greet Lindbergh at the John Rodgers Airport in Honolulu. He continued:

> IT IS NATURAL FOR ALL OF US IN HAWAII AS WELL AS ALL FOLLOWERS OF AVIATION THE WORLD OVER TO HOPE THAT THIS CONTEST MAY BE DOUBLY SUCCESSFUL FIRST THAT IT MAY COST NO BRAVE MAN EITHER LIFE OR LIMB AND SECOND THAT THE CONTINENT AND HAWAII MAY BE LINKED BY AIRPLANE.

There were few things more exciting to do on earth in the early twentieth century than to fly above it, cruising the skies for hours at a time with no master to heed save the airplane's fuel gauge. Early aviators soared among the clouds in open cockpits, the wind rushing through their hair. The freedom to cut through the heavens and float above roads, rivers, forests, and cities was intoxicating. Largely free of regulation, pilots flew and landed wherever they chose.

The first powered flight occurred on December 17, 1903, when brothers Wilbur and Orville Wright flew a powered glider of their own design off the top of the Kill Devil Hills at Kitty Hawk, North Carolina. The brothers had experimented with unpowered gliders for four years along North Carolina's Outer Banks before putting a small motor aboard their latest prototype. Then Orville took to the air, flying 120 feet at 34 miles per hour, aided by fierce coastal winds. The brothers made three more flights that day, including Wilbur Wright's powered glide of 852 feet in which he spent 59 seconds in the air.

Returning from North Carolina to their home in Dayton, Ohio, the Wright brothers refined their plane designs. After building prototypes in the bicycle workshop they owned, they tested the new aircraft at Huffman Prairie, a field just outside of town that could be reached by streetcar. By 1908 their designs were so successful that Wilbur Wright sailed across the Atlantic and made hundreds of flight demonstrations in Le Mans and Pau, France, flying in front of mesmerized crowds that included American industrialists and European royalty. According to the *Paris Herald*, the brothers' arrival in Pau caused the town along the northern section of the Pyrenees Mountains to "[go] mad about aviation."

"Nothing is talked about but mechanical flight," said the report. "Everyone is buying a new camera to snap aeroplanes, painters are busy at their canvases, the long-neglected roads are being repaired, and society is inviting the Wrights to many more gatherings than they can possibly attend."

Days later a photograph of the Wright brothers and their sister, Katharine, graced the front page of the newspaper. It was just one of their many appearances in the European press. "Every time we make a move, the people on the street stop and stare at us," wrote Katharine Wright in a letter home to her father. "We have our pictures taken every two minutes. . . . *The Daily Mirror* of London had a man here who got a dandy picture of Orv and me."

The press's full attention signified how thrilling the public considered the invention of the airplane. The Wright brothers had sparked the creation of a new industry—aviation—and many others soon joined their cause to dominate the skies. Progress came rapidly. A year after Wilbur Wright's demonstrations in Europe, Frenchman Louis Blériot made the first flight across the English Channel. Two years later, in 1911, the first airmail was delivered. A year later, the first parachute jump was made from a powered airplane. Then, during the First World War, airplanes made their combat debut, forever changing warfare as flying machines were used for reconnaissance, dogfighting, and the dropping of bombs.

At war's end, American pilots who survived their dogfights and scouting missions returned home heroes. Given a glut of warplanes and an enduring public fascination with flying, these pilots were encouraged to stay in the sky, and keep cheating death, by buying surplus airplanes from the government at bargain prices and barnstorming across the United States and Europe. Though the term *barnstormers* originally referred to traveling theater groups, some of whom might have indeed performed for rural audiences in farmers' barns, aerial barnstormers made their living by touring and performing in the sky.

One of the most common surplus planes sold was the Curtiss JN-4, commonly known as the Jenny. As the American military reduced its fighting force in peacetime, it divested of unneeded airplanes, including its many Jennys, which were used as a training craft by the US Army Air Service, the predecessor of the US Air Force. Civilians were happy to get their hands on the beginner's plane, especially since they were dirt cheap. The two-seat biplane proved extremely popular with wingwalkers, who could scramble around the small craft easily, grabbing hold of its many struts and wires.

The Jenny is credited with sparking America's romance with flight. It enabled a new generation of pilots and introduced the airplane to the masses through its ubiquity at air shows and flying circuses. In 1918 the US Postal Service honored the plane by featuring an image of a Jenny on a twenty-four-cent airmail stamp. During a print run about one hundred of the stamps were misprinted, producing an upside-down image of the aircraft. The mistake resulted in one of the world's most collectible stamps, with one Inverted Jenny selling at auction nearly a century later for more than a million dollars.

As valued as the Jenny was—by pilots, wingwalkers, and stamp collectors—the plane had its limitations. The aircraft, composed of wood and fabric, was relatively delicate. The Jenny was slow, its top speed just seventy-five miles per hour. The small plane had a small range, able to fly just two hours before needing to refuel. But that was enough for the barnstormer, who just needed to perform a few tricks to turn a dollar.

Typically barnstormers would fly low when arriving to a new town, skimming rooftops to announce the arrival of their flying circus. Experienced barnstormers, like veteran army flier Basil Lee Rowe, could size up the market instantly. As Rowe described his tactics:

> To test a town for its interest in flying, I would buzz it a couple of times. If the people continued about their business, I did the same. But if the animals and fowl took off for the woods and the kids tried to follow me, it indicated virgin territory. In that case I looked for a farmer's field from which to operate and, when I found one, buzzed the town to get the whole population following me out to the field like the children of Hamelin following the Pied Piper. The farmer usually let me use his field for a free ride for himself and his family.

Once they'd set up camp outside of town, barnstormers would give airplane rides to whoever had the courage, and fifteen dollars, to be taken into the air. They'd also sell tickets for their air shows, which featured any number of awe-inducing aerial maneuvers, including harrowing loops, rolls, and dives. Eventually these stunts became familiar to the public and airplane rides lost their luster.

To continue holding the attention of crowds, flying circuses employed wingwalkers—fearless men and women who left the safety of cockpits to amble around a plane's wings in midflight. Sometimes these daredevils maintained a grip on the plane with just their teeth clenched tight around a strut, delighting the audience hundreds of feet below. Other times they danced the Charleston, walked across the wing while blindfolded, or, incredibly, stepped from one plane's wing onto another's. When it became passé to simply walk between airplanes in midair, wingwalkers innovated, carrying a can of gasoline between the planes, for example, so as to top off the tank of the second aircraft. Some wingwalkers were fond of hanging upside down from a plane's landing gear at low altitudes before releasing their hold and dropping into a haystack.

One famous wingwalker, Gladys Ingle, practiced archery atop the wing of a moving plane, slinging arrows from the tip of a wing into a bull's-eye mounted at the other end. When Ingle tired of target practice, she turned to mimicking a tennis match, simulating racquet swings with an opponent as they both soared through the air standing on opposite ends of the wing. A small net was even stretched taut between the high-flying volleyers.

There seemed to be no limit on imagination when it came to the stunts barnstormers, wingwalkers, and their promoters devised. Some stunt flyers sat in chairs bolted atop a plane wing and played cards while flying through the sky. Another carried a live rattlesnake in his cockpit during an air race from Los Angeles to Phoenix. Then there was the wingwalker who slipped during a transfer between airplanes, tumbling into a death plunge before a horrified audience. At the last minute she deployed a concealed parachute and gently floated to earth, to the astonishment of the onlookers below.

Stunts like mile-high tennis matches and seemingly fatal freefalls made the boldest wingwalkers and their flying troupes minor celebrities. Ingle was the sole female member of the 13 Black Cats, a group whose name suggested the flippant attitude these fliers held in regard to their own mortality. Other flying troupes of the era included the Love Field Lunatics and the Flying Aces. During one memorable performance, Flying Ace wingwalker Jessie Woods lost her shirt in the slipstream while hanging from a plane's landing gear. She remained calm and climbed back into the open cockpit, greeting a wide-eyed pilot. The gentleman graciously loaned Woods his shirt for the remainder of the flight.

Not every mishap had a happy ending. In 1923 at least 179 aviation accidents were recorded in the United States, with 85 people killed and 126 injured. And the tally would certainly be much higher if not for safety measures wingwalkers employed that were disguised by sleight of hand. For example, when wingwalkers seemed to perilously hold onto an airplane with just their teeth clenched tight around a strut, they often had a cable connecting their body to the plane, too, though the lifeline was concealed beneath their clothing. And as for that live rattlesnake carried in a cockpit between Los Angeles and Phoenix, well, the serpent was defanged, a detail never disclosed to the public.

Despite these and other precautions, barnstorming and wingwalking was undoubtedly dangerous work. Crowds delighted in the risks pilots and wingwalkers took, entertained by both successful stunts and those that went awry. Pioneering pilot Ralph Johnstone, who flew for Wilbur and Orville Wright, once remarked on the morbid mood of air shows. "The people who go to see us want thrills. And, if we fall, do they think of us and go away weeping? Not by a long shot. They're too busy watching the next man and wondering if we will repeat the performance," said Johnstone, who later earned the distinction of being the first American pilot to die in a plane crash, after failing to recover his aircraft from a dive in Denver in 1910.

Falls and crashes were common hazards for early aviators, but one pilot quipped there was a greater danger when flying: "the risk of starving to death." On account of all the expenses associated with airplanes, barnstorming hardly paid the bills. When parking their aircrafts overnight, some barnstormers elected to sleep under the wings of their planes rather than pay for hotel rooms. Charles Lindbergh struggled as a barnstormer early in his aviation career, yet his love of airplanes never wavered:

> Science, freedom, beauty, adventure: what more could you ask of life?
> Aviation combined all the elements I loved. There was science in each
> curve of an airfoil, in each angle between strut and wire, in the gap of
> a spark plug or the color of the exhaust flame. There was freedom in
> the unlimited horizon, on the open fields where one landed. A pilot
> was surrounded by beauty of earth and sky. He brushed treetops with
> the birds, leapt valleys and rivers, explored the cloud canyons he had
> gazed at as a child. Adventure lay in each puff of wind.

While Lindbergh was pilloried as the "Flyin' Fool" for attempting to cross the Atlantic Ocean alone, he in turn pitied those people blind to the appeal and promise of aviation:

> I began to feel that I lived on a higher plane than the skeptics on the
> ground; one that was richer because of its very association with the
> element of danger they dreaded, because it was freer of the earth to
> which they were bound. In flying, I tasted a wine of the gods of which
> they could know nothing. Who valued life more highly, the aviators
> who spent it on the art they loved, or these misers who doled it out
> like pennies through their antlike days? I decided that if I could fly
> for ten years before I was killed in a crash, it would be a worthwhile
> trade for an ordinary lifetime.

If flying wasn't particularly useful for improving health or increasing wealth, Lindbergh and his peers affirmed it was at least a heap of fun. Pilots were often some combination of restless and reckless, eager to take to the air again and again no matter how many close calls and crash landings they survived. Glory and the novelty of flight were the only motivations needed for scores of men and women to launch themselves into the sky within fragile machines. Early aviators thought little of risking safety for progress and adventure. As flier Mickey Rupp exclaimed, "Air racing may not be better than your wedding night, but it's better than the second night."

The excitement an airplane provided was consistent with other thrills of the time, including jazz music, cabaret shows, the illicit consumption of alcohol within speakeasies, and relaxed sexual mores. In the wake of the First World War, social and technological changes transformed the world by enabling greater personal freedoms. American women in particular profited during this time, able now to cast their votes, slip on slinky dresses for visits to nightclubs, more easily obtain birth control, and pilot their own planes.

The Roaring Twenties were flush with innovations beyond the airplane. Radio programming grew in popularity, including the broadcast of sporting events, particularly baseball. Car ownership increased substantially, with manufacturers Chrysler, Ford, and General Motors rising to the top of the American auto industry. Movie palaces drew packed crowds when screening newsreels and silent films. By the end of the 1920s, theaters were showing talkies, or movies with sound, to great acclaim, further fueling the growth of the film industry and establishing scores of Hollywood stars. The printed press was in high demand, too, with magazines like *Time* and the *New Yorker* debuting and major American cities publishing multiple newspapers, almost all of which devotedly chronicled aviation, recounting the exploits and accidents of many a flier.

Spirited public enthusiasm for airplanes, as well as the breakneck innovation of flying machines, created a golden age of aviation. During this period between world wars, airplanes' capabilities began matching their creators' ambitions. For the first time, planes were fairly durable, could travel long distances, and could perform aggressive aerial maneuvers. Airplanes were also now mass-produced, meaning more and more fearless pilots could take to the skies and conquer new frontiers. Mirroring society at large, the golden age of aviation was infused with a sense of optimism, gaiety, and wonder, producing bold pilots and beautiful machines for them to fly.

But as enthusiasm for flight abounded among the general public and upstart pilots and plane manufacturers, the US military and government was much less keen on aviation. In the wake of the carnage and mass casualties incurred during World War I, there was scant public support to fund and develop new methods of aerial warfare. Some pacifists would have preferred to demilitarize the nation entirely. There remained a healthy skepticism, too, of the value of the airplane. Flying machines cost money, and occasionally human lives. When the War Department presented a request to purchase new airplanes, President Calvin Coolidge asked, "Why can't we just buy one airplane and let the pilots take turns flying it?"

Such dismissiveness wasn't limited to the White House. In 1920 Congress decided against creating an independent air force, preferring that the army and navy continue to administer their own flying divisions. Five years later US Army colonel William Mitchell, assistant chief of the US Army Air Service, loudly protested that army and navy leaders were reluctant to nurture air divisions, preferring to use limited resources to maintain and improve tried-and-true instruments of war, such as their divisions of tanks and fleets of ships. While the court of public opinion sided with Mitchell and his blistering critiques, the army responded to the criticism by court-martialing Mitchell, who had already been demoted from brigadier general. A military court ruled against the outspoken colonel in 1925, suspending him from rank and service and forfeiting his pay for five years. Mitchell resigned from the army the next year.

Mitchell was hardly the only man to leave the Army Air Service around this time. Within a year of Armistice Day on November 11, 1918, the Air Service reduced its manpower from 190,000 officers and enlisted men to a fighting force of less than 13,000. Just nine American aces from World War I remained in the army ranks. Though these personnel reductions were consistent with the general demobilization of the American military after the war, Army Air Service leaders felt this level of peacetime staffing was inadequate.

A similarly precipitous drop in funding also dismayed army aviators. Five months before the war came to a close, the US Congress appropriated $460 million for the Army Air Service at the onset of fiscal year 1919. A year later, during peacetime, that amount dropped to $25 million, forcing Air Service administrators to choose between purchasing new planes and equipment or using the money to maintain and repair the existing fleet. As this reduced level of monetary support remained consistent for the next couple of years, the Air Service survived by relying on its plane and parts inventory that had been inflated during wartime but since gone without replenishment. As time passed, this inventory dwindled and became outdated.

In 1925 the leader of the Army Air Service, Major General Mason Patrick, expressed disappointment with the continual underfunding and lack of growth, complaining that Congress should give enough "to supply safe flying equipment for at least existing units and personnel." Among the safety problems in the Army Air Service was a Standard biplane whose engine, the Hall-Scott A-7A, sometimes caught fire during flight. Army aviators also flew the DH-4 airplane, which had a tendency to fall over and crash onto its nose when making a landing on soft ground. To prevent overturning during landing, a passenger in the two-person plane crawled out of his cockpit seat and onto the tail as the DH-4 alighted on the runway, holding the rear of the plane down. It was a tactic that cost at least one army flyer his life.

Beyond money, manpower, and equipment shortages, there were other aggravations for Air Service administrators. Promotions within the army lagged and paychecks were typically less than civilian wages, leading to a high rate of turnover. More alarming, pilots were dying at a higher rate than during the First World War. Some of these deaths were attributable to poor equipment, but the bulk of such fatalities were the result of the many air shows, long-distance flights, and stunt flying that army flyers performed as they sought to promote aviation as part of their peacetime mission. Unwilling to forbid stunt flying entirely but obligated to restore discipline within the flying ranks, the army ordered its pilots to refrain from performing risky maneuvers and low flying above cities and near buildings. Any acrobatic flying, the army commanded, should occur above 1,500 feet. For good measure, the army also threatened to prosecute any pilot seen buzzing flocks of waterfowl or shooting birds with airplane-mounted machine guns.

Despite these challenges, the Air Service was hardly hopeless. For many aspiring pilots and mechanics, the army provided the best opportunity to receive aviation training. The Air Service counted among its ranks some of the best pilots in the world, with these aviators consistently winning air races and achieving records in distance and high-altitude flights, including the first round-the-world flight, accomplished in 1924. Yet Air Service officials believed they were capable of much more. They fretted about being unprepared for war and also hoped to better develop the combat capabilities of the airplane.

In 1926 Congress addressed some of these concerns through the Air Corps Act, which renamed the Army Air Service, created the Office of the Assistant Secretary of War for Air, and approved a five-year expansion plan for the new Army Air Corps. That same year the army established its Materiel Division at Dayton, Ohio, to control logistics within the Air Corps. With a new name and a new advocate in the War Department, aviation in the army finally showed the potential of renewed promise.

When a young man enlisted in the army during World War I and expressed interest in becoming a pilot, he was sent off to ground school at one of eight colleges across the country. Two months later the flying cadet shipped off again for primary flight training, donning a helmet, goggles, and leather coat as he learned to solo an airplane. If commissioned as an army pilot, the newly minted aviator then attended a specific type of advanced training, where he'd hone skills in pursuit piloting and dogfighting, observation and reconnaissance, bombing, or gunnery.

Such was the case for Lester James Maitland, who enlisted in the army in April 1917 just as the United States entered the war and Maitland graduated from high school in Milwaukee, Wisconsin. After ground school at the University of Texas in Austin, Maitland left for primary training at Rich Field in nearby Waco, Texas, where he was deemed a "born flier" by army aviators and commissioned as a second lieutenant in the Army Air Service Reserve. The war ended before he had the chance for combat and he was made a flight instructor at nineteen years old. Advanced training in gunnery followed, as well as a stint as a test pilot in Dayton, Ohio, where the second lieutenant flew with other top-notch army pilots. Two years after enlisting, Maitland was given an exotic, far-flung posting: flight duty with an army observation squadron in Hawaii.

Second Lieutenant Maitland began dreaming of making a flight to Hawaii before he even arrived to the islands. His eagerness to fly had a lot to do with his aversion to sailing. "I went over on an old army troop ship, and we wasted a lot of time," Maitland said of his voyage to Hawaii in 1919. "I immediately decided we could fly there."

Upon reaching the army's Luke Field on Ford Island in Pearl Harbor, Maitland was not shy about sharing his idea to pilot a twin-engine Martin bomber between Hawaii and the mainland. "I wrote a letter (to this effect) to the chief of the Air Corps," he said. "I didn't even get an answer; they ignored it." Not to be discouraged, Maitland repeated his request a year later. This time the army gave him an answer: no.

Maitland flew planes between the Hawaiian Islands until May 1921 when he shipped back to the mainland to work as an army squadron commander, test pilot, and racer. Now a first lieutenant in the Army Air Service, he was chosen as an aide to Brigadier General William "Billy" Mitchell, who had begun agitating for major improvements and investment in military aviation. As part of this campaign, Mitchell arranged for the army to join a navy aerial bombing exercise of unmanned ships in 1921, hoping to prove his controversial claim that airplanes had rendered battleships obsolete in modern warfare. During the experiment, which targeted German ships the United States captured as war trophies, Maitland flew an army bomber that helped sink the battleship *Ostfriesland*, giving much public credence to Mitchell's claims.

The next year Maitland won second place in the Pulitzer Race, averaging a speed of 198.8 miles per hour as he rounded the pylons along the fifty-kilometer course. The pilot took some of these turns so sharply and at such high speeds that he experienced short blackouts. The loss of consciousness at breakneck speeds did not spook the airman. His brain function returned to normal, he said, as soon as the plane pulled out of the turn. "It is like flying at night with not a star in the skies" he said of racing with a brain starved of oxygen.

He may have won first prize that year had his fuel pump not failed on the first lap of the race. Rather than bow out of the contest, Maitland kept competing, using one hand to manually pump fuel into his engine and the other to steer the plane as it whipped around the air course at nearly two hundred miles per hour. A year later he set a speed record using that same type of plane, a Curtiss R-6, by traveling 244.94 miles per hour.

"Blond, bumptious and a first class pilot," according to *Time* magazine, Maitland was a member of the "hard-living crew of swashbucklers" that comprised the Army Air Service and Air Corps after the First World War. These men, the magazine continued, "would fly anywhere in anything" and "kept the Corps on Page One, though in a way that might often give [another] pilot the cold sweats."

Known as Les among friends, Maitland delighted in pushing airplanes to the limit. Among his favorite testing grounds was Washington, DC, where he'd perform after hours in a black de Havilland airplane, zipping and looping along in the nighttime skies above the capital. Though he enjoyed thrills in the sky, he prided himself on his professionalism, drawing a hard line between aviators who were daring versus plain dumb. "The front pages of newspapers are a popular playground for those who have a 'spectacular complex,' but they are poor landing fields for airmen," he said. "The distance between a headline and a headstone is much too short. One is apt to overshoot the field, and that is fatal."

When stationed at Bolling Field along the Anacostia River, Maitland turned heads on the ground, too, as he made a number of impressive introductions in Washington. There he married Ruth Thurston, the daughter of a late US senator from Nebraska and the stepdaughter of Dr. William Alanson White, a prominent psychiatrist and superintendent of St. Elizabeth's Hospital in Washington. About the same time, Maitland became an aide and personal pilot to F. Trubee Davison, a wealthy, high-ranking official in the War Department responsible for air operations. Assistant secretary of war, Davison was an alumnus of Yale University, where, during the First World War, he had persuaded fellow classmates to join a student air reserve unit he created with part of his family's massive banking fortune. He sustained serious injuries in a navy plane accident in 1917, ending his flying career. But after earning a law degree from Columbia University and serving in New York's legislature from 1922 to 1926, he returned to aviation, nominated by President Calvin Coolidge to join the Army Air Corps leadership.

While working as Trubee's aide in the fall of 1926, Maitland was asked to dinner at the home of Major General Mason Patrick, chief of the newly reorganized Army Air Corps. Maitland saw the dinner as a golden opportunity to suggest the army attempt a nonstop flight to Hawaii, especially since Maitland had recently helped teach the sixty-two-year-old general how to fly. "I had a very fine chance to sell him the idea," he said of the evening.

Since his initial request in 1919 Maitland had made repeated pleas to fly across half the Pacific, always to be told that such a venture was premature, as no army plane was believed to be capable of making the treacherous hop. The young pilot did not lose faith, but kept up his requests as aviation advanced. As he wrote:

I waited patiently, constantly looking for the day when an airplane capable of carrying the necessary fuel load and equipped with motors that would stand the strain of a 2,400-mile non-stop flight would appear, hoping at the same time that when such a ship was an actuality I might be fortunate enough to draw the detail of piloting it across the Pacific. For seven years I studied and hoped. Whenever a new type of transport or bomber was purchased by the Army I considered it from every angle to see if it might be *the* ship.

At dinner Maitland seized his chance and proposed a flight to Hawaii. Patrick was receptive to the idea. He suggested Maitland look for a plane capable of crossing half an ocean, unaware that his ambitious young charge was already two steps ahead of him.

"I have the plane," Maitland told the air chief. "Tony Fokker's C-2."

What he did not mention to Patrick was he also had chosen a navigator.

Like Lester Maitland, Albert F. Hegenberger enlisted in the army in 1917, earned his wings in 1918, and served the remainder of the war as a flight instructor. But whereas Maitland was ordered to Hawaii at war's end, Hegenberger was sent to Boston. At the army's direction he enrolled in an aeronautical engineering course at the Massachusetts Institute of Technology.

The plum assignment amounted to a homecoming for the young second lieutenant. Hegenberger had grown up in Boston, the son of a German immigrant father and Swiss immigrant mother. Before taking this latest course for the army at MIT, Hegenberger had studied civil engineering at the university. The posting in Boston kept him close to his girlfriend, Louise Berchtold, whom he would soon marry.

After finishing his course at MIT, Hegenberger was assigned in February 1919 to McCook Field in Dayton, Ohio, and named chief of the Air Service's Instrument Branch. Here the Air Service gave Hegenberger license to pursue his passion: perfecting the operation of airplanes and all the gadgets they carry on board. In particular, the mechanically inclined Hegenberger was interested in improving instruments of aerial navigation and wanted to enable blind flying, or flying by instrument alone.

One way to test all his navigational methods and equipment, he knew, was flying at night on a long-distance course with few landmarks. So when he was just months on the job in Dayton, Hegenberger wrote to the leadership of the Army Air Service and requested the chance to make a nonstop flight from the West Coast to Hawaii. His letter arrived to Major General Mason Patrick the same year as one from a fellow airman stationed in Hawaii. Like Second Lieutenant Lester J. Maitland, Hegenberger was rebuffed. But Hegenberger, also like Maitland, refused to take no for an answer. He was intent on proving that the army possessed the flight and navigational capabilities to pilot a plane to its tiny Hawaiian outpost in the middle of the Pacific.

It was only fifteen years earlier that Wilbur and Orville Wright had made the first airplane flight. Since then, airplanes had changed tremendously. Whereas the Wright brothers laid precariously on top of the bottom wing of their original flyers, pilots now sat more securely in open-air cockpits or enclosed fuselages. Whereas many planes were made of wood framing wrapped tight in painted cloth, newer aircraft featured metal framing and experimented with aluminum paneling in place of cloth. And whereas biplanes originally ruled the skies, monoplanes were becoming increasingly popular, especially in larger aircraft. Hegenberger knew all these changes made Hawaii a viable new frontier for the airplane.

But while the design and construction of airplanes changed radically in a short amount of time, aerial navigation techniques and equipment were slower to develop. Many fliers refused any equipment beyond a parachute when they took to the air, considering most radio and navigational equipment bulky, heavy, and unreliable. Rather than get bogged down and distracted by fancy and temperamental gadgets, fliers overwhelmingly preferred to fly by the seat of their pants and navigate by landmarks they could spot from the air. The most reliable landmark was often the railroad, or so-called iron compass, that ran from city to city across the countryside, easily identified from the air. If railroad tracks were absent from the landscape, the pilots would spot other unique topographical features, say the curve of a river or mountain peak, and then attempt to match them on the maps they carried aloft.

Such methods were not foolproof, as a pilot busy flying his plane could easily misidentify a river, peak, or portion of railroad tracks, ending up hours later at an unintended destination. Navigating by landmark was more or less useless at night, during bad weather, and in places where there were no landmarks or even land, such as the middle of an ocean. And while pilots often employed time-tested sea navigation techniques in the air, the uneven results left a lot to be desired. Hegenberger knew firsthand how tricky it was to try to navigate a fast-moving plane:

> The operation of present avigation instruments and the reduction of the observations are by far the most difficult functions that are performed in the air. Because of the mental gymnastics involved, these operations never become instinctive, as does piloting. Fatigue, due largely to the noise and vibration in the airplane, reduces one's mental efficiency tremendously during a long flight. Under such conditions, the most simple mental activity becomes most difficult, and serious errors in results and decisions may be made.

In the mid-1920s it was only when an army plane traveled a great distance or at night that the most basic navigation instruments were commonly carried. For these flights army pilots would typically have on board a magnetic compass to establish direction; an altimeter to measure the plane's flying height; and a flight indicator, also known as an artificial horizon or attitude indicator, which could tell a pilot whether or not his wings and nose were level or in a bank or pitch. This was not enough, argued Hegenberger, who complained of the army's "false sense of confidence in its operating ability."

Instrumentation was even more primitive in aviation's civilian sector. An artificial horizon was oftentimes nothing more than a plum line, or a weight attached to a string tied to the dashboard. If the weight was not hanging exactly perpendicular to the dash, then the plane wasn't flying level. Centrifugal forces, however, could render the plum line useless.

Los Angeles stunt pilot Frank Clarke explained how he flew through California's notorious coastal fog by watching only his tachometer, which measured engine speed, and oil pressure gauge. If the tachometer showed engine revolutions to be increasing rapidly, he realized he was in a dive. When the revolutions slowed, the plane's nose was up and he was climbing. And if the oil pressure dropped to zero, it was time to land, and fast.

The strategy was certainly not perfect. Clarke was once forced to ditch in the ocean a half mile from shore after being enveloped by fog. Fortunately, a fishing boat rescued the aviator and towed his half-sunken plane to shore.

Taking charge of the Instrument Branch at McCook Field, Hegenberger was well aware of the navigation challenges facing aviators. He sought to improve assorted air indicators and instruments and popularize their presence on the pilot's cockpit dashboard. Specifically, he hoped to refine the operation of three little-used devices he thought could revolutionize air navigation, if only they could be made more reliable and earn pilots' trust. The first of these was the compass, which in its traditional design with a magnetic needle was susceptible to interference from a plane's metal parts. So Hegenberger and a colleague helped test a new technology, the induction compass, at McCook Field. Their tests culminated in a 1923 flight from Dayton in which Hegenberger and a companion, cruising high above the clouds in fierce winds and poor weather and out of sight of landmarks, navigated successfully to Boston.

The sextant, too, was underused by aviators because of the difficulty in adapting the sea navigation instrument for the air. In an airplane, it could be difficult to hold the sextant steady while aiming it toward the heavens. It could also be challenging for a navigator to discern a horizon, especially at night. Finally, if a pilot did not maintain a steady speed and course while a navigator used a sextant, it could cause errors in the navigator's readings. So Hegenberger experimented with a special sextant that featured a bubble level, or artificial horizon, in order to determine the plane's position. In 1922 he used a custom-made air sextant to fly from Dayton to New York, where he then related the merits of his invention to a gathering of the American Society of Mechanical Engineers.

Last, Hegenberger believed planes could benefit from radio technology. Besides directly exchanging messages with other operators using radio sets, Hegenberger was intrigued by radio beacons. He conducted numerous test flights in which a plane navigated by homing in on a radio beacon atop a tower, following the signal until reaching its destination.

He ultimately logged more than four hundred flight hours during this time period, testing assorted radios, compasses, sextants, flight indicators, and other army equipment in many types of planes in many types of weather. At least fifty hours of this experience was earned through nighttime flying, meaning he was also a very capable pilot.

Hegenberger's aerial navigation and instrument expertise extended so far that he attempted to coin new terminology related to his field of study, proposing the term *avigation*. In the spring of 1923 Hegenberger and his army colleagues in the Instrument Branch had decided that the word *navigation,* or *air navigation,* was improper to use with aircraft given the term's nautical implication. So the army men dropped the first letter, coining a new and similar-sounding word of which they were very proud. If navigation meant to journey by ship, then avigation, they reasoned, meant to go as a bird. In 1924 the hopeful army avigators wrote a letter to the National Advisory Committee for Aeronautics asking that this term be officially adopted to refer to "the science of directing an aircraft from one point to another." As a backup they suggested another homegrown word: *aerogation,* meaning to go by air.

The advisory board declined to endorse either term. That didn't stop Hegenberger and his acolytes from inserting their preferred phrasing into assorted articles about aviation. Eventually a report about the word *avigation* found its way into the journal *American Speech.* At least one journal reader was outraged enough by the army's reasoning and loose translation of Latin to write a letter declaring that "such an etymology is enough to make any thoroughbred philologist tear his hair in despair." Correcting the aviators, he proposed a much less elegant solution in its place: *aviaction.*

Whatever you called it, Hegenberger was enthralled. He took night courses to expand his navigation knowledge. He simulated flights to Hawaii, trying to anticipate how much more difficult it would be to fly over open ocean than land. In 1923, after fellow army lieutenants John Macready and Oakley Kelly made the first nonstop flight across the United States, Hegenberger renewed his proposal for a nonstop flight to Hawaii. Macready and Kelly's flight from Long Island, New York, to San Diego, California, had lasted nearly twenty-seven hours—roughly the same amount of time expected for the hop to the islands. Hegenberger argued the transcontinental flight could essentially be replicated, and in his unsolicited report to the top brass, he provided fuel estimates of the flight at different altitudes and detailed preparations for every type of mishap. It was still not enough to persuade Army Air Service leaders in Washington.

"The time is not yet ripe," Major General Patrick wrote to Hegenberger. It was a response Patrick would repeat over and over again to the ambitious lieutenant in the years to come. In fact, Hegenberger asked so often to fly to Hawaii that Patrick complained the young officer "bored me to death." But still Patrick would not budge.

In 1924 Hegenberger was reassigned to Hawaii and traveled there—by ship. Stationed at Luke Field in Pearl Harbor, he worked alongside navy commander John Rodgers, who would soon make his own attempt at the flight across the Pacific. Not long after Hegenberger arrived to Hawaii did he request permission from army superiors to fly to the island of Midway, more than a thousand miles away, in a bid to survey Pacific islands that could be home to airfields and fleets of scouting airplanes. On this request, too, Hegenberger was apparently denied, told to stick closer to home. He never made the flight.

Hegenberger passed three years in Hawaii before he was reassigned back to McCook Field, promoted to chief of the Instrument and Navigation Unit in the army's Materiel Division. In February 1927 he received a letter from Maitland, an airman stationed in Washington with whom he was well acquainted and who flew into Dayton quite often as an air chauffeur for army leaders. Maitland wanted to know if Hegenberger was still game to make the Hawaiian Hop:

"I have regularly requested permission to make this flight from the Chief of Air Corps; and, while my requests have heretofore been turned down, chiefly because we didn't have a suitable airplane, I was given assurance that if such a flight were made, my name would be considered [for] one of the pilots because I had made the initial request in 1919," wrote Maitland, indicating that the army had obtained a sufficient airplane. "The reason I am writing this letter is to ascertain whether you would be willing to make the flight with me—of course, to share any honors as well as any labors in connection with the flight on a fifty-fifty basis," he continued. "I hope you will keep this letter strictly confidential and advise me by wire to this office."

At the turn of the twentieth century, at about the same time the airplane was invented, another revolutionary device was being refined and popularized: the motion picture camera. It was not long before these two thrilling machines were brought together.

The first motion picture footage of an airplane flying, or at least nearly flying, appeared in 1905. A newsreel filmed that year, *Ludlow's Aerodrome*, features a biplane owned by New York attorney Israel Ludlow tied by a rope to an automobile. The car speeds off, the airplane takes flight, and then the airplane crashes. A second newsreel from 1905, *Ludlow's Aeroplane No. 2*, shows a plane being launched like a kite before it glides into water. The next year, with no cameras rolling, Ludlow was paralyzed when he crashed his plane in Florida.

In the early twentieth century, newsreels were popular with movie theater audiences and provided substantial, consistent income for some of the most daring pilots and wingwalkers. One aerial exhibitionist to find fame in newsreels was a Cherokee named John Miller, otherwise known by his stage name, Chief White Eagle. "Allow us to introduce the man with the world's strongest head of hair," begins one newsreel that features Chief White Eagle hanging calmly beneath a plane in flight, attached to the landing gear by a mere strap braided into his long dark tresses. The reel concludes with the chief combing flat his upright mane, quipping that "a hair in the head is worth two in the brush." The chief later perished when he jumped from a plane and attempted to launch ten parachutes in a row as he fell to earth, cutting the strings off one chute before deploying the next. He managed to open and slice away four parachutes before thudding into a barley patch, his fifth parachute not having time to open.

As the California film industry blossomed, airplanes began appearing in feature films as well. At first the airplane's role was minimal and basic, with a studio hiring a pilot to simply take off, perform a flyby, and then land in front of the cameras during the early 1910s. Then in 1915 the film *Out of the Air* featured one of the first true Hollywood airplane stunts when an actor dropped from a flying airplane onto a train. Variations of this stunt soon became commonplace. Pilots swooped their planes low to deposit villains on trains, where they'd rob passengers or loot jewels. Other pilots swooped in to make rescues, plucking a beleaguered character from a rolling railcar. Abandoning the train, pilots then made similar transfers of stuntmen to speeding cars and boats before changing course again to film scenes with wingwalkers shuttling between planes in midair.

One memorable wingwalking scene occurred during the making of *The Grim Game*, a 1919 film starring escape artist Harry Houdini. While filming a scene in the sky, a pilot attempted to drop Houdini's stunt double, dangling beneath his airplane from a rope, onto another plane. As the stuntman struggled with this stunt more than four thousand feet above Santa Monica,

California, the planes unintentionally collided and locked together. With the stuntman still clinging tightly to his lifeline, the planes began falling together toward earth, all while the camera rolled. Moments later the airplanes miraculously separated, enabling each pilot, one with the stuntman still in tow, to miraculously land without major injury.

The next year another aerial stunt for Hollywood did not end so happily. Ormer Locklear, who pioneered the midair transfer between planes in 1918 and who was fond of performing handstands on top of wings, tried in 1920 to simulate a flaming plane crash. While flying at night for a scene in *The Skywayman*, Locklear and his copilot lit magnesium flares about the plane and put the aircraft into a dive. But as they hurtled toward earth, the ground lights the film crew used apparently blinded the pilots, resulting in a truly fiery crash that killed them both.

Still the show went on. Hollywood aerial stuntmen created a trick where a man hung from a rope attached to a plane's landing gear and then began swinging like a pendulum from wingtip to wingtip. Later the pendulum trick was refined to feature two men fighting midflight atop the wingtip. When one man punched the other off the wing, the tethered recipient of the blow swung in a semicircle beneath the plane and reappeared atop the opposite wingtip. The fight then resumed.

In December 1920 Frank Clarke, the aviator known to fly with a rattlesnake in the cockpit and to navigate thick fog with a tachometer, engaged in what seemed like even more lunacy: flying off the roof of an unfinished ten-story building for a scene in the film *Stranger than Fiction*. Leaving his serpent copilot behind, Clarke dismantled a Jenny, somehow hoisted or smuggled the pieces to the roof of the Los Angeles Railway Building, and then reassembled the plane. Preparing to take off along a ramp built atop the roof, Clarke tied the plane down and began revving the engine to build up power. Then the rope was cut and Clarke's Jenny shot forward, bolting across the roof, and off the ramp, before plunging into a free fall above the streets of downtown Los Angeles.

Observers watched from the streets below, staring in disbelief, fearful of a crash. To their relief, the plane leveled out after plummeting halfway to the ground. Clarke flew away safely, though when he landed a few minutes later, he was nearly arrested by police on account of causing such a spectacle. Clarke

later performed as a stunt pilot in *Wings*, a 1927 film about two American aviators in the First World War that won the first Academy Award for Best Picture.

Dick Grace, a veteran naval aviator renowned in Hollywood for his ability
to stage and survive spectacular plane crashes, also performed flying stunts for
Wings. In 1918 the young American pilot earned a Purple Heart after being
wounded during a bombing run of a German island fortress—the first of many
injuries he'd suffer within an airplane. Returning home to Minnesota to finish
studies interrupted by the war, a bored Grace soon abandoned law school to
work as a stuntman in Los Angeles. He dived from cliffs, jumped from speeding cars, and once leaped ablaze from a building into a vat of water while clad
in gasoline-soaked clothes. That last stunt inflicted third-degree burns across
eight hundred square inches of his skin, necessitating skin grafts. "No death
is more horrible, more painful," he said of the searing experience.

Yet Grace's appetite for destruction did not subside. He began performing flying stunts and soon discovered his specialty and calling card—crashing
airplanes for the cameras. Moviemakers hired Grace to fly through church
steeples, burst into barns, and collide with cliffs. Most often he steered planes
into the ground, his chaotic crashes masking the disciplined preparations and
safety precautions he undertook before each stunt.

He preferred crashing at 11:45 AM. At this time of day, he explained, the
sun was high in the sky and posed little threat of blinding him as he made his
low approach to a crash site ringed with cameras and film crew. By midday,
too, said the aviator, winds were normally blowing at a consistent speed and
direction, less likely to gust or shift suddenly.

Once a director chose a crash site, Grace studied the terrain extensively,
devising exactly how he would violently ground the plane. He ensured that
a cordon was in place around the set and manned by strong guards. Film
crew and onlookers had a tendency to rush toward a crashed plane to check
on a pilot's safety, and Grace did not want the concerned and well-meaning
observers to ruin the shot. He made sure a doctor and nurse were on set,
and that a fast ambulance was nearby, its engine idling and a driver seated
behind the wheel. He confirmed that firefighting and rescue squads were in
place, the former toting extinguishers and the latter armed with large nip-
pers, steel cutters, sledgehammers, pliers, saws, and other tools that might be
needed to extract him from crumpled wreckage. When Grace crashed near

water, a pulmotor was on hand in case oxygen needed to be pumped by tube into his lungs.

Despite these measures, the stunt flyer acknowledged that most people thought him utterly reckless. Perhaps it was the eighty-one broken bones he suffered during forty-seven intentional plane crashes and other stunts that led his acquaintances to consider him a glutton for pain. "I've been called a fool. I know many people believe me insane," said Grace. "The companies I work for give me no credit; to them I am but a service to be used at times when a thrill is urgently needed."

He always fasted for a full day before he was scheduled to crash. It wasn't nerves that kept him from eating but rather his desire for his digestive system to be clear of food. Should his stomach or intestines rupture, he didn't want food and waste spilling into his body.

Before crashing, Grace always underwent a physical examination from a doctor to confirm he was in top shape. A clean bill of health in hand, he then poked and probed the airplane he would soon fly and destroy. He inspected the padding placed over the instrument panel and the horsehair that lined portions of the cockpit. He looked over the plane's wooden structural components, which had been wrapped in tape and reinforced with steel to prevent splintering. He checked that the main tank in the plane had been drained and an auxiliary tank installed on the wing was filled with just enough fuel to deliver him to his target. Grace was inclined to try to survive a crash but not a gasoline-fueled explosion or inferno as well.

When examining his aircraft, Grace considered not only himself but the engineering marvel he would obliterate. He could become sentimental about certain airplanes, reluctant to destroy aircraft he regarded as well engineered and enjoyable to fly. When observing fresh coats of paint applied to an aircraft destined to be crashed, he thought the situation analogous to "buying a new suit in which to bury a person."

"The linen was all smooth and the wings were taut," he remarked of one plane he would soon shatter. "It stood there awaiting the end aloofly."

When serving as a plane's executioner, he attired himself in leather helmet, leather jacket, corduroy pants, golf socks, and shoes. Boots, he explained, would be difficult to remove from an injured leg. Additional layers of clothing were also considered useless. "If I missed [the crash site], no matter what form of padding or armor I wore it would be no more protection than paper," said

Grace, who did don goggles when flying but made sure to remove them before crashing for fear of glass splinters piercing his eyes.

For the Academy Award–winning *Wings*, which was filmed in Texas, Grace was asked to crash twice. The first crash in the war film was to occur in a simulated no-man's-land—the unprotected territory between enemy trench lines in which no soldier ventured, lest they desired to be punched full of machine gun bullets. In an effort to spare Grace from harm, a film crew replaced a section of barbed wire fencing on the movie set with twine and balsa wood. Yet the substitute fencing was for naught. When Grace flew low for the cameras and purposely dipped a wing into the ground, his Spad airplane missed the twine and balsa wood and cartwheeled instead into the stiff fence posts and barbed wire. Somehow he was unhurt.

For the second stunt, Grace was to take off from an air base and then almost immediately crash when an enemy aircraft shot his plane as it lifted off the runway. In an effort to help the plane break apart upon impact, a film crew sawed through portions of the wing and landing gear on his German fighter airplane, a Fokker D.VII. No matter the weakened parts, the plane stayed intact when Grace took off and then plowed the Fokker into the ground at one hundred miles per hour from a height of twenty feet. What did fracture, however, were several vertebrae in the stunt flyer's neck.

Doctors advised Grace, with a cast wrapped tight around his throat, to stop crashing airplanes. He refused to stop flying, however, and soon found himself intrigued by the challenge posed by pineapple baron James Dole: to fly across the Pacific to Hawaii. Grace thought himself capable of claiming the $25,000 prize, but weeks remained before the contest was to commence on August 12, 1927. Whether due to restlessness or because he desired to make a trial run before the race, Grace decided to make an early attempt at the Pacific crossing with one twist—he'd fly from Hawaii to California, the reverse of the course Dole proposed. By the middle of June 1927, Grace was aboard the steamer SS *Manukai*, heading to Honolulu, his Waterhouse Cruzair airplane packed in the hold below and his fragile neck still enveloped by a brace.

After offering cash prizes for the first flights to Hawaii, James Dole left San Francisco by train for the East Coast. If the Honolulu tycoon was hoping for relaxation and anonymity traveling so far from home, he did not receive it. Coming on the heels of Charles Lindbergh's stunning flight across the Atlantic, Dole's prize offer for spanning the Pacific unleashed excitement across the country. The Pineapple King was besieged during his journey, repeatedly engaged by people with either a general interest in aviation or a specific desire to cross the Pacific and earn the promised prize. "It's the most popular topic of conversation on the mainland these days—aviation. In dining cars, hotel lobbies, at church, in the theaters—everywhere, they are talking about Lindbergh," said Dole.

Whereas it took eight years for someone to claim Raymond Orteig's $25,000 cash prize, Dole faced the prospect that he might need to pay out much sooner. There appeared to be no shortage of pilots interested in making the attempt to Hawaii, and almost all of them were preparing to leave as soon as possible. "I wouldn't be surprised to see a number of starters take off at the same time," said Dole during an interview at the Biltmore Hotel in Manhattan on June 7, 1927, less than three weeks after Lindbergh's flight to Paris. "All in all it looks as if it will be a real race."

Indeed, in order to corral all the aviators intent on winging it to Hawaii, the contest would have to be a race. Dole named a flight committee in Honolulu to govern the proceedings, removing himself from administration of the contest. Dole, who himself had never flown in an airplane, asked only that the committee consider certain safety requirements for participants, such as mandating planes to carry fuel reserves and emergency supplies in case of sea landings.

The basic rules of the Dole Air Race soon took shape, with race day set for August 15, 1927—a date selected to give Lindbergh enough time to prepare for the contest, even though he had yet to confirm his participation. Aviators could depart from any place on the mainland, though it was assumed most would leave from California, the state closest to Hawaii. Planes arriving to Oahu were expected to land within or near Pearl Harbor, with seaplanes directed to the harbor water and planes with conventional landing gear invited to nearby John Rodgers Airport, which opened months earlier and was still undergoing construction. Because of safety concerns, a proposal was nixed that required the aviators to first fly to the island of Lanai and drop a letter above Dole's massive pineapple plantation before finishing the race on Oahu.

That Dole's contest took the form of a derby only added to the public's intrigue. This would be the most significant air race in human history, claimed many newspapers and magazines, if not the most significant sporting event of the time. Such positive press thrilled Hawaiian Pineapple Company executives, who counted on even more attention come race time. "That the newspapers have seen fit to be so liberal in the use of the name of the company is gratifying, and I may say that little things we hear indicate that—well, it is really a wonderful program of publicity all the way through," wrote H. E. MacConaughey, manager of the company's San Francisco operation, to a colleague at headquarters in Honolulu in June. "Of course, there are a lot of cranks writing letters and we are saving them here so that we can send you some of the interesting ones."

A month later MacConaughey wrote again to Honolulu, celebrating the unending publicity: "We believe Mr. Dole's picture was printed in nearly every newspaper in the country, or should I say nearly every town in the country. And we further believe that the name 'Dole' is known to about every household in the United States—yes, and outside of the United States, too. To gain such publicity by advertising would have cost literally, well we should say a million dollars wouldn't begin to do it."

Hawaii's newspapers were especially bullish on the Dole Derby. The upcoming contest was already shining a bright light on distant Hawaii, said a *Honolulu Advertiser* editorial that made clear its writer had little appreciation for native Hawaiian civilization and history: "Our ports will henceforth mean something more than a string of unpronounceable names. Our islands will take on the importance of real places, not merely the storied, poetic, abiding place of barbaric kings and strange races. . . . And for this, our thanks to 'Jim' Dole, seizing opportunity. Acting. Taking time by the forelock. Doing the thing."

Another editorial in the English-language section of a Japanese newspaper printed in Hawaii shared the same enthusiasm for the air race. In creating this contest, said the *Hawaii Hochi* newspaper, Dole "steps up to the plate and socks the old pill over the fence for a home run!"

Boosters in Honolulu echoed these sentiments. The general manager of the Royal Hawaiian, Arthur Benaglia, offered the Waikiki hotel's finest suites to the derby's winning racers. He also offered to place a fifty-foot illuminated sign atop the hotel pointing the way to the finish line. "This is not too much to do for these brave fellows who are going to fly across the Pacific to Hawaii this summer," said Benaglia. "James Dole started it, and the rest of us will do our bit. The eyes of the world will be on Hawaii this summer, and we, at the new hotel, will do everything possible to give the successful flyers a royal reception."

One was arguably the army's best pilot, the other the army's top navigator. They had enlisted for military service the same year, become pilots and flight instructors in lockstep, and earned identical promotions, and both were posted overseas in Hawaii. They shared friends, took orders from the same generals, and displayed equally great passions for airplanes. After nearly nine years of military service, with one aviator famously breaking speed records and the other burnishing a reputation as an instruments whiz, the men were well aware of each other's accomplishments and saw each other regularly. Yet Lieutenants Lester Maitland and Albert Hegenberger had never flown together. That was about to change.

After Maitland extended the invitation to fly to Hawaii, Hegenberger was not entirely pleased. Annoyed that Maitland might undercut his own bid to lead a flight to Hawaii, he initially ignored Maitland and wrote to Washington himself, asking to make the flight and reminding his superiors of his long-standing requests to travel across the Pacific and the considerable amount of study he had devoted to the challenge. Only in the last paragraph of his five-page letter did Hegenberger disclose that he was in contact with Maitland and would support being paired together.

The jockeying was to no avail; army leaders wanted Maitland, twenty-eight, as pilot and mission commander. Hegenberger, thirty-one, would serve as secondary pilot, flight engineer, and navigator (or avigator, as the lieutenant liked to say). Maitland wrote to him again to subtly break this news. He also asked that Hegenberger remain discreet about their plans, especially since the navy could quickly mount their own second attempt to fly to the islands. "We are all afraid, this includes Gen. [James Edmond] Fechet, of the navy getting on to it and then our chances are nil," Maitland wrote to Hegenberger. "[Fechet] said that the only thing he could do was to turn down or disapprove your application officially but for me to tell you not to worry about your selection for the flight but you must absolutely be quiet on the subject."

The airmen were expected to leave for Hawaii in just a few months. Since secrecy was considered paramount to their success, the army designated a codename for the trip: Project Z. Only thirty people in the army were privy to the preparations, which began in earnest in February 1927, three months before Charles Lindbergh flew across the Atlantic Ocean and James Dole announced his cash prize.

As Maitland referenced, the army airmen would be flying a new aircraft—a military version of the Dutch-designed Fokker F.VII transport plane. Manufactured in the United States by Fokker's American subsidiary, the Atlantic Aircraft Corporation, the big plane was renamed the C-2 by the army and was powered by three 220-horsepower Wright J-5 Whirlwind radial air-cooled engines, each of which turned steel propellers. These new air-cooled engines were much lighter than their water-cooled predecessors, enabling planes to fly greater distances with the same amount of fuel. This innovation was critical in helping Maitland convince the army that the Fokker C-2 could make the jaunt to Hawaii.

The plane was exceptionally large for a crew of two, stretching forty-eight feet long and twelve feet high with a seventy-two-foot wing positioned across the top of the fuselage. The plane weighed six thousand pounds without fuel and equipment, cruised at 100 miles per hour, and could reach an estimated maximum speed of 116 miles per hour. It was painted green, though the color was so drab that some observers called the aircraft gray or black or brown. On the topside and underside of each wingtip was painted a white star. The tail, or vertical stabilizer, featured red and white stripes, a rare bit of ornament in the paint scheme.

While Maitland prepared for the journey by logging flight hours on a sister ship, Hegenberger took charge of refitting their C-2 for a journey to the islands. He had the passenger seating cleared from the fuselage, reinforced the plane, and removed or substituted components that were causing interference with compasses and radios. He had two large fuel tanks installed in the center of the plane, dividing the fuselage into a pilot's cockpit up front and a navigator's cabin in the rear. Though large, the fuel tanks did not reach the cabin ceiling, leaving a passage that Hegenberger could crawl across to reach the pilot's cockpit, where he could sit in a copilot's seat and relieve Maitland at the controls if necessary.

The center engine sat directly in front of the cockpit, limiting forward visibility, with a pilot better able to see through side windows. In front of him sat a dash full of dials and gauges, including engine controls, flight instruments, a clock, and two magnetic compasses. Maitland stared at this display through new sets of flying goggles, including one pair specially designed to eliminate glare and protect his eyes from harmful solar rays—an early type of sunglasses.

Behind the pilot's cockpit and the fuel tanks was the navigator's cabin, which Hegenberger packed with navigational equipment, batteries, and duplicates of the gauges and instruments installed in the pilot's cockpit. A swivel chair and two tables were placed inside, useful for viewing an oversized eight-foot-long map of their route. One table also served as a platform for Hegenberger, allowing him to stand tall and poke his head through a hatch in the ceiling of the cabin, from where he could use his sextant to gaze at the sky or toss smoke bombs to measure the wind.

The army plane carried fifty-five of these bombs, though half actually emitted flame instead of smoke and were designed for use at night. They were indeed shaped like a bomb, with a rounded aluminum nose and a balsa wood body that tapered back to fins. Standing fourteen inches high and weighing less than a pound, they would be easy for Hegenberger to activate and lob to the sea, where powder would combust and produce smoke or flame. Hegenberger referred to the smoke bombs as "miniature volcanoes." If all went well, his continual sighting of these small floating volcanoes would serve as a prelude to seeing full-sized versions in Hawaii.

As Hegenberger prepared for the trip, Maitland was impressed by his flying partner's thoroughness and industry, saying, "He is not only a fine pilot but a navigator without peer. While he gives the impression of being shy and retiring I know Hegenberger as a man of profound knowledge of navigation and tenacity of purpose that will carry him through any obstacles."

Hegenberger respected Maitland's skill as a pilot just as deeply. The army fliers complemented—and complimented—each other nicely, both in respect to their personalities and aviation proficiencies. Maitland was composed of electricity, their peers said, and Hegenberger of cold steel. "Maitland's the high strung youngster, a remarkable and brilliant pilot, with a gallant fighting heart," said an acquaintance of the army pilots. "But Hegenberger is the cool, unexcited fighter, the ideal balance to keep Maitland in check."

US Army Air Corps lieutenants Albert F. Hegenberger (left) and Lester J. Maitland in front of the trimotored Fokker C-2 *Bird of Paradise*. Maitland was one of the Air Corps' top pilots and Hegenberger one of the Air Corps' best navigators, as well as a talented pilot. *Courtesy of the National Museum of the US Air Force*

By June 16, 1927, Maitland and Hegenberger had finished modifying and testing the Fokker C-2 and were ready to fly to the West Coast to make their final preparations for the flight to Hawaii. After bidding farewell to their wives and children in Dayton, the army pilots and a temporary crew of three civilians climbed into the modified Fokker C-2 and took off, stopping at Scott Field in Belleville, Illinois, before flying again that day to Hatbox Field in Muskogee, Oklahoma. Though the army aviators planned to fly nonstop to Hawaii, they followed a piecemeal route to the West Coast, stopping every few hours at army airfields, careful to shield their plane from public view.

By the time they reached Texas the next day, the secret was out—the War Department had suddenly announced the army was attempting the Hawaiian

Hop! Landing at Kelly Field in San Antonio by way of Dallas, the crew fastened the doors to the cabin and covered the plane's windows with curtains, shielding the equipment inside from prying eyes. No, Maitland and Hegenberger told a waiting throng of reporters, they were not going to compete in the Dole Derby. The army was making its own attempt at the islands.

Next the army fliers stopped in El Paso, Texas, and Tucson, Arizona, before arriving to Rockwell Field in San Diego, where Maitland and Hegenberger parked themselves for five days as they fine-tuned their airplane and installed another gasoline tank. The C-2 was kept in a closed concrete hangar, surrounded by guards who kept the hundreds of sightseers at bay. The newspaper headlines about the flight, as well as the mobs of aviation enthusiasts hoping to get a glimpse of the C-2, persuaded Maitland to be more forthcoming about the army's plans. "Well, since everyone seems to know about it, I guess it's not a secret," said Maitland. "All we need now is permission from the War Department and some adjustments on the ship."

The army explained to the press how it had been preparing this flight for months, that its timing close to the Dole Derby was coincidental. Its aviators were not seeking to pioneer a route for publicity purposes, but rather to accomplish military objectives, namely testing navigation and communication equipment and establishing an air route between military facilities in Hawaii and the mainland. The flight to Hawaii might also boost commercial aviation, which was an Army Air Corps peacetime objective.

At Rockwell Field, Maitland also broke the unpopular news that the flight would depart from San Francisco, not San Diego. "From here the distance to Diamond Head is approximately 2,700 miles, while from San Francisco it is but 2,418," said the pilot. "The 200 miles is worth saving—we might need it if we got a bit off our course and had to circle around looking for the islands."

This fear of getting lost may have been prompted, in part, by the welcome extended to them in San Diego by Lieutenant Byron J. Connell, the naval aviator who had piloted PN-9 No. 1 during the first flight attempt to Hawaii two years earlier. Maitland and Hegenberger were extremely familiar with PN-9 No. 1's flight and miraculous sea voyage, as well as the courage the late Commander John Rodgers had displayed. Maitland later praised Rodgers as the "type of man who never ordered a subordinate upon a mission he would not venture on himself. A brave, stout-hearted man who had the blue of the sky in his eyes and the tang of the sea in his heart."

Mindful of the hardships Rodgers and his crew endured, Maitland stated that he and his flying companion were devoting the days ahead to ensuring they were properly prepared for their estimated twenty-six-hour journey. "We believe that the hazard of accurate navigation is the gravest problem we shall have to face," said Maitland. "In order that we may become proficient to the Nth degree we shall concentrate most of our attention from now until the date of our hopoff on checking the instruments for precision and reliability and in familiarizing ourselves with the charting detail and mathematical compilations to the end that our speed, distance, load, drift and position may be known exactly throughout the flight."

The army fliers headed north on Saturday, June 25, 1927, piloting the C-2 toward San Francisco. Hundreds of people awaited them at Crissy Field along the bay, and scores more were parked along the hills of the Presidio, craning their necks to catch a first glimpse of the plane. About 2:30 PM a speck appeared in the distance, barely visible against the backdrop of the Contra Costa Mountains.

"There she is!" yelled someone in the crowd.

A man holding field glasses to his eyes confirmed the sighting: "It's the Fokker, all right! I can see the three motors."

The crowd watched the C-2 come closer and circle Oakland across the bay before landing at Crissy Field. As onlookers surged forward, soldiers prevented all but a few speedy photographers from rushing the plane. Cheers erupted when Maitland exited the C-2 and flashed a huge grin. Hegenberger emerged next, appearing more bookish than his tall, smiling flying partner.

Addressing the crowd of admirers and journalists, Maitland faced the cameras and told of his satisfaction with the plane's performance that day on the flight from San Diego. Newspapermen—who had been busy labeling the army pilots as birdmen, air vikings, and argonauts of the air, among other descriptors—clamored to know when the fliers would be heading for Hawaii. Maitland suddenly became coy, willing only to say their plans were "uncertain" after Sunday.

The army was due to hop off any minute. Nearly ready to leave, too, albeit in reverse fashion, was Hollywood stunt flier Dick Grace, who was now in Hawaii reassembling his crated aircraft. And across the country dozens of other pilots began gearing up to participate in the Dole Derby, hoping to nab the big prize that would be available in just six weeks. In the summer of 1927, one more challenger jumped into this ocean-crossing scrum. Unlike his competitors, he did not have the military's resources behind him, nor any kind of high public profile from appearing in motion pictures. But what Ernie Smith did possess would carry him far: pluck and determination.

Later memorialized as a "hard-living and utterly charming pilot," the free-wheeling Smith endeared himself to nearly everyone he met, including those who occasionally sought his arrest. As a young speed demon in California, Smith once blazed down a highway to Sacramento in his Essex automobile, outpacing a number of policemen who tried to pull him over. The patrolmen ultimately caught up with him at the state capitol, where Smith admitted to racing the Essex to 104 miles per hour. Rather than lock Smith up, the police asked to borrow the keys and have a turn themselves in the powerful car. He obliged, but the patrolmen grew timid as the speedometer needle climbed, not daring to push the Essex past ninety miles per hour.

Smith did earn a trip to the station when, in the midst of Prohibition, he punched a San Francisco policeman. There a precinct captain took pity on the young man, suggesting to him and the clocked cop, "Why don't you fellows have a drink and forget about it?" Because gin sounded better than jail, Smith and the cop headed to a local speakeasy. But minutes later his luck ran out when federal agents raided the bar and arrested both him and the city copper.

Smith, thirty-four, had grown up in Nevada before his family moved to the San Francisco area, where he graduated high school and enrolled in college to study dentistry. Like two of the aviators he hoped to soon be racing across the Pacific, Smith's college education was interrupted by the First World War. On account of his dental training, he enlisted in the army's medical corps, though he soon transferred to the Army Air Service because it was more thrilling. He attended ground school at the University of California, Berkeley, before heading to Rockwell Field to train as a flight cadet. After being commissioned as a second lieutenant, Smith served the last fourteen months of the war as a flight instructor, just like his potential army rivals Lieutenants Maitland and Hegenberger.

Favoring the flying of airplanes over the fixing of teeth, Smith ditched the dentistry plans at war's end and started work as a civilian pilot in Seattle. For years he flew as part of a forest air patrol operated by the US Department of Agriculture. In 1926 he began flying for the early airline Pacific Air Transport, delivering airmail, and occasionally passengers, along the West Coast.

While most aviators hoping to fly to Hawaii were content to compete in the Dole Derby, Smith lacked their patience. The brash flyer saw greater value in cutting in front of his competitors and setting out for the islands as soon as possible. In his mind, the celebrity attached to being the first aviator to reach Hawaii would outweigh the value of Dole's cash prize. Assembling a team of investors, the aviator soon hired navigator Charles H. Carter and procured a plane he was very comfortable flying: a Travel Air 5000 he bought from his employer, Pacific Air Transport.

Smith's insistence on being the first to fly to Hawaii upset a number of officials and observers associated with the planned transpacific flights. In Honolulu a newspaper complained that pilots taking off ahead of the Dole Derby were "bum sports" guilty of trying to "crab the game."

In San Francisco a citizen flight committee helping to govern the Dole Derby complained that Smith's behavior was both unsportsmanlike and reckless. Committee chairman Milo D. Kent wrote to US secretary of commerce Herbert Hoover, begging for the federal government to intervene and prevent Smith's "suicide" over the Pacific in a "second hand" plane. Added committee secretary Frank A. Flynn, "Six men died in attempts to cross the Atlantic before Lindbergh accomplished it. We don't want to be responsible if anything like that happens in the Pacific flights."

The flight committee's comments infuriated Smith's financial backers, who quickly came to the pilot's defense and cast aspersions on the committee, accusing them of trying to sabotage Smith's flight for the benefit of the army and racers in the Dole Derby. "Smith and Carter are going to hop off the minute their plane is ready, and neither Kent nor anybody else can stop them," said Smith sponsor Anthony Parente of San Francisco.

Another backer and the manager of the flight, Edmund J. Moffett, chimed in with his own disapproval: "Those are the dirtiest tactics I ever heard of. Doesn't any sane man imagine that we would send these boys out over the ocean in a 'suicide ship,' or that two experienced flyers like Smith and Carter would take off in one?"

But even a friend and fellow pilot questioned Smith's motivation for flying so soon, wondering why he wouldn't simply wait to race with the rest of the civilian aviators. "It seems to me that aviators contemplating the flight should wait until then," said Livingston Irving, an entrant in the Dole Derby and a former college fraternity brother to Smith. "The transpacific flight, more than the transatlantic flight, is a competitive undertaking. Before Lindbergh crossed nobody could have stated definitively the feat was possible. Today it is an assured fact a flyer can travel across the Pacific to his goal."

Shrugging off this criticism, Smith and a team of mechanics modified his plane in a small engine shop in San Francisco as he readied himself for the transpacific flight. Though the silver plane had been delivered new to Pacific Air Transport just months earlier in April 1927, Smith elected to install a new engine. He chose a Wright J-5 Whirlwind, the same air-cooled engine on the army's plane and the same engine that had powered Charles Lindbergh's *Spirit of St. Louis* across the Atlantic Ocean just weeks earlier.

Smith also had large fuel tanks installed within the fuselage. Together with fuel tanks in the wings, the plane could hold up to 370 gallons of gasoline. Much like within the army's C-2, the tanks separated the pilot's cockpit from the navigator's cabin, with a small corridor left between them to allow for communication and passage. Spirits were high in the machine shop in San Francisco's North Beach as the silver plane received its new engine and fuel tanks. Smith, often appearing wild with his long windswept hair blown back, removed four silver dollars from his vest pocket and boasted of his imminent success. "I'll bet this against one cent that I get away from here and get to Honolulu," he said.

Smith's slim, blond, soft-spoken navigator, Carter, seconded the claim: "Just keep that old engine going and I'll land you in Honolulu."

"Honolulu!" said another in the machine shop. "Charley Carter could land you in a back yard!"

"He could land on a banana peel," added the sponsor Parente.

For all the confidence, there also existed a few worries. Smith was desperate to embark before, or at least at the same time, as the army. He and his team monitored the army's progress and announcements closely, grateful for each day that passed without the C-2 taking flight. They also feared sabotage, prompting investors to hire armed guards to stand sentry outside the machine shop.

Beyond subversion, the team fretted about interference from the government, which had announced it would inspect Smith's plane prior to the flight. A year earlier, in 1926, Congress had passed the Air Commerce Act, which charged the US Department of Commerce with promoting the commercial aviation industry and enforcing safety standards. As Smith prepared his airplane, inspector Walter F. Parkin was en route from Los Angeles to verify the craft could safely make the flight to Hawaii. Smith's backers were not pleased at the possibility that he might forbid the trip. "I am not questioning the integrity of Captain Parkins [sic] or intimating that he would be a party to any scheme to throw obstacles in our way," said Moffett. "Nevertheless, for our own protection we are going to keep a close check on Captain Parkin's contracts and associations while he is in San Francisco."

Parente suggested the team might ignore any Commerce Department rulings and proceed with the flight to Hawaii regardless of government disapproval. He was unfazed by the possibility of a $500 fine: "We have already spent more than $20,000 so I guess we could stand that much more."

Last, Smith's team was unsure from where their plane would take off, having been refused permission to use the army's Crissy Field, which Smith had been allowed to use when carrying airmail for Pacific Air Transport. The refusal irritated his sponsors and fueled their theories of a government conspiracy to thwart their flight—accusations the military denied. Just days away from an anticipated takeoff, his sponsors scrambled to find a new runway long enough to accommodate a plane weighed down by so much fuel. They found a solution in a newly flattened seven-thousand-foot airfield on Bay Farm Island in Oakland, situated along marshland across the bay from San Francisco. As a sign of gratitude for use of the airfield, Smith's team announced their plane would be named City of Oakland.

With a spot at the new Oakland airport secured, mechanics labored through the night in San Francisco to have City of Oakland ready for transport across the bay by boat on the morning of Saturday, June 25, 1927. Three trucks were needed to move the plane, which was separated into pieces. A first truck towed the fuselage, which rolled along the Embarcadero on its landing gear toward the Ferry Building at the end of Market Street. Two other trucks—one carrying the wings, the other carrying the propeller and plane's tail—joined the motorcade, which was escorted by a crowd of mechanics, newspapermen, and Smith's friends. As the caravan approached the waterfront, three lit cigarette butts were discovered in the fuselage. Fearing he was the victim of a sabotage attempt, Smith prevailed upon policemen to stand guard and forbid smoking near the aircraft.

After carefully maneuvering the plane through the Ferry Building, Smith's team placed the plane pieces onto three boats and floated east across the bay. In Oakland a crowd greeted the plane and its entourage, which then proceeded to Bay Farm Island. Waiting at the airfield was Smith's father, who had been surprised to learn his "boy" would soon be departing on a twenty-six-hour nonstop flight to Hawaii. "First thing I knew about this was when I read the paper this morning. I have been away on a vacation and just got back," said Ernest W. Smith.

Yet the elder Smith did not express alarm over the prospect of his son mimicking Lindbergh and becoming only the second person to make a transoceanic flight of such magnitude. In fact, he offered to come along. "I've been up [in an airplane] several times, but never with my son," he said. "However, if he wants a passenger this trip he can count me in."

An uncle who came to see Ernie Smith take off was less gung ho, stating he was excited for his nephew but that he would remain at home, "at least for this trip." Ernie Smith's brother, Morris, later expressed a similar sentiment, stating, "I believe he'll make it if anyone can. I would like to go along, but I can't swim well enough."

When the plane pieces concluded their journey to the airfield, crews of mechanics immediately began attaching the wings, tail, and propeller to the fuselage. Smith remained optimistic about his chances of reaching the islands, claiming he was ready to leave as soon as possible. "I'll hop off Sunday night if the ship is ready," he said.

"But you haven't made any trial flights," cautioned a friend.

"I'll go without any trial flights," replied Smith. "I'll try her out on the way to Honolulu."

Upon arriving in San Francisco, Army Air Corps lieutenants Lester Maitland and Albert Hegenberger met with the local weather bureau to receive a forecast for the next few days. Predictions were generally favorable for the flight; the fliers were told to expect winds at their back and only passing showers. The skies would likely be cloudy, though, and dark, as a new moon was due to begin soon, on Tuesday, June 28, 1927. Though it would be advantageous to wait for a full moon, as the navy did two years earlier in its own attempt with flying boats, the army was not timid about flying in total darkness. The purpose of the trip, as Maitland and Hegenberger had started explaining to the press the last few days, was in part to test the army's ability to fly blindly using instruments. For the Air Corps to function most effectively, its pilots would need to learn to fly safely in nearly any conditions.

Hegenberger planned to use several familiar forms of navigation during the flight, which included celestial fixing using an air sextant, dead reckoning using smoke bombs, and pilotage, which involved matching landmarks to a map. Since the only natural landmark on their overseas route was the Farallon Islands thirty-two miles off the coast of San Francisco, the army coordinated with steamship lines operating between Hawaii and California, learning the routes and schedules of their vessels. When the army fliers sighted a steamship on their journey, they could therefore obtain a general idea of their location. They also asked steamers to signal via semaphore the longitude and latitude of their location, providing the aviators a precise location through signal flags hoisted on each side of the ship, with latitude displayed to starboard and longitude to port. Since the army fliers had no maritime training nor a strong familiarity with semaphores, they pasted the inside of the C-2's fuselage with lists of the International Code of Signals so they could decipher the flags the steamers flew. Finally, the ships and plane could communicate by radio, exchanging coordinates and weather information. Steamships could also provide a radio bearing to the plane, should Hegenberger request it. Of course, the navigator knew through navy commander John Rodgers's experience that radio bearings could sometimes be inaccurate.

But if radio bearings were a last resort for Hegenberger, a similar technology held more promise: radio beacons. Hegenberger and the Army's Signal Corps Aircraft Radio Laboratory had been working feverishly in the last few months to establish this new means of air navigation, erecting ninety-three-foot radio towers on the opposite ends of the flight. In San Francisco a location was easily found at Fort Winfield Scott, just beside Crissy Field. In Hawaii it was more of a challenge, with Hegenberger insisting the tower be placed in the center of the island chain, on either Maui or Molokai, to allow him and Maitland the greatest range of error without dooming the flight.

Since Molokai lacked a good port and required pack animals to haul equipment across the mountainous island, the army opted for placing its radio tower on the northern side of Maui in a sugarcane field between the communities of Haiku and Paia. The field, and power for the tower, was provided by the Maui Agricultural Company, who also volunteered to burn a number of nearby sugarcane fields to provide the army fliers with a large visible beacon of smoke and flames as they approached the islands. The army declined the bonfire but gratefully accepted the chance to erect its radio beacon tower in the sugarcane field, constructing a small shack beside it to house radio equipment.

Hegenberger was confident that aiming for Maui was a wise choice. By steering south of Honolulu along a slightly longer route of 2,418 miles, the army airmen also hoped to avoid flying over the seventy miles of ocean separating Oahu and Kauai, where they might miss spying both islands, especially if passing in darkness or bad weather. "Both Maitland and I know every foot of the islands, and are thoroughly familiar with the Oahu-Kauai Channel," said Hegenberger. "With our complete navigation equipment we expect to fly direct to Paia, then head northward for Honolulu. . . . Maui is a little off our course but sane navigation is better than risking flying a few miles shorter."

To use the radio beacons positioned on each end of the flight route, Hegenberger had a special radio receiver installed aboard the C-2 the day after he and Maitland landed at Crissy Field. The navigator planned to don a pair of headphones and use this receiver to listen to the continuous Morse code signals being broadcast from each tower across the ocean. The radio towers had been engineered to each simultaneously broadcast two inverse tones: the letters *A* (a dot followed by a dash) and *N* (a dash followed by a dot). When the plane traveled directly between the towers, the Morse code signals combined to make the sound of the letter *T*, or an uninterrupted long dash. Should the C-2 veer off course, the *T* signal would diminish as only one letter would intone strongly while the other tapered off. So should the C-2 drift south of the route, the *A* signal would become more prominent, the continuous tone broken. Should the plane travel north of its path, the *N* sound would begin to dominate, indicating to the navigator that the plane should correct course.

The radio beacons were described as lighthouses for aviators, helping guide a plane to (air)port. Maitland was clearly appreciative of the devices, referring to the beacons as an "electric highway" and as "the faithful little jinni who, in dots or dashes, flings out an airway in Morse code that guides the airman to his goal."

"To the pilot," he said, "the intermittent buzz-buzz-buzz of the letter T he hears when he is on his course is sweeter music than a moonlight sonata."

A day after landing in San Francisco, he and Hegenberger flew above the Farallon Islands and tested the beacon system, as well as other radio equipment. The aviators were hopeful the beacons would work as designed, though they were mindful that mishaps could occur, and that the system would function more effectively the closer they were to the beacons on the Californian and Hawaiian coasts, where the signals would be strongest. "In a new instrument like this it is probable several things may go wrong," said Hegenberger. "It will take time to work out the bugs, but I believe from our past experiments it will work. We will fly down this radio path much the same as one would pour water which must come out of the neck of a bottle."

Maitland was less tolerant of potential malfunction, considering the radio beacons critical to the job of finding the small Hawaiian Islands amid a sprawl-ing, sloshing ocean. At one point before takeoff he placed his finger atop a map of the Pacific Ocean and traced the flight route. Upon reaching Hawaii he drew his fingers into a fist and pounded the table. "From here, those islands look like a bunch of rocks!" he said. "I just hope the Signal Corps did a good job on that radio beacon."

Hegenberger, from across the table, responded by flashing a smile.

The two army aviators had formed a friendship in the last few months as they prepared to cross the Pacific. While waiting in San Francisco for final approval for their flight from the Air Corps, Maitland invited Hegenberger to his parents' home in the suburb of Burlingame, where they could enjoy a home-cooked meal and conversation, and obtain a good night's sleep. Because of their proximity to the flight's starting point, the Maitlands had recently been swamped by phone calls and visits from well-wishers and reporters. Everyone wanted to know what they thought of their son taking off across an ocean.

"It will be fine—if he makes it," said Maitland's mother, Bertha. "I'd rather not talk about it."

Maitland's father, too, tried to limit the questioning. "We don't want to talk about ourselves. We are not making the flight to Hawaii; the boy is," said J. W. Maitland. "But we are confident he will make it, for he doesn't start anything unless he is pretty certain to finish."

Two days after the army fliers' arrival in San Francisco, J.W. went to see the aircraft his son would pilot across the Pacific. Observing the C-2 at Crissy Field, he disclosed that he'd yet to muster the courage required to join his son in the sky: "I've never been up. I've always found an excuse not to when I was invited. I'm not a lighter than air person. But my son lives off the ground. That is his life. He belongs to a new race—the flying race."

⸺•⸺

City of Oakland sat reassembled on a dusty airfield on Bay Farm Island, its nose pointed west toward Hawaii. The engine was running like clockwork and its pilot was eager to take to the air. Upon arriving to the Oakland airfield on Sunday, June 26, 1927, Ernie Smith manically checked his instruments and airplane, climbing in and out of *City of Oakland* repeatedly to confer with his mechanics and sponsors. As one observer noted, "Smith himself was here, there, and everywhere. His eye was on every detail. . . . The pilot appeared to be temperamentally incapable of standing still for more than a second at a time. The strain of waiting was telling on him."

The US Department of Commerce had forbid Smith to leave before Tuesday—two long days away. As he waited he fretted, worried his competitors in the army would beat him to Hawaii. Earlier that Sunday morning, before Smith arrived to fine-tune his plane, army lieutenants Lester Maitland and Albert Hegenberger had flown over to Bay Farm Island in an army de Havilland airplane, leaving their C-2 behind at Crissy Field in San Francisco. Borrowing an automobile after they landed the de Havilland, the army flyers drove up and down the long dirt runway, inspecting it for depressions and other potential trouble. Pleased with its conditions, the lieutenants flew back across the bay, deciding they would depart for Hawaii from Bay Farm Island as well.

The Army Air Corps leader, Major General Mason Patrick, was expected to arrive that day in San Francisco from Washington, DC. Maitland and Hegenberger were reportedly waiting for his final approval before leaving for the islands. Smith feared that approval could come at any moment, that their flight was imminent and could happen as early as Monday morning. "Maitland and Hegenberger might fuel up, hop over here, and take off before daylight," he worried aloud while milling about the airfield.

"Let 'em," said backer Edmund Moffett, who had earned the nickname "optimist-in-chief" for the *City of Oakland* flight attempt. "You and Carter can 'spot' the army six hours and beat them to Honolulu. Your ship can fly thirty miles an hour faster than theirs."

Newspapermen salivated over the prospect of the army and Ernie Smith racing head-to-head to Hawaii. The *San Francisco Chronicle* wrote of "two planes, their engines driven madly, tearing out over the long stretches of the Pacific, with vast throngs lining the sandy island shores to wreathe the shoulders of the winners with Hawaiian blossoms."

Should stunt flier Dick Grace begin his own transpacific flight in the opposite direction, the drama would heighten tenfold. News reports from Hawaii told of Grace tuning his plane's engine, awaiting a replacement propeller, and arranging for the clearing of trees and filling of holes alongside Barking Sands beach on Kauai—the only runway in Hawaii long enough to launch a plane loaded down with the fuel supply required to cross half the Pacific. The *Chronicle* continued, "And perchance, if this thrilling thing should come to pass, they might meet along the way a third plane, headed toward the rising sun, piloted by that lone eagle, 'Dick' Grace, he of the broken neck and the unbroken spirit."

The newspaper coverage endeared Smith to the general public, who regarded him as an undaunted underdog. The single-engine *City of Oakland* was a little more than half the size of the army's trimotor C-2, allowing Smith to neatly play David to the military's Goliath. When Smith finished testing the engine on the Bay Farm Island runway that Sunday afternoon, a throng of admirers rushed out to greet him as he exited the plane, eager to shake his hand.

Smith enjoyed the adulation, but late in the afternoon he endured another scare. The pilot's ears had picked up a steady and distinct droning sound emanating from the clouds, prompting him to dash out from under the wing of his plane and look to the sky. Circling above the airfield was the army's C-2. Smith shaded his eyes with his hand and watched the army plane's every move. He relaxed only when the C-2 flew east, back across the bay to San Francisco.

While Smith worried over the competition, his navigator, Charles Carter, calmly checked his instruments and monitored weather forecasts, which promised good flying conditions in the days ahead. Of potential concern were the gusty crosswinds that sometimes plagued the runway at Bay Farm Island. No windbreaks—neither trees nor substantial buildings—existed at the dusty new airfield along the marshy bay. But Carter wasn't bothered by the crosswinds, thinking them perhaps troublesome only to the army. "We can weather them without much trouble," he said "They might bother the big Fokker more than us."

The army was similarly concerned about crosswinds buffeting their large plane at takeoff, contemplating the use of an airfield near Sacramento should there be fierce gusts in Oakland. Yet on Monday morning the C-2 was flown from Crissy Field to Bay Farm Island in preparation for the flight. To Smith's relief, the army plane remained on the runway after landing, apparently staying put for another day, though one could never be sure. "They are watching each other like hawks, these entrants in an epic race, even though they fly like eagles," noted a report in the *Chronicle*.

Despite the newspaper claiming, "This race will be a more classic sporting event than all the Derbies ever run, championship fights that were ever fought, and world series ball games ever played put together," Smith's team and the army fliers were exceedingly cordial to each other. That Monday, as each team made final tune-ups beside each other and took their planes to the air for trial runs, the pilots and navigators chatted, laughed, and shook hands as they discussed their upcoming flights, which were expected to begin as soon as the next day—Tuesday morning. Later this camaraderie among aviators deepened when the army graciously loaned Smith a pressure gauge and radio antenna for *City of Oakland*. And when Major General Patrick arrived to Bay Farm Island to inspect the C-2, he expressed a desire to meet Smith, who had just left the airfield on a short trip to Oakland. "I'm sorry. I would liked to have met the brave young man," said Patrick. "Tell him he has my heartiest wishes for the success of his flight."

Patrick wasn't the only person seeking an audience with Smith. On the eve of his expected flight, so many visitors came to Bay Farm Field that policemen were forced to corral and contain the crowd. Some of these people planned to sleep in their cars through the night in order to witness the takeoffs early the next morning. Tents had been set up to accommodate the many news reporters and photographers at the airfield, and special telephone lines were installed for the correspondents, too. A vendor did brisk business peddling weenies to the masses.

Among those who penetrated the police cordon was six-year-old Sallie Hutchinson of nearby Berkeley, California, who gifted Smith a fairy stone to ensure safe travels. Sallie explained that fairy stones are found in Patrick County, Virginia. Legend has it that the cross-shaped stones were formed from the tears of fairies in the Blue Ridge Mountains who cried when an angel flew over them and announced the crucifixion of Christ. Smith thanked the little girl with a peck on the cheek and promised to bring the stone aboard *City of Oakland.* "As surely as the angel flew over the world," said Smith, "I will be sure to fly across the Pacific to Hawaii."

Smith also received the mother, wife, and daughter of Livingston Irving, his friend, fraternity brother, and fellow pilot. Irving's mother said farewell and gave Smith a blessing—the same blessing she promised to give her son before he competed in the upcoming Dole Derby. Irving's eight-year-old daughter, Madeline, hugged and kissed Smith while Irving's wife shook the aviator's hand and smiled through her tears as she said goodbye. Conspicuously absent was Irving himself, who was perhaps still sore that Smith would not wait to compete in the Dole Derby.

With Smith's preparations complete, the plane running perfectly, and night soon falling, there was just one thing left to do: christen *City of Oakland.* Optimist-in-chief Moffett launched into a speech comparing Smith's Hawaii-bound plane to the wooden ships European explorers Vasco Núñez de Balboa, Christopher Columbus, and Ferdinand Magellan sailed four centuries earlier. Then Irene Parente, the pretty daughter of sponsor Anthony, smashed a bottle of champagne across the nose of the plane, wowing a crowd unaccustomed to seeing the public appearance of alcohol. The people surrounding *City of Oakland* roared with delight, their cheers echoed by a contingent of nearby soldiers standing guard around the C-2.

Meanwhile, the army fliers and top brass had left the airfield, Patrick having given his blessing to the military flight after making a thorough inspection of the C-2. Satisfied, the major general and the army fliers addressed reporters at the field before their departure. "The ship's all right. And the men are all right. We're ready to go the minute the weather is just right," said Patrick, causing Maitland and Hegenberger to blush.

Upon Maitland and Hegenberger's suggestion, the cheerful major general also gave his approval to name the C-2 *Bird of Paradise*, though it was against army policy to have a name painted on the aircraft. With that the army was done for the day. Maitland, relieved that months of preparation had finally come to an end, retired to the nearby Hotel Oakland to take an afternoon nap.

As evening came, word arrived from the War Department in Washington that the flight would almost certainly proceed in the morning. The army then delivered orders to airport officials: "Give us a clear field at 7 o'clock." *Bird of Paradise* would soon be winging its way to the islands. *City of Oakland* promised to be on her tail.

At 5:30 in the morning on June 28, 1927, Lester Maitland and Albert Hegenberger rose from their beds in a shared room in the Hotel Oakland, refreshed after nine hours of sleep. It was wise for the army officers to stockpile some slumber—in minutes they would begin more than a full day's flight across the Pacific Ocean to Hawaii, with no opportunity to shut their eyes.

Descending to the lobby for breakfast, the men were surprised to see two familiar, smiling faces: Les's parents. The Maitlands had come to the hotel the night before, explained Bertha Maitland, to avoid the considerable traffic they would have encountered driving into Oakland from their home across the bay. The Maitlands had spent the night in a room beside the one their son and Hegenberger occupied. Les's father suggested that it was more than traffic worries that prompted their proximity, claiming about his wife, "She wouldn't have missed spending that night near Lester for anything in the world." Hegenberger was touched by their devotion to their son, deeming their presence at the hotel "one of those rare little incidents which are treasured in men's lives for forever after."

"With all the consideration of parents, they had not disturbed us, although we immediately knew how longingly they must have looked forward to the morning and an opportunity to bid us godspeed," said the navigator. Lester was considerably less emotional as they breakfasted, expressing confidence to his parents but otherwise saying little. He asked his mother and father to stay away from the airfield for fear of a crash at takeoff. At this request his father looked him over before instructing him "not to worry."

Maitland next hopped into a taxi. Hegenberger soon followed, en route to Bay Farm Island with a police motorcycle escort. The scene awaiting the army pilots was festive, with people and parked cars lining both sides of the runway, which ran for nearly one and a half miles to the edge of San Francisco Bay. Hundreds of people had spent the night to claim their front-row vantage points. Sitting by bonfires or in the glow of automobile headlamps, the revelers smoked cigarettes, roasted hot dogs, and sipped coffee out of thermoses. If they needed to snooze, they lay down in cars. At daybreak they woke as thousands more aviation enthusiasts joined them at the airfield, all eager to witness the historic first flights to Hawaii.

At the far eastern end of the runway stood the big green *Bird of Paradise* beside Ernie Smith's tiny silver *City of Oakland*, their wings nearly touching. Judging from appearances alone, it didn't seem like a fair fight. The bigger army plane held three times as much fuel as Smith's aircraft. The army plane had three motors; Smith's had just one. The army plane contained radios, compasses, altimeters, and other air instruments galore; Smith had just one of those instruments each, some of them borrowed from the army. Yet with a top speed of 140 miles per hour and a cruising speed of 125 miles per hour, *City of Oakland* was twenty-five miles per hour faster than *Bird of Paradise*. It was perhaps Smith's single advantage.

The usual morning haze hung over the field as mechanics worked feverishly about the planes, using rags to wipe dew off the fuselages. Both aircraft were parked at the extreme end of the runway, nearly touching a row of automobiles parked along a levee that formed the eastern terminus of the airfield. The pilots wished to have as much runway available to them as possible.

The US Army Air Corps' *Bird of Paradise*, with stars atop its wings, beside Ernie Smith's smaller *City of Oakland* at the Oakland airport on Bay Farm Island. The rival planes both took off for Hawaii on June 28, 1927. *Courtesy of the National Museum of the US Air Force*

To the mechanics' surprise, the army plane—filled with 1,129 gallons of gasoline and weighing 13,774 pounds—had sunk four inches into the ground overnight. The men stared at the half-buried wheels in disbelief before devising and executing a plan to jack up the wheels one at a time and fill the small craters beneath them. About that time, police sirens sounded as the army fliers' taxis arrived two minutes apart, their police escorts weaving in and out of the traffic jam clogging the road to the airport.

Maitland and Hegenberger were greeted with cheers as they exited the taxis and strode toward *Bird of Paradise* to make final inspections and adjustments. Still and motion picture cameras clicked and whirred all around them while the crowd buzzed with excitement. The hubbub would have been dizzying if not for the aviators' intense concentration and commitment to ensuring that every aspect of the plane was properly adjusted before takeoff. They soon were satisfied *Bird of Paradise* was in top working order, with Maitland stating, "We have every confidence in the plane and the success of the radio direction. If the flight is successful it will mean much to aviation. We will do our best and expect to make it."

"Yes," added Hegenberger, half yawning. "Just tell them we expect to get there."

A lucky few in the crowd were able to chat with the aviators before they departed for the islands. This included army lieutenant Oakley Kelly, who made the first nonstop coast-to-coast flight in the United States in 1923. Standing on the runway in Oakland, Maitland quizzed Kelly about his preferred technique for keeping the plane's tail from hitting the ground while taking off with such a heavy fuel load aboard.

The army fliers also greeted Mary E. Tusch, a local regarded as a patron saint of aviators. Tusch lived in Berkeley, across the street from the University of California, in a white bungalow known as the Hangar. When the military established a flying school on campus during World War I, Tusch founded the University Mothers' Club to provide support for the young combat aviators in training. She regularly hosted the fliers at her home, serving coffee and doughnuts. The fliers, whom she called her "boys," reciprocated by sending her souvenirs from war. She even received a pair of silver wings from a German ace, inscribed, "To the Mother of us all, with love from Capt. Willie Mauss."

Even as the flying school shut down after the war, Tusch remained popular with fliers and transformed her home into a shrine to aviation. A piece of fuselage from an army plane sat in the bungalow and rooms were covered with framed pictures of pilots. Wallpaper featuring the silhouettes of airplanes also covered the interior, much of it covered in names. Before aviators departed the Hangar, Tusch required them to leave their autographs on the wall. Among the hundreds of signatures scribbled on the walls were those of the late navy commander John Rodgers, the army pilots who flew round the world, and Amelia Earhart.

As Maitland and Hegenberger readied for takeoff, Tusch gave them each a silver dollar for good luck. They promised to pen their own names on her wallpaper once they returned from Hawaii. "God bless you," she told them, adding that they should heed the instructions stamped on the silver dollars: "IN GOD WE TRUST."

Staring at the cheering throng surrounding him, Maitland spied two familiar faces a hundred feet away behind the police rope lines—his parents, who had ignored his pleas again. The young pilot motioned for a police officer to allow them to come close. Maitland kissed his mother, put an arm around his father, and then shook his pa's hand.

Army planes from Crissy Field began to land on Bay Farm Island, preparing to escort *Bird of Paradise* out of the Golden Gate. Major General Mason Patrick arrived by car about the same time, a few minutes after seven o'clock. Maitland had helped teach the Army Air Corps chief to fly just two years earlier, and the general was hoping his superiors would allow him to tag along on the flight. But this morning he arrived with bad news: the army had grounded him. "Sorry I can't go myself . . . but Washington won't let me," said Patrick, dressed in an aviator's jumpsuit. "Permission is denied."

The general's disappointment elicited much sympathy. A poem, "The Man Who Couldn't Go," was published the next day in the *San Francisco Examiner.* Among the lines of verse from poet Miles Overholt:

> All heroes do not soar to heights, or lead the battle's flare
> And see their names emblazoned in the headlines everywhere.
> Not everyone's a Paul Revere for hist'ry to acclaim;
> Not everyone is called to hear the public chant his name.
> While others laud the flyers who sail through the limelight's glow,
> Let's honor him, the tragic one—The Man Who Couldn't Go!

Standing on the runway, Patrick tenderly shook each lieutenant's hand. All three army men struggled to hold back their emotions. "God bless you, my boys," said Patrick. "I know you'll make it."

"General, you know we're going to do our best," replied Maitland, bending down to speak to the more diminutive officer.

With that Maitland and Hegenberger donned their own flying suits and helmets. Some observers thought they were preparing for a photograph, but instead the lieutenants bade farewell as they climbed into the plane with Patrick, who wanted to make one last inspection, if not possibly stow himself away.

"Goodbye, boys, we're off," said Maitland and Hegenberger as cameras photographed and filmed their final moves on the mainland.

Within the plane the aviators sat side by side in the cockpit. Maitland adjusted controls as *Bird of Paradise*'s three engines came roaring to life. The pilot chewed gum furiously as he tested each motor. Patrick exited the airplane, and the cabin door was zippered shut. The plane motors screamed. So, too, did the mob surrounding the planes and airfield. Policemen labored to keep spectators behind the rope lines. The observers could hardly believe the plane was already preparing to depart; Maitland and Hegenberger had arrived less than a half hour earlier.

Maitland gunned the motors, kicking up dust and pebbles onto the cars and people standing behind the planes. Before he sent the plane barreling down the runway, a car pulled up and a man in a blue sweater and gray knickerbockers jumped out, rushing in front of *Bird of Paradise*. It was Smith, just in time for takeoff. Standing in front of the army plane, with all eyes watching, Smith clasped his hands together, raised them high, and mimicked a handshake between him and his army rivals. "Good luck!" he shouted toward the airplane. Maitland waved and smiled back from the cockpit.

Police motorcycles, their sirens drowned out by the plane motors, raced down both sides of the runway, keeping the lines of spectators in place. The army plane followed, picking up speed as it charged down the dirt airfield along the marsh, leaving a suffocating cloud of dust in its wake. People honked their car horns and threw hats, confetti, and overcoats into the air as the plane tore down the runway. An ambulance trailed the plane, in case of accident.

At 7:09 AM *Bird of Paradise* lifted into the air having used just a little more than half of the runway. The dust cloud behind it was so thick that only those at the far western end of the runway could see the plane rise off the ground.

Army planes buzzing about the airport fell into line behind the big green cargo plane, ready to escort Maitland and Hegenberger to the Pacific Ocean just a few miles away. *Bird of Paradise*, rising slowly because of its immense fuel load, cleared warehouses in nearby Alameda by just fifty feet. Minutes later it burst through the black haze that hung low in the air and entered sunny skies. The army fliers flew past Alcatraz, then downtown San Francisco and Crissy Field, until land and bay gave way to the ocean at the Golden Gate.

Back at Bay Farm Island, Ernie Smith stood in the center of the runway, looking out at the army plane, which grew smaller by the second. The dust had settled and mechanics were hard at work on his own plane, preparing the silver aircraft for an imminent takeoff. But for the moment Smith could not peel himself away from the runway. He stared hard into the western sky at the spot where the army plane had just vanished. There were tears in his eyes.

As the army's *Bird of Paradise* was in the midst of its long flight to Hawaii on June 28, 1927, Dick Grace idled about on Kauai, supposedly ready to race in the opposite direction toward California. The stunt flier had arrived by steamship to Honolulu four days earlier. Upon reaching the islands, Hollywood's king of crack-ups let it be known that he had sated his appetite for destruction, at least temporarily, and hoped to safely fly across the Pacific. "I may have a reputation for doing dangerous stunts for the movies," said the twenty-nine-year-old, "but I'm not going to start on this trip with the idea of crashing."

Grace soon flew his reassembled Waterhouse Cruzair monoplane to Kauai, where he planned to take off on the long airstrip running along Barking Sands beach on the western side of the island. While the airfield had been cleared, depressions and bumps remained, some of them marked with red flags planted in the ground. It seemed as much a runway as an obstacle course, though a beautiful one. The runway stretched for a mile and a half, running parallel to the beach and crashing surf while mountain cliffs loomed about a mile inland.

Grace's small, twenty-four-foot-long airplane was bare bones in almost every way. Most of the airplane dope slathered on its wings and fuselage lacked pigment, resulting in an unfinished-looking coat atop the cloth wrapping. The plane also lacked nearly all of the navigation equipment contained within the army's flying science laboratory. Beyond some basic flying instruments, the Waterhouse Cruzair contained just one compass and a clock.

Rather than carry a drift meter or smoke bombs to measure the effects of the wind, Grace said he planned to toss rolls of toilet paper over the side of the plane and observe their fluttering descent. And the plane was in need of a new propeller, a replacement having just arrived to Honolulu from the mainland that morning. Grace could not lift off before the new propeller was shipped to Kauai and installed on his plane.

When plane and pilot were ready, he planned to take off from Barking Sands and hug the island shoreline, skirting the high cliffs of the Nā Pali Coast before spying the Kilauea Lighthouse on the northern tip of Kauai. From the lighthouse Grace would then head northeast on a bearing leading straight to San Francisco. Should the wind blow him north or south of the City by the Bay, it would not matter, he reasoned, as he would still intercept the California coast somewhere. If enough fuel remained in his tanks, he said he would then turn south and finish the long flight by landing in Los Angeles. After that, Grace boasted, he'd pick up a navigator and make a return trip to Hawaii.

It was an ambitious route, especially for an airplane with fuel tanks capable of holding only 320 gallons of gasoline and being piloted by a man whose neck was held tight in a brace. Grace would be fortunate, in fact, if he made it to California at all with that small fuel load, let alone have time to head south to Los Angeles. A stiff headwind on the way to California would almost certainly cause his tanks to run dry, in which case he would need to ready the inflatable raft and flares and unpack his four-day supply of canned brown raisin bread, chocolate, and water.

What did Grace plan to take aboard his airplane instead of extra fuel, a navigator, and additional flight instruments? A gift of a Hawaiian feather cape, for one thing, to be delivered to San Francisco mayor James Rolph. Once worn by Hawaiian royalty and chiefs, feather capes were and remain elaborate and prized historic garments, composed of netting decorated with thousands of red, yellow, and black feathers plucked from small birds. Also going to California: a wirehair fox terrier by the name of Kauai Leilani. Perhaps the pup dreamed of becoming the canine Lindbergh. "When I fly, my dog flies," said Grace.

As the army continued winging its way to the islands on June 28, Grace, his underfueled plane, and his four-legged passenger all remained on Kauai. Though the broken-necked flier had promised to take off and race the army men, he was still awaiting his new propeller. Unprepared to travel across the Pacific as quickly as he had hoped, he decided to shut his eyes and catch up on sleep.

As the army plane passed through the Golden Gate and its escorts peeled back toward San Francisco, Lieutenants Maitland and Hegenberger settled in for the long haul. Hegenberger left his seat in the cockpit and crawled back to the navigator's cabin, sliding over the large fuel tank that separated the two sections of the plane. The aviators expected to see the Farallon Islands within twenty minutes. It would be the last landmark of the journey. After that, they would not see land again until reaching Hawaii.

Leaving Oakland, and then California entirely, behind him, Maitland relaxed, overcome by a "feeling of absolute safety." "Every instinct in me told me as I sat at the controls of the plane that meticulous inspection had made it perfect in every detail," said the pilot. For the first time in what felt like a long time, his mind was not distracted, his mission straightforward. All he was expected to do was fly. "After all the years of effort to win the detail, and after all the months of study, preparation, and anxiety, it seemed a blessing to be free from any other responsibility than that of keeping the ship on its course," he said. "I had perfect faith in the ship, in Hegenberger, and in myself, and if there was any worry in my head it was that for the first time since 1922 I was flying without a parachute."

While the army pilots deemed parachutes useless for a flight across an ocean, they did pack an inflatable raft with oars and a telescoping aluminum mast. Should they make an emergency landing atop the waves, they estimated *Bird of Paradise* would float for a few hours before sinking. Then they would need to move to the raft, taking along the limited rations on the plane. Fearful of becoming drowsy after eating, the aviators had elected not to bring along too much food.

The Farallon Islands soon appeared to the north as *Bird of Paradise* bolted across the Pacific. Minutes later the plane flew over the army transport ship USS *Chateau Thierry*, which was heading to San Francisco. Then, as open ocean spread out before them, they passed through the first of many rain squalls they'd encounter on their journey, all while a strong crosswind buffeted the fuselage. Yet the weather would be the least of their problems.

The interior of the Fokker C-2 *Bird of Paradise*, looking from the navigator's cabin forward to the pilot's cockpit. A large, boxy fuel tank separated the pilot from the navigator and his equipment, including a radio set, compasses, and a plotting table. *Courtesy of the National Museum of the US Air Force*

The induction compass in the rear of the plane failed within the first hour, and Hegenberger labored to repair a broken plug on the equipment without success. Next to fail was the radio beacon that the Army Air Corps had so highly touted. As soon as the flyers tuned in, Hegenberger heard the beacon loud and clear, intercepting the overlapping tones broadcast between radio towers on Maui and in San Francisco. Less than an hour later, however, the tones inexplicably went silent. Hegenberger again attempted a fix, switching out the radio receiver's filament tubes and batteries in an effort to resuscitate the tones. But this device, too, could not be immediately repaired.

The failure of the induction compass and radio beacon left Hegenberger annoyed, but not doomed. Although Hegenberger had looked forward to testing the special compass, two traditional compasses remained in the plane for

Maitland to consult as he steered a course for Hawaii. Hegenberger could also use a sextant to determine their position through celestial navigation. What's more, the plane was well supplied with smoke bombs and float lights that he could toss overboard to measure the plane's drift on account of the wind.

Maitland flew beneath the clouds, often just three hundred feet above the water, to allow Hegenberger to periodically heave the smoke bombs out of the plane, observe the drift, and adjust course through dead reckoning. But as Hegenberger stared back at the first smoke bomb he tossed atop the waves, eager to see how sharply the plane was being pushed by the gusty wind, the glare of the rising sun shone hard into his eyes. It would be impossible to use the smoke bombs until the sun climbed higher into the sky.

Unwilling to wait that long, Hegenberger devised a novel way to estimate drift: by sighting clumps of sea-foam atop the rolling water. Bits of sea-foam remained stationary atop the water even as waves washed underneath. By focusing on a bit of foam through a glass window in the bottom of the plane, he believed he could observe how severely the plane was being pushed from its intended path.

His innovation seemed to hold promise. After all, what was the difference between spotting a smoke bomb or blob of sea-foam? Either should be able to function as a reference point for the navigator, so long as the foam truly stayed in place while the ocean undulated below. That was Hegenberger's theory, at least, and the drift observations he made in this fashion seemed consistent with his position about noon, when he used an air sextant to establish the plane's location.

It was one thing for these positions—determined independently—to coincide on the chart spread across Hegenberger's navigator's table. It was another thing to have these estimates check against some kind of landmark. Though the aviators were now long gone from any visible land, a chance to confirm their position did loom ahead. Maitland passed Hegenberger a note asking how long it would be until they saw a steamer. Ten minutes, replied the navigator, knowing the passenger liner *Sonoma* was scheduled to be cruising east in the shipping lane between Honolulu and San Francisco.

Nine minutes later, at 2:44 PM, they spotted the ship emerging from the mist. Maitland was elated. "I have seen many beautiful liners in my day," he said, "but never a craft that looked as pretty as the *Sonoma* at two forty o'clock that afternoon." With Hegenberger now sitting beside him, he steered *Bird of Paradise* low over *Sonoma*, causing a stir below. Ship passengers left their lunches in the dining room and scrambled to the deck to shout greetings to the fast-approaching aircraft. The radio operator aboard *Sonoma* described the rendezvous in a message sent over the airwaves: "THE PLANE CAME UP LOW ON THE HORIZON, NEARLY DEAD AHEAD. DINING ROOM WAS CROWDED WHEN SIREN BLEW. STEWARDS DROPPED TRAYS. PILOTS OF PLANE WAVED TO PASSENGERS AS PLANE PASSED ON STARBOARD SIDE."

An airplane was exciting enough in any place but especially so when seen over open ocean more than seven hundred miles from the California coast. *Sonoma*'s passengers were electrified by the flyover. "It was a tremendous thrill," said W. S. Beekman, a passenger from Seattle. "Everyone on board had time to get on deck. Many brought cameras, but few were sufficiently collected to get a picture. The plane passed almost on a level with the *Sonoma*'s masts and so close that we felt we could almost reach out and touch it. The two airmen waved to us. 'Those poor boys,' several women said. We felt so secure on our big ship while they seemed to have so little between them and the ocean."

Captain R. R. Drummond also pitied the men. "We could clearly distinguish the two officers as they waved to us from the control cabin of their big plane, which looked mighty small and frail against the face of the sea," he said.

The captain and passengers need not have worried about the army lieutenants cutting through the sky above. They were both relieved to have spotted the steamer, which validated Hegenberger's navigation thus far. Neither, it seemed, would have wanted to trade places with those aboard *Sonoma*. Maitland had previously been anxious about flying over open ocean—a feat he had never attempted—but by midafternoon he was enjoying himself. "I forgot all about it when the plane started through the Golden Gate," he said. "All through the day both Hegenberger and myself admired the beautiful water below our ship."

Ernie Smith had been itching to leave for days, desperate to become the first man to fly across the Pacific Ocean. Since his airplane *City of Oakland* was considerably faster than the army's *Bird of Paradise*, he could afford to give them a bit of a head start, though not too much of a lead. After watching *Bird of Paradise* vanish in the sky, he and his crew hustled to ready their own plane.

Before being permitted to fly by the US Department of Commerce, an inspector was requiring that Smith replace an altimeter, reinstall a bank indicator, and obtain a reel to allow for the retraction of the long radio antenna that would trail behind and below the plane. Smith, navigator Charles Carter, and the rest of their team raced to make these adjustments so *City of Oakland* could take to the air that morning. Again the army lent a helping hand, retrieving an antenna reel from a spare plane at Crissy Field and transporting it across San Francisco Bay to Smith. Meanwhile, a mechanic scoured San Francisco from the back of a hired taxicab, desperate to find a more sensitive altimeter that would satisfy the Commerce Department.

There was little for Smith to do as he waited for the parts to arrive and be installed by his mechanics. One of *Bird of Paradise*'s sponsors, Edmund Moffett, insisted he stay inside a tent and calm his nerves. Smith, who observers compared to a caged lion, balked at this treatment and repeatedly left the tent, becoming furious with Moffett. At one point Smith met Army Air Corps major general Mason Patrick outside the tent. Patrick was beaming, ecstatic that *Bird of Paradise* took off that morning without incident. He was curious to know if Smith would soon follow in the army plane's wake.

"Yes, sir," replied Smith.

"Right away?"

"Yes, sir"

"Good for you," said Patrick, patting Smith on his back. "And good luck to you."

Smith returned to the tent, the tension between him and Moffett rising. Smith's many friends at the airfield began cursing Moffett, upset with his treatment of the pilot. "If Moffett doesn't leave that boy alone he won't be fit to fly a plane across the bay, let alone to Hawaii," said one admirer.

By 9 o'clock, two hours after the army plane departed, all the needed equipment had been found, brought to Bay Farm Island, and installed on *City of Oakland*. The engine was started and warmed as Smith and Carter rushed to the plane, making final, hasty farewells. Before the men climbed into *City of Oakland*, a young woman placed elaborate floral leis around their necks—a sweet but premature gesture.

At 9:37 AM Smith's small silver airplane hurtled down the runway, slowly gaining speed before taking off perfectly. Though *City of Oakland* was two hundred miles or so behind *Bird of Paradise*, Smith and Carter were bullish on their chances, commenting just before takeoff that the army's head start made the race more sporting. The crowd of fifty thousand lining the airfield cheered on the underdog pilot and his navigator as they lifted into the sky, shouting, "Attaboy! Go get 'em, Ernie," and, "Beat the army!"

The optimism did not last long inside *City of Oakland*. A wind deflector above the navigator's hatch tore loose soon after takeoff and began flapping and bulging, much to Carter's alarm. If the deflector was damaged and continually shifting, he feared he could not take accurate celestial observations and they might get lost. Unable to secure the wind deflector in midflight, he attempted to communicate the problem to Smith in the pilot's seat.

Smith, who initially thought his navigator had indicated something was wrong with the radio antenna, replied, "Let's go anyway. Let's stay with it, please." Carter again tried to motion that the problem was the wind deflector, finally convincing Smith to turn the plane around for repairs. *City of Oakland* had traveled a mere two miles, and the crowd on Bay Farm Island emitted a collective groan when it circled back toward the airfield less than ten minutes after taking off. Smith was none happier. Not only would he suffer another delay, but now he needed to attempt a dangerous maneuver—to land a plane fully loaded with gasoline. He compared the task to "dropping a crate of eggs on a sidewalk without breaking any" and "like jumping off a table with a one-ton block of concrete on your shoulders."

As *City of Oakland* came in for a landing and was just feet off the ground, a crosswind gusted, sending the "flying gas truck," as Smith called it, into a terrifying sideslip toward the crowd along one side of the runway. The talented aviator somehow recovered, bringing the plane in for a bumpy yet safe landing clear of any onlookers.

When *City of Oakland* rolled to a stop, the crowd rushed forward and surrounded it, eager to know what plagued the aircraft or its occupants. Mechanics descended on the plane, too, hoping to make a quick fix of the wind deflector and enable Smith and Carter's return to the clouds. While Smith waited for the repairs, he searched for a drink of water under police escort. "We'll make it yet," he shouted as he ambled about the airfield.

As the minutes crawled on, Smith looked unnerved. His father insisted he lie down inside an automobile to recover. Two policemen stood guard outside the car, ensuring the pilot would not be bothered. Some people at the airfield thought the pilot had collapsed. Losing confidence that Smith would again lift off, the crowd at the airfield began to thin.

Two hours later, close to noon, a new wind deflector, ripped from an army plane, was installed. It did not matter. Carter now refused to attempt the flight, at least immediately. The navigator conceded the race to the army, thinking it unlikely *City of Oakland* could catch up. "It was all simply unfortunate for after these various delays the army had such a head-start that there would have been no point to our starting out again," he said. "If the army should fail I am willing to go out with Smith again in the morning. If the army succeeds it will have accomplished what we wanted to accomplish and there will be no necessity for it. There is no logic in saying that the army is a different sort of organization and that it doesn't count. The army flyers are men, just as we are." Smith, his eyes moist, begged the navigator to reconsider. Carter was unmoved: "It's too late now. The sun's too high! I can't get my bearings!"

Smith walked away with his head in his hands and tears streaming down his cheeks. "I'm going home," he said, climbing into a friend's automobile.

Carter's refusal to fly did not endear him to anyone on the airfield. Accusations of cowardice were hurled, and some claimed during the short flight that Carter threatened Smith with opening a valve and emptying the plane's fuel tanks in midair, essentially forcing Smith to turn back to Bay Farm Island. Carter hotly denied having "cold feet" or making any vow to sabotage the plane. "If he wanted to proceed under the circumstances it was all right with me," said the navigator. "I made no threat to dump the gasoline or anything else. It was up to him, and he chose rightly—to turn back. . . . I had set my heart on this trip, and on getting to Honolulu first. I had no thought of glory or fame; just the adventure of being first. If the wind deflector hadn't collapsed, we'd have continued on our way. However, under the circumstances, I felt it best to turn back. I couldn't handle my instruments, and so couldn't navigate, could I?"

In any case, *City of Oakland*'s sponsors stated their intent to continue the flight in the near future. If Carter would not accompany Smith, it was of no consequence: six other potential navigators had already volunteered their services that day on the airfield. "We're not going to quit," said optimist-in-chief Moffett. "We're going on, even if the army flyers get there unless some other civilian plane beats us to it. Our boys may be the first civilian flyers to make the flight."

Smith was less certain the show would go on. Before leaving the airfield, the distraught pilot said he was unsure if he would take off again for Hawaii: "I'll make a definite decision within 24 hours. I can't say more now; there's no use putting my head in the noose—I mean there's no use being silly. Let's all get a good rest and talk it over then."

Bird of Paradise proceeded briskly across the Pacific, traveling just below one hundred miles per hour. Lester Maitland had piloted the army plane for most of the flight, occasionally yielding the controls to his flying partner. As Maitland flew, Albert Hegenberger kept busy charting their course. After more frustrating attempts to use the smoke bombs, he abandoned the idea completely. Although the sun was no longer low on the horizon and blinding him, turbulence prevented the navigator from making accurate observations. Every time Hegenberger sought to track the drift, the bumpy air tossed the tail of the plane about so much that it proved impossible to take a measurement.

The plane droned on westward as the sun sank lower and lower on the horizon, almost directly ahead of them. As darkness came over the ocean, the aviators decided to climb above the clouds, where Hegenberger could see the stars and make celestial observations with his air sextant. The army plane climbed blindly through the sky, enveloped by clouds. Gone now was the sun. Moonlight was absent as well on account of the new moon beginning that morning. The men prepared themselves for one of the most challenging periods of the flight, when their eyelids would droop from drowsiness, yawning would be frequent, and visual stimulation would be almost nonexistent.

A contemporary to the army pilots, aviator Beryl Markham, wrote of the challenges of flying at night in the skies above Africa, where she grew up on a farm in Kenya after her father moved her family from England. As her memoir, *West with the Night*, reads:

> Night flying over charted country by the aid of instruments and radio guidance can still be a lonely business, but to fly in unbroken darkness without even the cold companionship of a pair of ear-phones or the knowledge that somewhere ahead are lights and life and a well-marked airport is something more than just lonely. It is at times unreal to the

point where the existence of other people seems not even a reasonable probability. The hills, the forests, the rocks, and the plains are one with the darkness, and the darkness is infinite. The earth is no more your planet than is a distant star—if a star is shining; the plane is your planet and you are its sole inhabitant.

Higher and higher the plane climbed, its occupants eager to break free of the clouds. *Bird of Paradise* reached an altitude of one thousand feet, then two thousand, three thousand. . . . It was not until the aviators reached 10,200 feet above sea level that they could again see the night sky and its stars. Still, some clouds reached even higher.

At this great height the fuselage was frigid. Maitland and Hegenberger shivered inside their uniforms and coveralls, surprised that the air temperature was nearly freezing. Wasn't it supposed to become warmer as they neared the tropics? Maitland thought some soup and coffee might warm him up and fill his empty belly. He asked Hegenberger to pass some forward. His flying companion promptly turned the cabin over, searching for the chicken sandwiches, soup, and coffee supposedly stowed aboard the plane, but could not find a bite to eat. For all the preparation for this nonstop flight to Hawaii, somehow the army had apparently forgotten to pack food for its fliers.

More aggravation ensued when Hegenberger realized most of the precomputed tables he had brought along to quickly establish their position through celestial navigation were useless. In planning for the flight, the army never imagined their aviators would have to fly so high to spot the stars. Because the bulk of the tables had assumed a lower altitude, Hegenberger could only use his sextant with the North Star, forfeiting the chance to confirm his estimate with sightings of Venus, Jupiter, or other stars. The North Star could only help with establishing latitude, leaving Hegenberger to rely on dead reckoning for longitude.

Then a more alarming failure eclipsed this frustration: the center engine began to run roughly, soon dropping to an idling speed. Unable to float such a heavy fuel load on the strength of the two remaining engines, *Bird of Paradise* slowly started to descend back into the thick clouds as Maitland and Hegenberger tried to resuscitate the center engine and preserve the remaining motors. The seasoned fliers did not panic, but of course recognized that losing an engine over the Pacific was potentially disastrous. Complete darkness surrounded them as they dropped through the clouds, mirroring their ascent an hour or two earlier, although this change in altitude was involuntary. The plane fell to nine thousand feet, then eight thousand, seven thousand. . . . If the center engine did not soon spring back to life, it would not be long before Maitland and Hegenberger prepared to make a nighttime landing atop the ocean.

Jazz played from the radio while Mr. and Mrs. Maitland sat quietly in their living room, nervously passing time. J. W. Maitland occupied an easy chair in front of the fireplace; Bertha sat upon the davenport. Earlier in the evening they had visited friends, eager to avoid the many callers knocking on their door and ringing their phone to offer support for their son and his flying companion. At this late hour they were now back at their home in Burlingame. The only phone calls now were coming from the newspapers, whose correspondents shared updates they had received via radio communications sent from *Bird of Paradise*.

Just two nights ago, recalled the Maitlands, their son Lester and fellow army lieutenant Albert Hegenberger had gathered with them in this same room. Lester had sat on the davenport while "Hegy" parked himself near the table. Now they were cruising above the Pacific Ocean, halfway along their journey to Hawaii. "You can't expect any news before 11 [AM]," Hegy had told the Maitlands, attempting to manage their expectations. "We'll land between 9 and 11, but you won't hear right away."

The phone rang, causing both Maitlands to spring from their seats. Bertha Maitland retrieved the phone. J. W. Maitland returned uneasily to his chair as his wife listened to a routine update concerning the plane's position. Desperate to hear the latest, J.W. leaned forward, gripping the armrests tightly, attempting to discern what was being said.

Afterward he adjusted the radio, switching away from jazz to find news bulletins about his son and Hegenberger. Just as the caller had said, all reports indicated the army pilots and their plane were whizzing across the Pacific. The good news put the Maitlands' minds at ease, at least temporarily, raising their spirits after hours of sitting quietly and crying.

"Say, whoever named that big Fokker 'The *Bird of Paradise*' had the right idea," said J.W. "That's a fine name for it—a wonderful machine. It's making better time than the boys thought it would. Beautiful takeoff—she just sailed into the air. We were there, mother and I, watching. Lester didn't want us to come. But we had to see our boy—our boy. Why, I couldn't believe it was my own little lad in the cockpit of that great plane as it leaped into the air from the field." Reminiscing about the scene at Bay Farm Island, he offered praise for the army's competition, too. "That Ernie Smith has sand," he said. "I looked over that silver-nosed little plane of his. Anyone who was willing to take a chance in a small plane like that, has real backbone. Anyone who goes up in a plane has backbone. It's no joke, this flying business."

Bertha, meanwhile, looked out into the dark night sky. She imagined her son and Hegenberger tucked inside their airplane, in search of "those pinpoint islands." Sleep, she decided, would not come to her until *Bird of Paradise* landed in Hawaii.

Lieutenants Maitland and Hegenberger had sat in darkness in their airplane for nearly two hours. Every which way they looked was black, save the dim lighting in front of them on instrument panels. The center engine continued to limp along and the plane had lost half its altitude. *Bird of Paradise* continued to fall from five thousand feet above the ocean.

The aviators shone flashlights out the windows, peering through the glass at instrument gauges installed outside the cabin on the left and right engines. Frost covered these gauges, obscuring the dials, as well as other parts of the plane. As the men sat puzzled over their predicament and the plane kept losing altitude, the center engine roared back to life. Maitland halted their descent and the fliers discovered the cause of their troubles: their high altitude had caused the center engine's carburetor intake to ice over. Only when *Bird of Paradise* dropped to a lower elevation, where the temperature was warmer, did enough ice melt away to allow the engine to revive itself.

The return of the center engine caused the fliers great relief. Emboldened and eager to leave the clouds and enjoy starlight, as faint as it might be, Maitland climbed back toward the heavens. The clouds broke apart at seven thousand feet, and here Maitland held the line, unwilling to risk the engine refreezing by flying any higher. Hegenberger stood on the navigator's table and poked his head through a hatch to take two sightings with a sextant. His observations showed they were on course to reach Kauai, that northernmost island in Hawaii where Commander John Rodgers and his crew sailed the flying boat PN-9 No. 1 two years earlier. After flying for nearly twenty-four hours, the Garden Isle was just one hundred miles away.

Rather than adjust course south toward Oahu, Maitland kept steering for Kauai. It was raining and still dark, with dawn still hours away. The army fliers, having benefited from a substantial tailwind at high altitudes, had not expected to be this close to Hawaii so early in the morning. If they turned for Oahu, Maitland and Hegenberger reasoned, they might slip through the seventy-two-mile-wide Kauai Channel and miss both islands, just as Rodgers had feared when he was sailing the navy seaplane for landfall. Maitland reduced the plane's speed to a crawl—just sixty-five miles per hour. He and Hegenberger wanted the sun to be shining when they prepared to land, so they needed to slow down.

Confident in his navigation and with *Bird of Paradise*'s arrival in Hawaii seemingly imminent, Hegenberger crawled across the fuel tank in the center of the fuselage and sat beside Maitland in the pilot's cockpit. Enjoying this brief respite from flying and navigating duties, Hegenberger succumbed to sleep and promptly nodded off.

Drowsiness had plagued Charles Lindbergh, too, on his solo journey a month earlier across the Atlantic. He had tried a number of tricks and strategies to stave off sleep, from shaking his head violently to running in place to unpacking and repacking the cotton balls in his ears to swerving the plane side to side in an effort to allow fresh air to breeze in through the cabin windows. Beyond this Lindbergh continually chanted a warning to himself as he kept his eyes open: "No alternative but death and failure. . . . No alternative but death and failure. . . . No alternative but death and failure."

The pilot later described his agonizing battle against slumber:

> I've lost command of my eyelids. When they start to close, I can't restrain them. They are shut, and I shake myself, and lift them with my fingers. I stare at the instruments, wrinkle forehead muscles tense. Lids close again regardless, stick tight as though with glue. My body has revolted from the rule of its mind. Like salt in wounds, the light of day brings back my pains. Every cell of my being is on strike, sulking in protest, claiming that nothing, nothing in the world, could be

worth such effort; that man's tissue was never made for such abuse. My back is stiff; my shoulders ache; my face burns; my eyes smart. It seems impossible to go on longer. All I want in life is to throw myself down flat, stretch out—and sleep.

While Hegenberger snoozed, Maitland remained alert at the controls, content to let his partner enjoy a short rest. At about 3:20 AM in Hawaii, the pilot spotted a light in the distance, five degrees to the left of the nose. The light was yellow, too warm looking to be a star. He initially guessed it was a steamer, then reconsidered and decided it was a lighthouse. He nudged Hegenberger in the ribs. "Wake up," said Maitland. "There is a light ahead."

He pointed out the window. Then he and Hegenberger each scribbled down the same note: "Kauai." As the plane drew closer Maitland realized he was seeing the lighthouse at Kilauea Point on Kauai's north shore. They could each breathe a deep sigh of relief, encountering land again after flying above nearly 2,400 miles of ocean. The aviators did not dwell on the fact that they intercepted Hawaii along the northern shore of the territory's northernmost major island.

The true wonder, in their eyes, was not that they had found Hawaii but that they reached the islands so quickly, in less than a day. The tailwind had helped them zip across the Pacific so briskly that they now needed to kill time as they waited for dawn to break. They thought it unwise to fly across the channel to Oahu in darkness, wary of meeting clouds, rainstorms, or either of Oahu's two mountain ranges. So instead they circled Kauai slowly at three thousand feet, patiently waiting for the sun to rise. "We had plenty of gas and [Kauai] had no place to land," said Maitland. "We took our time and sort of drifted around."

The army fliers shot flares from the plane, in case anyone might be watching the sky from below. As dawn broke *Bird of Paradise* flew above Barking Sands beach, where Dick Grace was preparing for his own flight across the Pacific to California. Maitland and Hegenberger spied the light of his camp at the crude airstrip.

As the sun rose from the sea, Maitland and Hegenberger marveled at the sight illuminated before them through cockpit windows. It was a fantastic sunrise, one that signaled not only a new day but a new era of aviation and travel across the Pacific. They were mesmerized. "The morning light struck off grotesque cloud shapes, turned grays and purples into vivid pinks, crimsons, and lavenders," they later wrote in a joint account of the flight. "We thought we never had seen such a magnificent sunrise and doubly welcomed it after the lonely darkness through which we had passed."

With darkness dispelled, the men set course for Oahu. Maitland increased the throttle to full speed. *Bird of Paradise* charged over Kauai Channel at 130 miles per hour, closing in on Oahu, which sat dead ahead. Maitland steered the plane toward Wheeler Field, situated on a plateau between the Waianae and Koolau mountain ranges.

As *Bird of Paradise* approached its destination, two dozen army pilots based in Hawaii searched the skies in vain for the ocean-hopping transport, hoping to escort Maitland and Hegenberger to the army airfield. The pilots had set out east that morning, toward California, unaware *Bird of Paradise* had made such good time, already visited Kauai, and was approaching from the west. So when *Bird of Paradise* suddenly swooped down out of the mist above Wheeler Field, alone and unannounced, everyone on the ground was stunned.

As startled spectators strained to catch sight of the airplane in the mist, an army artillery cannon boomed. Maitland and Hegenberger circled the field, in awe of the crowd of fifteen thousand or so people below who had gathered throughout the night listening sleepily to the nonstop sounds of the Twenty-First Infantry Band. The aviators had not counted on any reception, writing later, "We fully expected to find a deserted airdrome and land unheralded. Just as we swung around the corner of the first big hangar we saw the broad field walled with motor cars and thousands of people. All at once it flashed on us that they were waiting to see us land. It was certainly the biggest surprise of our lives."

Maitland landed the heavy plane with ease, arriving on Oahu at 6:29 AM on June 29, 1927. After a flight of twenty-five hours and forty-nine minutes, Lester J. Maitland and Albert F. Hegenberger had become the first men to fly across the Pacific to Hawaii.

With the crowd cheering and rushing toward the plane, Maitland taxied *Bird of Paradise* in front of a reviewing stand and shut off the motors. Soldiers surrounded the plane as the lieutenants stiffly climbed out of the fuselage. "Hegenberger, old kid, we made it," said Maitland. Then, "How about a cigarette?" to the dozens of well-wishers rushing toward him.

The US Army Air Corps' *Bird of Paradise* being greeted at Wheeler Field on the island of Oahu on June 29, 1927, as it completed the first flight to Hawaii. Lieutenants Lester J. Maitland and Albert F. Hegenberger flew between Oakland, California, and Oahu in twenty-five hours and forty-nine minutes.
Courtesy of the National Museum of the US Air Force

Hegenberger's body ached with desire, too, but for something more substantial than a smoke. "I'm hungry," said the navigator. "They put in coffee and sandwiches but we couldn't find them." Hearing this, a fellow army officer climbed into the plane. A minute later he reemerged with the missing food; it had been placed below the navigator's table and covered with a tarp, right under Hegenberger's nose. Maitland quipped that while Hegenberger was the "best navigator," he was also "the world's worst waiter."

Moving past their hunger, Maitland addressed the personal significance of their flight across half an ocean. "Our dream of a lifetime has been realized," he said. "We've both wanted for a long time to fly from the mainland, and now we have accomplished it." The pilot mentioned the failure of the radio beacon and how the "old-type compass" proved most reliable among their navigational instruments: "Our compass is what got us here. If we hadn't that we should have been out of luck."

Old friends greeted the fliers, including fellow military aviators now stationed in Hawaii. Just as touching to Maitland and Hegenberger was the boisterous reception offered by the many locals who had forgone sleep and endured rain to witness the first landing of an overseas flight to Hawaii. The crowd, representative of Hawaii's ethnic diversity, was unified in their support of the aviators. "Soldiers and civilians in tuxedos and sweaters, dainty slippered and high-topped boots, rain-soaked and dry, Chinese and Japanese, Portuguese and Filipinos, Caucasians and Hawaiians—that is about the only way we can describe those loyal people who had stood throughout the night to welcome us," wrote the army lieutenants.

After removing their flying coveralls to reveal immaculate uniforms, the aviators were piled high with leis. A giant garland, too, was placed around *Bird of Paradise*, as mounted officers closely guarded the plane. Maitland and Hegenberger then climbed the reviewing stand to receive congratulations from army and navy commanders, as well as greetings from Hawaii's territorial governor, Wallace Rider Farrington.

The brief reception on the review stand was the beginning of much praise and attention directed toward the army fliers. Just ten minutes after *Bird of Paradise* landed, the *Honolulu Advertiser* published an extra announcing the news—the first of eight they'd print about the flight. In Hawaii, Maitland and Hegenberger received approximately one thousand congratulatory telegrams, including messages from their families, leaders of the army and navy, the US secretary of state, and President Calvin Coolidge. "YOU HAVE ADDED A NEW CHAPTER TO THE BRILLIANT HISTORY OF AMERICAN AVIATION, OF WHICH WE ARE PROUD," read a portion of Coolidge's message. "YOUR SUCCESS MARKS A FURTHER STEP IN THE ART OF FLYING, COMBINING AS IT DOES THE SUPREME SKILL OF THE PILOT WITH THE WONDERFUL ACCURACY OF THE NAVIGATOR, AND FURNISHES A STRIKING EVIDENCE OF THE EFFICIENCY OF OUR AIR FORCES."

More congratulations arrived from James Dole, still traveling on the mainland. "YOUR ACHIEVEMENT WILL GIVE CONFIDENCE TO THOSE WHO FOLLOW," said the pineapple tycoon, mindful of his own upcoming air derby.

The fliers were soon escorted through the crowd to army headquarters, where they breakfasted on orange juice, coffee, and water. It was hardly enough food for the famished aviators. Then they were taken by car to Honolulu, twenty-six miles away. At least four thousand cars and huge crowds of scream-ing people clogged the road to town. Some of these people jumped on the running boards of the aviators' car, trying to touch the fliers' coats.

Upon their arrival to the beach in Waikiki, Maitland and Hegenberger were shown to a luxury suite in the Royal Hawaiian. They invited journalists and dignitaries to their room, recounting for them the trip across the ocean. The army fliers begged for more food, complained of headaches, and asked their visitors to speak loudly—more than an hour after landing, both were still partially deaf from the engine noise. Finally, they called for an end to the questions and politely requested their guests to leave. "Please let's have some sleep; we're tired," they said. And with that they went to bed, resting soundly in their suite behind guarded doors.

⊂━•━⊃

The little blonde poked her head inside the Maitland home at 7:00 AM on June 29, 1927.

"Tan I tum in?" asked four-year-old Babs, a piece of toast clutched in her hand.

J. W. Maitland scooped up his little neighbor and placed the girl on his knee.

"It seems only a few weeks ago when Lester and Frank were about the size of Babs. And now Lester is a man grown. He has realized his ambition to fly to Hawaii. Of course he'll get there," said J.W. to a reporter also visiting his home that morning.

J.W.'s wife, Bertha, kept silent, overwhelmed with worry. She and J.W. had forfeited a night's sleep to listen to radio reports that now placed their son Lester and his flying companion, Albert Hegenberger, very close to Hawaii. The exhausted mother hoped the boys would make the final leg of the flight.

Time passed slowly as the sun rose. Two hours after Babs's arrival the Maitlands' phone rang. Bertha lifted the receiver to hear the happy news she had been awaiting all night.

"They've arrived—oh, Daddy—they've arrived," she exclaimed to her hus-band.

"By George—by George—arrived, eh?—And it's just after 9. Well, Lester's dream of years has been realized," said J.W. "Boy, that's a relief." Tears fell from his eyes as the news took hold in his mind. Composing himself, J.W. reflected on the significance of the flight Lester and Albert just completed. "My boy's aid to science makes me very happy. His flight, like Lindbergh's, is a distinct contribution to scientific knowledge," he said. "We have profoundly admired Lindbergh as a man and as an aviator and we are very proud that our son's feat is comparable with his. . . . Both have done a lot for the nation, for science, for aerial navigation, and for the morale of the younger generation."

"Gee—I bet those boys are happy," added the proud father.

Meanwhile, similar scenes filled with joy and tearful relief occurred in Washington, DC, and Boston, where Maitland and Hegenberger's wives had been monitoring the flight. Louise Hegenberger listened to radio reports with her two sons at her mother's home on Castle Island in Boston Harbor. Upon hearing news of the flight's success, she began to cry and hugged her two young boys. "Oh! Isn't that wonderful? I know how happy they must be," said Louise before crossing the channel to South Boston to send her husband a congratulatory radiogram.

In Washington, at her own parents' home, Ruth Maitland had listened stoically to news reports throughout the night, waiting "for every scrap of information as it came by telephone." "Long ago," she said, "I determined no fears of mine, no nervous tremors, no hesitations should interfere with my husband's career. I was not afraid. Somehow I had a real conviction that this glorious, long-dreamed adventure would end as it did, in victory. From the moment I said my last goodbye in Dayton just three and a half weeks ago when Lieutenant Maitland started west, until I received the word of his safe landing in Hawaii, I was conscious of a deep conviction that all would be well with him."

A phone call advised Ruth Maitland that her husband and Hegenberger had reached Hawaii. "I can hardly remember now what I did, but I know I did not cry. I just hugged Patricia, our little 3-year-old, and knew I had never been quite so happy before," said Ruth. "I was thrilled—thrilled beyond words—when the news came. Nothing seems quite real yet, and somehow I did not quite realize what the accomplishment of this flight would mean—my husband's name to go down in history and this national acclamation! It is all still like a dream."

Back in Burlingame, California, Maitland's parents were finally free of worry, too. Their worst fears unrealized, Bertha's and J.W.'s thoughts turned to the same thing their son 2,400 miles away had just become fixated upon:

slumber. "Well, mother, I guess we can get a little sleep now," said J.W., smiling and laying a hand on his wife's shoulder.

Bertha agreed that sleep sounded soothing after an exceptionally emotional evening and morning. "It was an awfully long night, though the radio helped us to get through it. We weren't exactly anxious for we knew down deep in our hearts, Lester would make it, but—" she said, unable to finish her thought as she choked up and began to cry. Moments later she collected herself, saying, "We'll just stay home. After a bit, when they've had a rest, we'll have a cable from the boys. Now, they're too tired. And, yes, come to think about it, I guess we're a little tired now, too. But he's there safely. Daddy, our boy has flown across the Pacific!"

As soon as the transoceanic fliers awoke in their Honolulu hotel suite, they headed for the one place they had been trying to avoid the last day and a half: the Pacific Ocean. Exchanging their flight suits for swimsuits, Lester Maitland and Albert Hegenberger made a run for the water, delighted to frolic and swim in the surf off Waikiki Beach. More fun was to come during their week in Hawaii, as they enjoyed luncheons, receptions, and luaus thrown in their honor. The birdmen surfed, paddled outrigger canoes, and were even gifted feather capes. There was so much hoopla in Honolulu concerning their flight that the aviators said the deluge of invitations was more stressful than their flight across the ocean. Still, all the attention only added luster to an experience Maitland deemed "the happiest day of my life." "I had planned and hoped and worked for that day ever since I first joined the service," he added. "When I saw Kauai and then Oahu I was the happiest boy in America."

The congratulations sent from around the world included those from fellow army men. The assistant secretary of war, Trubee Davison, praised the *Bird of Paradise* flight as "unquestionably one of the greatest of aerial accomplishments ever made." Davison added he was "particularly pleased that two Army Air Corps officers, operating an army plane built for no other purpose than regular army use, were the first to negotiate the flight to Hawaii." Charles Lindbergh declared the army's ocean crossing as "the most perfectly organized and carefully planned flight ever attempted." New York newspapers offered praise as well, with the *World* stating, "If ranked in terms of danger and difficulty . . . the Hawaiian flight will stand high in the list of gallant air achievements."

US Army Air Corps lieutenants Albert F. Hegenberger (left) and Lester J. Maitland modeling Hawaiian feather capes awarded to them after completing the first flight to Hawaii. Made of thousands of small feathers, the precious capes were traditionally worn by Hawaiian chiefs and warriors. *Courtesy of the Hawaii Department of Transportation Airports*

Even the broken-necked Dick Grace came over to Oahu from Kauai and congratulated the men he had almost raced across the Pacific. But Grace's congratulations did not mean he was giving up his own flight across the ocean. Days later, early in the morning of July 4, 1927, Grace took off beside Barking Sands beach on Kauai with his puppy, Kauai Leilani, in tow—the first time in three days of takeoff attempts that he was able to get airborne off the bumpy field.

Despite a successful takeoff, Grace's flight was short-lived. He returned to the airfield in less than an hour, making a rough landing that devolved into a ground loop that severely damaged his aircraft. The plane had become unmanageable in the air, he said, forcing him to give up on his attempt to fly to California. News reports indicated that Grace's ego was bruised more than his airplane. "Grace seemed less concerned over the loss of the plane than over the impression his failure to make the flight might produce among the public throughout the world," noted one.

About a week after landing on Oahu, just after Grace faltered a final time on Kauai, Maitland and Hegenberger began their return trip to the mainland aboard the steamship *Maui*. Fellow passengers regarded the aviators as celebrities, asking for their autographs and insisting they take photographs. The army men gamely accepted every woman's invitation to dance on the weeklong cruise, revealing themselves to be much better at flying than moving their feet. The aviators' courage even reportedly inspired one young doctor to work up the nerve to ask a fellow passenger for her hand in marriage.

When *Maui* reached the Golden Gate, the aviators were received in much the same fashion as navy commander John Rodgers and his crew were two years earlier in San Francisco. An assortment of civilian and military welcome planes buzzed the steamship and dropped laurel wreaths, a few of which landed on deck at the fliers' feet. One sleek plane in the sky belonged to the *San Francisco Examiner* and was destined to compete in the Dole Air Race weeks later. On board the Lockheed Vega were pilot Jack Frost, *Examiner* publisher George Hearst, and three journalists, including reporter Harry Lang, all eager to provide some of the first accounts of the heroes' homecoming.

While working on a portable typewriter he had lugged aboard, Lang composed an account of his exhilarating experience aboard the speedy monoplane, which enabled a bird's-eye view of San Francisco and the heavy automobile traffic streaming into the city to welcome the Hawaii fliers. From the perch of an airplane, Lang wrote, the hills of San Francisco "look as flat as yesterday's near-beer." Continuing with the alcohol theme despite the imposition of Prohibition, Lang described how the plane zigged and zagged across the city, "like a Volstead ignorer trying to find his way home."

Looking down from a height of several hundred feet, where navy warships and streetcars looked like toys, Lang captured the spectacle awaiting the army fliers: "The ships below us are alive with flags, and waiting with boilers full of steam to toot their welcome to the *Maui*. And now we're over the Presidio— and the parade ground is alive with a lot of little olive drab beings, all lined up in pretty formations, getting ready for the Maitland-Hegenberger parade that's to follow in an hour or two."

While assorted watercraft escorted the steamship into port, fireboats shot arcing streams of water into the sky. A band played aboard a nearby tugboat while other steamships blew their whistles and flew flags in celebration. A greeting party steamed out to meet *Maui* from San Francisco, counting among its ranks Mayor James Rolph, navy lieutenant Allen P. Snody, and two carrier pigeons named King Sperry and Princess Drifted Snow.

"I'm mighty glad you're back," said Rolph, stepping aboard *Maui*.

"We're mighty glad to be back," replied Maitland "Aren't we Hegy?"

"You bet we're glad," said Hegenberger, receiving a hug from the mayor.

Snody, whose own attempt to fly to Hawaii aboard the navy's PN-9 No. 3 was cut short by a broken oil line two years earlier, was gracious when greeting the aviators. "I'm glad you made it, Les. Since I couldn't make it myself I'd rather see you make it than anybody else I can think of right now," he said.

"I'm just as sorry about your not making it," Maitland sympathized.

As for the pigeons, messages were attached to their legs and they were set loose, free to fly home from the Golden Gate to their lofts along the Embarcadero within buildings owned by the Sperry Flour Company. The trip took the birds just three minutes. "Greetings to San Francisco. Wonderful trip both ways. Reception wonderful," said the message attached to the pigeons, which was then broadcast over the radio.

As *Maui* prepared to dock along Pier 32, tens of thousands of excited Californians gathered to cheer the flying men. At the front of the pack were the aviators' families, including their wives, who had not seen them in a month. The long, nervous wait had been taxing on the women. "Boats and trains are so slow," Louise Hegenberger had remarked hours earlier as she left Oakland for San Francisco. "It has taken me four times as long to come from Boston as it took my husband to fly to Honolulu. And this last hundred miles was the longest. But I have only a few more hours to wait and I am so very happy to be here at last."

As *Maui* drew closer the parties on land and water could at last distinguish each other's faces. "Hello, Dad. Hello, Mother," said Maitland. A moment later both fliers recognized their spouses standing side by side and holding hands. "Hello, dear!" said the aviators, who upon docking were the first off the ship. They ran straight down the runway and into the arms of their wives.

The intimate moment was short-lived. Because fog had delayed *Maui*'s arrival, officials were in a hurry to begin the parade leading to festivities at city hall. The aviators were shooed into open-air automobiles as a procession traveled up Market Street. Maitland and Hegenberger sat with the mayor in a car at the front, waving to the many people lining the street, watching from windows, and sitting atop balconies, ledges, fire escapes, and rooftops. A brass band and mounted police followed behind the automobiles as confetti rained through the air. As the *Examiner* noted, "Not Penelope herself was more overcome with joy to have her Ulysses back than were San Francisco and Oakland to have their two back from this modern Odyssey."

At a luncheon at city hall, Maitland and Hegenberger were awarded medals and commended in speech after speech. "These boys are leaders among super-men who are working to weld together the peoples of the earth," said San Francisco supervisor Warren Shannon. "They opened the longest oceanic airway ever traversed. They carved, thereby, a golden path of fame across the sky. And the story of their deeds will forever be written in the stars." Added US senator Hiram Johnson, who sat to one side of the army fliers at the luncheon, "They shook dice with death in the Pacific and won. . . . They have written an epic that has come down to us. They need no bard to sing their praise. They have written their song in the sky." And added California's other US senator, Samuel Shortridge, who sat to the other side of the aviators, "Your heroic flight has placed your name among the Magellans of the sky. You realized the hazard of your undertaking, but with a fine contempt for death you challenged storm and distance, and won over them all." Following every bit of praise, Maitland and Hegenberger remained humble, crediting each other's talents and thanking the army for providing sufficient training and equipment to arrive to Hawaii safely.

Senators and city supervisors were not the only ones wishing to venerate the air heroes. In the hours and days that followed, Maitland and Hegenberger juggled an overwhelming amount of requests for their appearance. They paid a visit to Mother Tusch in Berkeley, making good on their promise to sign their names beside other aviators' upon a wall of her home. In Oakland they revisited Bay Farm Island, partook in another elaborate parade, and witnessed an air show. There, too, they met would-be competitor Ernie Smith at a luncheon, where he warmly congratulated them. Meanwhile, the movie theaters in San Francisco played newsreels featuring footage of *Bird of Paradise*. In short, the entire Bay Area pulsated with pleasure and excitement over the army's incredible flight to Hawaii.

The first pilots to fly to Hawaii were celebrated with a parade upon their return to San Francisco on July 12, 1927. US Army Air Corps lieutenants Lester J. Maitland (seated in car at left with hat in hand) and Albert F. Hegenberger (to the right) were feted throughout the country after making the transpacific flight, ultimately being awarded the Distinguished Flying Cross at the White House during a ceremony with President Calvin Coolidge. *Courtesy of the California History Room, California State Library, Sacramento*

Knowing that they were just the first of many men who would cross the Pacific by air, the fliers offered reflections on their flight. They emphasized the importance of preparation and provided encouragement for air travel to other far-flung destinations. "In spite of the fact that we had all known types of navigation instruments, and although many of them failed, we still feel that, with an ordinary compass and a few solar and celestial observations, it is possible to fly anywhere," wrote the aviators.

With Ernie Smith readying for another attempt and the Dole Air Race slated to begin in a month's time, Maitland and Hegenberger also offered a strong caution to those winging their own way to the islands. "And yet, for all that our course was adhered to so closely, these Hawaiian islands are a mighty small spot on a mighty big ocean, and it is entirely possible that a plane might miss the group if navigation were not good or for some other reason, and might fly on and into the Pacific, unable to find land until failing gasoline would force it to the sea. This possibility must be taken into consideration by any man who tries the transpacific hop."

James Dole arrived home to Honolulu on July 12, 1927, following the same 2,400-mile track across the Pacific that many participants of the Dole Derby would soon follow, just in a different mode of transportation—a steamship. By this point at least three pilots had formally entered the Dole Air Race and dozens more promised to join, though a few of them were hard to take seriously. This included the pilot of the first steam-powered plane, a famed Hollywood shimmy dancer, and a Cleveland pharmacist who advertised laxatives on the wings of his aircraft.

Dole's desk was piled high with mail that arrived during his absence on the mainland. Never mind that he ran one of Hawaii's largest companies, almost all of the correspondence related to the Dole Derby, not pineapples. A few of the letters were from the same woman, Rose Anne Schalski of Bartlesville, Oklahoma, who desperately wanted to compete in the Dole Derby. As one of Schalski's notes, addressed to a "James D. Doyle," read: "So there is a $35,000 [prize] offered for Hops to Hawaii. Please entered [*sic*] my name if ladies can enter. I am no aviator. But I sure can learn and take a chance for the prize. Can't I[?] I can be ready by the 15th of Aug 1927 or with in the next twelve months thereafter. Hope to see my name on your list."

Schalski was one of the "cranks" that HAPCO's San Francisco manager, H. E. MacConaughey, mentioned to Dole. She was hardly the only unqualified person to express interest in the air race. Dole marveled over the amount of appeals he received in the span of a few weeks, especially from people claiming to be his relatives:

> I didn't know there were so many Doles in the United States until now—and even with all this evidence believe me, I am still inclined to

> doubt it. Why, every Dole from San Francisco to Boston, it seems, has written me a letter. Some have congratulated me, some are reminding me of kinship, others would like to borrow a little money, still others need financial assistance, from which investments I shall receive ample returns. . . . They want me to finance everything—from divorce cases to cellos for prodigy sons.

He also mentioned a man in Germany who asked for help paying his monthly rent.

Though the army had stolen the spotlight two weeks earlier when Lester Maitland and Albert Hegenberger completed the first flight to Hawaii, Dole was upbeat about the air race and praised the army for its performance. He refused to condemn the army, or the other civilian aviators such as Dick Grace and Ernie Smith, for their attempts across the Pacific. "This is a free country," he said, smiling. "I had hoped all the serious contestants would enter the contest as planned, but if these earlier flights are a success they will but stimulate interest in the main event. It will be a great race, even if a few persons run it ahead of time."

The race's greatness would suffer, however, from the absence of Charles Lindbergh. Prior to crossing the Atlantic, Lindbergh had contemplated a flight to Hawaii and even purchased maps of the islands, worried that well-financed rivals attempting the flight across the Atlantic would beat him to Paris. But after besting the competition to France, he decided against trying to traverse the Pacific as well. While his flight across the ocean was no fluke, Lindbergh knew he was fortunate to triumph. After all, when "Lucky Lindy" returned home to the United States, he and *Spirit of St. Louis* took a steamer back west across the Atlantic instead of crossing it again by air. In regard to the Pacific crossing, there was little for him to gain now, save for the cash prizes. But a head-to-head sprint between other aviators across near-virgin flying territory did not appeal to the famous young aviator, no matter which body of water he was hopping. "I never wanted to race across the ocean," Lindbergh later wrote. "There are hazards enough without adding human competition."

Ernie Smith was down but not out. Since being humiliated on the runway two weeks earlier when his flying companion refused to chase after the army, infighting had erupted among his team. The plane's sponsors openly feuded on the runway in Oakland and threatened lawsuits against each other. Smith stayed above the fray and was unbothered when navigator Charles Carter and sponsor and optimist-in-chief Ed Moffett were jettisoned from the team. "I still want to fly that plane to Honolulu!" said Smith. "I've always wanted to, and I've never changed my mind, no matter what has happened. I'm not licked yet!"

In the days following the army's flight, Smith and his remaining team sought a new navigator for *City of Oakland*. The pilot soon interviewed twenty-five-year-old Emory Bronte, a native of New York City living in San Francisco who had been inspired by the army flight, watching *Bird of Paradise* take off for Hawaii from a local rooftop. Despite his youth, the mustachioed Bronte was an ace navigator and master-rated merchant marine captain, having been at sea since age fifteen. He served in the navy during World War I and later aboard commercial ships. Bronte was also the author of a marine navigation textbook and had recently begun taking flying lessons. Smith admired the young man's spunk and had little doubt Bronte could deliver them to the islands. As Bronte enthusiastically boomed, "As far as I'm concerned, it's heaven, hell, or Honolulu for me—and I know it'll be Honolulu!"

The young navigator's earnestness and expertise improved the morale in the Smith camp by leaps and bounds. He quickly got to work, assessing *City of Oakland* and discovering a number of shortcomings. "I had looked the plane over and was shocked to find it didn't even have a radio and very little else in the way of navigational equipment," said Bronte. "To make the trip, we needed charts, compasses, a sextant, and many other items. I could see why Carter bowed out. The windshield just cinched it for him. Smith was fortunate, because had they gone out with such a lack of equipment they'd have ended up in the water."

Bronte enlisted the army's help, persuading the communications officer at Crissy Field to custom build a radio set for *City of Oakland* that would allow the plane to home in on the radio beacon signals being broadcast by the army between Maui and San Francisco. "Two weeks later, we not only had a radio but it was a first class piece of apparatus," he said. "As for the compass, we had three of them installed, with the master compass calibrated so finely that a deviation was eliminated on the westerly headings [the only important headings because that's the direction we were going to fly]."

By July 14, 1927, *City of Oakland* was again ready to fly to Hawaii and parked at one end of the runway along Bay Farm Island. Early that morning Smith enjoyed a big breakfast with his father and fiancée at Oakland's Hotel Coit, chowing down on cantaloupe, scrambled eggs, sausages, rolls, and milk. The whole crew was upbeat and jolly, expressing confidence in the flight to come as they left for the airfield a few miles away. "I think Ernie is a great flyer and Bronte is a great navigator, from all that I can learn," Smith's father told a stranger in the hotel lobby. "Unless something goes wrong with the plane they'll get there."

Smith's fiancée, Marjorie Brown, claimed she and Smith would be married when he returned, though he hesitated to confirm such plans, and at one point referred to her as a "friend, only." Brown was nevertheless fearless about losing her man, to the ocean or anyone else, saying, "I'm not a bit afraid. I wouldn't be worthy to be his girl if I were afraid. He'll get there, all right."

Navigator Emory Bronte (left) and pilot Ernie Smith playfully demonstrating use of their emergency life raft before leaving for Hawaii in *City of Oakland* on July 14, 1927. *Courtesy of the California History Room, California State Library, Sacramento*

Upon arriving to Bay Farm Island about 8:00 AM, Smith and Bronte received two distinguished visitors—army lieutenants Lester Maitland and Albert Hegenberger. Gathering in a tent at the airfield, the army officers shook the hands of their fellow fliers, wished them luck, and offered a few words of friendly advice. While Hegenberger touted the army's radio beacon and described the distinct silhouettes of each island and their major landmarks, Maitland urged his former competitor to pack smelling salts. "It'll help to keep you awake and that night'll be long, don't forget it," said the army pilot, who inspected *City of Oakland* with Hegenberger.

Maitland also emphasized the importance of division of labor aboard the long flight.

"Don't watch the instrument board too much—if you do, you'll get batty. It bothers the eye and makes you nervous. Let your navigator worry about that," he advised as Hegenberger reviewed the flight plan with Bronte in such detail that they seemed to be examining it mile by mile.

Eventually Smith and Bronte thanked the fliers, who were obliged to return to San Francisco immediately, unable to witness the takeoff. "You fellows sure have been nice," said Bronte. "We won't forget to follow your advice. We'll make the grade all right if Ernie keeps awake. Between the aid we get from the army radio beacons, dead reckoning and my celestial observations, we can't go wrong."

As Maitland and Hegenberger departed, many others at the airfield called out for Smith's and Bronte's attention. Anywhere from five thousand to twenty thousand people were estimated to have arrived to Bay Farm Island that morning to see *City of Oakland* make the flight. Though the crowd seemed smaller than two weeks earlier when both the army and Smith were preparing to leave for Hawaii, it was still plenty large enough to distract and delay Smith and Bronte, who had previously hoped to make a quick and uneventful takeoff that morning.

One little boy asked Smith to autograph a baseball. Another gave him a rabbit's foot for good luck. Two young women gifted the aviators a floral horseshoe, which was placed on the runway and pointed toward Hawaii, not to be removed until the trip was complete. Another woman broke through police lines to give the fliers two special tokens: Smith received a cross and Bronte a medal that had kept the woman's brother safe through World War I. Someone else gave Bronte an army pistol before takeoff; he promised to use it to shoot sharks. Smith also still carried the fairy stone the little girl had given him the last time he prepared to fly to Hawaii. By the time Smith and Bronte made it to their plane, *City of Oakland* was chock-full of lucky charms.

Also on board were four carrier pigeons, including Princess Drifted Snow and King Sperry, the two pigeons used to deliver messages during Maitland and Hegenberger's homecoming. Bronte planned to release the pigeons at intervals during the flight, attaching to their legs small aluminum tubes containing notes that detailed the plane's position. Upon being released from the silver plane, the pigeons were expected to return to their lofts along the Embarcadero, with Princess Drifted Snow and King Sperry triggering an electronic alarm when they reentered their cubicles in San Francisco.

At about ten o'clock in the morning, Smith said his goodbyes. His father, hoping to dissuade his son from flying back to California from Hawaii, counseled Ernie not to "do anything rash: one flight's enough." Brown, clad in a yellow dress and appearing "lissome and trim," threw her arms around her fiancé and kissed him repeatedly. Smith counseled her in return on the proper way to watch their takeoff and flight for Hawaii: "Hold your breath for the first two minutes and then pray like the devil."

Bronte was also leaving a female admirer behind. Just before takeoff he called out to a young woman in the crowd. Mary Rose McGlynn of New York City ran to the plane, gave Bronte a smile, and grabbed his hand through a cabin window, giving it a squeeze. Then, with the help of spectators pushing the nearly overloaded plane from behind, the aviators were off, with *City of Oakland* charging down the runway.

But just moments later, the plane came to an abrupt stop. A gust had blown it sideways during takeoff, pushing its wheels into a depression, which then caused it to swerve wildly before Smith shut off the engine and brought the craft, loaded with 369 gallons of gasoline, to a halt. Crews spent the next half hour digging the plane's tail skid out of the ground and wheeling it back to its start line. Fortunately, *City of Oakland* suffered no damage.

The near crash unnerved Smith's father and fiancée. While Smith's father fidgeted nervously, Brown could hardly compose herself sitting beside her sweetheart on the running board of a sedan as the pilot waited to make another takeoff attempt. "You're not downhearted, are you, Ernie?" someone in the crowd shouted to Smith.

"Don't you ever think it," he replied. "I'll be out of here again inside half an hour. I won't come back this time. I'll be in Honolulu in the morning, or—or somewhere."

True to his word, Smith and Bronte were back in the plane thirty minutes later, again hurtling down the airfield. *City of Oakland* ran along much of the runway before lifting off the ground and heading across the bay toward San Francisco. At first Smith kept the plane low, just fifty feet off the water, to gain speed. Then he began circling and climbing, slowly gaining altitude. Onlookers below watched in alarm, wondering if he was circling back because of more mechanical malfunctions. Then, at a height of seven hundred feet, *City of Oakland* disappeared into the fog. Navy escort planes followed until Smith straightened out the plane and flew through the Golden Gate, en route to Hawaii.

The fog did not abate offshore. For ninety minutes Smith and Bronte flew above or through hazy conditions, finally breaking through shortly after noon at an altitude of two thousand feet. But a half hour later, they were back in the thick of it. "More fog," Bronte noted at 12:45 PM in the flight log. In the hours that followed, Bronte's observations testified to the challenging weather *City of Oakland* encountered. He logged notes every hour, offering descriptions like "Thick fog below," "Foggy," "Foggy as hell," "Still foggy," "Fog breaking slightly," and "Damn the fog."

Finally, at 8:00 PM, just after the sun dipped below the horizon, Bronte noted, "And still fog. We'll be out of luck if it doesn't clear soon." While the fog was one annoyance, the army's radio beacon became another. Bronte gave up on the beacon just a few hours into the flight, guessing the radio receiver aboard the plane was broken. Given his expertise in dead reckoning and celestial navigation, however, the malfunction caused little worry aboard the airplane. He knew there was more than one way to find Hawaii, so long as they could eventually see the through the haze at the stars above and the islands below.

Smith seemed unfazed by the fog, as well. Messages sent back to shore were upbeat, with one radio communication indicating that *City of Oakland* and its two occupants were "GOING STRONG." Late in the afternoon Bronte released two of the pigeons, hoping they'd make their way back home to San Francisco. Tossed into the slipstream, the pigeons tumbled head over tail until they righted themselves and flew away through the thick fog. By nine o'clock that evening *City of Oakland* was cruising at 2,600 feet, flying between the fog below and a full moon above. As the night progressed Smith fought off drowsiness and climbed higher, giving Bronte a clear view of the skies for his celestial observations.

Less than two months earlier, Charles Lindbergh sat similarly in an airplane above a different ocean, reflecting on his daring attempt to cross the Atlantic in a contraption invented less than twenty-four years earlier. While he flew without the aid of a navigator, he at least could spy the waves below. "Looking ahead at the unbroken horizon and limitless expanse of water, I'm struck by my arrogance in attempting such a flight," Lindbergh later wrote. "I'm giving up a continent, and heading out to sea in the most fragile vehicle ever devised by man. Why should I be so certain that a swinging compass needle will lead me to land and safety?"

Bronte wondered, too, how certain he could afford to feel when it came to navigating through the fog on the final approach to the islands. Unwilling to take any chances, he broadcast a radio message early in the morning asking for the help of escort planes when they neared Hawaii. As the night progressed, he signaled course corrections to Smith by shining a flashlight to the pilot's left or right. Smith would then turn in the direction of the light until Bronte shined the flashlight again, indicating he should stop. When midnight rolled around, Smith grew chilly and put on a sweater. He began to get sleepy and bored. "There was nothing to do except to keep on and watch the instruments so she didn't stall and slip into a spin," he said. "Sometimes it was pretty hard to believe that those little dial needles are telling the truth."

Staring at compasses and flight indicators did not sharpen his senses. Neither did looking at the stars. Smith began to nod off, falling asleep at one point long enough for *City of Oakland* to fall into a dive. When he jerked awake seconds later, the interior of the plane seemed to be assaulted by a strobe light, as Bronte was turning the flashlight on and off furiously to wake him up. As Smith regained his wits, he pulled the plane out of the dive and leveled out.

Later that morning, just before dawn or so, Smith heard a sound that "felt like I was hit in the head with a sledgehammer." The airplane's engine was misfiring and the fuel gauge had dropped alarmingly low. The plane was apparently out of gas. Bronte began broadcasting distress signals. "WE ARE GOING TO LAND IN THE SEA. WE HAVE A RUBBER LIFEBOAT, BUT SEND HELP," he radioed, also broadcasting the plane's location above the Pacific. Believing a water landing imminent, the navigator released the remaining two carrier pigeons, reasoning there was "no use drowning them."

While Bronte readied the lifeboat and survival gear, Smith dived toward the ocean. If forced to make a sea landing, he desperately wanted the plane's engine running at full power as he tried to make the difficult touchdown atop the waves. He also hoped a ship might be within sight, though chances were slim. As he dived, he switched the fuel supply to a small auxiliary tank and began pumping fuel to the engine by hand, surmising that perhaps the automatic fuel pump had failed. To his delight, *City of Oakland*'s engine roared back to life as he and Bronte cruised just above the Pacific. Disaster averted, the aviators collected themselves and reevaluated their fuel supply, sending out an amended emergency call that estimated they could fly an additional four hours.

The message never transmitted. When Smith flew low over the water, he and Bronte soon realized, the long radio antenna dangling beneath the plane dipped into the ocean and tore away. As he braced for an emergency landing, Bronte had forgotten to reel the 150-foot antenna inside. His subsequent attempts to rig a replacement were unsuccessful.

As nearby ships heeded the original SOS call and steamed toward the plane's supposed location, *City of Oakland* motored on, unable to send another communication advising that the plane was still flying and no longer in severe distress. With no more communications emanating from the airplane, radio observers following the flight assumed the plane had indeed landed or crashed in the drink. The aviators aboard *City of Oakland* now found themselves in a predicament much like the one experienced by the late John Rodgers and his crew aboard PN-9 No. 1: they were assumed lost at sea with no working radio. *City of Oakland*, at least, was still flying, though perhaps not for much longer.

Smith eased the throttle to conserve fuel, which he was still manually pumping into the engine. "The way I worked that pump was nobody's business," he said. "If it had been hooked up to the prop we wouldn't have needed the engine." Bronte scanned the seas for nearby land or ships, focusing so intensely through a pair of binoculars that his eyes throbbed with pain. With the sun rising behind them and the fog finally lifting below, the aviators saw the ocean for the first time in approximately twenty hours of flying. But with fuel running precariously low, they would have much rather sighted land.

The engine still running strong, Smith began climbing to a higher altitude. Visibility was poor close to the water, and a higher vantage point would lift them out of the spotty fog and allow them to see farther. At an altitude of 7,200 feet they spotted a mountain, or at least what might have been a mountain. The pair had spotted so many mirages during their flight—seeing houses, farms, and people among the clouds—that they no longer trusted their eyes. But when a second mountain peak came into sight, they felt assured they were spotting volcanoes on the Hawaiian Islands, likely the nearly fourteen-thousand-foot peak of Mauna Kea on the Big Island and then the ten-thousand-foot peak of Haleakalā on Maui.

Minutes later they were flying close to Haleakalā, which loomed large and close to the plane even when cruising at eleven thousand feet. With gas still in the tank, Smith was hopeful they could reach their intended destination, Wheeler Field on Oahu, 120 miles away. He could tell Maui wasn't the most hospitable terrain for an airplane to touch down, with much of the island covered in mountains, forest, and sugarcane fields, all of which guaranteed a rough landing.

Heading north, *City of Oakland* descended rapidly and flew across the Pailolo Channel to Molokai, home to a famous leper colony. This island was mountainous and forested, too, and also covered in low-hanging clouds, mist, and rain that made much of Molokai "invisible," according to Bronte's note in the flight log. Rather than proceed directly over the island en route to Oahu and Wheeler Field, Smith flew along the island's southern shoreline to avoid the poor weather. Conditions along the coast were only marginally better than the interior, presenting Smith with few places to make an emergency landing, which now seemed imminent.

Flying above the surf along Molokai's shore at a height of seventy-five feet, *City of Oakland*'s engine sputtered and then stopped. Smith turned toward the island and pointed the plane downward, which allowed the last bit of remaining fuel to drain into the engine, reviving the motor for an additional thirty seconds of flying time. Then the propeller stopped spinning for good as *City of Oakland* began a gliding descent. The shore and forest below appeared larger by the second as the plane lost altitude.

As Smith flew over Molokai's southern shore his eyes darted desperately across the landscape. There were no good options. He considered landing atop the shallow ocean water, except extensive coral formations rested conspicuously below the surface. A muddy beach stretched alongside the water, but the soft soil promised to suck up the plane's landing gear upon touchdown and cause the plane to flip. Farther inland was a forest of kiawe trees and beyond that a narrow, severely rutted, and uneven dirt road.

With time running out, Smith decided to steer *City of Oakland* atop a grove of kiawe trees. Mynah birds and quail scattered in panic as the plane clipped branches and plowed through the treetops, the thorns on the kiawe trees shredding the fabric wrapping the plane. *City of Oakland* came to a halt fifty yards later suspended between two trees, its wings battered and partly torn, its propeller partially buried, its landing gear badly mangled, and its fuselage broken in two. Nearly unscathed, however, were Smith and Bronte, who exited the wreckage slowly with mere scratches at about nine o'clock in the morning, Hawaiian time. Together they became the first civilians to fly to Hawaii, by their own account reaching the islands twenty-five hours and two minutes after leaving Oakland, or forty-seven minutes faster than the army fliers, though the army flew about one hundred miles farther to reach Oahu.

The wrecked *City of Oakland*, which pilot Ernie Smith crash-landed into a thicket of thorny kiawe trees on the Hawaiian island of Molokai on July 15, 1927. Smith and navigator Emory Bronte survived the rough landing after running out of gas and falling short of their target, the nearby island of Oahu.
Courtesy of the Hawaii Department of Transportation Airports

Before jumping down from the plane, Smith sat still in his battered cockpit and relaxed for a moment as relief washed over him. *Thank God, it was all over*, he thought. The fear of losing fuel over the ocean seemed to have spooked him worse than the crash landing, which he later described as "one of the old army landings." "[I] picked out two trees and flew between them to shear off the wings," he described. "All was well until a third tree loomed up between the two. The crate was pretty well washed out and we got shook up some."

A Japanese farmhand from a nearby pineapple plantation was the first to arrive to the wrecked plane. Smith and Bronte, eager to broadcast news of their safe arrival, asked him and other locals gathering around the wreckage for directions to the nearest radio station. The aviators initially treated these locals with caution, mistakenly believing that all of Molokai was inhabited by lepers, or those afflicted with Hansen's disease. Still the locals persisted with warm greetings, assuring the aviators that lepers lived only in a colony on the other side of the island. Smith dropped his reservations and was soon grateful to the farmhand for a taste of tobacco, which was especially sweet after spending more than a day in the clouds. "He couldn't speak any English, but he took out a pack of cigarettes and I grabbed one. It tasted good. It was the first puff I'd had since I left Oakland," said Smith. "I threw my cigarettes away before we left. I was afraid I'd be tempted and light one on the way and, maybe, set the plane afire."

While the farmhand shared a cigarette, other locals began stripping the crippled plane of its contents. Smith and Bronte gave away a flying helmet and smelling salts but then had to reacquire their flight instruments, navigation equipment, and personal papers from aggressive souvenir seekers. Then they were driven to a radio station ten miles away. "Boy, doesn't that dust feel good in your eyes," said Smith, sitting in the cab of a truck with a missing windshield as it bounced violently along a rutted island road.

Arriving to the radio station, the aviators sent word of their arrival and canceled their SOS call for help, mindful that ships would still be searching the ocean for a downed aircraft. "FORCED LANDING NEAR RADIO STATION," said the radio transmission. "BOTH O.K. SEND SOME ONE FOR US. NOTIFY OTHERS WE ARE O.K."

The army responded to the happy news by immediately dispatching two de Havillands, a Martin bomber, and other planes to Molokai to retrieve the fliers. While waiting for the army to arrive, news correspondent and Molokai judge Ed McCorriston hosted Smith and Bronte at his home. McCorriston had witnessed the plane crash-land atop the kiawe trees and had been one of the first to greet the fliers on the island. He prepared an exceptionally hearty Hawaiian feast at his home, serving poi, fish, sweet potatoes, roast pig, cured seaweed, shellfish, chicken, and more. At the same time he collected the details of the flight in order to write the first news reports of the epic journey.

Smith and Bronte detailed the considerable challenges they encountered flying across the Pacific, namely the extreme fog and cloudiness, drowsiness, loss of radio communication, a failed fuel pump, and, last and most critically, a shortage of gasoline that precipitated their crash landing. They claimed bad weather and poor visibility disoriented them considerably, to the point that they first believed Molokai to also be a mirage and then apparently mistook it for Oahu, where they had hoped to land at Wheeler Field. "But it wasn't possible," said Bronte, whose arrival to Molokai so impressed the locals that a pregnant Hawaiian woman would soon name her newborn son after him. (It would prove a popular name, as Smith would name his own son after Bronte about four years later.) "We saw the kiawe and the mudhole. It didn't look like a choice, then. It looked like a funeral. We made it a choice, however, and it was the bush."

"At any rate," Smith added, "[the kiawe trees] looked better than the mudhole and infinitely better than putting back to sea."

The aviators said their crash landing was no less terrifying than the earlier failure of their fuel pump over the ocean and an apparent total loss of fuel. "We believed we faced certain death if we remained in the air," said Bronte. "We prepared to take a chance on the ocean and while I was wondering what I would really say to St. Peter, Smith, in some miraculous manner, revived the motor and we climbed."

Bronte bristled at critics who complained *City of Oakland*'s distress call was premature and born of inexperience at sea. "I am a navigator and Smith is a flying genius and a gentleman," he said. "We know the sea's ethics. We were both aware of the consequences of sending an SOS and we certainly would have kept all ships informed of our condition and position had we been able to do so."

Yet save for those few sticklers, the response to *City of Oakland*'s transpacific flight was otherwise exuberant, with praise rolling in from every which way. On Molokai, Pearl Harbor naval commander M. B. McComb inspected the airplane wreckage and lauded Smith and Bronte for accomplishing the near impossible. "There wasn't a drop of gasoline left in the tank. It was dry as a bone. There was almost no oil left," said McComb, who would die months later in a plane crash off Oahu. "The fliers made what I consider the finest piece of aerial navigation yet made in a Pacific flight—above the clouds and all the way not seeing water yet hitting Molokai smack on the nose. Their landing under the circumstances was excellently done."

Back in Oakland, Smith's sponsor Anthony Parente, acting in typical showman fashion, deemed Smith and Bronte's feat an unqualified success. "Whether they went to Honolulu or Molokai is a mere technicality," he insisted. "The fact is that they took off from the mainland and landed in Hawaii. I don't care what happened to the plane so long as they got there with it."

Marjorie Brown burst into tears of joy and relief when she heard news of the aviators' safe arrival. She then hugged and kissed all of *City of Oakland*'s mechanics and sponsors, whom she had stayed with overnight in San Francisco, listening to radio updates of Smith and Bronte's jaunt across the ocean. Once her emotions subsided a bit she sent a message to her fiancé while he waited on Molokai: "Darling: You have all my love. I am proud of your heroic flight against so many obstacles. Tons of love." She then sent another to Bronte: "Thanks for getting Ernie over there. I owe it to you."

Smith's short response minimized the dangers he had faced and the accomplishment he achieved: "Dearest: Hard trip, but put it over. Lots of love. ERNIE" Brown wasn't surprised to read Smith's muted message. "That sounds just like Ernie," she said. "Neither of us is particularly sentimental, and that's just the way he would take to tell me about something wonderful he accomplished."

In a cabled communication to the *San Francisco Call*, Smith was a bit more expressive: "Reached Hula land up a tree. Cold, tired, whiskery, but glad we skipped the shark puddles. Haven't seen any grass skirts yet, but hoping. Almost missed islands. They should be larger so fliers can find them." On Molokai, army planes soon picked the two men up and transported them in separate planes to Oahu. Flying in formation, twelve army aircraft flew over Honolulu before landing at nearby Wheeler Field about four o'clock in the afternoon. An artillery gun blasted in salute as the planes landed and a crowd of locals cheered. Stepping out of their respective aircraft, Bronte and Smith approached each other on the airfield, shook hands, and clapped each other on the back. Smith then triumphantly addressed the boisterous crowd: "Well, here we are. I want to say right here that all credit for this flight should go to Bronte. He kept us on our course and plotted our route through. The trip was mighty well worth while in every way. But it was hard to have the ship wrecked after it had carried us so far. We'll never be able to fly her again."

Pilot Ernie Smith celebrating on Oahu's Wheeler Field after being retrieved by army fliers from the island of Molokai. Smith and navigator Emory Bronte became the first civilians to fly to Hawaii, cruising between Oakland, California, and Molokai in twenty-five hours and two minutes. *Courtesy of the Hawaii Department of Transportation Airports*

Eventually Smith and Bronte were released to the Royal Hawaiian—the same hotel where army lieutenants Maitland and Hegenberger rested their similarly weary heads two weeks earlier. Smith woke up early the next day to tour Honolulu, but Bronte slept in. The exhausted navigator had to be woken, in fact, to make a late-morning visit with territorial governor Wallace Farrington. And so began two weeks of feting in Honolulu and California, as Smith and Bronte received many of the same honors given to Maitland and Hegenberger for making the Hawaiian Hop. Smith gushed over the attention and explained his and Bronte's motivation for crossing half the Pacific: "We made the flight to prove to the world that a commercial plane could accomplish the job, and I think we've proved that. Every man who flies does it to boost the profession he loves. We don't go in for this personal glory business. An aviator never grows up. We're all a bunch of kids and I think everyone who flies does it because he loves the game."

In Honolulu, beyond the attention of local boosters and dignitaries, the *City of Oakland* aviators received congratulations from their former rival, Hollywood flier Dick Grace, who was planning to return to California by ship to prepare for the upcoming Dole Air Race. They also met James Dole. The Pineapple King wondered aloud why Smith and Bronte couldn't have waited a few weeks later for his race.

Upon Smith and Bronte's return to the Golden State, they were greeted by a band at the pier in San Francisco as well as by scores of family, friends, journalists, and supporters. Smith characterized their reception on the mainland as "parades, banquets, dizzy offers and daffy compliments, mail by the truckload, a lot of wild hero-worship, mass hysteria—and also a lot of sincere admiration and friendship." An official welcoming party escorted the aviators to Oakland for congratulatory ceremonies before the fliers returned to San Francisco the next day to be lauded at city hall. "Not only are you aviators of great experience, note, and ability, but you are typical of red-blooded Americanism. We are mighty proud of you," said San Francisco mayor James Rolph, labeling the fliers "heavenly twins."

"We may have been heavenly twins," Bronte replied, "but we sure went through a lot of hell."

In the weeks to follow there was no sign of any of the carrier pigeons released during the flight. Lovebirds Smith and Brown suffered a tragic fate, too, when Smith broke off their engagement and married another woman. Brown took the heartbreak in stride, gamely laughing off the change in plans. "I'm a good loser," she said nobly. "Why, I wish Ernie all the happiness in the world. I stuck by him when he needed me, but now that he has found happiness with someone else, I can still be his friend."

Smith was asked about the upcoming Dole Derby and the wisdom of some pilots considering making the attempt alone and serving as their own navigators. "All I can say is they'd better trust in God," he responded. "Not only is it a two-man job, but, as Maitland and Hegenberger told us before we hopped off, it's really a four-man job."

Smith had no plans to enter the air race himself. His harrowing trip to Hawaii had exhausted his enthusiasm for long-distance flights. "I want to go back to flying mail again," he said.

PART III

THE DOLE DERBY

THE COLORADO STREET BRIDGE opened in 1913 to great acclaim. Observers admired the handsome, mighty concrete arches that spanned the Arroyo Seco canyon in Pasadena, California. Motorists enjoyed the shorter drive into Los Angeles. And Art C. Goebel, a leading Hollywood stunt pilot, appreciated the chance to daringly swoop his biplane beneath the bridge one day with two women crouching perilously atop his aircraft's upper wing.

A photograph taken on June 14, 1926, shows Goebel in the cockpit, threading his speeding plane through one of the bridge's 150-foot-tall concrete arches, while wingwalkers Gladys Ingle and Babe Kalishek coolly hang on for dear life. Though the photograph shows the plane with plenty of clearance, the passage felt like a tight squeeze to the stunt fliers. Ingle and Kalishek both ducked as they passed under the arch of the bridge, and Goebel flew low enough that he brushed treetops with the underside of his plane.

To many the stunt was astonishing, but to Goebel it was routine. The talented flier was known in Hollywood by the nickname "Upside Down" because of his ability to pilot an inverted airplane for minutes at a time. If anything, flying beneath the Colorado Street Bridge only encouraged him to do more of the same in other places, including Peoria, Illinois. A boy in that small midwestern city once witnessed a magical event when Goebel arrived to visit a girlfriend. "The first time I saw him, his plane came flying up the Illinois River low over the water," recalled W. J. Weisbruk. "Just before he reached the Cedar Street Bridge, he turned on his red smoke, flew under the bridge, pulled up in a perfect loop, and flew under the

169

bridge again. When he finished, the bridge ran right through the middle of a perfect pink circle."

Goebel dreamed of threading the Eiffel Tower, too, and once offered to fly a loop around the Brooklyn Bridge. He balked over the latter, however, when a man in New York offered a fee Goebel found insulting. Yet most of the time people were happy to pay the prices the stunt flier demanded. Only a few others in Hollywood rivaled Goebel's daring and talent.

Tall, dark, and handsome, he was a good fit for a city flush with pretty faces and physiques. When posing for photographs, the affable stuntman was impeccably dressed and likely to flash a big, teeth-baring grin. If he wasn't sporting a three-piece suit, then Goebel was likely clad in racing gear, complete with leather boots that laced up to his knees. Somehow oil stains were always absent from his fancy flying attire.

Hollywood stunt pilot Art "Upside Down" Goebel, pilot of *Woolaroc* in the Dole Air Race. *Courtesy of the California History Room, California State Library, Sacramento*

Goebel was a member of the 13 Black Cats, the famed flying troupe in Los Angeles that made death-defying aerial stunt services available to the Hollywood movie industry. Promising they would "do anything" with an airplane, the flying circus thumbed its nose at fate and doubled down on symbols of bad luck, choosing a logo that prominently featured the number *13* and a black cat. The troupe published a long menu of stunts and prices. Some of these stunts were common maneuvers that could be seen at almost any air show across the country; others were designed to satisfy the most ambitious screenwriters and directors. For $50 the troupe would make a plane catch fire. For $100 a member of the 13 Black Cats would amble from one airplane's wings to another in midflight. For $450 the 13 Black Cats would loop a plane while two men stood on the wingtips. And for $1,500 the flying troupe would blow up a plane in midair, just after a pilot bailed out and floated down to earth via parachute.

Much better at flying planes than crawling about them in midair, Goebel's piloting contributed much to the 13 Black Cats' success. Wingwalkers were lucky to have the calm and quick-thinking Goebel at the controls. Once he flew low over an automobile speeding seventy miles per hour down Los Angeles Boulevard, intent on picking up wingwalker Gene LaVock, who planned to grab hold of a ladder dangling from the plane. LaVock made the transfer from the car to the ladder successfully, but as she was dragged through the air, the twenty-year-old lacked the strength to climb up into the cockpit. As the minutes passed and LaVock precariously stayed put, clinging tightly to the swinging ladder, Goebel considered flying out over the ocean, cutting his speed and dropping to just a few feet above the waves, where LaVock could drop and make a safe splash before swimming for shore. Then another idea struck him, and Goebel unfastened his seatbelt, tossing one end of the restraint to LaVock before heaving her upward into the plane.

Another time, from the ground, Goebel witnessed a wheel fall off of a plane right after it took to the air. He sprang into action, taking off in his own plane while carrying a wingwalker lugging a spare wheel. Goebel caught up with the disabled plane, allowing for the spare wheel to be transferred and installed in midair. After saving the day Goebel and his daredevil companions didn't count their blessings. Instead they decided to replicate the incident as a stunt for their audiences. Soon enough he and his stunting cohorts were purposefully shaking loose a wheel after takeoff and then, while onlookers watched nervously, waited for a rescue flier to bring them a spare.

Goebel had long enjoyed making mischief. During his first day at school in his birthplace of Belen, New Mexico, he ran home to his mother as soon as class broke for recess. Later, after moving to the farming community of Rocky Ford in eastern Colorado, he skipped school by hopping out the classroom window when his teacher turned her back. His escapes were remedied only when the teacher forced him to sit in the center of the room, far from windows and doors.

Goebel found other paths to freedom. One day he brought a skunk to class on a leash, forcing the whole school's closure. Other times he teased and started fights in order to be sent home. His behavior only improved when his father made him work the sugar beet fields on the family farm—hard labor with foul-smelling produce. Goebel detested the work.

Yet the youngster was not hopeless. He showed great mechanical ability after buying his first bicycle in 1907, at age twelve. After dismantling and rebuilding his own bike, he started making repairs for friends, learning the ins and outs of the simple machine. When Goebel was fifteen years old, his father surprised him on Christmas Day by taking him to Pueblo, Colorado, which seemed a metropolis to a country boy growing up on a beet farm. Goebel saw his first airplane in Pueblo, a Farman biplane that circled a race track four times before crashing during its landing. The mishap hardly fazed Goebel, who was smitten. "I cannot express the feelings with which I returned to Rocky Ford and the farm," he later wrote. "I was in a sort of daze. My eyes had seen a thing I could not otherwise have believed."

Even if he could have found another airplane in rural Colorado in 1910, he could not have afforded it. In fact, he didn't lay eyes on another plane for almost seven years. So instead the teenager bought the next best thing—a motorcycle—and began riding with friends through the Arkansas River valley and into Kansas, occasionally entering races for prize money. He also worked stints as a farmhand and mailman, earning just enough to get by and take frequent long-distance motorcycle trips. "I had something now that fascinated me far beyond anything I had ever before owned—a gasoline engine," wrote Goebel. "In time I knew every part by heart, every sound of engine ills, every emergency precaution to take with this little but mighty power plant."

Again Goebel became a mechanic for friends, learning how to fix not only his own vehicle but also any kind of motorcycle. Then his fascination shifted to automobiles, which were becoming more common on American roads. Unable to afford a car, he built one, trading his possessions one by one for assorted auto parts, many of which did not belong to the same make of vehicle. Nevertheless, within a year or so, Goebel assembled these parts into a functional but humble jalopy. "Maybe it was without doors or cowl—maybe the short wooden step was hung to the chassis with castings from broken down farm machinery and the rear springs taken from a neighbor's cast-off carriage—but it ran," he wrote.

In early 1918 he joined the army to fight in World War I. A crack shot and avid hunter, he served as a rifle instructor during the war, teaching in training camps in America and France before the war ended that same year. Returning home from Europe, a restless Goebel took mechanic jobs in Fort Worth, Texas, and Denver, Colorado, before leaving for California, where he found work as an aviation motor mechanic in Los Angeles. Finally reunited with the airplane, he decided he must learn to fly. The mechanical expertise he had honed building and tuning bicycles, motorcycles, and automobiles aided his aviation education considerably. He wrote of learning the mechanics of flight, "In no other work is it so important to know the why of things, to inspect and reinspect, to be master of machinery, as in aviation. I came to know every inch of a ship—every strut, every bolt, every part, and why it was there. I learned, in endless lessons, its operation and what to do in any emergency."

While learning to fly in Los Angeles, Goebel became friends with Juan Leguía Swayne, a pilot and the son of the president of Peru. When Peru seemed on the verge of war with Chile, Leguía Swayne persuaded his friend to head south and join the Peruvian military as a combat pilot. Peru and Chile soon settled their differences, however, leaving Goebel to work as an air courier and flight instructor in South America.

By 1923 Goebel had returned to Los Angeles. With help from his father, he bought a pair of surplus Jennys from the army, parking one plane at Clover Field in Santa Monica, on the northern edge of Los Angeles. He joined the 13 Black Cats and began working for movie studios, performing established stunts for the cameras and continually trying to sell directors on new ones of his own device. He opened a stunt flying school and worked for newsreel companies, taking photographers up for aerial shots and footage. He also joined the Army Air Service Reserve and performed tailspin tests for the Douglas Aircraft Company, one of which nearly cost him his life. The near-death experience after a nine-thousand-foot tailspin hardly shook Goebel; aviation was everything to the young man.

In January 1927 he and a few fellow members of the 13 Black Cats took a steamer to Honolulu for a brief vacation. They rented a plane and cruised the island, flying over Oahu's beaches, mountains, and fields. Goebel was proud to state he had never crashed an airplane, but when coming in for a landing on a beach in Hawaii, the plane's landing gear caught in the soft sand, snapping it from the fuselage. That night, while sitting around a campfire, his buddies ribbed him about the incident. He ignored their kidding, though, and made a bold prediction: "The next time I come to Hawaii, I'm going to fly."

Four months later, pineapple tycoon James Dole invited aviators to Hawaii, promising cash prizes to the first and second pilots to reach its shores. Goebel, now back home in Los Angeles, jumped at the chance to make good on his vow to fly to the islands. He soon submitted his registration form and $100 entry fee, becoming the first aviator to officially enter the Dole Derby. Now he just needed a plane that could fly 2,400 miles without stopping, not to mention the money to pay for it.

⌐—•—⊃

While Art Goebel and dozens of other male pilots scrambled to find a suitable plane to take to Hawaii, a number of women sought to make sure they, too, were included in the exciting air race. Aviation was overwhelmingly a man's game in 1927, though from aviation's earliest days there existed a number of impressive female pilots and wingwalkers.

In 1911 journalist Harriet Quimby became the first American woman to earn a pilot's license. The next year she became the first woman to fly across the English Channel. Her aerial accomplishments led Vin Fiz soda to hire her as a spokeswoman, replacing the late Calbraith Perry Rodgers, the cross-country-flying cousin to navy commander John Rodgers who perished in a crash off Long Beach, California, when his plane collided with a flock of birds. Print advertisements for the grape soda featured a smiling Quimby clad in purple aviator's coveralls.

In 1922 Bessie Coleman became both the first woman of black descent and the first woman of Native American descent to earn a pilot's license. She grew up picking cotton in Texas before moving to Chicago, where she decided to learn to fly after becoming enthralled with the tales of aviators fighting in World War I. Since American flying schools would not admit her on account of her race and sex, a determined Coleman left for France to learn how to fly. After earning her license, she returned to the United States to dazzle crowds as a barnstormer and parachutist. "Queen Bess" refused to perform for segregated audiences and raised money to open an American flying school for black students. "The air is the only place free from prejudices," she said.

Neither of these women, however, would participate in the Dole Derby. By the time the air race was announced in 1927, Quimby and Coleman were dead. Quimby had been tossed from a plane in Massachusetts in 1912, just a year after obtaining her license and months after crossing the English Channel. Coleman also fell to her death from an airplane, dropping out of a cockpit above Florida in 1926. And another famous American aviatrix of the time period, Amelia Earhart, was relatively unknown and just beginning her flying career when James Dole advertised his contest to Hawaii.

In the absence of seasoned female fliers entering the race across the Pacific, other brave women lobbied to compete, no matter their total unfamiliarity with aviation. These laywomen could not fly, could not navigate, and could not offer to contribute any money or equipment for the expensive overseas journey. They couldn't even offer pilots their company on the trek over the waves, as the oversized fuel tanks required for the long flight would split fuselages in half, with pilots seated up front and any navigators or passengers accommodated in the rear of the plane. About all these women could offer pilots entering the Dole Derby, in fact, was extra weight, which was hardly appealing.

Still they tried. Two women in Dallas proclaimed that they'd be willing to fly to Hawaii with any pilot that would take them. One of these women obtained a signed waiver from her husband allowing her to fly; the other said she'd go despite her hubby's objections. Meanwhile, in San Francisco, a twenty-six-year-old named Jessica Day begged to be brought along: "I've always wanted to fly and I've always wanted to see the Hawaiian Islands. I'm not in the least afraid." And down in Bartlesville, Oklahoma, Rose Anne Schalski was still waiting for her chance to be included in the race, much to the delight of the Hawaiian Pineapple Company executives who chuckled over her letters. None of these women had much chance of being included in the race. Yet in Michigan one young airplane enthusiast with lofty intentions spied an opportunity to make the trip to Hawaii, even if her flying knowledge and capabilities were scant.

Mildred Doran was twenty-two years old, living in Flint, Michigan, with her father and three siblings. Her mother had died eight years earlier, leaving Doran, with the help of extended family, to more or less raise a younger brother and sister herself in a working-class neighborhood while her grief-stricken father earned a living for the family. "Oh how I missed my mother in those days!" she recalled. "We were so lonely without her, and I didn't dare show my longing for her old-time care, for if I did, my father and the others felt all the worse. . . . I used to get Floyd and Helen to play games in the morning—competing to see who could get dressed first, and who could be at the breakfast table first—anything to keep them from remembering mother, and crying for her."

Maternal responsibilities did not squelch Doran's gay spirit. The wide-eyed teenager had a mirthful and witty reputation, and Michigan boys were bowled over by her charm. Flint resident Edmund G. Love recalled having the Doran family as a customer along his paper route when he was fifteen years old. The teenager looked forward each morning to handing a newspaper to Mildred Doran, a woman he described as "extremely attractive" and "the classic flapper of her time." With big warm eyes, wavy curls, and a mischievous smile that seemed ever present, there were few people, especially fifteen-year-old boys, immune to Doran's good looks. "She wore short dresses with her stockings rolled just below her knee and she had a tendency to sashay when she walked," said Love.

After graduating from high school in Flint, Doran attended nearby Ypsilanti Normal College for a year, training to become a teacher. The next year she taught fifth grade in rural Caro, Michigan, where she was beloved by her students.

She was sometimes chauffeured home to Flint by airplane from both Ypsilanti and Caro, a perk courtesy of William F. Malloska, a longtime family friend and Doran's godfather. Malloska owned Lincoln Petroleum Products Company, which operated or supplied more than fifty automobile service stations in Michigan. He also owned a small airline and Flint's Lincoln Field, which became a regular hangout for Doran, who had caught the aviation bug after attending an air show with a college roommate, Leona Marshall. Doran had initially resisted attending, accepting Marshall's invitation only after staring at the airplanes through a fence. "Finally we went on the field and walked from plane to plane, admiring them," said Doran. "I didn't have a ghost of an idea about how they worked, and machinery never interested me, but the planes themselves looked so alive that I loved looking at them."

Ultimately, Marshall challenged Doran to pay $2.50 for an airplane ride. "You're always afraid," said Marshall. "When are you ever going to stop being a coward, Mildred?" The shaming worked. After taking to the air, Doran returned to earth a transformed woman—one keenly interested in aviation. "After we began rushing through the air, twisting and turning, it seemed like some particularly glorious ride on some miraculously smooth highway," she said of her first flight.

Doran began befriending pilots at Malloska's airfield, persuading them to take her aloft as often as they could. She had no apprehension of taking to the sky and occasionally took control of an airplane in mid-flight, though this experience hardly made her a competent flier. But when the pilots needed a courageous volunteer to accompany them on public demonstrations of dives, Doran eagerly stepped forward. She was happy to plummet to earth within the belly of a plane, confident that neither pilot nor plane would fail her.

Among her favorite aviators in Flint were E. L. "Slonnie" Sloniger, who flew for the Army Air Service in World War I, and John A. "Auggy" Pedlar, a young pilot and wingwalker who performed with handcuffs around his wrists and who had a talent for diving off moving airplanes into the ocean. Pedlar learned to fly in the West, though he so badly crashed one airplane that he walked away from the wreck with a lasting and pronounced limp. Friendly and well liked, Pedlar was recognizable at the Flint airfield for his toothy grin and beloved headwear—a straw hat that covered his thin hair.

One evening in May 1927, after Pedlar ferried Doran home to the Flint airfield from her job in Caro, the young schoolteacher began conversing with Pedlar and Sloniger about the airmail pilot Charles Lindbergh and his preparations for an imminent attempt to cross the Atlantic Ocean. Excited for Lindbergh, Doran exclaimed that she'd like to be the first woman to cross the Pacific. The two pilots seconded her idea, both volunteering to make the flight with her, however improbable it may have seemed. And then the airfield owner Malloska, who overheard Doran and his pilots, offered to buy a plane. Doran did not hesitate to accept his proposition. "I told Mildred that if she was serious I'd finance the plan and would order a plane built tomorrow," said Malloska. "She snapped me up immediately and the next day I made a deposit with the Buhl Aircraft Company of Marysville for the construction of the plane. This was the day before Lindbergh took off [for Paris]."

While some people believed an airplane was no place for a woman, others cheered Doran's ambition to make the Hawaiian Hop, if only as a passenger. American women had made great strides in the last decade when it came to gender equality, including earning the right to vote, obtaining access to birth control, and securing greater social freedoms. Doran matured into womanhood while the flapper era was in full swing, with women donning revealing and sultry clothing, bobbing their hair, and dancing nights away at jazz clubs and speakeasies. So why shouldn't they ride in airplanes, too?

Defending Doran's decision to fly to Hawaii, Malloska praised the young woman's resilience:

> I have all the confidence in the world in Miss Doran. I know of the hardships she endured after the death of her mother. She was able to go to school only a half of each day, worked in a telephone office the other half, and in addition took care of all the housework and was a mother to her younger sister and a young brother. She will go through this flight just as she has gone through other hardships.

In the days to come, Lindbergh landed safely in France, James Dole offered prizes to entice the first Pacific fliers to Hawaii, and Malloska's new biplane began to be assembled in Michigan. Doran was ecstatic, giddy over the prospect of traveling the world and becoming Lindbergh's equal. "I was so thrilled," she gushed, "I jumped into my car and dashed all over town to tell all my aunts, uncles, and friends. Then we began to plan carefully what should be done."

One of the first decisions to make about the journey was a hard one: Who would pilot the plane? It was an uncomfortable question given the intense interest of both Pedlar and Sloniger. Finally, it was suggested that the pilots flip a coin for the honor. The men agreed and headed off with Doran to the *Flint Journal* to settle the question on a Saturday afternoon. There in the newsroom Doran flipped a fifty-cent piece into the air. Sloniger called heads; Pedlar tails. The coin dropped to the ground, rolled across the floor, and disappeared beneath a desk before settling out of sight. Very carefully the desk was then removed, revealing the coin with tails side up. Pedlar would be flying to Hawaii. Sloniger graciously shook hands with his rival and offered congratulations. His disappointment was severe, though, and Malloska closed his airport for the day to allow his dejected pilot the chance to take off work and cheer up.

Doran, meanwhile, glowed with excitement for the coming race, though she conceded that, should her mother still be alive, "I would never have thought of doing a thing like this." She added, "I simply desire to do something different and to be the first woman to do it. I am sure we will win, but if we don't life is nothing but a chance, anyway."

In towns across the country, and in places as far away as Australia, Canada, France, and Germany, aviators shared the same dream as Mildred Doran: to wing their way to Hawaii and collect a cash prize. Dozens of these men expressed interest in the Dole Derby, though only two pilots had submitted the entry fee by the end of June 1927, when the Army Air Corps made the first flight to Hawaii. Despite the army stealing the show, interest in the race did not flag among civilian aviators. If James Dole was still willing to spend $35,000 on the winners, then plenty of pilots promised to try for the islands.

The race rules had been modified slightly after Lindbergh declined his invitation to compete in the derby. Aviators could now leave the mainland as early as noontime on August 12, 1927. Beyond offering a full moon to the aviators that night, the date was symbolically important as the twenty-ninth anniversary of Hawaii being annexed into the United States. And though pilots would have preferred to leave at daybreak that day, James Dole insisted on a noon takeoff. Otherwise the pilots would likely land at Oahu before dawn the next day, denying the people of Hawaii the eagerly awaited spectacle of arriving airplanes and the finish to the Dole Derby.

As race day approached during the summer of 1927, the Hawaiian public's already strong appetite for aviation was whetted further by the arrival of the army fliers and the crash landing of Ernie Smith and Emory Bronte on Molokai. As the island newspapers lauded Dole for establishing the air race and directing the world's attention to Hawaii, locals rallied around pilot Martin Jensen, a twenty-seven-year-old Honolulu resident desperate to enter the competition. He would likely be Hawaii's only representative in the race and therefore became the hometown favorite.

Jensen had grown up far from the Paradise of the Pacific in Jamestown, Kansas, the son of a farmer who had emigrated from Denmark. Jensen had no patience for working the plow, though, and at age fifteen or so, following a fight with his father, he hopped a boxcar heading to Sioux City, Iowa. There he lived with a brother and worked as an auto mechanic while finishing high school. A stint in the Iowa National Guard followed, where he was tasked with guarding airplanes that arrived to the local airfield. It was his first meaningful interaction with aircraft.

Jensen then joined the navy and worked as a mechanic, transferring to Naval Air Station San Diego on North Island following basic training along the Great Lakes. In San Diego he saw more airplanes, but only dared ride in one after being ridiculed by his peers. The day of that first flight, he was among a group of fifteen young men watching an airplane and taking turns hitching a ride into the sky. "One by one the other fellows went up in it, until I was the last," he recalled. "I was afraid to try it, but they made such fun of me that I finally went up, and then I realized what a chump I was to remain on the ground."

Jensen soon started trading naval aviators flying lessons for mechanical work on their automobiles, slowly gaining time at the controls of airplanes. He first soloed in 1922, after leaving the navy, and then opened a winter flying school in San Diego. During warmer months he barnstormed across the country, once taking along his new bride, Marguerite, called "Peg," an accomplished and flamboyant wingwalker and parachutist. The Jensens had been married in 1925 in the air above Yuma, Arizona, the happy couple standing together atop the wing of a flying airplane. Minutes earlier Martin had taken off from the airfield below with Peg in his lap and a judge in the passenger seat.

A flying plane may not have provided the most solid foundation for the start of a marriage, but there was no denying the strong passion between Martin and Peg Jensen. Redheaded Peg was endearingly emotional and outspoken, effusive in her constant support of her high-flying husband. Martin was impulsive, scrappy, and unflappable, seemingly incapable of losing his nerve, no matter what went wrong aloft. As might be expected, the trim and fearless flier's hair was constantly windswept. This hint of dishevelment was countered by a small, neat, and fashionable toothbrush mustache that Jensen kept neatly trimmed in the style favored by celebrity comedians like Charlie Chaplin and Oliver Hardy.

The Jensens claimed to be the first couple to honeymoon by airplane, though not the first to be wed in the air. Couples had been wed aloft in hot air balloons for decades. During one part of the Jensens' honeymoon they landed near the Jensen family farm in Kansas, surprising Martin's father, who had not seen his son in ten years. The old family feud was soon forgotten when Martin showed off his wingwalker wife and very own flying machine.

"It was a thrill to see an airplane in the pasture," said Nils Jensen. "I knew it was Martin when I saw that queer contraption."

Though the Jensens kept barnstorming in their ninety-horsepower Jenny, traveling across the country with forty pounds of fuel at a time and fifty pounds of luggage, they never made much money. Martin offered the common complaint that he spent one too many nights sleeping under the wing of his airplane, though he'd have it no other way. "I had never considered flying as a glamorous field of endeavor," he said. "Rather it was a case of hardship . . . but we did it for love."

Settling back in Southern California, the couple operated an aerial lobster supply business, picking up the crustaceans in Mexico and flying them north in a plane equipped with a moistening device designed to keep the animals alive. Months later they left the lobsters behind and sailed for Honolulu, starting anew on the islands at the beginning of 1927. Martin Jensen was hired by the airline Lewis Hawaiian Tours and kept a busy schedule with sightseers and travelers, making more than one hundred inter-island flights during his first six months in Honolulu.

He piloted the airplane *Malolo*, which is Hawaiian for "flying fish." But *Malolo* was a misnomer, as the aircraft was not a seaplane and could not swim like a fish, or even float. Jensen would become nervous when taking the plane over water, especially if visibility was poor. When booked to fly to another island, he had the habit of flying out over open water "until the island I was leaving was just disappearing on the horizon. . . . If I couldn't see the island I was going to by then, I'd turn back." The unreliable reputation of *Malolo*'s engine amplified the worry of a sea landing. "I was carrying passengers to the other islands and I remembered sometimes this type of engine just quit on you," Jensen once remarked. "I didn't like the idea of it quitting on me between here and Kauai." "When I am flying over these channels with people I have a responsibility, which I take seriously," he added.

When he wasn't fretting about falling into the sea, Jensen was able to enjoy a virgin aerial paradise. The barnstormer from Kansas was one of the first to routinely fly between the Hawaiian Islands, hopping from one gorgeous green tropical isle to the next as his plane cut through warm air. Flying facilities were still extremely basic on many of the major Hawaiian Islands, if they existed at all. When flying to Maui, he would land at the Maui Country Club golf course. Golfers there fumed over the small trench *Malolo*'s tail skid made as it touched down and tore through the ground.

On Molokai the people were considerably friendlier. Jensen regularly dropped newspapers down to the island's leper colony and once unloaded a doctor, a visit that required the pilot to obtain a permit from state health officials. As a condition of his visit, lepers were free to look at *Malolo* so long as they did not touch the plane. He felt bad that the lepers were ostracized.

When Jensen flew between islands, the big blue Pacific just hundreds of feet below his wings, its surface rippling with waves and breached repeatedly by the humpback whales wintering in Hawaii's warm waters, he sometimes considered the possibility of a much longer flight over the ocean, one that stretched between Hawaii and the mainland. The notion was merely a daydream, a fuzzy, vague possibility that occurred to him as he piloted *Malolo* over open water for less than an hour's stretch at a time. But on May 21, 1927, when he was five months on the job in Hawaii, he returned to Honolulu from a trip to the Big Island, surprised to hear the din of bells and whistles as he arrived at the airfield. Stunning news had just reached Hawaii—Charles Lindbergh had flown across the Atlantic! Lindbergh's flight proved not only that an ocean crossing was possible but also that its requirements for success were surprisingly minimal: one man in one plane with one engine—just bring along enough fuel and the smelling salts.

Days later James Dole announced his cash prizes for the first aviators to reach Hawaii from the mainland. Now an idea that Jensen had considered rather abstractly was pushed to the forefront of his mind, demanding a decision. Did the flyer really have the courage and ability to cross an ocean by airplane? He knew that if he forfeited this chance, then surely others would make the attempt.

He agonized over his decision. The longest flight he had completed over water was the seventy-two miles between Oahu and Kauai, a distance that would account for just 3 percent of the journey between San Francisco and Honolulu. Jensen knew, too, that he possessed little navigational training, which was essential for finding the Hawaiian Islands. On the other hand, this was the chance every barnstormer lived for, to finally make it as a flier, to earn acclaim and fortune through manipulation of an airplane. "I spent several sleepless nights deciding what to do," he said. "I knew if I decided to enter, it meant the die was cast and that I would be entering a most dangerous flight."

Ultimately, he decided the overseas flight to Hawaii was a chance too good to pass up. He said goodbye to Peg, leaving his energetic wife behind in Honolulu to raise money for the flight. Then he stepped onto a steamer and sailed for Los Angeles in June, desperate to find a plane before race day on August 12.

George Hearst sat inside the sleek new airplane he had just purchased, gazing down at San Francisco Bay. The steam liner SS *Maui* was somewhere below, arriving from Hawaii with Lieutenants Lester Maitland and Albert Hegenberger, who two weeks earlier had flown across the Pacific to Hawaii. The army fliers were on the verge of being the toast of the town, with a massive homecoming celebration kicking off as their ship approached the Golden Gate en route to downtown San Francisco. But right now Hearst and his companions in his Lockheed Vega monoplane couldn't find *Maui* and its famous passengers—the morning haze and fog were too thick.

As the portly Hearst and his companions strained their eyes and sought to spy the steamer between breaks in the haze, fuel spilled from an overhead valve into the plane cabin and soaked his shoes. He quickly passed a note to pilot Jack Frost, who could not hear for the plane's roaring engine. "What kind of a ship is this?" said the note.

"Don't worry," replied Frost in his own note. "That's just overflow. It'll stop in a minute. Don't strike a match. Ship and squadron right ahead."

The soggy-socked Hearst had good reason to wonder about the leaking gasoline. He had just paid $12,500 for the gold-colored plane, and that price reflected a steep discount from its manufacturer, the Lockheed Aircraft Company. Moreover, the Vega, conceived by young aircraft designer John K. Northrop, was reputed to be a revolutionary model of airplane, its cutting-edge design and engineering resulting in high speed. *So why was such a masterpiece leaking fuel?* thought Hearst, publisher of the *San Francisco Examiner.*

Examiner reporter Harry Lang wondered the same thing sitting in the Vega's cabin. Like Hearst, he had become saturated with gasoline very quickly on this early morning flight. His skin reddened and burned as the gasoline dripped down his back, causing a four-inch blister. Besides the skin irritation, turbulence bothered Lang as he tapped out a report on the typewriter in his lap. Nonetheless, it was exhilarating to cruise above the city and bay. The excitement of the flight so overwhelmed him that he momentarily lost his way with words: "Down the runway at a hundred an hour, and up into the stratum of black mist that hugs the surface of these mornings. . . . Our shadow goes scooting ahead of us, along the ground below, like something-or-other— I'm too busy enjoying this, right now, to think up similes."

Lang regained his literary footing in the clouds, marveling at the calmness within the cabin of a speeding plane:

> Sounds fast, doesn't it? 125 miles an hour! But get up in an airplane and do it, and you don't realize you're moving. That sensation of speed, which one imagines an aviator has, simply isn't, that's all! You just seem to hang motionless in the air—and the ground glides by below, ever so gently. . . . And you don't realize, until you look at your watch and consider how many miles of terrain you've left behind, that you're doing better than two miles a minute!

The Lockheed Vega was indeed fast, courtesy of its bold engineering and unique construction materials and methods. Whereas most contemporary planes were made of steel-and-wood skeletons wrapped in fabric and painted with dope, the Vega comprised a twenty-seven-foot-long, cigar-shaped fuselage made of bonded wood. Called a monocoque, this laminated skin was much stronger than conventional fuselages, requiring no internal skeleton or bracing. The Vega also featured a cantilevered forty-one-foot wing, bare of any struts or additional supports connected to the fuselage. The result was a sleek machine that resembled a torpedo with a wing and tail fin glued on top.

If anyone was in need of a discount on this airplane, it was not George Randolph Hearst. The twenty-three-year-old publisher was the oldest son of the powerful media magnate William Randolph Hearst, a former New York congressman who owned more than two dozen newspapers and magazines across the country, a number of which earned reputations for engaging in sensationalistic journalism. But the Lockheed Aircraft Company of Hollywood, California, offered the discount nonetheless, hoping that Hearst's purchase would lead to free publicity for the young aircraft manufacturer.

The first Lockheed Vega, *Golden Eagle*, featured a wooden monocoque fuselage and cantilevered wings, which eliminated the skeleton framing and exterior struts common to other contemporary planes. *Golden Eagle* was piloted by Jack Frost, navigated by Gordon Scott, and sponsored by newspaper publisher George Hearst. Later versions of the speedy Lockheed Vega would prove popular with daring fliers such as Amelia Earhart and Wiley Post. *Courtesy of the California History Room, California State Library, Sacramento*

Sometime shortly after the Vega's first flight from its factory on July 4, 1927, the airplane flew to William Randolph Hearst's vast coastal estate in San Simeon, California. The 250,000-acre property boasted its own airfield, 127 acres of gardens, and, most famously, Hearst Castle, a fifty-six-bedroom compound that had commenced construction eight years earlier (and which would take twenty more years to finish). When the Vega arrived to the Hearst airfield, George's wife, Blanche, an aviation enthusiast herself who would soon earn her own pilot's license and form an airplane company, christened the craft *Golden Eagle*.

While George Hearst, who also later became a pilot himself, displayed clear enthusiasm for aviation, his father's feelings were harder to decipher. Beyond hosting *Golden Eagle*'s christening ceremony on his estate, the elder Hearst had recently bought a Fokker airplane to commute between Hearst Castle and Los Angeles. But on July 24, 1927, he sent a telegram to his second-eldest son and namesake, William Randolph Hearst Jr., warning him not to take to the air:

> Please keep out of airplanes Bill. Am afraid you will break your neck just as you are getting to be useful newspaper man. Am serious about this. Answer.
> —Pop

It was twenty-nine-year-old pilot Frost who had persuaded George Hearst to buy *Golden Eagle* by taking the spiffy plane up for an early test flight. A Chicago native, Frost was a veteran army flier and instructor, though he had apparently given up flying in recent years while working as a bond salesman on Wall Street in New York, where two of his brothers operated a stock brokerage firm. Before that, he had served as an assistant to the postmaster general and also was one of New York's first aerial policemen, sworn in with nineteen other fliers to form the aviation section of the New York City Police Reserve in April 1919.

That same year, while flying for the army, Lieutenant Frost crashed a Curtiss Model H into Oyster Bay beside Long Island, New York. The biplane's engine had sparked and become disabled at two thousand feet, causing it to drop into a tailspin. Frost recovered and leveled out two hundred feet above the water, but then the plane nosedived into the bay, plunging him and a companion beneath the water. Moments later both men bobbed to the surface and were rescued by oystermen.

Such a splash did not discourage Frost from wanting to fly over water again. The slightly stocky and mustachioed aviator, partial to bow ties and three-piece suits, convinced Hearst to sponsor him as pilot of the *Golden Eagle* in the Dole Air Race. Possessing one of the fastest planes in the country, Frost and Hearst were bullish on their chances. So bullish, in fact, that they even suggested Frost might compete in the Dole Derby as a prelude to an even bigger air contest across the Pacific. After capturing the prize in Hawaii, Frost was considering flying *Golden Eagle* back to California, switching to a seaplane, and then cruising across the entire Pacific, landing finally in Australia. He practiced for these anticipated flights by flying up and down the California coast, pushing *Golden Eagle* to its maximum speed of 135 miles per hour as he traveled between San Francisco and Los Angeles in a mere three hours.

Both pilot and sponsor were elated with the plane's speedy performance. "We're going in to win first money," boasted Hearst.

While Jack Frost buzzed about California preparing for the Dole Derby, his plane secured and his expenses covered by a wealthy sponsor, his potential competitors scrambled to obtain their own aircraft and hightail it to Oakland before race day. Entry fees and registration forms were due August 2, 1927—ten days before planes were allowed to leave for the islands. That left a little more than nine weeks between James Dole's air race announcement and the deadline for pilots to have their plane and cash in hand.

As the deadline approached, some of the more exotic competitors bowed out of the race. No shimmy dancers would be flying to the islands, nor the laxative-advertising dentist, nor anyone in a plane powered by a steam engine. But that didn't mean the race would be devoid of all oddities. In Illinois a team prepared *City of Peoria*, a biplane that planned to carry a caged owl named Colonel Pineapple. Because the animal was nocturnal, explained pilot Charles W. Parkhurst, the owl would stare at him and the plane's navigator throughout the night, helping them keep awake.

In Southern California, veteran British aviator Arthur V. Rogers conducted test flights in *Angel of Los Angeles*, a twin-tailed, twin-engine plane whose two motors were configured to work in tandem, with one pushing the plane and the other pulling it in the same direction. The similarly named *Pride of Los Angeles*, which counted movie star Hoot Gibson as a sponsor, was also striking in appearance—it had three wings. Snarky observers labeled the triplane the "Stack of Wheats."

And in San Diego, Royal Flying Corps veteran Arthur Goddard installed a bulging gas tank in the belly of *El Encanto*, whose name translates from Spanish to mean "charm." The modification not only made the Englishman's silver monoplane look pregnant but also precariously placed the plane's fuel load extremely close to the ground. Goddard designed and supervised the construction of *El Encanto* himself, bankrolling his entry into the Dole Derby by selling the airport he owned and operated in San Diego. On the fuselage he painted "HBH," an initialism meaning "Hell-Bent for Honolulu." In early August he flew his plane north to begin preparations for the race, joining other pilots arriving from around the country to the airport on Bay Farm Island in Oakland.

In Los Angeles, Art Goebel held a sale in his hangar, offloading a few Jenny planes, personal belongings, and flying gear to raise money for a plane to fly across the Pacific. He leaned on friends for loans, too, and then flew east to the Travel Air factory in Wichita, Kansas, where he placed an order for a new Travel Air 5000—the same plane that Ernie Smith used to reach Molokai. Though it wasn't the fastest plane, Goebel valued the Travel Air's reliability, especially since the race entailed such a long flight.

After the plane's completion and test flights, it was time for Goebel to pay for his plane. He was suddenly short on cash, owing to one of his backers in California reneging on his support. The executives at Travel Air suggested that Goebel make a short flight south from Wichita to Bartlesville, Oklahoma, to see if he could scrounge up the difference owed. He was not flying to see Rose Anne Schalski, the aviation booster who had written James Dole of her desperate desire to fly to Hawaii. No, Goebel was told to visit oilman Frank Phillips and ask him for a loan.

Phillips, fifty-three, was twenty-two years older than the Hollywood pilot, but the two men formed a fast friendship. They had some things in common: both came of humble beginnings in the western United States and displayed considerable ambition to excel in their professions. Phillips was born in a log cabin in Nebraska. To make extra money as a kid he dug potatoes and then as a young man worked as a barber in Iowa. Soon he owned a number of barber shops in Iowa, then sold bonds out East, then became a small-town banker when he moved to Bartlesville in Indian Territory, a region that three years later would become the state of Oklahoma.

In Oklahoma, Phillips obtained oil leases, formed the Phillips Petroleum Company, and became a rich man through the sale of natural gas and Phillips 66 gasoline, as well as the operation of iconic Phillips 66 gas stations across the country. Phillips, who was later made an honorary chief by the Osage Indians from whom he leased land, established a ranch outside of Bartlesville in the Osage Hills and built an eight-bedroom home there in 1927. He named his ranch Woolaroc. Some people have erroneously believed this unusual name was that of a local Native American, or that the term was a Native American word for "good luck." In fact, *Woolaroc* is a portmanteau of the prominent features of the ranch's surrounding landscape, namely woods, lakes, and rocks.

When Goebel arrived to Woolaroc, his proposition for Phillips was straightforward: invest in the flight in exchange for publicity. The two quickly struck a deal, with Phillips giving Goebel about $5,000, enough for Goebel to purchase the airplane, which was then named *Woolaroc*. The agreement required the pilot to use Phillips's Nu-Aviation gasoline.

Goebel soon headed west in his new airplane, eager to reach Oakland and have sufficient time for the fast-approaching Dole Derby, in which he planned to fly alone, acting as both pilot and navigator. About the same time, an identical Travel Air 5000 was leaving the Midwest for Oakland, too, also sponsored by the Phillips Petroleum Company. This was *Oklahoma*, navigated by Al Henley and piloted by former Oklahoma University football star and veteran army flier Bennett Griffin.

The two aviators from Oklahoma City had hoped to fly the nearly 1,500 miles from Oklahoma to California in a single hop, essentially staging a dry run of their upcoming trip to Hawaii. But at takeoff they lost a wheel and then several rivets sprung loose on the plane. Later, after somehow landing safely and restarting with repaired landing gear, *Oklahoma* was forced down at the border between Arizona and California on account of overheated exhaust pipes that threatened to burn the plane. After making more repairs, the duo continued up the California coast to Santa Monica, where fog grounded their plane. Finally, they arrived in Oakland.

Oklahoma wasn't the only Dole Air Race craft experiencing problems in flight. In Southern California, navy lieutenant commander George D. Covell cut short a flight in his *Spirit of John Rodgers* because of fog. Ernie Smith's old friend Livingston Irving, a native of Berkeley, California, was forced to land his *Pabco Pacific Flyer* forty miles south of Monterey because of a bad gasoline feed pipe. And *City of Peoria*, with the feathered and wide-eyed Colonel Pineapple aboard, nearly smashed into the Rockies as they flew east from Illinois. "While we were passing over the most mountainous part of our route," said pilot Charles Parkhurst, "our engine went dead. We began to fall rapidly. I looked over the side, but as far as I could see there was not a level place large enough to hold the ship even could I have done the impossible and landed on it.

[Navigator Ralph C.] Lowes and I had about decided that it was all over, when the engine picked up again and we came on through without further trouble."

Meanwhile, from Dallas came Bill Erwin, thirty-one, who unveiled his airplane, *Dallas Spirit*, from beneath a white cloth during a ceremony at Love Field in front of ten thousand Texans. The governor of Texas and mayor of Dallas were both on hand to praise Erwin before a band played "The Star-Spangled Banner" and the silver and green *Dallas Spirit* was undraped. Boosters in Dallas were fiercely proud of Erwin, a veteran American war ace who was credited with downing nine German planes and surviving five forced crashes. Once, Erwin completed a combat mission despite his comrade lying dead in the seat before him, having been fatally shot in the head.

Among the dignitaries at the Dallas event was William E. Easterwood, a Texan offering $25,000 to the first person to fly from Dallas to Hong Kong in no more than three stops. The opportunistic Erwin was trying to combine this contest with the Dole Derby, planning to fly his Swallow monoplane from Dallas to San Francisco to Honolulu to Manila before landing in Hong Kong. Should all go well, Erwin would collect a total of $50,000."We are going to do our best on this flight," he told the crowd. "We are going to make every possible preparation to assure success. We are not going off half-cocked and are not going to attempt the impossible." But even Hong Kong would not be the end of the trip. Erwin then planned to fly around the world. Accompanying him the entire time would be his pregnant twenty-year-old wife, Connie, who would serve as navigator and radio operator.

In early August 1927 *Dallas Spirit* left for California, the first of three legs permitted to obtain Easterwood's Hong Kong prize. Erwin didn't even make it out of Texas before fuel problems forced a return to Love Field. Easterwood graciously allowed Erwin to restart the flight the next evening, though the pilot's problems persisted. Flying through the night, he encountered three storms over west Texas and New Mexico, experiencing much lightning and rain before nearly colliding with a mountainside. "While I was plowing through this deluge of water, almost blinded, I noticed a black wall rising suddenly before the nose of the ship," he said later. "It was the mountains and I just did pull her up in time to get over. They talk about the southern route, but after I saw those mountains, I said southern route be darned, and I pulled *Dallas Spirit* up to ten or twelve thousand feet and came on through at that altitude."

Following the electrical storms, the fuel problem recurred, forcing *Dallas Spirit* to land in a California wheat field to the east of Los Angeles. Erwin took off again the next morning, flying with one hand while continually operating a wobble pump with the other to deliver fuel to the engine. He was relieved by the time he reached Oakland six hours later, and also so stiff he could hardly exit his plane. "The worst part of the trip to Honolulu is over," he boasted, perhaps prematurely. "I would rather take a trip across the water any time than make it across the mountains to California from Texas."

Mildred Doran's journey to Oakland from Michigan was similarly protracted and aggravating. Soon after Auggy Pedlar won the coin toss to pilot Doran across the Pacific, the new red-white-and-blue Buhl Airsedan ordered for the schoolteacher was delivered to Flint. With the mayor and hundreds of residents looking on, the biplane was christened *Miss Doran* as a bottle of ginger ale was cracked across its propeller—champagne being forbidden because of Prohibition. Then Doran and Pedlar, with Malloska in tow, prepared to embark on their journey west to Oakland, and after that Honolulu.

Though E. L. Sloniger had lost the coin toss to Pedlar and would be staying home in Flint, he still cared passionately about *Miss Doran*'s chances. Before the plane left, he urged Pedlar to simulate the race during his trek to California, arguing a nonstop run to Oakland was the best preparation for the ocean flight. Specifically, Sloniger hoped for *Miss Doran* to take off one evening in Flint, fly through the night, arrive at the Rockies by daybreak, and then cruise into Oakland later that day. It would have been a two-thousand-mile flight—four hundred miles short of the span between Oakland and Honolulu, but nonetheless plenty of distance to put plane, pilot, and navigator to the test before heading out over open ocean. But Pedlar disregarded the idea, opting to instead hopscotch across the country, visiting six cities over three weeks before arriving in Oakland. Some observers thought the snail's pace of *Miss Doran* was due to sponsor William Malloska's insistence on generating maximum publicity for the flight, but mechanical snafus and bad weather also contributed to the slow going. In any case, it was not an auspicious beginning for the biplane and its inhabitants: Doran, Pedlar, Malloska, and a three-week-old Great Dane named Honolulu who would also be traveling to the islands.

Embarking on the cross-country flight, *Miss Doran* flew into the edge of a horrible storm before even leaving Michigan. The plane was tossed so violently that its cabin door popped open and luggage tumbled out and plummeted to the ground. Doran, Malloska, and Honolulu the pup nearly followed, with Malloska later claiming, "We were shaken about in that plane for five minutes as popcorn is shaken in a popper." While his flying companions ricocheted around the fuselage, Pedlar steered *Miss Doran* back to the airfield he had just departed, reportedly flying 150 miles per hour in his haste to escape the high winds. "Auggie stepped on the gas," Doran wrote to a fellow schoolteacher in Caro days later. "We arrived a little ahead of the storm. I'm sure the plane would never have stood the storm, no doubt crashed to earth. We were flipped over once, then the door flew open and baggage started to go out."

The brush with death did not discourage *Miss Doran*'s cross-country crew, however. In fact, they were inspired by Pedlar's astute decision to reverse course and speed away from such a violent storm. *Miss Doran* was soon again on its way, introducing its increasingly famous passenger, Mildred Doran, to every community in which the plane landed. Still, the poor weather persisted. "We stayed in Mount Clemens that night and Wednesday arrived in Chicago," Doran continued in her letter to her colleague. "Fifteen reporters and photographers were waiting to chase me. We went to St. Louis Thursday. A very disagreeable ride. It rained so hard we were forced to land once in a hayfield. We were all very tired. Friday we went to Tulsa, Oklahoma."

After Tulsa came stops in Texas at Fort Worth and El Paso, at Tucson, Arizona, and then at Long Beach, California. Doran was reportedly tired from all the flying, though three weeks remained for her to recover before attempting to cross the Pacific. Still, despite any fatigue, the "Flying Schoolma'am" or "Flying Schoolmarm," as she was becoming known, was quite chipper with newspapermen. "We will be the first ones off on August 12," she said in Long Beach, where Pedlar addressed a chamber of commerce meeting. "I'm really tickled to pieces to be here, and I haven't the slightest misgivings about the coming jaunt to Hawaii. I've always wanted to do something different and to be the first woman to do it. Even if Auggy and I don't pick up first money, I will still be the first woman to make a trip like that."

The next week *Miss Doran* made a detour south to San Diego. Here again the crew members were feted by locals, invited to suppers and social and civic events. Doran attended a dinner in her honor hosted by the San Diego Hawaiian Club, which had given the late navy commander John Rodgers a hearty send-off two years earlier before he embarked on his own pioneering flight to Hawaii. Doran told the crowd she refused to pack a life preserver on her plane, claiming, "We are not going down out there; we are going to stay up until we reach land."

She was so inundated with invitations and interview requests on her whirl-wind trip out West that she fell behind in her correspondence. She finally took time at the San Diego Hotel on July 31 to write eight letters, the last of which went to her family in Flint, Michigan:

> Everything is going fine with us. [Malloska] left last nite for the Hawaiian Islands. He will be wearing a grass skirt and doing the Hula Hula when we arrive. The western cities have treated us in a royal fashion. Lots of things given in our honor.
>
> We are leaving for San Francisco next week. I'm anxious to get started on our trip. I have been studying navigation. I, and the other navigator, will both navigate. I'll send you all a grass skirt from Hono-lulu. Guess you could do quite a stroke of farming them.
>
> Now dear folks, my hand is getting tired of pushing this pen so will send you another edition tomorrow. Heaps love, Mildred

But no matter how much time Doran allotted to returning notes, she'd never get ahead. Newspaper reporters made huge demands of her time, hound-ing her for far more photos and interviews than any of her male competi-tors. Then, each time Doran's name and picture appeared in the newspaper it prompted young men across the country to jot mash notes to the cute, aspiring aviator and send them by post out West to reach the Flying Schoolma'am. Boys loved her grin, her wavy dark hair, her sweet mannerisms, and, perhaps most of all, her eyes, even if observers weren't quite sure what color they were, with reports listing her irises as blue, gray, and brown. Also hazel, though pictures don't seem to do her eyes or face justice, according to one newspaper reporter: "Although she photographs remarkably well, it's hard for a camera to suggest her wide hazel eyes and warm olive coloring, or the dimple that comes with her infrequent smiles."

While in San Diego, Auggy Pedlar recruited navigator Manley Lawing, a naval officer on North Island, to join the crew. Though Doran professed to be learning navigation techniques, a seasoned navigator was needed to assure the plane kept on its course. Doran, Pedlar, Lawing, and Honolulu then embarked for Oakland, eager to begin final preparations for the Dole Derby.

As *Miss Doran* cruised north over California, its tools rattled noisily on the cabin floor. The reverberations came to annoy the plane crew so much so that they tossed the offending tools out of the plane, letting them fall to the ground below. As Doran explained, "We threw them off at Long Beach because they were in the way and cluttering things up."

Sometime later in the flight the engine began misfiring. Pedlar made a landing in a field, but crashed into an unseen rut, causing a wheel and portion of the landing gear to shear away from the plane. Now Pedlar and Lawing had two problems to fix, and fewer tools with which to do it. They labored in the sunshine of Mendota, California, while Doran continued on to her destination, the *Oakland Tribune* having sent a carful of journalists down to retrieve her. The newsmen took full advantage of the long drive back to Oakland, peppering Doran with question after question so as to feed their readers details of her life and ambition to fly. Despite being the only official entrant in the Dole Derby who could neither truly fly nor navigate, Doran was by far the most popular competitor, especially among the press. "She's a pretty girl, Mildred Doran," wrote the same reporter who praised her olive complexion and wide eyes. "A thousand city editors all over the United States must have beamed in satisfaction when they first saw her photographs, sent out from Flint, shortly after the announcement was made that she would fly the Dole race."

When Martin Jensen stepped off the steamer in Los Angeles, he cast about the city, looking for a spare airplane. He found none. Or at least none that he could afford.

He was willing to pay around $10,000 for a new plane, an amount that did not inspire plane manufacturers to disrupt their assembly lines to accommodate the pilot's request for a rush job. To complicate matters, Jensen only possessed a portion of the money, as fund-raising efforts back home in Honolulu had been waylaid since he left Hawaii and his wife, Peg, was admitted to a hospital for treatment of a nervous breakdown. Despite Jensen promising glory for Honolulu if he should win the Dole Derby, few people were willing to pay for that possibility.

When Jensen had first set sail for Los Angeles, Peg tore through the Hawaiian Islands in search of benefactors. She traveled to Maui and Molokai for donations, canvassed Oahu, and staged a benefit concert as well as a performance at a Honolulu theater—all to raise cash for the Jensen Flight Fund. In the middle of this frenzy she fell victim to a breakdown, worried not only over money but the safety of her spouse. But even on bed rest Peg Jensen demonstrated tenacity and devotion to her high-flying husband. "I'm going to leave the hospital tomorrow and renew the campaign for the $10,000 Jensen fund—and we're going to get it—this week!" she exclaimed. Making good on her promise, Peg left the hospital to perform as a wingwalker in a local air show, fainting fifteen minutes after she landed.

Yet still the Jensens were coming up short. A discouraged Martin declared in San Diego that he'd be returning to Hawaii by steamship very soon, unable to find a new airplane he could afford. This pronouncement spurred Peg to redouble her efforts, and she soon raised a few thousand dollars more for Honolulu's hometown flier. These last-minute donations from a state senator and Japanese women's groups allowed Martin to stay in California and continue rooting around for an airplane. With the race less than two weeks away, he decided he better head to San Francisco and search for a plane there.

But first his official race application was due, and officials wanted to know what plane he'd be flying. Jensen fibbed when providing these details, inventing a fictitious monoplane with a forty-two-foot wing and Wright J-5 engine. The fib and $100 entry fee bought him a little time, but he knew that soon enough he'd have to present an actual plane to race officials. He hoped San Francisco contained a machine to carry him across the Pacific.

His persistence was finally rewarded when he stepped into Vance Breese's airplane factory on Seventh Street. One of Breese's customers had recently ceased payment on a plane, forfeiting a diamond ring he had put down as a deposit. The plane was now available to Jensen, said Breese, although it was only partially finished, and the Dole Derby was set to begin in ten days. With no other option, the pilot said he'd take it. "It had no wheels, no fabric, no propeller, no control wires," said Jensen. "I wish to point out that it did have an engine."

Beyond an engine, the plane was well designed, another creation of John K. Northrop, the chief engineer for the Lockheed Aircraft Company who had designed two other Dole Derby airplanes—George Hearst's Lockheed Vega

Golden Eagle and *Pabco Pacific Flyer*, a Breese monoplane and sister ship to Jensen's aircraft. Northrop, who would become one of America's leading aviation industrialists, came to design many impressive airplanes, including the first flying wing, an aircraft without a tail or fuselage, which led to the creation of the B-2 stealth bomber.

Sometime after meeting Breese, Jensen gave him a check for $15,000, just three hours before another woman arrived to purchase the plane with cash. Jensen was ecstatic. He praised Peg for her fund-raising efforts in Honolulu, especially since the plane had cost more than expected. "God bless that darling wife of mine," said Martin.

Happily for Jensen, the half-finished Breese monoplane, with its Wright J-5 engine, was almost as exactly as he had described on the race application. Even the wingspan was almost spot on, just one foot shorter than the forty-two feet he had listed. Beyond these details, the plane measured twenty-seven feet long and had a fuselage made of steel tubing and a wood-framed wing. The plane's top speed was projected to be 110 miles per hour, with a cruising speed of 84. These speeds were impressive, but certainly did not make the plane the fastest in the race.

Jensen worked day and night alongside Breese's employees to finish the plane. Since there was not enough time to fashion a new fuel tank to accommodate the heavy load of gasoline he would need to reach Hawaii, he elected to keep the stock version in place and supplement his fuel supply by carrying five-gallon gas tins in the rear cabin. At first he planned to just toss the cans overboard when emptied. But he then thought better of their disposal, reasoning that if he corked a depleted can and kept it inside, it could help keep the plane afloat in case of a water landing.

Jensen had not planned on bringing along a navigator on the flight, confident in his own abilities to reach Hawaii, despite a total lack of navigational experience. To him, a flying companion meant extra weight and less prize money. Besides, he said, he'd been "boning up" on navigation. The plane's fuel system, however, forced a change in plans. He now needed another set of hands in the plane to replenish the gasoline, someone able to lift and empty the thirty-pound tin cans in midflight. Instantly Jensen thought of taking along his wife and reliving their barnstorming days. But with the race fast approaching, ensuring Peg's timely arrival to Oakland would be a challenge. "My wife is waiting now in Honolulu for a cable from me telling her to take Saturday's boat and get here to make the flight with me," said Martin. "The ship doesn't get in [to San Francisco] until noon Friday, starting time of the race, but she suggested I have a seaplane go out, take her off and bring her to the field." Beyond the possibility of a delayed arrival, he worried that his wife might lack the strength to repeatedly replenish the fuel supply. "I don't know—I'd like to have her with me—she's a good flyer," he continued, "but I guess I'd better get a male navigator, especially when I think of [the cans] of gasoline."

Jensen had additional motivation to find a navigator other than his wife: race officials would soon be administering a navigation test to every entry, disqualifying any plane devoid of occupants able to demonstrate basic navigation know-how and celestial navigation techniques. Despite personal confidence in his abilities, he recognized it was essential that he recruit a professional navigator, as he certainly couldn't navigate by the stars. It seemed a sound decision, as earlier in the summer he boasted about being able to travel between Oakland and Honolulu in fifteen hours, failing to explain how his airplane would arrive to Hawaii ten hours faster than the trips by the army's *Bird of Paradise* and the civilian flyers in *City of Oakland*.

The Honolulu pilot knew almost no one in San Francisco, and certainly no navigators. So with just days remaining before the race, he placed a classified ad in a newspaper. The copy read, quite plainly: "Wanted, Navigator to fly with pilot to Hawaii."

When registration for the Dole Air Race ended on August 2, 1927, fifteen pilots had officially entered the contest. Six days later these pilots or their proxies gathered in the office of C. W. Saunders in the Matson Building in downtown San Francisco. The aviators were ready to draw lots and determine the race's starting lineup.

Earlier that summer James Dole had charged Saunders with leading a race committee in San Francisco, appointing him because of his experience as an executive with the Matson Navigation Company, which operated passenger and cargo ships between California and Hawaii, and because of his position as director of the California chapter of the National Aeronautics Association, the American branch of the Fédération Aéronautique Internationale, which governed all aeronautics competitions at the time. Dole also appointed a race committee in Honolulu, and together the two committees set rules for the race. In San Francisco, Saunders's chief concern was qualifying all entries and making certain each plane was airworthy, carrying sufficient fuel, and crewed by a competent pilot and navigator.

The San Francisco race committee also had to establish the race lineup. So when all parties arrived to Saunders's office on August 8, a wastebasket was placed atop a table and numbered pieces of paper placed inside. One by one these paper scraps were plucked out of the receptacle, aviators and proxies grinning or grimacing based on the numeral that greeted their eyes. *Miss Doran* nabbed the fourth spot, while Art Goebel in *Woolaroc* snatched the ninth position and Jensen the eleventh. Unlucky number thirteen fell to naval aviators George Covell and Richard Waggener, who were still in San Diego, making repairs to *Spirit of John Rodgers*. Meanwhile, the boys in *Oklahoma* grabbed the top spot and Jack Frost in his lightning-quick *Golden Eagle* settled for the fifteenth and last position.

With the race now four days away, the final stragglers began to arrive to Bay Farm Island, where all planes would depart for Hawaii. Infrastructure remained basic at the months-old Oakland airfield, with not much to boast of besides a dusty seven-thousand-foot runway along the bay. Given the lack of buildings, aviators erected tents at one end of the airfield, parking their planes outside. Meanwhile, the ever-present newspapermen took their shelter in a wooden shack.

Among these makeshift facilities a carnival-like atmosphere reigned, with pilots, navigators, mechanics, sponsors, and observers milling about the airfield, watching planes come and go, making practice runs after each tune-up. Mechanics worked outside on the planes, without protection from the sun or the considerable dust at the airfield. Technicians from the Pioneer Instrument Company and Wright Aeronautical kept busy running between aircrafts and making adjustments, as nearly all the entries relied on Pioneer compasses and Wright engines. "Night and day, every day, I'm adjusting and installing and repairing instruments," said John D. Peace of Pioneer Instrument.

Operating from their shack, newsmen covered nearly every conceivable angle to the story. One writer compared the Dole Derby to a horse race, with the pilots standing in as jockeys, the navigators as trainers, and the planes as the galloping thoroughbreds. "This race should be the greatest sky race on any track," said the report. "Every ether steed should be primed at post time." The article even facilitated gambling, with three favorites—*Golden Eagle*, *Miss Doran*, and *El Encanto*—listed as even bets, though it's hard to deduce any scientific reasoning behind these selections. Poor Martin Jensen and his unfinished airplane faced forty to one odds. Livingston Irving and his *Pabco Pacific Flyer* fared better in the oddsmaker's eyes, given a two-to-one shot: "*Pacific Flyer*, with 'Lone Eagle' Irving handling the reins and probable rains, will be backed heavily."

Among the Dole birds, as the papers began calling the aviators, Irving was regarded as the Lone Eagle because of his insistence on flying to Hawaii by himself. Irving served in the Lafayette Escadrille during World War I, joining a squadron of American pilots fighting and flying for the French Air Service prior to the United States entering the conflict. Lately he worked for the Paraffine Companies, makers of paints and roofing materials, which sponsored his entry into the Dole Derby, buying him an orange Breese monoplane named *Pabco Pacific Flyer* in honor of the company. Instead of taking a navigator along, Irving intended to bring a radio receiver aboard and follow the army's radio signal to Hawaii, using celestial navigation only if necessary. A radio set, he knew, weighed less than a human navigator and wouldn't clamor for a share of the prize money, either.

But for the other Dole birds, it was clear that only cuckoos would fly to Hawaii alone. Jack Frost chose Gordon Scott of Santa Monica, California, to accompany him as navigator, prizing the twenty-six-year-old for his knowledge of the sea and air. Scott, who worked as an engineer for Douglas Aircraft Company, had recently competed in a yacht race between Los Angeles and Hawaii, navigating a boat to the islands and back. *Golden Eagle*'s sponsor, the Hearst newspaper empire, applauded the selection, as both Scott's and Frost's surnames were short and would fit well in any headlines they published about the men. And Frost was so pleased with his flying companion and aircraft that he shrugged off a potential omen of bad luck when the US Department of Commerce awarded *Golden Eagle* its experimental license. "Your number, Jack, will be NX-913—you haven't any objections to the 13 in that number, have you?" said Walter Parkin, an inspector with the Commerce Department.

"Heck, no!" said Frost, smiling. "As a matter of fact, I've got a police badge with number 13 in it. There'll be about 13 starters when this race begins, and we've got to land the 13th of the month—what's one more 13 in my life?"

Similarly giddy, and also goofy, was "Lone Star Bill" Erwin, also known as "the fat boy from Texas." After arriving in Oakland following his tortuous journey from Dallas, when he nearly collided with mountains and was forced down at least twice due to mechanical mishaps, Erwin learned race officials were forbidding his twenty-year-old wife from serving as his navigator. Contestants needed to be twenty-one years of age, said race officials, who were perhaps also uncomfortable with the fact that Connie Erwin was pregnant.

In Connie's stead would go Alvin "Ike" Eichwaldt, a mariner and navy veteran who lived with his mother in nearby Hayward, California, when he wasn't at sea. Erwin and Eichwaldt, both veterans of World War I, formed a fast friendship at the Oakland airfield as they prepared *Dallas Spirit* for the race. While tooling around the airplane, Erwin quickly bestowed a nickname on his new navigator: "Old I.A.O.D."

"Stands for In Addition to Other Duties," explained Erwin a few days before the race. "Every time I think of something else we ought to do, I ask Eichwaldt to do it, I.A.O.D."

After playfully calling Erwin a "nut," Eichwaldt asked for clarification of his many duties. Who, Eichwaldt asked Erwin, was responsible for paddling the life raft in case of an ocean landing? "Me!" said Erwin. "That's one job you won't have to do, Al. Because if you don't navigate me to Honolulu I'll see that you never get on that raft, so you won't have to work the paddles."

Continuing in the same vein, Erwin told a crowd he had just one paddle for his life raft. When Eichwaldt was hired as navigator, Erwin obtained a second paddle. "For Eichwaldt?" someone asked.

"No: to hit Eichwaldt with if I have to use the other one to paddle."

A gentle threat of violence was also heard from the crew of *Miss Doran*, which had finally reached the Oakland airport after its breakdown in Mendota. Since arriving to Bay Farm Island, *Miss Doran*'s navigator, Manley Lawing, failed navigation tests and was disqualified from the race. Navy lieutenant Vilas R. Knope, stationed at Naval Air Station San Diego, was soon hired to take his place. While Knope was initially a stranger to Auggy Pedlar and Mildred Doran, he did spy two familiar faces in Oakland. The navigators of *El Encanto* and *City of Peoria*, Kenneth C. Hawkins and Ralph C. Lowes, had graduated with Knope from the US Naval Academy in 1920.

Knope established a quick rapport with his new crewmates. Soon after being hired, the navigator stalked the airfield with a long stick in his hands, a pin protruding from one end and a feather attached to the other. He called this device the Auggy Agitator, and then offered an explanation: "If Auggy gets sleepy I reach forward from my cabin, across the gas tanks, and tickle him with the feather."

So what about the pin, people asked.

"Auggy might get too sleepy," said Knope.

While Knope was recognizable for his intimidating agitator, "Straw Hat" Pedlar was easily identified by his plaid knickers, mackinaw jacket, and distinctive headwear. At twenty-four years old, he was the youngest pilot competing in the race. He was also among the most energetic and lively of the pilots, observed to be "a bundle of optimism" and the "gayest showman of the Dole Derby." He flitted about the airfield, offering thousand-dollar bets that he would be the first to arrive to Hawaii. "I have two advantages. One is I'm absolutely fearless," said Pedlar. His second advantage, he added, was traveling with Mildred Doran, "the prettiest little pigeon on wings."

The jolly crew of *Miss Doran*: (left to right) US Navy lieutenant Vilas R. Knope, "Flying Schoolma'am" Mildred Doran, and John "Auggy" Pedlar. *Courtesy of the Hawaii Department of Transportation Airports*

Despite Pedlar's attraction to Doran, their relationship was strictly platonic. Doran dismissed any chance of romance, at least at this point in their young lives. "I admire Auggy more than any man I ever knew. Nothing can ever change our friendship—but, truly, we're not in love with each other," said Doran. "I don't want to fall in love and marry, and neither does Auggy. He and I both want to do a lot of things, see a lot of things."

As race day neared, Doran still outshone all her competitors. The recipient of many invitations from admiring fans, she was wheeled about town, "caught in a social whirl," quickly becoming a favorite of the San Francisco press and national reporters who gathered each day at the Oakland airport. Like Pedlar, Doran turned heads with her attire: an olive drab flying suit that resembled a military uniform. Tailored for her in Michigan, the ensemble featured a military-style coat, tight-fitting riding pants, and tall, tan riding boots, though sometimes she wore shoes with golf stockings instead. Accessories of a flying cap and Sam Browne belt, which stretched across her waist and shoulder, completed the look, much to tailor Carl T. Walter's satisfaction. "Miss Doran was a lady with a fine build, with more than average beauty," said Walter. "When the whole job was complete, she was truly an eye catcher."

Doran was well aware of her feminine charm and the unique advantages it brought her in the realm of aviation. "Why is it people always expect you to act noisy and masculine if you are interested in flying? Femininity is a girl's biggest asset, no matter what kind of work she does, nor what kind of sport she chooses for a hobby," she said, explaining how her looks obtained her free airplane rides. "Why, if I hadn't been—well, feminine—I never would have had all the lovely hours in the air which I managed to obtain at Flint. I never even would have had this trip."

Beyond good looks, Doran's breezy demeanor and frank admissions endeared her to strangers. She was the girl next door, but exciting! "I'm not interested in business or politics," said Doran. "Most girls are, or pretend they are. But I don't even care who becomes president! This flight is all I care about now!"

Adding even more to her allure was her nonchalance, even in the face of so much media attention in the lead-up to an exceedingly dangerous flight across the Pacific. "I'm not a bit worried about the flight although I suppose I should be," she remarked. Her aloofness extended to her romantic life, where she liked to keep the upper hand. When asked about a handful of fraternity pins she proudly wore on the breast of her flying jacket, where military commendations would normally be displayed, Doran acted the minx. "They represent dead scalps and show what I got out of a college education. They *were* all fine fellows," she said, emphasizing the past tense.

While Doran gallivanted around San Francisco, Martin Jensen worked furiously to finish his airplane while also interviewing candidates for the navigator position he had advertised. Despite the dangers that could easily be imagined on a 2,400-mile overnight trip across an ocean to small islands, many people responded with interest to Jensen. In order to vet the candidates, he enlisted a navy navigator to question the men and women seeking to become his flying mate. Some were easier to dismiss than others.

Among the hopefuls was a Boy Scout who tried to convince Jensen that his use of a compass on treks through the local woods was sufficient navigational training for finding the Hawaiian Islands. Jensen passed on this applicant, just as he passed on the aspiring twenty-year-old starlet who was convinced that her participation in the Dole Race would assure her a place in Hollywood movies. Of course, neither satisfied the age requirement for the race, anyway. Then there was an elderly woman who conceded that while she possessed no navigational abilities herself, she did have full faith in the ability of the pilot.

Jensen soon settled on Paul Schluter as the best candidate, despite the fact that the thirty-seven-year-old, who worked as a navigator aboard a merchant ship, had never been in an airplane. Just to make sure Schluter had the stomach for the race, Jensen took him aloft in his finished plane. Instructing Schluter to "get a firm grip," he then performed a series of aggressive aerial maneuvers. "He stayed with me," said Jensen, "and took the stunts in stride."

After failing to spook his newfound navigator in the air, Jensen tried one other way to scare him off: he confided to Schluter that he would not be able to pay him for his navigational help. He already owed too many debts relating to the purchase and fine-tuning of his plane. Even if they placed first, he explained, there would be nothing left over for pilot or navigator. Schluter said he was not flying for any monetary prize. "I will go for the glory," he told Jensen, impressed with the pilot's confidence.

Like Jensen, Art Goebel also fretted about finding the islands by himself. But unlike his competitor from Honolulu, Goebel did not need to advertise for a flying companion and navigator; already he had received plenty of offers. As the Tinseltown flyer prepared for the race, he pulled a sheaf of telegrams from his pocket and detailed their contents to the press, explaining that assorted gals, aged anywhere from about six to sixty years old, had invited themselves along for the trip. Three of these telegrams came from a single Hollywood actress. The first communicated greetings and well wishes. The second volunteered the actress as a passenger aboard the plane. And then the third made the same request in more pointed fashion. "Will you take me with you, Art?" she pleaded. "I am serious about this."

Goebel's answer, to every woman, was no. "Girls and aviation don't mix," he said, having just arrived in Oakland with his new airplane, *Woolaroc*. "Wouldn't take a woman under any circumstances," he added. "Auggy Pedlar sure is braver than I am, taking that little school teacher with him." In fact, Goebel declared, "I wouldn't even marry as long as I'm flying. I feel so certain of that. There's a story out that I'm engaged to a mighty fine girl in Beverly Hills who helped me with my financial backing. Well, I'm not, and what's more, I never will be engaged, either!"

Casting about for a navigator, he spread the word at Naval Air Station San Diego that he was in need of a flying companion. When Lieutenant William V. Davis Jr. heard the call, he responded quickly, barely beating out a rival flier. The Dole Derby was a hot topic of conversation at the military base, with a good portion of the competitors currently serving or having served in the navy. "We all wanted a crack at it," said Davis, twenty-five, who had graduated from the US Naval Academy three years earlier. "Knowing Art's reputation for physical strength and nerve, and his skill and experience at the controls, I felt no hesitancy about joining him in any aerial venture."

Goebel hired Davis on August 9, 1927—just three days before the race was to begin. Davis immediately put in a request to the navy to take leave and packed clothes in a suitcase. Then he gathered flight data about the trip across the ocean and consulted with one of the few people who had made the trip successfully, navy lieutenant Byron Connell, who piloted and sailed the flying boat PN-9 No. 1 to Hawaii two years earlier with Commander John Rodgers. After his discussions with Connell, and knowing that the army's radio beacons would be operating, Davis felt confident he could hit his target within thirty to forty miles.

Also planning to leave Naval Air Station San Diego for the Dole Race were Lieutenants George D. Covell and Richard S. Waggener. Davis had hoped to catch a ride to Oakland with them aboard *Spirit of John Rodgers* and then meet Goebel at the airfield on Bay Farm Island. But as Covell and Waggener prepared to depart the morning of August 10, Davis was still awaiting approval of his leave request. Hours later a message of approval was finally transmitted from Washington, DC, and Davis hurried to the airfield, only to watch Covell and Waggener taking off into a hazy and foggy sky.

As it turned out, he was fortunate to have missed the flight; fifteen minutes later the eerily named *Spirit of John Rodgers* collided into a cliff at Point Loma, the peninsula separating San Diego Bay and the Pacific Ocean. The plane exploded against the cliff, its fuselage and occupants incinerated as it crashed down into a gully. Thick fog was blamed for the accident.

No matter the loss, Davis resolved to race to Hawaii. Worried he would not reach Oakland in time, he chartered a private plane to Los Angeles and then caught a train to San Francisco. "Their price for the [plane] ride staggered my financial standing considerably," he said, "but it had to be done."

Sitting comfortably in the seat of a train car chugging north, he reflected on his hasty departure, the crash of *Spirit of John Rodgers*, and his grim interactions that morning with fellow naval aviators. When he had packed his belongings hours earlier, friends and squadron mates stopped by his room to chat and say farewell, some unable to resist teasing Davis. Most conversations went like this:

"Hear you're flying to Honolulu," said a chum.

"Yeah, hope so," said Davis.

"If you decide not to go, how's for your place?"

"Oh, I'm going all right."

"Then, how's for your khaki shirts if you don't come back?"

The morbid kidding struck a nerve, even in a fearless military flier. "I didn't sleep much that night," confessed Davis.

The Dole Air Race was still two days away when its first competitors died. *Spirit of John Rodgers* took off at a sluggish pace, leaving observers to wonder whether the plane's two occupants fell victim to poor visibility or a mechanical problem that prevented the plane from climbing. The scorched wreckage at Point Loma left few clues behind.

Five days earlier there was tragedy close to Oakland, when a twenty-six-year-old student from Stanford University crashed and died in front of a crowd that had gathered at Bay Farm Island to see the Dole racers arrive. While flying one hundred feet above the nearby Alameda airport, the left wing of the plane suddenly crumpled, causing the aircraft to plunge to earth. Doctors claimed every bone in the student's body was broken.

On August 11, 1927, the eve of the race and just one day after *Spirit of John Rodgers* slammed into Point Loma in San Diego, another Dole Derby entrant fell from the sky. After a brisk trip north from Long Beach in which *Pride of Los Angeles* averaged a speed of one hundred miles per hour, the triplane faltered in its final approach to the Oakland airport, dropping into San Francisco Bay just before reaching the airfield. The plane was wrecked when it collided with the water, but its three-man crew was spared any injury. A fireman on shore soon tied a rope around his waist and swam to the soggy Stack of Wheats, rescuing crew and airship, the latter of which was hauled to shore for salvage.

And on race day, August 12, hours before the scheduled takeoff, the unusual twin-tailed, tandem-engine airplane *Angel of Los Angeles* made its final flight. Already delayed and unlikely to compete in the Dole Race, pilot Arthur Rogers was testing his plane above Los Angeles when he lost control. As his wife held their baby and watched from the airport below, Rogers leaped from the falling plane and pulled open his parachute. Yet he was too close to the ground; he crumpled to the earth before the parachute could fill with air and slow his fall. Another Dole Derby contestant had perished.

Already the previous accidents, as well as the general nonchalance of the remaining competitors, had unnerved race officials. They weren't alone. Lloyd's of London refused to insure any of the flights, characterizing them as "entirely too dangerous." "That old story that Lloyd's will insure anything is all the bunk, you know," said Charles Vornholt, a Lloyd's representative in San Francisco. "Lloyd's is in business to make money, not lose it."

After navy lieutenants George Covell and Richard Waggener perished within *Spirit of John Rodgers*, an editorial in the *San Francisco Chronicle* warned that the success of the recent flights to Hawaii concealed the many dangers of the transpacific crossing:

> Their mishap comes just in time to drop a necessary note of caution
> into the preparations for the August marathon to the islands. [Army

lieutenant Lester] Maitland's flight perhaps made it appear a little too easy. [Ernie] Smith's gas failure goes to show that it's not easy. He and [Emory] Bronte were really very lucky. A quart or two less of gasoline and they might have come down in the sea. And forced as they were to land in a tree their guardian angels were surely on the job there.

With an eye to preventing further accidents and injury, the newspaper urged race officials to weed out any fliers unfit for the long ocean hop. "The Hawaiian islands make a very small target to hit on the middle of the Pacific, and, aside from pure chance, only competent navigation can make the bullseye," said the *Chronicle*. "The Hawaiian flight is for nerve, daring, skill, and adequate equipment. There is no place in it for foolhardiness. Let us hope that the prize race will have some supervision that will prevent any reckless participation."

The responsibility of qualifying the final lineup of competitors fell to navy lieutenant Ben H. Wyatt. As a 1917 graduate of the US Naval Academy and a well-respected pilot and aerial navigator stationed at Naval Air Station San Diego, Wyatt was well versed in the challenges the Dole birds would face as they cruised toward Hawaii. "This flight is something different from other trans-oceanic flights. This is a supreme test of aerial navigation," he said. "The planes are shooting at a target 300 miles wide in the middle of the Pacific ocean and an error of but a couple of degrees on the part of the navigator would send a plane at least 200 miles off the course, and such would spell disaster for the fliers."

In an effort to minimize the chance of failure, race officials set forth a number of requirements to be met before takeoff. Planes were obligated to carry a 10 percent gasoline reserve and make a test flight carrying half a load of fuel. Pilots were required to undergo a physical examination and submit their flying credentials for review. And Wyatt asked navigators to fly a compass course above the Bay Area to demonstrate their abilities. But as race day quickly approached, few of the airplanes were qualified to compete. The majority of the competitors had only arrived in Oakland in the last few days, their planes in need of repairs after tough flights across the country or up the California coast. Beyond missing parts, some of these planes were also awaiting the last-minute addition of navigators. Others needed auxiliary fuel tanks installed to meet the gasoline requirements, or spare compasses put on board, or the compasses oriented, or damaged landing gear fixed . . . the list was long and time was short. The hasty atmosphere worried race officials in San Francisco so much that on the eve of the flight they cabled James Dole and their race committee counterparts in Honolulu, recommending the race be postponed. "The planes and participants which have thus far presented themselves are not now properly equipped or qualified," said the San Francisco race committee. "To start August 12, the scheduled date, would present hazards never contemplated by the donor or the committee and the result could easily be unfavorable."

Privately, committee chairman C. W. Saunders used much stronger language, claiming an imminent takeoff would be "nothing short of suicide." His comment mirrored the feelings of Hawaiian Pineapple Company executive H. E. MacConaughey, who penned a panicky letter from San Francisco to his boss in Honolulu two days before the race was to begin:

> I am not writing much of anything by this mail for the simple reason that I have not had time. I can say to you from the bottom of my heart that I will be glad when this flight is over. There are a lot of things I should like to write about, and after Friday they will be old. Frankly, I am hoping that the majority of the planes entered will be disqualified, and it will be better for all of us if they are.

MacConaughey detailed a few of the incidents that were causing his distress. Infighting among the race committee had been distracting. One navigator arrived drunk to his qualifying test. And the other night, a federal aviation official called on MacConaughey at his home in an attempt to lobby Dole to cancel the derby and perhaps sponsor an air race across the country instead. "He said if it were in his hands he would call the flight off because of the fact that some of these hair-brained [sic] pilots were going into the flight with planes ill prepared and without a realization of the difficulty of their undertaking," wrote MacConaughey.

When pilots and navigators heard of a possible delay, many were hopeful for a reprieve and the chance to better prepare their planes. A few competitors, however, were upset by the delay, considering it unsporting and capricious. A day before the race was supposed to begin, Auggy Pedlar protested angrily to Wyatt, complaining about the potential postponement and Wyatt's administration of the navigation tests, which *Miss Doran* had previously failed. "Let those who are ready to go, go," said Pedlar.

"You know you were 40 degrees off," said Wyatt, mentioning how badly *Miss Doran* had fared during the examination.

"You know I made an appointment with you for eight this morning to make another test," Pedlar replied. "Here it is after 11, and I'm still waiting; you haven't been ready for me."

"You know you'd be a damn fool to fly now," said Wyatt, smiling.

"No, I'd not. The ship is OK. And I want my test. I want to fly," Pedlar said sorely before walking away. Later Pedlar voiced a threat: "We may go anyway, particularly if they postpone the flight for a fortnight. . . . To hell with the prize money! I have a girl to take over there, and I'm going whether there is money in it or not."

Speaking of that girl destined for Hawaii, sunny Mildred Doran was agnostic about when her eponymous airplane would leave for the islands. "It doesn't matter much when we start," she boasted, "because we're going to make it even if I have to get out and push."

But Livingston "Lone Eagle" Irving was none happier than Pedlar with Wyatt and other race officials, wiring the committee in Honolulu that "preparation is part of the competition." The sole occupant of *Pabco Pacific Flyer* confronted the increasingly unpopular navy lieutenant about disparaging comments Wyatt supposedly made to the press regarding Irving's ability to fly and navigate at the same time. "Did you say I can't fly alone?" he asked Wyatt.

"If you want to, it's all OK with me," the unflappable Wyatt responded, denying he had been critical of Irving. But when Jack Frost complained that he'd be ready to depart in *Golden Eagle* if not for the pesky navigation test he'd yet to pass with Gordon Scott, Wyatt felt compelled to defend the standards he was enforcing. "As a matter of fact, it's my personal belief that at least three or four of the navigators . . . aren't competent to act as navigators," he said, declining to name those he deemed inept.

Hours before the noontime race was to begin, San Francisco officials received a message from the islands: the Dole Air Race would go on! Race officials in Honolulu decided to ignore the recommendation from their California counterparts. Prize money was now available to the first person to fly nonstop to Hawaii.

The pilots, though, had other plans. Rather than have a chaotic and controversial beginning to the race, for which many planes and their occupants had still not officially qualified, the pilots struck a gentlemen's agreement to delay it four days. The Dole Derby, they decided, would now begin at noon on Tuesday, August, 16, 1927. Every pilot signed on to the agreement, with navigator Kenneth Hawkins of *El Encanto* predicting the racers would travel in a swarm across the ocean, no more than two miles apart from any other plane, before each pilot increased the throttle and made a mad dash to the finish line at Wheeler Field on Oahu. In the meantime, pilots, navigators, and their crews hustled to make last-minute repairs and modifications to their airplanes. They also prepared for further scrutiny from race officials, who vowed to only let professional pilots, able navigators, and sufficiently equipped airplanes into the final lineup.

MacConaughey believed close examination of the potential competitors would absolve his boss should disaster unfold during the race, writing to Dole, "In this way the responsibility is placed where it belongs, and that there can be no reaction unfavorable to you." Still, he worried for the future. The race entrants were young, cocky, and impatient, all assured they were contenders for the top prize. Unlike MacConaughey, few, if any, of these aviators fretted that Hawaii might be out of reach:

> With the usual oft-mentioned hind sight, I do not hesitate to say to you that if I had had any realization of what was coming when you made the offer, I certainly would have voted "No". If they all get there, then all of this anxiety is for nothing—which is one thing that was mentioned by Lieut. Wyatt yesterday—but if you could hear them talk you would not blame me for my anxiety.

On the morning of August 10, navy lieutenant Bill Davis opened his eyes in San Diego, where he watched *Spirit of John Rodgers* take off on its final flight, destined to slam into a fog-shrouded cliff fifteen minutes later. The next morning he awoke in San Francisco, rendezvoused with pilot Art Goebel, and traveled across the bay to the Oakland airport on Bay Farm Island. There Davis arrived right on time to witness the triplane *Pride of Los Angeles* dive into the water and cripple itself as it failed its landing attempt. Yet still Davis wanted to fly to Hawaii.

When he reached the opposite end of the airfield, he caught sight of the plane that promised to carry him across the Pacific. With its boxy blue fuselage and yellow wings, *Woolaroc* made a handsome appearance. The airplane was also intact, which was more than could be claimed about the other two Dole Derby competitors he had laid eyes on in the last twenty-four or so hours. Looking over *Woolaroc* with Goebel, Davis stated he was "highly pleased with her appearance." "A Travel Air Transport of a tried and proven model, she was a sight to gladden the eye of any pilot," he added.

He soon toured his wood-trimmed navigator's cockpit in the rear of the fuselage, which measured about four feet long and wide. A large metal fuel tank filled the center of the plane, separating pilot and navigator. There was a window on each side of the cabin, as well as a hatch on top that he could use to make celestial observations. A clothesline wrapped around two pulley wheels ran down the left side of the cabin, slipping just between the fabric of the fuselage and the fuel tank, to provide a system for Davis and Goebel to transfer written messages to each other.

Davis got to work immediately, given free rein by Goebel to modify the navigator's compartment. In contrast to some of his more freewheeling competitors in the Dole Air Race, the navy lieutenant was methodical, creating a checklist of equipment needed for him to navigate *Woolaroc* and ensuring that each component was installed correctly and performing as expected. To enable navigation by dead reckoning, Davis ensured a healthy supply of smoke bombs was stowed aboard. To navigate by the stars, he calibrated a bubble sextant. He attached a flashlight to the instrument so he could use the sextant at night, spending much time experimenting with assorted bulbs to find the perfect illumination for viewing the bubble—channeling Goldilocks when judging bulbs to be too bright or too dim. Then he tested four different radio sets, and rejected them all, before borrowing the radio Ernie Smith and Emory Bronte used in *City of Oakland* to follow the army's radio beacon. If nothing else, Davis knew this particular radio set was resilient, having survived a Pacific flight, crash landing on Molokai, and return voyage to California by steamer. With so much to do, he said the days before the race passed quickly "in a blur of impressions and feverish activity":

I had had enough training in, and experience with, the gentle art of navigation to realize that we were cramming literally weeks of work into the space of a few days. However, our determination was not so much to race to Honolulu as it was to get there, so we made it our working principle to make all the speed possible, but to allow no mistakes, and take no chances, never "That'll do," but "That's the best that can be done."

The four-day postponement of the race was crucial for Davis to get *Woolaroc* in order. Progress was slow going, especially since many modifications affected the four compasses on board. Any addition or relocation of a metal object on the plane threatened to bend the compass needles and disrupt accurate readings. With every change made to *Woolaroc*, the plane had to be taxied atop a compass rose painted on the airfield and turned in each direction, making necessary compass adjustments and recording any deviations. The process could be exhausting. "The compasses had to be checked and rechecked, the plane being swung around through successive arcs of azimuth to find the error of each of the four compasses on every heading," said Davis. "A new arrangement of any apparatus, a change in the radio, and the compasses had to be gone over again—a tedious, tiresome job, and every minute precious."

Davis's constant presence about and within *Woolaroc* did not escape attention. While he had hoped to delay the announcement of his participation in the race until he told his family on the eve of takeoff, the pushy press contingent at the Oakland airport would not be so patient. Finally, reporters stopped believing Davis when he claimed to be only a mechanic. "I was finally forced to break down and confess my name, rank, age, color, home town, previous condition of servitude, and favorite flower," said the navigator. "I asked one charming young lady reporter, after she had extracted every possible item of my past history and future hopes, just what she intended doing with all this miscellaneous information. She answered, 'Oh I know it's a lot of bother, but we have to have all this dope on you birds for obituaries.'" The reporter's honesty was unsettling. Her story also forced Davis's hand, requiring him to notify his family back home in Georgia before they read about him in the newspaper.

The Davises, at home in Atlanta, were chatting about the race. The much-publicized Dole Derby became a topic of conversation in many American households at the time, including theirs. Flying to Hawaii sounded exotic and exciting, but also dangerous. Who would be crazy enough to risk their lives on such a flight? Thomas Davis thought of his aviator brother stationed in San Diego. "I am glad that the navy isn't entering the race, as I would hate to see Bill in it," said Thomas. At that very moment a telegram arrived from Bill. He advised his family he was in San Francisco and that he would be competing in the Dole Derby, serving as a navigator to pilot Art Goebel aboard *Woolaroc*. Upon hearing this news Thomas pivoted a bit, attempting to put a positive spin on his brother's announcement. "Well, Goebel is a good conservative flyer," he rationalized. "It's only these stunt flyers that get into trouble, so Bill is safe enough." Then William Sr. read part of a newspaper report that said Goebel was known as a Hollywood stunt flyer. After that, says another family member, "Thomas attempted no more helpful remarks!"

But the Davis family would have been pleased with Goebel, had they known his daredevil instincts and considerable courage would soon save both aviators' lives during a test flight two days before the race. Taking to the air for the navigation test required by race officials, Goebel and Davis embarked on a fifty-mile course over the ocean. The flight started poorly, with the landing gear's shock absorbers damaged at takeoff. "I could feel them slip and [realized] that unless repaired," said Goebel, "serious [damage] would result in landing."

While Davis sat in the navigator's cabin at the back of the plane, oblivious to the damaged landing gear and Goebel's concerns, Goebel decided to make repairs immediately. After tying *Woolaroc*'s controls in place to ensure a straight and steady flight above the waves, he opened his cockpit door in midair, leaned out of the plane, and lowered his inverted body toward the landing gear. With one hand holding on to the plane and the other gripping a pocketknife, he hacked away at the housing surrounding the shock absorbers so he could repair the damage, all while the improvised autopilot system kept *Woolaroc* cruising steadily.

Forty-five minutes later, after surviving a jolt from an air pocket that nearly tossed him from the plane, Goebel finished making the fix. The pilot then lifted himself back into the tiny cockpit, resumed operation of the plane, and returned *Woolaroc* to the airport. The men had passed the test. It was only after landing that Goebel could inform Davis about the risky midflight repairs he had made. Davis didn't seem perturbed; he was grateful the rest of *Woolaroc*'s parts and equipment had performed well.

That same day, Martin Jensen and Paul Schluter took flight for their own navigation test. The duo earned a near-perfect rating, which was especially impressive considering Schluter had never been inside an airplane until a week earlier. Based on these results, race official Lieutenant Ben Wyatt made the impulsive Jensen promise to listen to Schluter and obey his navigational instructions. "And if you do you will get there," said Wyatt.

The certification of these final aviators meant at least eight planes would compete in the Dole Derby. A ninth entrant, *City of Peoria*, was also a possible contender, though officials were unhappy with the biplane's limited fuel capacity and threatened to disqualify it, and Colonel Pineapple the owl, unless it was augmented.

During the race's four-day delay, Jensen had heeded race officials' advice and improved his own fuel system. Discarding the forty-seven tin cans he had planned to loosely stack in the navigator's cabin, he installed large permanent auxiliary tanks, increasing his fuel supply to 405 gallons. The modification was viewed as an obvious safety improvement in and of itself, but all the more so because Schluter had a reputation as a chain-smoker.

To celebrate their qualification for the Dole Derby, Jensen arranged a ceremony at the airfield to christen his hastily constructed new plane. Canary yellow with a flower lei painted across the nose, the airplane featured big red letters on each side of its fuselage, spelling out its name: *Aloha*. As a stringed orchestra played nearby and performers sang Hawaiian songs and danced a hula, Oakland beauty queen Ruby Smith, clad in grass skirt, cracked a bottle of seawater from Waikiki Beach across the airplane's nose. "I now christen you, *Aloha*," said Smith, who proceeded to stand on a wing and sprinkle the remaining water on Jensen and Schluter. When a reporter pointed out that the bottle of Hawaiian seawater resembled a container Jensen had filled from a hotel room faucet that morning, the *Aloha* pilot could only smile in reply.

Later he sat in the plane's open-air cockpit as messages of support from Hawaii were read aloud. "Tell the people of Hawaii that I'm flying for them and that I will do my best to get to Wheeler Field first," he said in response. "I think I can do it." The aviator then took care to thank his wife, Peg, who had worked through sickness to help secure a plane. "My wife did it all. She stayed there in Honolulu and raised all that money," said Jensen. "I'll make the hop to Honolulu or die in the attempt. But I will not fail. She'll be there to meet me and greet me when I land at Wheeler Field. God bless her soul."

Jensen was hardly the only flier feeling bullish. Pilots and navigators for the Dole Derby laughed and joked as they milled about the airport before race day. They hardly acknowledged the chance of failure, though the palpable nervousness of some hinted at hidden apprehension. Overwhelmingly, though, a "gay and nonchalant spirit" prevailed among the "company of gallant gentlemen" at the airport, said one news report. Almost every aviator felt assured they would safely cross the Pacific, and a number of competitors boasted of their plans for the tropics after claiming the top prize.

Dole Derby competitors (left to right) Kenneth Hawkins, Mildred Doran, Norman Goddard, and Livingston Irving enjoying an escape from the Oakland airfield on August 15, 1927, the day before the race. *Courtesy of the California History Room, California State Library, Sacramento, California*

"When I get to Honolulu I'm going to find the dancing party wearing the reed skirt and thank her for guiding me in, because when I pass the halfway mark I'm going to listen for the rustling in the breezes and use it as a beacon," said Livingston Irving, the pilot and navigator of *Pabco Pacific Flyer*.

Navy lieutenant Kenneth Hawkins, navigator for *El Encanto*, declared he'd use his margin of victory to familiarize himself with Hawaiian water sports: "When we get over to Honolulu we're going to reserve rooms for the rest of the racers. After that I'm going to rent a surf board and an outrigger canoe and practice up so I can show the boys a few tricks when they arrive."

Pilot Jack Frost of *Golden Eagle* was like-minded, asking, "Please have the executives in Honolulu have their surf boards ready, because Gordon Scott, my navigator, and myself, want to try out surf riding." Not only would *Golden Eagle* reach Hawaii, boasted Frost, the plane would cross the Pacific in record time, shaving at least four hours from the previous flights by *Bird of Paradise* and *City of Oakland*. "I expect to make this flight in from twenty to twenty-one hours," said Frost. "And I expect to have a late breakfast in Honolulu tomorrow morning."

Goebel predicted that in a day's time he'd be wearing a thick necklace of congratulatory leis. Jensen imagined biting into a thick chicken dinner he claimed to have reserved in Honolulu. Bennett Griffin, pilot of *Oklahoma*, dreamed of completing the flight "and having my life's ambition realized." And Auggy Pedlar, the young pilot of *Miss Doran*, was eager to finish the race and take in some sights. "I don't know just how I'm going to feel physically when I land in Honolulu," said Pedlar, "but I hope they hold the bands down until I get some sleep. We all have been wanting to look at a few of Hawaii's attractions and we are going to make the best of our visit after we get over there."

As the crew of *Miss Doran* prepared to leave the Oakland airport a day before the race, Pedlar teased Mildred Doran, asking that she not spend too much time in the morning primping for the cameras. "No, I won't keep the race waiting," Doran replied. "I'll be first in the plane and we'll be first in Honolulu." The Flying Schoolma'am's father in Michigan echoed her bravado, affirming his daughter's grit. "My daughter is not yellow, nor is there one member in the family with a yellow streak; the Doran name stands for courage," said William Doran Sr.

Hardly any competitors expressed concerns for their own safety. No one had died in the previous flights to Hawaii, so why would the Dole Derby be any different? The exception was Davis, the *Woolaroc* navigator who had already watched two Dole Derby planes take their final flights and who unwittingly traveled for forty-five minutes aboard an airplane whose pilot temporarily abandoned the cockpit. "Scared? Sure," said Davis. "Anyone that doesn't feel a few chills along the spinal column at the prospect of starting out over a 2,400-mile expanse of water with only the perfect functioning of a man-made, and therefore fallible piece of mechanism between himself and eternity, is made of sterner stuff than I am."

Early in the morning on August 16, 1927, as fog hung high in the sky, heavy machinery rumbled up and down the runway at the Oakland airport. First the Caterpillar tractors rolled the seven-thousand-foot runway, smoothing any bumps. Next came the water trucks, spraying mist onto the dirt airfield in order to limit the dust eight speeding airplanes would kick up. In just a few hours, at noon sharp, the Dole Air Race to Hawaii was scheduled to begin. In the opinion of one reporter for the *San Francisco Examiner*, never before had there been such a consequential and thrilling contest. "The greatest race in the history of the world—San Francisco to Honolulu by air! The biggest sporting event ever since the Roman gladiators went into the arena—a score of men and one woman playing on a tenuous line between life and death," said the newspaper, which happened to be a sponsor of the airplane *Golden Eagle*.

As many as one hundred thousand spectators were estimated to be in attendance at the Bay Farm Island airfield. They lined the length of each side of the runway, packed tight in a crowd twenty-five feet deep, standing in front of rows and rows of parked automobiles. Motorcycle policemen zipped up and down the runway sidelines to keep order. Public interest in the race was so intense that Oakland had forbid its police officers from requesting any leave in the days before the Dole Derby, requiring all hands on deck.

The airport crowd represented just a portion of the air race audience that morning. As was the case with the transpacific flights attempted in the previous two years, every bit of high ground around San Francisco had been claimed on the morning of race day. Each of San Francisco's storied seven hills were thronged by aviation enthusiasts, many of whom clutched binoculars. Others gathered on rooftops, in skyscrapers, along the Great Highway, or atop the upper deck of ferries in San Francisco Bay to watch the air race begin. And within the Presidio, patients at the Letterman Army Hospital and US Marine Hospital were rolled outside in their wheelchairs to be given a view of the race. Patients in worse health were moved beside windows inside the hospitals, allowed to catch a glimpse through the glass. "All San Francisco was a grandstand," said the *Chronicle*, estimating half a million people watched the Dole Air Race unfold.

Elsewhere, people read the morning paper or tuned in to the radio to learn the latest about the air race. From Washington, DC, came the approval of the federal government, as voiced by US secretary of commerce Herbert Hoover:

> The Department of Commerce is not interested in air races as races. Flights by inferior pilots in inferior planes are serious setbacks to aviation. [But] I believe the race from San Francisco to Hawaii, while it is a sporting competition, nevertheless has its value. The pilots qualified for the event are capable men. Their ships have been expertly examined by the Department of Commerce. Under such supervision, flights such as the San Francisco–Hawaii race ... should result in benefits in trans-Pacific and other oceanic aerial navigation.

As the morning passed, attention focused on the single airplane, *Oklahoma*, resting alone at the starting line. By 10:00 AM *Oklahoma*'s rivals had rolled into place, these other aircraft arranged in a semicircle behind the starting line. Missing from their ranks was *City of Peoria*, which had been officially disqualified that morning for insufficient fuel capacity, much to the annoyance of its investors. That left eight planes ready to fly to Hawaii, each due to leave two minutes apart once the starter fired his gun at noontime. The race lineup, which had been revised since the Dole Derby pilots had pulled lots from a wastebasket, featured the following contenders:

1. *Oklahoma*, piloted by Bennett Griffin and navigated by Al Henley
2. *El Encanto*, piloted by Norman Goddard and navigated by navy lieutenant Kenneth Hawkins

3. *Pabco Pacific Flyer*, piloted and navigated by Livingston Irving
4. *Golden Eagle*, piloted by Jack Frost and navigated by Gordon Scott
5. *Miss Doran*, piloted by Auggy Pedlar, navigated by navy lieutenant Vilas Knope, and carrying passenger Mildred Doran
6. *Aloha*, piloted by Martin Jensen and navigated by Paul Schluter
7. *Woolaroc*, piloted by Art Goebel and navigated by navy lieutenant William V. Davis Jr.
8. *Dallas Spirit*, piloted by Bill Erwin and navigated by Alvin Eichwaldt

All eight airplanes were powered by the same type of motor that pushed *Bird of Paradise* and *City of Oakland* across the Pacific, the reliable Wright Whirlwind J-5. All these planes flew on a single wing save *Miss Doran*, the only biplane. When it came to communications systems, four planes carried two-way radio equipment, three planes opted against hauling any radio devices, and one plane, *Golden Eagle*, featured a receiving set only, meaning it could hear radio messages but not respond.

The first pilot to arrive at the airfield that morning was Martin Jensen, who promptly took *Aloha* on test flights while carrying two-thirds of his fuel supply—probably the heaviest load he attempted in any of his practice runs before the race. Despite all the assorted race preparations at the Oakland airport in the previous few weeks, few, if any, of the aviators had attempted taking off with a full fuel load. As other aviators' fiery mishaps had demonstrated in recent years, taking off in an airplane stuffed to the gills with gasoline could be extremely dangerous. And it was even more hazardous to try to land such a heavily laden aircraft, which was why the Dole birds waited until race day to see if their fully loaded planes could actually take to the sky.

Jensen and navigator Schluter had spent the night at the Clift Hotel in San Francisco. Schluter couldn't catch a wink and paced the hotel room all night, but Jensen slept solidly, waking up energized and giddy. Leaving the hotel the next morning with sixteen sandwiches packed into a bag for the flight, the upbeat pilot crowed to the front desk clerks, "I'm a homing pigeon, going home." His confidence was just as pronounced at the airport. When asked if he had bought life insurance or made a will in preparation for the flight, Jensen asked, "What the hell for?"

Other aviators soon followed him, arriving by police escort so as to cut through the thick automobile traffic and large crowds that had descended on the Oakland airport. "The biggest kick I got before leaving Oakland was to ride in an automobile at 65 miles an hour preceded by a motorcycle cop with a loud and strident siren," said *Woolaroc*'s navigator, Bill Davis. "We finally wormed through the biggest crowd of people I ever saw in my life and reached the side of our crate."

Davis said he slept soundly the night before, "without a care in the world—which was simply the reaction of five days' frantic effort and worry." But a wake-up call the next morning from a member of *Woolaroc*'s flight team rattled the navigator's calmness, as Davis did not appreciate the "solemn air about him." Then, at breakfast, he sensed more of the same foreboding. Every waiter was extremely attentive, he observed, but the staff all performed their jobs with the "same solemn air that had chilled the atmosphere around the fellow that had wakened me." "Why all this 'last few moments' attitude—was it really as bad as all that? Had I underestimated some difficulty?" he wondered. "Why did I keep thinking of the title of that infernal book *Last Days of a Condemned Man*?" That morning's breakfast, said Davis, was "the least enjoyable meal of my life."

His spirits recovered as he reached the airport, leaving the funereal hotel behind for the frenzied exuberance of the crowd gathered on Bay Farm Island. Upon reaching *Woolaroc*, he double-checked every instrument and piece of equipment in the plane. Learning from the experience of the *Bird of Paradise* army aviators, Davis ascertained that sandwiches and coffee were aboard the plane and that he knew exactly where to find them. Then he smoked cigarettes and chatted, counting down the minutes until noontime.

Other aviators were busy saying farewell to friends and family. Livingston Irving of *Pabco Pacific Flyer* was seen off by his wife and young daughter. Pilot Bennett Griffin of *Oklahoma* said goodbye to his fiancée, Juanita Herod, whom he had attempted to marry the day before, only to be told that California required a three-day waiting period for a marriage license. Their plans thwarted, Herod cheerfully agreed to take a steam liner to Hawaii and marry Griffin in the islands.

Alongside *Golden Eagle*, pilot Jack Frost and navigator Gordon Scott received a visit from George Hearst's wife, Blanche, who handed the aviators velvet-lined boxes. Inside his box Frost discovered a gold miniature of *Golden Eagle* with his initials engraved on the wings. Scott received a gold compass.

The favored winners of the Dole Derby also received a surprise visit by Sheila Scott, the navigator's redheaded younger sister. She had traveled to Oakland from Santa Monica, where she worked for a bank. It did not matter that she was out of vacation days. "I just went to the president of the bank and I reminded him that one doesn't have a brother flying across the Pacific every day, and didn't he think I ought to come up here and see him off," said Sheila. "And he did think so—and here I am." Gordon rewarded his sister with an open-mouthed kiss that a news photographer caught on camera. Also by his side that morning was his brother Denham, who had slept in the plane the night before as a watchman, even as policemen were stationed outside the plane. In the morning Denham related to his brother that three men had strangely approached *Golden Eagle* the previous night at 10:00 PM, claiming to be representatives of the Pioneer Instrument Company. Denham refused to let them touch the plane.

That morning navy lieutenant and navigator Vilas Knope also suspected a possible sabotage attempt when he discovered two magnets missing from a compass on board *Miss Doran*. After borrowing a spare pair of magnets from *Oklahoma*, he and pilot Auggy Pedlar quietly told other aviators about the possibility of tampering. The incident left Knope shaken:

> Who could do such a thing? It would have to be a man familiar with the technical details of such things. But if anyone wanted us out of the race, why didn't they damage us so we couldn't start, rather than do a thing like that that might send us to certain death, hundreds of miles out at sea. For I might not have discovered this until we were on our way—and when the magnetic compass failed to check with our other two—the earth inductor and the periodic—I'd not have known which to trust, and we'd have been in a terrible situation.

When Art Goebel learned of the magnet theft he became incensed. "Anyone who interferes with the instruments or the motors of these planes is a menace to life and property and should be instantly deprived of their own," said the pilot of *Woolaroc*, looking sharp in a brown linen suit he had chosen for the flight.

The crew of *Miss Doran* looked even snazzier. Pedlar, already bedecked in leis, wore a busy outfit featuring plaid mackinaw jacket, plaid knickers, plaid socks, and a tie with a leaf pattern. Stowed away in the plane was his trademark straw hat. Knope was more subdued, sporting a gray vest, bow tie, and knickers with golf socks. Mildred Doran, meanwhile, looked snappy in her tailored flying outfit. She walked the airfield cheerily with her leather flying helmet in one hand and a bouquet of carnations and ferns in the other. A crowd of admirers, reporters, and photographers followed in her wake. She was chatty and playful as she signed autographs, shook hands, and answered newsmen's unending questions. "Afraid? Hmm, not a bit . . . ," said Doran. "I conceived this flight before Lindbergh conceived his to Paris. Well, Maitland and Hegenberger have stolen our thunder by flying the Pacific, but I'll be the first woman to fly across the Pacific—and that's something."

Michigan schoolteacher Mildred Doran, twenty-two, looked the part of the dashing aviator as she waited to race across the Pacific, sporting a leather flying helmet, military-type jacket, Sam Browne belt across her chest and waist, jodhpurs, and golf socks. Fraternity pins from her suitors decorate the flap over her left breast pocket. *Courtesy of the California History Room, California State Library, Sacramento*

The audience at the airfield scrutinized Doran as she claimed to not "feel a bit different than as if I were going on an automobile ride." But observers noticed "dancing lights" in her eyes, trembling lips, and were generally impressed that she looked "scared to death." She was wise to their perceptions, warning her entourage of drawing too many conclusions from her appearance alone. "Excited? I'm so excited I'm boiling over, inside—but I don't always show how I feel," said the young schoolteacher. The questions kept coming. Doran stayed calm, answering gently with crisp enunciation.

Did she pack food for the flight?

"I should say not! I make terrible sandwiches, and the boys wouldn't have eaten them if I had."

What about a vanity case?

"Why, of course. I'll doll up just before landing and look my best when I meet Governor Farrington and accept the check from Mr. James D. Dole."

Did she have a restful night?

"I tried to sleep but I woke up early. I had breakfast in my room—just raspberries and toast and coffee. I never eat more than that, and especially now, when there's so much excitement."

A reporter asked about the color of Doran's eyes, that mysterious hue that befuddled newsmen across the country. She replied by turning to the man and impishly opening her eyes wide. And then someone else asked, "What are your last words to the world—in case you don't come back?"

"Why, I AM coming back," she said.

Beneath her mirthful appearance and lively rapport, Doran was suppressing her emotions. The constant barrage of attention—from the press, from individual fans, from letter writers, from civic and social clubs, and from her own friends and family—had overwhelmed the otherwise indefatigable and cheery Flying Schoolma'am. After enduring a whirl of social engagements and news interviews as she traveled across the country and prepared for the flight in Oakland, she spent the two days before the race in her hotel room, resting and receiving just a few friends. She had become homesick and lonely, no matter all the invitations to come her way in California and all the telegrams from friends, family, and others that poured in daily. "I really will be glad to see my family," she said, tearing up. "I don't suppose there'll be much sleep at the Dorans' tonight. I'd have almost given up the trip the other night. I was so anxious to see them." In Hawaii she at least would have one friend. "I'll be so glad to see Mr. Malloska. He's someone I know," she said of her sponsor and close family friend, who had already arrived by steam liner to Hawaii and brought along Doran's spare luggage.

While outwardly displaying excitement, there were hints of nervousness in her behavior. Such uneasiness was to be expected among all the competitors in the Dole Air Race, but Doran's emotions were arguably unique. She was the youngest person in the race, the only woman, and the only passenger. While the male Dole birds and other transpacific fliers were labeled eagles and hawks, the innocent and earnest Doran was compared to a pigeon, hinting at vulnerability. Pigeons had not fared well recently over the Pacific. While King Sperry and Princess Drifted Snow did fly safely between the Golden Gate and the Embarcadero during San Francisco's homecoming celebration of Lester Maitland and Albert Hegenberger, their subsequent journey to Hawaii aboard *City of Oakland* resulted in their disappearance above the Pacific, along with two other carrier pigeons. Would Doran enjoy better luck?

The morning of the race, as Doran prepared to leave for the airport, she placed a bible in her pocket. Every aviator in the Dole Air Race, in fact, had received a lightweight copy. "I'm taking this with me," she said quietly. "I can leave most of the other things that people sent me right here in the room, but I think I'll feel more comfortable with this along, and I like to read that part beginning, 'Wings of the morning . . .'"

Doran, a practicing Methodist, was referring to Psalm 139, a portion of which reads:

> If I take the wings of the morning, and dwell in the uttermost parts
> of the sea;
> Even there shall thy hand lead me, and thy right hand shall hold me.

The verse was comforting, especially when interpreted literally by someone about to fly over an ocean. The bible was just one of many gifts sent to soothe and entertain Doran in the few weeks since she left Michigan. "I think I've received a little bit of everything that's ever been made, from candy bars to public speaking courses," she said. "No one has sent me a cook book yet—of course I can cook, but not too well. The funny part of it is that no one has thought to send me a book on *The Insides of an Airplane and Why*. To tell you the truth I don't know anything about the mechanics of a plane—no more than most women know about the insides of their ears—but I can answer all the questions without batting an eyelash."

Doran's frank admission was alarming. On the eve of a flight across 2,400 miles of open ocean, after spending weeks aboard an airplane and at airports, she conceded she had not bothered to bolster her knowledge of aviation and learn the basic operations of the vehicle designed to lift her across the water. Doran also admitted to being unable to swim or even paddle an oar. "If we have to use the rubber raft, I won't even know how to row," she confessed.

Given the talents of Pedlar and Knope, maybe she thought it pointless to duplicate efforts, or far-fetched to expect that a month's worth of study would qualify her even as a basic pilot or navigator. So Doran left most responsibilities to her teammates, even deciding the assembling of sandwiches was better left to others. Her role, she decided, was to put on a brave face as she blazed a trail for women across the world's largest ocean.

As the time until takeoff dwindled at the Oakland airport, she powdered her nose and straightened her hair a final time. She was eager to reach Hawaii. "I'm tickled to death," Doran exclaimed. "We can't leave too soon to suit me."

It was nearly noontime on August 16, 1927. The fog had cleared around Oakland and the sun was shining high in the sky, casting its rays down on the dusty airport on Bay Farm Island through a somewhat hazy sky. Ernie Smith walked among the planes assembled near the starting lines, inspecting the aircraft and chatting with the assorted Dole birds. "Don't you wish you were going along, Ernie?" someone asked Smith.

"Not me," he replied. "Once is enough."

Smith had been invited to the beginning of the Dole Air Race as the honorary starter. Emory Bronte, Smith's companion and navigator on *City of Oakland*'s flight to Hawaii, was on hand, too, tasked with being an honorary timekeeper. Within minutes Smith was due to fire a starting gun into the air, signifying the beginning of the Dole Derby. The lead racer, *Oklahoma*, would then roll down the runway and take flight for Hawaii. Seven planes would follow in *Oklahoma*'s wake. The first plane to reach Wheeler Field on Oahu would win, no matter its starting position.

Twenty minutes before noon, pilot Bennet Griffin and navigator Al Henley began their walk to *Oklahoma* and the starting line. They smiled to the reporters in the small shacks forming Newspaper Row. They shook hands with their fellow fliers in the air race. Then they walked across the dusty field to their plane, climbed aboard, and started *Oklahoma*'s engines.

All eyes rested on *Oklahoma*. Tens of thousands watched the small blue-and-yellow airplane from each side of the airfield. Tens of thousands more watched from around the bay, in downtown San Francisco and nearby Marin County, across the Golden Gate, waiting to see a tiny object rise in the sky from Oakland. Among the crowd was Jack Northrop, the young and brilliant airplane designer who had helped create both the sleek *Golden Eagle* and the more traditional-looking *Pabco Pacific Flyer* and *Aloha*. Marveling at the collection of "beautiful, well-designed ships" on the airfield, Northrop also lamented the presence of a handful of "poor little backyard jobs that didn't stand a chance." He remembered the start of the Dole Derby as "the most emotionally thrilling thing I have ever seen."

In Hawaii thousands waited, too, preparing to gather at Wheeler Field in less than a day's time to see who would collect James Dole's first- and second-place prizes. One Hawaiian resident baked an elaborate cake decorated with airplanes, a pineapple plantation, waterfalls, and an electric, illuminated moon to welcome the aviators, while a Honolulu music teacher offered free ukuleles and lessons to the winning teams. And scores of people flew banners, carried signs, or wrote on automobiles, offering happy wishes and prayers for derby competitors.

Just minutes remained until noon. Then the unprecedented and eagerly anticipated air race, featuring eight planes soaring over the Pacific in a dead heat to Hawaii, would begin. Tension increased with each passing second, observed *Woolaroc*'s navigator, Lieutenant Bill Davis:

> The excitement gradually heightened, the messengers made more speed on their dashes here and there, the cameras clicked more frantically from every angle and direction, and the crowd milled outside the ropes in a tighter and tighter jam. Engines began to sputter, last-minute touches were made by sweating mechanics, and the *Oklahoma*'s engine settled down to a heavy drone as the starter raised his flag.

When Griffin and Henley waved a final goodbye from *Oklahoma*, a hush fell over the crowd. Mechanics dropped their wrenches and policemen, who moments ago were pushing back against the encroaching crowd, turned around so they, too, could watch the hop-off of the first plane.

At noon exactly the official starter dropped his checkered flag while honorary starter Smith fired a shot from the starting gun. *Oklahoma*'s motor roared as Griffin increased the throttle. Meanwhile, a team of men pushed on *Oklahoma*'s wing struts, helping the heavy plane gain momentum. More than four hundred gallons of Phillips Nu-Aviation gasoline filled *Oklahoma*'s tanks, adding 2,400 pounds. The plane would hardly budge without a push from behind.

Slowly *Oklahoma* rolled forward, its propeller chopping furiously through the air. The plane picked up speed, pulling forward on its own strength and soon outdistancing the mechanics who helped it off the starting line. *Oklahoma* sped down the runway along San Francisco Bay for nearly its entire length, kicking up an extensive cloud of dust. Then it took to the air, ascending slowly above its own dust cloud and into the mist above the bay. People watching from San Francisco rooftops saw a black speck move across the bay, the flying object slowly becoming recognizable as a blue airplane cutting through the fog. As *Oklahoma* approached the Golden Gate, many downtown observers saw the plane disappear briefly behind the twenty-six-story Pacific Telephone Building, which opened two years earlier as one of San Francisco's first skyscrapers. Emerging on the opposite side of the building, it passed through the Golden Gate and cruised out over the Pacific, fading away to a tiny black speck once again. The first of the Dole birds was on its way to Hawaii.

Back at the Oakland airport *El Encanto* was wheeled into place at the start line. At 12:03 PM the silver plane tore down the runway, piloted at takeoff by its navigator, Kenneth Hawkins, who possessed a set of controls in his rear cabin. Hawkins had a superior view at takeoff from his cabin, as well as better control of the rudder. But as *El Encanto* gained speed and lifted slightly in the air, it was buffeted by a gusting crosswind that caused the plane to falter. Returning to the runway, the plane hit a bump, tilted to one side and veered sharply toward a group of newspapermen standing along the sidelines of the runway. The journalists scrambled to evade the out-of-control plane, with some reporters falling flat on their stomachs to avoid being swept by *El Encanto*'s wings. The plane narrowly missed the newspapermen and then entered a ground loop, turning so sharply that its left wing dipped to the ground and crumpled. Meanwhile, the plane's landing gear tore away from the fuselage, causing *El Encanto* to plow nose-first into the dirt runway, its motor burying itself as the plane ground to a violent halt. Miraculously, the large fuel tank, which bulged below the fuselage, did not explode.

Moments later Goddard and Hawkins crawled out of the wreckage and waved to the astonished crowd, signaling they were without injury. Goddard extended both arms upward in a gesture of surrender, a pained smile across his face. *El Encanto*, for which the Englishman had sold his airport in San Diego, would not be flying to Hawaii, if ever again. He was so stunned and saddened he could not speak. Hawkins found some words, which he grumbled while tears fell from his eyes: "I would rather have crashed in midocean than to have had this happen." Then their wives consoled them, before *El Encanto*'s pilot and navigator started to bicker and assign blame to each other for the crash.

The wreck caused a short delay, preventing Livingston Irving from taking off in *Pabco Pacific Flyer* until 12:11 PM. The former World War I pilot struggled with the heavily loaded plane, repeatedly lifting into the air as he charged down the runway, only to fall back to the airfield each time. *Pabco Pacific Flyer* bounced up and down about seven times before the orange airplane ran out of room, forcing Irving to cut the ignition and roll to a stop near the end of the runway, right before the bayside airfield transitioned to muck and marsh. A disappointed Irving vowed to refuel his plane and try to take off again.

Before any refueling could start, *Pabco Pacific Flyer* needed to be moved. When Irving cut the plane's engine, the gasoline-laden plane rolled to a stop square in the middle of the runway. No other Dole birds would be able to take off from the Oakland airport until tractors towed *Pabco Pacific Flyer* away.

It was only at 12:31, a half hour after *Oklahoma* left for Hawaii, that the runway was cleared and the fourth plane attempted its departure for the islands. Pilot Jack Frost and navigator Gordon Scott waved as they hurtled down the runway in their speedy cigar-shaped Lockheed Vega. *Golden Eagle* lifted into the air easily and climbed high as it flew across the bay toward San Francisco, the aviators inside eager to make up for lost time.

Next in line was *Miss Doran*. While the plane's namesake had received scores of telegrams in the preceding weeks, including a thick sheaf the morning of the race, Mildred Doran stepped into her red-white-and-blue biplane with a single message tucked into a pocket, a note of good luck from her father in Michigan. She requested one favor before departing, stating, "I would like the *Tribune* to wire my father and tell him goodbye for me until I send the cable from Honolulu tomorrow." Moments later, at 12:33 PM, Doran, pilot Auggy Pedlar, and navigator Vilas Knope were airborne as *Miss Doran* took off without incident. Now three planes were winging their way to Hawaii.

A crowd cheering as *Pabco Pacific Flyer* got airborne during the Dole Derby, only to drop back to the runway moments later, unable to take off due to its heavy load of fuel. The failed takeoff was preceded by another mishap, when *El Encanto* (seen in the background with its wing jutting upward) lost control at takeoff and ground looped, destroying the plane. *Courtesy of the San Diego Air and Space Museum*

A moment later *Aloha* was sprinting down the runway, its pilot, Martin Jensen, intent on avoiding the fate of *Aloha*'s sister ship, *Pabco Pacific Flyer*. While Jensen had been waiting for the race to begin that morning, a Western Union bank messenger had tried repeatedly to reach him at the airport. Police and guards ejected the messenger three times before he reached the pilot and was able to hand over $300—a final payment from Jensen's wife in Honolulu. The last-minute cash delivery enabled him to settle his debts with mechanics and *Aloha*'s manufacturer—men he had been working with day and night for the previous ten days to get the plane in flying shape. He found it hard to bid them all farewell, stating, "It was an emotional day with joy, sorrow, fear, and love."

After rolling down the runway in his yellow plane, Jensen took to the sky at 12:34 PM, flying low over the bay on account of *Aloha*'s heavy fuel load. A wide, mischievous grin covered his face as he flew away from Oakland. Inside his pocket were 125 telegrams—all unread. As *Aloha* passed over the crowd of spectators at the airport, Jensen dropped leis from his open-air cockpit, causing a skirmish below that police struggled to contain.

A minute later *Woolaroc* was on the starting line. Pilot Art Goebel and navigator Bill Davis had closely watched the other planes at takeoff, at first encouraged by how smoothly *Woolaroc*'s sister ship, *Oklahoma*, departed the airfield. But the crash of *El Encanto* and *Pabco Pacific Flyer*'s failed takeoff had alarmed the aviators, who worried their own plane might be too heavy to lift off the runway. Their anxiety ebbed, however, when *Golden Eagle, Miss Doran*, and *Aloha* all took off successfully.

Sitting inside *Woolaroc* at the start line, Davis, clad in his khaki navy uniform, closed the windows in the fuselage. The plane seemed to move slowly to him as it rolled down the runway, though he eventually felt it lift from the ground so gently that a thermos bottle sitting on the floor of the cabin remained undisturbed. Opening the cabin windows, he could see the large crowd of people below, lined up along each side of the runway. He waved from the navigator's cabin and was surprised to hear the crowd roar back, their enthusiasm audible over the drone of *Woolaroc*'s engine.

Goebel piloted the blue-and-yellow plane across the bay, climbing to rise above a layer of haze. Within the navigator's cabin Davis unspooled the radio antenna, letting it trail below the plane. He then unrolled his charts, tuned in to the army's radio beacon, and set up speed and drift indicators, readying himself for a twenty-six-hour flight. Goebel steered *Woolaroc* above Market Street as it flew west across San Francisco, toward the Pacific Ocean, at a height of 1,500 feet. A handful of planes carrying news photographers followed closely behind.

Back in Oakland, the final competitors in the Dole Derby readied for take-off. Bill Erwin and Alvin Eichwaldt sat in the silver-and-green *Dallas Spirit*, preparing not only to travel to Hawaii, but also to Hong Kong in a bid to win another prize, and then around the world. Erwin, the former World War I ace whose pregnant wife was waiting back home in Texas on account of being too young to fly in the race, left for Hawaii buoyed by the support of his family, not to mention the thousands of people that had recently crowded Love Field to see him off from Dallas. Just days earlier his mother had sent him a note

Woolaroc, the seventh plane to depart for Hawaii, as it lifted off the runway during the start of the Dole Derby with pilot Art Goebel and navy navigator Lieutenant William V. Davis tucked inside. *Courtesy of the California History Room, California State Library, Sacramento*

from Oklahoma, where he had grown up as the son of a preacher. The note read, "Dearest Old Big Boy, Read Luke, Chapter 1, Thirty-seventh verse, and go on and around the world with your navigator. Easterwood prize is nothing compared to the reward of carrying out your original program. This great opportunity comes only once. Grab it. Your friends believe you will. I love you." The Bible verse referenced by Erwin's mother advised that "for with God, nothing shall be impossible."

Steadied by his faith, Erwin gunned *Dallas Spirit*'s throttle and tore down the runway at 12:37 PM. A minute later the plane was in the air, flying across the bay, in hot pursuit of the other Dole birds, one of six airplanes desperate to reach Hawaii and claim the $25,000 first-place prize. As *Dallas Spirit* zoomed toward the Golden Gate, a siren atop Aloha Tower on the Honolulu waterfront blared, alerting Hawaii residents that the Dole Derby racers were en route. In a day's time, residents of Oahu should be able to see the Dole birds overhead, as the aviators finished the final portion of their long journey and prepared to land at Wheeler Field.

With the last plane, *Dallas Spirit*, gone, Irving was permitted to attempt another takeoff in *Pabco Pacific Flyer*. But as Irving's plane was being refueled, cries of alarm could be heard from the crowd. "The *Miss Doran*, the *Miss Doran!*" said excited observers. "She's coming back!" Others groaned at the sight of *Miss Doran*, which Pedlar piloted in circles above the airfield to allow police the chance to clear the runway. The biplane had only been in the air for twelve minutes, and its quick return at 12:46 PM meant that it would have to attempt a dangerous landing with a nearly full load of fuel. As Pedlar brought the airplane down for a landing, navigator Knope stood in the open doorway of the fuselage, his hands gripping the body of the Flying Schoolma'am. Should the plane catch fire during its landing, Knope was prepared to try and hurl the petite twenty-two-year-old out of the plane and clear of any wreckage or explosion. Yet Pedlar landed the plane expertly and taxied toward the starting line. "Motor trouble," he explained, his engine spurting gasoline. "Let's get busy."

Doran exited the airplane sobbing as Pedlar described how the aircraft's engine had started sputtering and backfiring as they cruised along at eight hundred feet. Doran was not crying because she was unnerved by the mechanical problems and dangerous landing. Rather, she was bawling because she was disappointed she might not fly to Hawaii after all. "It was a great thrill, going down the runway, and out over the bay. Everyone waved to us from the shores, and from the ferries and other ships out on the bay," she said. "The only scare I had was when we turned back—I was afraid they weren't going to take me along after all."

Meeting Doran on the runway, Ernie Smith escorted her from the plane to a waiting car. More than a month ago Smith himself returned to the Oakland airport after a failed attempt to fly to Hawaii, his spirits crushed when his navigator bowed out because of equipment failure. But he had redeemed himself two weeks later with another navigator, successfully flying across half the Pacific to Hawaii. He begged Doran to calm herself. "Now don't let it upset you. For heaven's sake, don't get excited. Everything will be all right," said Smith. "P-please, Miss Doran, keep cool!" Doran was driven a short distance and given shelter within a shack along Newspaper Row. There the teary-eyed adventurer expressed her disappointment to friends and reporters. "I didn't want to come back. . . . Oh, isn't it a pity we had to come back," she said.

As Pedlar, Knope, and a team of mechanics worked to replace the spark plugs in *Miss Doran*'s engine, Doran waited in Newspaper Row, her emotions vacillating wildly. Initially she was hopeful that she would be airborne again at any moment, saying, "I hope we can get away right again. We're not out yet. Nothing to do but make repairs and start off again." Then, when urged to eat her packed lunch at the airport because repairs were ongoing, she reacted angrily, crying, "No! No!" Her mood worsened further when told that *Miss Doran* might not attempt another flight that day. But then Doran perked up considerably when it seemed likely *Miss Doran* would soon take off again for Hawaii after all. "Scared—frightened? I should say not. If they force us down seven times, I'll go up again the eighth," she told reporters. "I'd make any number of starts when Auggy was at the controls."

Despite the brave words, reporters buzzing around Newspaper Row noticed Doran talking in a nervous, clipped tone—an obvious departure from her normal habit of speaking slowly and sweetly. The engine problems, the forced return, the uncertain prospects of reentering the race, and the continual bother of journalists agitated the otherwise unflappable and affable Michigan schoolteacher. Finally, she begged for some privacy within Newspaper Row: "Please let me alone. All I want is to have Auggy know I'm waiting—tell him, somebody. I'm going to rest."

While Pedlar and Knope continued to tinker with *Miss Doran*'s engine, the remaining crowd at the airfield began chattering excitedly as another plane suddenly reappeared in the distance, apparently returning for a landing. It was *Oklahoma*, which a moment before was presumed cruising across the Pacific in first place, with a half hour head start. Griffin landed *Oklahoma* safely at 1:12 PM, a little more than an hour after he took off for Hawaii.

When *Oklahoma* taxied to a stop, Henley was found standing in the navigator's cabin with a fire extinguisher in hand. "The damned ship was burning up," he said. The plane's engine housing had restricted airflow, causing the engine to overheat considerably. Never mind any disappointment over failing to reach Hawaii; the boys from Oklahoma were fortunate to have safely returned to Oakland. Plus, now Griffin didn't have to wait any longer to get married. "I guess we can go ahead with those original plans after all," said his fiancée, Juanita Herod.

Henley, however, had no such consolation. He sobbed over their misfortune and begged Griffin to start again, lacking an appreciation for the sorry state of *Oklahoma*'s engine. "We can't," Griffin responded. "Our cylinders are melting. Don't feel so bad. There's Erwin coming back, too, and he's the greatest pilot of them all."

As Griffin noted, flying back at that very moment was *Dallas Spirit*, piloted by war ace Erwin. Erwin and Eichwaldt had been airborne for less than a half hour, but their reason for returning was obvious even from the ground: a huge swatch of tattered fabric at the rear portion of the fuselage was flapping loosely in the wind, exposing almost the entire interior of the navigator's compartment and tail. As Erwin lined the plane up for a return to the Oakland airport, Eichwaldt asked him if he thought *Dallas Spirit* could be landed safely. "We'll be goddamned lucky to get back!" came the reply from the pilot's cockpit.

Dallas Spirit circled the airport to allow people to clear the runway. Spectators, including *Dallas Spirit* manager Ted Dealey and chief mechanic Eddy Blom, watched the plane nervously from below. "Don't look Mr. Dealey. He's going to crash. He can't land it," said Blom. Dealey continued to look, unable to turn his eyes away from the potential horror of a fiery crash. "Don't look, please!" begged Blom. "They're going to get killed. He has 425 gallons of gasoline in his tanks and he can't land it."

Yet Erwin did land the plane. After he taxied to a stop on runway, the war veteran let loose a deep sigh of relief. "Well, by God," he said, "we're down!" Erwin and Eichwaldt grinned as they exited the plane, explaining that the plane's fabric had ripped away after a hatch in the bottom of the fuselage had torn open during their flight. While mechanics assessed the plane, the aviators walked away, joining Dealey in a search for some bananas that the business manager had left in his car.

Minutes later, at 1:19 PM or so, Livingston Irving was ready to try to take off again in *Pabco Pacific Flyer*. The orange airplane had been towed back to the start line, topped off with fuel, and its engine started. Again Irving plowed forward down the runway, eager to pull away from the ground. As before, his airplane accelerated and lifted a few feet from the runway, only to stall and fall back down to the dirt. Then the fast-moving *Pabco Pacific Flyer* entered a ground loop, tearing off its landing gear, breaking its propeller, and dislodging its engine as the plane smashed into the ground. A crowd rushed to the wreck, including Irving's wife and five-year-old daughter. Irving emerged from the battered plane with tears in his eyes. He was not seriously injured, but severely disappointed. "Now it's impossible for me to take off," he said, hugging his wife and sobbing. "I can't get off this runway. I can't do it."

Determined to race to Hawaii, pilot Livingston Irving made a second takeoff attempt during the Dole Derby on August 16, 1927. He crashed his *Pabco Pacific Flyer* but was not seriously injured. *Courtesy of the Hawaii Department of Transportation Airports*

The carcasses of disabled planes now littered the airfield. *El Encanto* lay on its side some distance down the runway, one wing broken and the other pointing awkwardly into the air. *Pabco Pacific Flyer* sat nearby, its belly having scraped along the runway until it ground to a halt. Closer to the starting line stood *Oklahoma*, whose engine had started to melt, as well as *Dallas Spirit*, whose fabric had torn away. Such a scene was hardly encouraging for the crew of *Miss Doran*, who were readying for their second takeoff attempt to Hawaii after replacing engine spark plugs.

As Doran waited for the repairs to be completed, many people begged her to reconsider the flight. The Flying Schoolma'am refused. Some observers thought she appeared nervous before the flight; yet others caught sight of her dazzling smile as she waited to fly away. In any case, just after 2:00 PM Doran left Newspaper Row and walked out to the runway. Waving cheerfully to the crowd, she again stepped into the rear cabin of *Miss Doran*. "We'll make it this time," said the fearless passenger before *Miss Doran* barreled down the runway.

Then the red-white-and-blue biplane took to the sky, pointed toward Hawaii, and faded into the distance as it flew west across San Francisco and the Pacific.

While *Miss Doran* restarted her attempt across the bay and ocean, *Golden Eagle* blazed ahead. Pilot Jack Frost kept the throttle high, pushing his airplane along at the swift clip of 115 miles per hour. An escort plane had followed *Golden Eagle* out to sea more than one hundred miles, but then finally had enough and peeled away. Frost waved to his fellow pilot as the escort plane returned to California, leaving him and navigator Gordon Scott alone at two thousand feet as they continued their long flight to Hawaii.

Golden Eagle was likely in the lead, given the plane's high rate of speed and early starting position. But it was impossible to know for sure, especially since the plane only carried a radio receiver, and no transmitter, and therefore issued no broadcasts concerning its position. And while a few ships traveling the shipping lanes between San Francisco and Honolulu reported sightings of specific airplanes in the hours after the start of the Dole Air Race, these observations were regarded skeptically. It would have been easy for any observer to confuse airplanes, especially if any of these sightings occurred during the night or at a great distance.

Woolaroc, on the other hand, was well equipped, using the radio set borrowed from *City of Oakland*. Almost immediately after taking off, navigator Bill Davis tuned into the radio beacon and discovered they were slightly north of the base course that ran between Maui and San Francisco. Putting his mouth to a speaking tube that ran between the pilot and navigator cockpits, he instructed Goebel to correct course to the south.

The radio beacon proved to be a godsend for the two-man crew aboard *Woolaroc*. The thick fog had not abated since they left the California coast, prompting pilot Art Goebel to climb to six thousand feet to fly above it. Since Davis could not see the ocean through the "wooly" fog below, he could not drop smoke bombs to determine the plane's drift. So instead he ordered course adjustments based on the US Weather Bureau's predictions of wind speed and wind direction across the Pacific, as noted in a forecast issued that morning to all the Dole fliers. This strategy seemed to work, and *Woolaroc* stayed on course for Maui, as indicated by the constant tone of the radio beacon's signal.

Not entirely trusting of the device, Davis planned to verify their course and position that evening using celestial navigation.

The afternoon passed quickly as Goebel flew at a steady ninety miles per hour, considerably slower than *Golden Eagle*. Davis monitored the radio and issued hourly reports of their position, which nearby ships received and relayed to shore. Hour after hour, *Woolaroc* flew across the Pacific, with gray fog and clouds below and bright-blue sky above. Goebel's eyes grew irritated as the sun began to sink low in the western sky, almost directly in front of him. The smoked glasses he brought along offered some relief.

Beyond being somewhat blinded, the pilot's hearing had deteriorated, too. Engine noise penetrated the leather flying helmet he wore over his ears, deafening him. In order to communicate, he and Davis had to forgo the speaking tube and instead exchange written messages clipped to the clothesline running beside their massive fuel tank and between their respective cockpits. The notes they passed were short and to the point, especially those coming from Goebel, whose hands were busy flying the plane from within his cramped cockpit. "There was plenty of time to think," said Goebel. "Lieutenant Davis and I were as completely separated as if we had been at extreme ends of the earth. We could not see or talk to one another. Not ten feet apart, we were strangers together in the air over mid-ocean."

In the rear of the plane, Davis's only frustration was the weakening radio beacon signal. Though he had expected the signal to grow fainter the farther *Woolaroc* flew from the shore-based beacons, it had become so weak that he dared not tune away to listen to radio messages from nearby ships. Once he tuned away from the beacon, he feared, he might not find it again.

Yet this potential loss was no reason to panic. In time, Davis believed, the radio beacon's signal would come through again. And in a few hours, he knew, he would be able to take sightings with his air sextant. And sooner or later, whether this evening or the next day, he and Goebel would see water again, which would allow him to use smoke bombs to determine the plane's drift. As the sun began to set over the Pacific, Davis was relaxed enough to send a surprise message back home to his family in Atlanta: "SEVEN HOURS OUT. EVERYTHING GOING WELL. LOVE TO ALL." His mother received the message—which traveled across the Pacific and United States by radio, telegraph, and telephone—nearly two hours later.

As Goebel sat in the pilot's cockpit, watching the sun dip below the horizon, a grimness overcame him. He knew objectively that *Woolaroc*'s engine was performing perfectly, that their navigation so far was accurate, and that the assortment of instruments spread before him on the dash were functioning. Yet the disappearing sun unsettled the Hollywood stunt pilot, who feared "the long hours of darkness ahead." "The sun went down. It had been a good friend, and the weather had been fine," he said. "Now night was coming on, and with it a loneliness that cannot be described and which has not been experienced by any except those who, like us, have headed a plane into darkness over water." "I prayed in my heart," he added, "that nothing would keep me from seeing that golden sun again."

After taking off again from the Oakland airport, *Miss Doran* flew across the bay, past San Francisco and the Golden Gate, before reaching the Pacific Ocean. At about three in the afternoon the biplane was seen passing the Farallon Islands, the last specks of earth the crew would encounter until landing in Hawaii. Escort planes spied Pedlar sitting in the pilot's cockpit, his straw hat atop his head. In the rear of the plane sat Lieutenant Knope and the famous Doran. The Flying Schoolma'am gave a friendly wave as the escort planes dipped their wings in a final salute and turned back to the California coast.

Martin Jensen and Paul Schluter had passed the Farallones more than an hour earlier in *Aloha*, tearing across the sky at one hundred miles per hour. While *Woolaroc* and *Golden Eagle* had elected to fly above the thick fog blanketing the Pacific, Jensen deferred to his navigator's wishes and flew below the haze. "I happened to have a ship's navigator for the flight," Jensen explained. "To direct us he had to be within 100 feet of sea level."

Beyond Schluter fearing that his sightings with a mariner's sextant would be inaccurate if taken at higher altitudes, pilot and navigator observed the needles in some of *Aloha*'s compasses spun continuously when they climbed into the sky. So Jensen flew low, just forty feet above the waves. At times he dipped even lower, once becoming distracted and nearly crashing into a steamship on the open ocean. Only at the last minute did he yank hard on *Aloha*'s stick and avoid a collision with SS *Silver Fir*. Disaster had been averted, but more problems loomed.

Almost immediately *Aloha* experienced hiccups with its fuel systems, which Jensen conceded were "crude affairs" that had been hastily constructed. Excessive pressure in the fuel feed caused overflows of gasoline. He estimated he lost twenty gallons of fuel before reaching the Farallon Islands. Then the oil feed went dry, requiring a coordinated effort between pilot and navigator to keep the engine lubricated. To push oil through the system, Jensen put his mouth to an oil line and blew into it, all while Schluter released a valve to allow the oil to flow toward the engine. When Jensen had exhausted himself he removed his mouth and signaled that Schluter should immediately close the valve. When the oil had been consumed by the engine, they'd do it again. "When [the oil] emptied we had to go through the same procedure and were obliged to continue in this way the remainder of the trip," said Jensen. "I blew oil through that piece of rubber hose until I thought I'd go crazy."

While Jensen feared losing his mind over the oil line hiccup, Schluter feared losing his life. Later the fuel pump failed, requiring the aviators to hand pump gasoline through the plane's fuel system, worrying all the time if they had enough fuel to reach Hawaii. Because of these continual problems, Schluter spent much of the flight across the Pacific Ocean partially undressed. He had unpacked the life raft, stripped himself of shoes and some clothes to make for an easy exit, and strapped assorted tools and instruments to his body, expecting an ocean landing at any moment.

Jensen felt no better in the open-air pilot's cockpit. Though he did not plan to eat anything during the flight for fear of becoming drowsy, he kept food beside him in case he needed to grab it quickly while escaping to the raft. No longer was he giddy. In fact he could not shake the regret that continually overcame him as he cruised farther and farther from the mainland. For the first time in his life, Martin Jensen was scared.

When Jensen and Schluter left Oakland, they had agreed to fly west at a bearing of 248 degrees. As each hour or so of the flight passed, Jensen planned to adjust course south by a degree, the gradual turns leading them to the islands. Schluter, meanwhile, planned to periodically check *Aloha*'s position with his sextant, letting Jensen know if further correction was needed due to the wind drift. An hour into the flight, Jensen heard almost nothing from Schluter. Mindful of the promise he had made to navy lieutenant Ben Wyatt to listen to his talented ocean navigator, he flew on without adjusting course. Then another hour passed, and still there was no indication from Schluter to bear south. Jensen might have pressed his navigator on this, but the failure of the oil and gasoline systems, along with constant flying duties, such as keeping the plane on course and adjusting its engine controls, distracted him. And so the plane flew unguided across the Pacific Ocean, never making the necessary turns for the shortest route to Hawaii.

Schluter did not communicate any course changes to Jensen because he had performed little navigational work. He was stymied by the bad weather and his ignorance of other aerial navigation methods. Though smoke bombs were on board, Schluter apparently did not know how to use them to determine the plane's drift. Same with the drift meter. And with continual fog cover overhead, he could not use his sextant at sunset to establish their position. So with no basis to order course corrections, Schluter stayed quiet and allowed Jensen to keep flying straight ahead, despite the likelihood that Hawaii loomed farther to the south.

Communicating with his pilot was a chore, anyway. Schluter was confined to a small spot in the tail of the plane, hemmed in on three sides by fuel tanks. To reach Jensen in the front of the plane, he had to rattle the large stick they placed on top of the main fuel tank to attract his attention. Then he had to attach a handwritten note to the clothesline that ran between the two sections of the plane along pulley wheels. And each time they used this messaging system the clothesline inevitably ran off its track, requiring its repair by Schluter. Even the simplest machines were causing problems within *Aloha*.

As nightfall came and the horizon began to fade, Jensen was eager to climb above the fog and see the stars. He did not want to fly blind in the dark at low altitude, just skimming the tops of waves, especially since it would still be a few hours before the moon rose, offering at least some faint light by which to steer and discern the horizon. Until then, sea, sky, and fog all blurred into a near-total darkness, confusing the aviator, who could not tell which way was up. The only source of light, in fact, was the orange flame of the engine exhaust in front of him. This light was so intense it caused more visibility problems.

Jensen's task was complicated further because of his lack of experience flying blind, by instrument alone. Though he had previously used turn and bank indicators when flying through clouds, he soon discovered the additional rigors of flying through complete and inescapable darkness and fog.

Aloha climbed to four thousand feet through the darkening sky, Jensen wondering how high he must fly to see the twinkling heavens. He glanced at the instruments on the dash as he climbed, trying to keep level but also on course. Yet all the dials did was make him feel dizzy. As his head spun, *Aloha* began banking into a turn with increasing speed. Next thing Jensen knew the airplane was diving downward in a violent spin. He pulled back on the stick, but this only made the plane spin faster in a plunge toward the black ocean below. His mind raced as he tried to think of a solution that might save his and Schluter's lives. Then . . . eureka! He described how he drew on his barnstorming experience to avert disaster:

> If we were in a spin [as opposed to a spiral], I thought wildly, I could recover. I had made a living as a county fair stunt flier and knew how to get out of a spin. An idea suddenly occurred to me; it seemed crazy, but it was the only way. I chopped the throttle, eased the stick back into my stomach until the *Aloha* shuddered, then slammed on full right rudder. The ship seemed to hang there in the black night, until with a sickening plunge the nose dropped and we were whipping wildly around and around, heading straight for hell.
>
> I let her spin for maybe a thousand feet. Then I dumped the stick forward, got off the rudder and pulled out of the spin into level flight once more. My disorientation subsided and I exhaled slowly, wiped the sweat from my face, and settled down to the toughest flying job of my life. I had to learn to fly on instruments, there in mid-Pacific, or die trying.

This was the first of three consecutive vertigo-induced "graveyard" dives Jensen and Schluter endured. After each dive Jensen would seek to regain altitude, only to dive unwillingly again minutes later, with poor Schluter in back being tossed against the fuel tanks, clueless as to why they were flying so hazardously. During the third dive *Aloha* was only flying a few hundred feet above the water. When Jensen recovered, the airplane was cruising just above the waves.

After the third near-death dive, Jensen was finished trying to reach the stars. Should *Aloha* dive again from this low an altitude, it would surely be into the ocean. So he kept close to the invisible sea below, his eyes glued to the turn and bank indicator, ensuring that the plane flew level atop the ocean. Jensen estimated it would be four hours until the moon cast its glow over the waves.

"I knew this instrument would bring me through if I would use it properly," said the pilot. "There was years of flying knowhow, determination, and a lot of luck that saw me through those long four hours."

Another instrument Jensen eyed continuously was the altimeter. The instrument gave a reading of one hundred feet above sea level, which allowed him to relax a bit as he cruised in darkness. In time the moon began to rise, casting a glow that barely penetrated the fog bank, allowing him to spy at least a little bit of water.

Eventually Schluter asked him for his flashlight. Jensen reached backward to hand him the tool, inadvertently pushing forward on *Aloha*'s stick. The plane soon felt a bump as a wave crashed against its left wheel. A startled Jensen yanked back on the stick, sending *Aloha* skyward. The sudden climb caused Schluter to nearly pop out of the navigator's hatch on top of the plane. Other things went airborne within the fuselage, too, including Schluter's small telescope, which settled into some hidden recess of the plane. Now Schluter would have to sight the islands with his bare eyes, that is, if they ever made it through the night.

Jensen blamed the lower pressure over the ocean for causing the altimeter to overestimate *Aloha*'s altitude. He of course flew higher after the near crash atop the ocean, climbing to one thousand feet as the horizon became distinguishable with more moonlight. For mile after mile he piloted *Aloha* across the Pacific, though not exactly toward Hawaii. Schluter still had not instructed him to adjust course.

The night proved long and lonely, and Jensen was desperate to see daybreak. Not only would the sun restore visibility across the seemingly endless ocean, it would allow Schluter to take a sighting with his sextant. For the first time in nearly twenty hours of flying, the aviators aboard *Aloha* would know their position over the Pacific.

When daybreak finally came, it revealed heavy cloud cover in the sky above. Without climbing above the clouds, Schluter could not use his sextant. So *Aloha* blazed onward, waiting for its next chance to learn its position. As the time passed Jensen witnessed mirages, with distant clouds and rain squalls ahead appearing as islands. The pilot even cheered when he thought he spotted an island roamed by ducks and geese. But as *Aloha* drew closer these supposed islands were exposed, with the horizon eventually appearing beneath the clouds and precipitation splattering Jensen's face as he flew through the rain squalls.

Throughout the morning, Schluter passed no messages forward to the pilot. Jensen began wondering if his navigator was asleep. He wiggled the stick atop the fuel tank and then sent a note back to the navigator, indicating they should be spying the islands by now. "Which way from here?" asked Jensen. He was asking for guidance. But instead of providing a directional bearing for *Aloha* to strike out upon, Schluter sent forward a reply on the clothesline that astonished and infuriated Jensen. The veteran marine navigator wanted Jensen to circle until noon, which was more than two hours away! Only then could Schluter use his sextant to establish their position, so long as it wasn't cloudy.

Jensen was flabbergasted. Schluter had seemed to forget that they were in a race. The navigator also seemed to forget that *Aloha*'s fuel supply had become a source of concern. Crumpling up the note and tossing it on the floor, as was his habit with all of the messages traded aboard *Aloha*, the pilot sent a logical follow-up question. If they had to circle for more than two hours, the pilot asked, how much gas would they have in the tanks? Schluter's reply again astounded Jensen: "NONE!"

Since *Aloha* was still flying, there was at least *some* gasoline left in the plane's tanks, though apparently none that Schluter could see. Jensen soon realized that a broken fuel pump and other quirks of the fuel system led Schluter to underestimate the plane's true fuel supply. The pilot used his free hand to operate a wobble pump and push gasoline through the fuel system as he throttled down to the lowest possible flying speed in order to conserve fuel. He felt he had no other choice. As much as he wanted to set off for Hawaii, he only had a vague guess as to which direction the islands might lie. Only Schluter could tell him the exact course to follow, and apparently not until noon. "It was deadly, flying in circles hour after hour, draining one auxiliary tank after another and perhaps throwing away any chance we had of making landfall," said Jensen. "But any plan was better than none, so we continued flying in circles."

When news reached Hawaii that four airplanes had taken off from California and were streaming across the Pacific as part of the Dole Air Race, thousands of people mobilized to welcome the aviators. Residents of Oahu began arriving to Wheeler Field as early as 9:00 PM, even though the Dole racers were not expected for another fifteen or so hours. By midnight the crowd had grown to two thousand people; by 2:30 AM the count was up to six thousand. Ultimately twenty to thirty thousand people came to Wheeler Field to watch the Dole birds land. Most arrived by car, with an estimated ten thousand automobiles lining a two-mile section of road leading to the airfield. Others came on motorcycles, bicycles, and two trains that ran from Honolulu to the airfield. Together they formed a microcosm of Hawaiian society, as noted by a news account: "All races in the territory were represented. Pretty little Japanese women in sashed kimonos; Chinese in jackets and pajama pants; Polynesians and Koreans; Filipinos and Nordic blondes made up the welcoming multitude. These elbowed each other fraternally for vantage points."

The crowd could easily have been larger. Pineapple tycoon James Dole had originally planned on giving 3,500 employees at the Hawaiian Pineapple Company the day off to watch the air race's conclusion. Warm temperatures in recent days, however, had ripened so many fruits that these employees were needed in the fields and cannery, their vacation day rescinded. And over on Kauai, a group of youngsters watched the skies closely, intent on watching the race from their own island even if the planes were landing elsewhere. "Kauai's boydom is what might conservatively be termed agog," said one report. "If any of the Dole planes pass over Kauai or land here, the probabilities are they will be sighted first by a small boy, for there'll be a surplus of them along the coast from Haena on the north, clear around to Mana at the other end of the road."

As the crowd at Wheeler Field swelled, it became slightly unruly, spurring army leaders to order infantry units from nearby Schofield Barracks to stand guard and restore order. Despite the soldiers affixing bayonets to their rifles, the atmosphere at the airfield was jubilant and festive, and the army accommodating. The Twenty-First Infantry band played for the crowd throughout the night while other soldiers worked in field kitchens, serving hot dogs, hamburgers, soda pop, and coffee.

Supplementing the army's soundtrack, two Hawaiian boys strummed a ukulele and steel guitar. Soon a man with a portable phonograph player replaced them. He played the same two records a half dozen times apiece before the crowd ran him off to another part of the airfield. Occasional rainstorms passed over throughout the early morning, sending people scrambling for cover in airplane hangars or the insides of their cars, where they wrapped themselves in blankets to lessen the chill of the dark and escape the annoyance of mosquitoes. Searchlights shone in the sky throughout the night and morning, ready to illuminate any fast-moving plane, such as *Golden Eagle*, that might possibly complete the flight before dawn. To provide updates on the race, the army distributed bulletins and maps to the crowd.

At daybreak the army sent planes into the air to entertain the assembled. More than three thousand people filled bleachers along the airfield, paying a quarter apiece for their seats. A smaller reviewing stand for officials was set up close to the airfield. Fresh leis sat beneath the reviewing stand in big boxes, waiting to be tossed around the necks of aviators.

Peg Jensen had arrived to Wheeler Field at 2:00 AM wearing a sleeveless green dress and white hat. She put on a brave face for journalists, disguising her considerable nerves. There were unconfirmed reports her husband had crashed in a number of places—at sea, into Koko Head, or closer to Wheeler Field in Oahu's Nuuanu Valley. She didn't know what to believe, but hoped her husband was still flying. "I'm confident Martin will be first to arrive," she said. "Martin got off to a good start and he's going to bring the *Aloha* into the field first."

Dole arrived with his family a little later, coming to the airfield at 5:30 AM. As the race sponsor took his seat in the reviewing stand, the crowd gave him a cheer. Like everyone else, he was eager to see the planes land. "I am glad the flight is nearing the finish," said Dole. "It has been an exciting night. I tried to sleep but couldn't. I hope that all will arrive safely."

As darkness enveloped *Woolaroc*, pilot Art Goebel kept the plane flying above the clouds at an altitude of six thousand feet. He reduced the throttle slightly, to about eighty-three miles per hour, and settled into his seat for a long night under the stars. *Woolaroc*'s motor was running perfectly, thanks in part to the continual adjustments Goebel made to the choke and throttle. In the navigator's cabin, Lieutenant Bill Davis sat on the floor, holding his bubble sextant steady and gazing up through a hatch in the ceiling to find the North Star. The latitudinal positions he established from these sightings showed that *Woolaroc* was steadily crossing the Pacific en route to Hawaii. What's more, the radio beacon had started working intermittently in the dark, its steady tone confirming that they were flying along the base course between the radio beacons on Maui and in San Francisco.

Goebel and Davis had just one complaint as they traveled through the night—the never-ending clouds. The fog and cloud cover above the Pacific was so thick and far-reaching that *Woolaroc*'s two-man crew had yet to spot the ocean. The last bit of water they had laid eyes on was San Francisco Bay, which they passed over as soon as they left the Oakland airport. Continuing to fly at six thousand feet, Goebel eventually came to be annoyed and unnerved by the clouds, which were fully revealed beneath *Woolaroc* about 10:30 PM, just after moonrise. "At first the stars lighted them dimly, giving a somewhat ghostly effect. Then the moon came up and the fleecy floor took on a beautiful but cold and menacing brilliancy," said the pilot. "For a time they gave me a sense of false security and mystery but as the hours passed, twenty hours, mind you, they became a real menace for they blotted out everything."

The cloud cover thwarted Davis's attempts to use flares and smoke bombs as a check against his celestial navigation and the radio beacon. He looked out the plane continually for a hole in the clouds to drop a flare at night, eager to use the brightly burning flame as a reference point atop the waves to measure the plane's drift and ground speed. Occasionally he did spy a small break in the cloud cover, but he was uncertain these openings tunneled all the way down to the ocean. And though he judged it unlikely a ship could see them from the ocean below, Davis nonetheless periodically flipped on and off a powerful flashlight as they flew through the night, flashing signals identifying the plane as *Woolaroc*.

As the night passed, the navigator occupied himself with other chores, including oiling the earth inductor compass located in the tail of the plane. Every two hours he would pass a note up to Goebel, alerting him that he was about to crawl into the back recesses of the fuselage, where there was no flooring. Balancing atop cross wires that braced *Woolaroc*'s frame, Davis would be careful not to step through the fabric wrapping the tail as he oiled the compass.

During one of these oiling excursions in the middle of the night, Davis was startled by the sudden sound of intense sputtering. The naval aviator's trained ears immediately led him to suspect some type of major problem in the engine: likely a damaged valve, bad spark plug, or blown piston. Any of those problems could be disastrous for the airplane, meaning he and Goebel would probably soon be making a water landing. A chill ran down Davis's spine as he dropped the compass's cover and quickly turned himself around, crawling at top speed toward the front of the plane. He hurriedly gathered all the emergency equipment he could, loading life jackets, rations, and flares into *Woolaroc*'s life raft. "I heard the noise, quit oiling the compass, and listened," said Davis. "Then I made up my mind that our valves had gone bad and that we were in for a swim. I worked aft to our life raft, got it in shape, and loaded aboard the emergency rations and water. . . . Then I waited for Art to nose her down and light on the water."

The tense moments passed slowly until Davis glimpsed a small object pop out from underneath the floorboards just as the sputtering sound ceased. The navigator instantly recognized the object as a commutator brush—a spare part for the earth inductor compass. He deduced that the brush must have fallen out of his pocket and slipped between the floorboards and fuselage fabric, where it began rattling due to the vibration of the plane. "It was only the suspense of a moment or two, but it seemed like an age when suddenly the brush slid into view and I breathed the biggest sigh of relief of my life," he said. "I threw that brush out of the plane as far as I could and it's probably floating out there some 700 miles from Oahu." Calamity avoided, he stowed the emergency gear again. So grateful was he to be flying above the Pacific, instead of bobbing on top of the waves, that for the next few hours he stuck his head out his hatch a handful of times just to hear the smooth, steady, and satisfying drone of *Woolaroc*'s motor.

By 4:00 AM Davis had finished the last of his sandwiches and coffee. In the coming hours he glanced backward out the plane repeatedly, hoping to spy the first ray of morning light. Goebel did the same from the pilot's cockpit, eager to see the sun rise in the east. It had been a long night.

At 7:30 AM dawn broke above the ocean, revealing scattered cloud cover below. After twenty hours of flying across the Pacific, Goebel and Davis saw seawater for the first time. Though Davis had longed to see the waves, his initial impression of the Pacific was not positive. He regarded the ocean water as "cold, dark, and forbidding looking."

Though the long night had passed, hours of flying remained for the exhausted aviators. The pair kept constant lookout for the islands, desperate for a visual confirmation of Hawaii, no matter Davis's estimates of keeping course so far. Rain squalls reduced visibility across the ocean. Clouds, too, still cluttered the air, including long lines of cumulus clouds, which Davis had been told typically hover above the Hawaiian Islands. But every time they passed through one of these lines of clouds, no land was revealed on the other side—just more water and clouds. Davis's nerves began to fray. He wondered if *Woolaroc* would ever reach Hawaii.

> I don't believe anyone who had not flown over water out of sight of land can understand the feeling of absolute immobility that gradually grows upon you. There is nothing by which to gauge relative motion—the clouds roll slowly by, just as they do when you are on shore, the waves roll underneath as they do past a pier, but the plane does not seem to move at all—the horizon remains the same unbroken line, and your progress seems to be nil. A hopeless, helpless feeling creeps over you that you will remain suspended over the same spot until the engine stops and lets you down into the water. . . . When you are looking for a tiny spot, and all you can see is clouds and more clouds. Well, there is no feeling like it.

By early afternoon, after twenty-four hours of flying, Goebel grew anxious as he thought the islands should be within sight. His worry deepened when Davis began ordering a number of course corrections via the clothesline, many of them necessary to get back on course after deviations Goebel made to dodge rain squalls. But when the navigator suddenly ordered a twenty-five-degree course change to accommodate shifting winds, Goebel panicked and, by his own admission, grew "a bit pissed" over the substantial change in direction. "Are you sure?" the irritated pilot wrote back in reply before peppering Davis with other questions and commands. "Have you a beacon signal on this course? Can you reach a station in Honolulu? Check the earth inductor and give me the exact course."

Davis assured Goebel that all was well and *Woolaroc* was on track to reach Hawaii. Then, when he estimated they were three hours away from Hawaii, he sent Goebel a note of his own, inquiring how much gasoline remained on board. Goebel's casual reply caused him to panic: "2 hours."

Worried again that a water landing was inevitable, Davis began examining their radio, which had grown increasingly unreliable as the flight progressed. He first tackled the radio's transmitter, which would be necessary to issue an

SOS and to broadcast their position should they have to land at sea. By adding a flashlight battery to the radio, he was able to boost its range. Next he tackled the receiver, finding a broken electrical connection, which was likely caused by the plane's continual vibration. He made a fix and was relieved to instantly hear the radio beacon. The tone coming through the headset was solid, indicating they were right on course for the islands.

Despite Davis's mechanical breakthrough, the mood was tense and grim aboard *Woolaroc*. Inside the navigator's compartment, Davis dwelled on the apparent fuel shortage. In the cramped pilot's cockpit, meanwhile, Goebel fretted over all the course changes he had been asked to make. "We were in a funny fix," said Goebel. "There we were, both above the clouds, one thinking that we were flying away from our course, the other thinking that our fuel was running out."

As *Woolaroc* motored on, Goebel turned in his seat and passed back a note asking Davis to double-check the headings displayed by the compasses in the rear of the plane. As Goebel resumed facing forward, he spotted a speck in the distance along the horizon. Staring hard at the speck, he wondered if it was a cloud or an island. As the minutes passed, the speck loomed larger. Soon he could discern the outline of an island. He had spotted Molokai, the same island where Ernie Smith and Emory Bronte had crash-landed a month earlier in *City of Oakland*. An ecstatic Goebel uttered a celebratory whoop barely audible over the noisy engine. "I saw Molokai, a dim shore in the distance and oh, boy, what a joyful feeling it was," he said.

A moment or so later, Davis looked out a window in his navigator's cockpit and glimpsed a dark-blue smudge on the horizon. He stared hopefully ahead as the smudge morphed into the island Maui, sitting about seventy miles away. The navigator emitted his own shout of joy. "A more beautiful sight I have never witnessed," he said. Davis passed forward to Goebel a map of the Hawaiian Islands marked with *Woolaroc*'s position and the finish line at Wheeler Field. Then he sat down on the floor and relaxed, no longer overwhelmed with worry over the possible fuel shortage. "Here we are," he said. "By gosh, my job's done."

Davis instructed Goebel to set a course taking them past Molokai before turning toward Oahu. He radioed ahead advising of their position and imminent arrival, so long as their plane contained enough fuel. As Goebel piloted *Woolaroc* across the twenty-six-mile channel separating Molokai and Oahu,

Davis began celebrating their arrival. Though he did not know how many other airplanes might have already landed and claimed prizes, he was thrilled to have made the journey alive:

> Was I happy. I started shooting off our Very pistols and dropping smoke bombs all the way across the channel and even after we had passed Diamond Head. We left a trail all across the channel. When we were in mid-channel, Art looked back and pointed to Oahu. What he was doing was asking if it really was Oahu. But I thought he was asking me whether we should try to make it despite a shortage of fuel. Nothing mattered then. I gave him the signal to cut her loose and decided that if we went down we could swim the rest of the way.

Minutes later *Woolaroc* was cruising at 2,500 feet above Koko Crater and then Diamond Head, the frowning, extinct volcano at the southern end of Oahu, right below Waikiki Beach. Next Goebel and Davis flew above Honolulu, which seemed eerily devoid of people, save the luncheon crowd in the roof garden atop the Alexander Young Hotel. Davis was perplexed. "Honolulu looked deserted as we crossed the city. Was the race all over? Didn't they expect us?" he asked. "Then, as we approached Wheeler Field and army and navy planes began wheeling and zooming around us, I saw the reason for Honolulu's quiet. *Everyone* was out at the field."

As military escort planes buzzed about *Woolaroc*, one army pilot pulled close alongside it, extended his hand, and raised a single finger to the sky. His message was unmistakable: Goebel and Davis were the first to arrive to Hawaii. Davis was stunned, unaware that many of their fellow racers had returned to the Oakland airport with mechanical problems. The prize was theirs, if only Goebel would hurry up and land. Goebel himself hardly believed they could be the first to arrive, knowing he flew at a relatively modest pace across the ocean. "I banged on the cowling behind Art's head and made him understand, but he calmly and slowly circled while I hopped up and down in the tail like a monkey on a string being afraid that someone would shoot in and touch their wheels ahead of us," said Davis.

Finally, after twenty-six hours and seventeen minutes, Goebel turned into the wind and landed on Wheeler Field at 12:23 PM, Hawaiian time, on August 17, 1927. *Woolaroc* was the third plane to fly to Hawaii, the second to reach

Oahu, and the first to place in the Dole Air Race. After taxiing in front of the reviewing stand, Goebel stepped stiffly from the cockpit, removed his flying helmet, and waved to the crowd. A mighty cheer erupted in his and Davis's honor as the aviators walked across the airfield.

Local officials and dignitaries, including James Dole and Hawaii's territorial governor, left their seats to greet the winners. Excited spectators soon overtook these men as the crowd surged forward toward the aviators and plane, coursing past the soldiers standing guard. "Say, folks, it certainly is great to land here. How many others are in ahead of me?" asked Goebel, who just completed the longest flight of his life. The crowd surrounding him confirmed he was in first place. "Honest, gosh, do you mean that I am the first one here?" said the astonished pilot in response. "I thought surely some were ahead of us."

As Goebel was mobbed by the shrieking spectators, the army fired artillery to celebrate *Woolaroc*'s arrival. Goebel, already deafened from his exposure

Bedecked in leis, Art Goebel (center) celebrating his victory in the Dole Derby with navigator Bill Davis (left) and Hawaii territorial governor Wallace Farrington (far right) after flying *Woolaroc* from Oakland to Oahu in twenty-six hours and seventeen minutes. *Courtesy of the Hawaii Department of Transportation Airports*

to twenty-six hours of uninterrupted engine noise, could hardly hear a thing above the noisy crowd and bursting shells. As he shook hands and greeted those congratulating him, a woman in a green dress and white hat made a beeline for the aviator, wrapped him in a crushing embrace, and showered him with kisses. Unsteady on her feet, she then nearly fell into the still-spinning propeller before people grabbed her arms to steady her. "God bless you," cried Peg Jensen. "Oh! Can't you tell me something about Martin? Is he still in the air? Did you pass him? Where do you think he can be?"

Goebel and Davis confessed they had not seen Martin Jensen, or any other Dole flier, since leaving Oakland. This news so distressed Peg that she fainted and collapsed on the spot, requiring friends to take the emotionally exhausted woman away to recover. Meanwhile, Hawaiian women were now offering the aviators kisses, singing native songs, and placing flower leis around their necks. Goebel and Davis shook hands with each other as the celebration unfolded around them. "Oh boy! We did it!" they said.

Finally, territorial governor Wallace Farrington made his way to the front of the crowd and shook Goebel's hand. Not far behind was Dole, who greeted the winners by placing even more leis around their necks. "I'm mighty happy, boys, that you arrived safely," said Dole.

As they continued to be cheered, Goebel uttered praise for his airplane, the army's radio beacon, and his companion and navigator. "We didn't have a bit of trouble the entire trip," he said, dancing on the airfield, unable to stand still. "Old man Davis kept us right on the course and we never faltered." The Hollywood stunt flier then claimed that *Woolaroc*'s arrival was a boon to aviation, as the flight demonstrated long-distance travel across oceans is feasible and practical, saying, "I wanted to fly to Honolulu to prove to the world that airplane travel, even over 2,400 miles of water, can be made safely if proper precautions and preparations are made beforehand."

Goebel and Davis would soon be shuttled to their suite at the Royal Hawaiian, where Goebel looked forward to a clean shave and a dip in the ocean off Waikiki Beach. Goebel and Davis were encouraged to head to Honolulu to obtain some rest and food, rather than await the three other planes expected at Wheeler Field at any minute. But before leaving the airfield, in a brief moment when the winning Dole birds weren't being assaulted by all the well-wishers who had flooded the airfield, Davis turned to Goebel and asked him how he could have so badly underestimated *Woolaroc*'s fuel supply. At least one hundred gallons of fuel remained in the airplane's tanks after landing on Oahu, which would have allowed for much longer than two hours of flying time. Goebel reacted with surprise to his navigator's confusion. Then he offered an explanation for the handwritten note he had passed back to the navigator as they neared Hawaii: "Why man, that wasn't a '2.' 'That was meant for a '5'!"

It was a lonely spot of ocean Martin Jensen had chosen to circle. After a day and night of being unable to escape the clouds, now there was not a single one in the sky. No ships were visible, either, or any other airplanes, and of course no land. For more than two hours, he flew one hundred feet above the water, seemingly all alone atop the vast ocean, with mile after mile of blue water extending in every direction. Finally, after this excruciating wait in which *Aloha*'s gasoline supply might have given out at any minute, it was noontime. Navigator Paul Schluter could now establish their position atop the Pacific. "This was going to be our first celestial sighting," said Jensen, "and also our last."

Within minutes Schluter took three sightings, averaged them out, and passed forward a note indicating they were off course two hundred miles to the north. It was a great distance to travel with little fuel, but Jensen could only hope for the best. The pilot immediately turned the plane due south, increased speed, and set off for Oahu.

After two hours of flying, Jensen saw an island. Flying closer, he recognized it as his home—Oahu! He passed a note back to Schluter, advising him that he had spotted Hawaii. The navigator could cease his lookout duties, said Jensen, and no longer needed to stick his head out the hatch to help try to spy their destination. "You can now sit down. We are near Oahu," wrote Jensen.

Despite the good news, Schluter's written reply was less than enthusiastic: "For God's sake don't do any stunts. We are lucky to be here."

As *Aloha* neared Oahu, the Waianae Mountains loomed in front of the airplane. Jensen, flying close to the water for fear the engine might suddenly stop operating on account of no fuel, pulled back on his stick to lift the plane above the low-lying range. Then, dead ahead, sitting in the center of the island, was Wheeler Field. Jensen flew over the airfield once, observing a giant crowd and one other airplane parked close to a reviewing stand. Then, after turning into the wind, he made a landing at 2:22 PM, capping a flight of twenty-eight hours and sixteen minutes. Soldiers on the airfield greeted the taxiing airplane, grabbed hold of its wing struts, and helped push *Aloha* to the reviewing stand. The crowd at Wheeler Field could hardly believe their eyes. *Aloha* had sneaked in from the north, above the Waianae Mountains, an unexpected direction for a plane traveling west from California.

Peg Jensen was among those who could hardly believe *Aloha* had finished the race, what with all the reports of her husband crashing across the Pacific Ocean and Hawaii. She had spent the morning with a pair of binoculars glued to her eyes, scanning the skies for a telltale yellow plane, always disappointed. Yet there on the airfield was the yellow plane her husband had described, with "ALOHA" written in big red letters along each side of its fuselage. Realizing her husband had finally arrived safely, Peg fainted again.

When his plane rolled to a stop in front of the reviewing stand, Martin Jensen briefly sat still in the open-air cockpit. His face appeared drawn and haggard after the long flight. He attempted to stand but then slumped down again. A moment later he stepped out of the airplane and onto the airfield below. The cheering crowd surrounded him, celebrating *Aloha*'s second-place finish. At the front of the pack was Martin's hysterical wife, being delivered to her husband in the arms of military police. These MPs were so determined to reunite the Jensens they even pushed aside Governor Farrington, who himself was heading to congratulate the second-place fliers.

Seeing her husband, Peg Jensen broke free of the MPs and grabbed him in a tight hug. As she cried and showered her sweetheart with kisses, she screamed at him the question everyone was wondering: "Martin Jensen, where the hell have you been?" The pilot was oblivious to her inquiry. After twenty-eight hours behind an engine, Martin could not hear a thing.

"I'm sorry to keep you waiting," he told his wife innocently. Peg then collapsed for the third time that day, at least falling into her husband's arms this time. The crowd marveled over the tender reunion, as recorded in a report by the *Honolulu Advertiser*:

> As [the] two greeted each other, the man smiling, the woman weeping, the vast throng, as though comprising an audience at some epoch-making play, applauded to the echo. They applauded long and loud— and kept on applauding.

Jensen's homecoming will never be forgotten by that crowd, Jensen's homecoming will never be forgotten by Jensen, nor by Mrs. Jensen. It will never be forgotten by the newspaper men who covered the story—for few stories, such as this, ever race across the pages of life.

Leis were draped around the Jensens' shoulders as they soaked up the adulation. Martin endeared himself further to his fans when he reminded them that his airplane, *Aloha*, was financed by the men and women of Hawaii. "I'm certainly glad to see you all," he said, addressing the crowd with a sweeping hand. "I flew for you." The crowd screamed even louder.

Meanwhile, Schluter exited *Aloha*. Hawaiian songs filled the air around him, but the navigator was not in a festive mood. Clutching a bible and his sextant as he stepped to the airfield, he vowed to never fly to Hawaii again.

(Left to right) Navigator Paul Schluter, Peg Jensen, and pilot Martin Jensen grinning at Wheeler Field after *Aloha* took second place in the Dole Derby. After getting lost and nearly running out of gas, Jensen piloted *Aloha* to Hawaii in twenty-eight hours and fifteen minutes. He was greeted by his wife, Peg, who asked him, "Martin Jensen, where the hell have you been?" *Courtesy of the Hawaii Department of Transportation Airports*

Hawaii territorial governor Wallace Farrington inspected *Aloha* at Wheeler Field on Oahu at the conclusion of the Dole Derby. The governor discovered, and then ate, pilot Martin Jensen's untouched lunch. *Courtesy of the Hawaii Department of Transportation Airports*

Similarly agitated was James Dole, who greeted the two aviators shortly after their landing. The race sponsor was obviously worried about the planes that had yet to arrive: *Golden Eagle* and *Miss Doran*. "That's fine! Now for the other two," he said tersely to Jensen and Schluter.

But the other two airplanes did not arrive to Hawaii. Not that day, not that night, not the next day, or any day after that. *Golden Eagle* and *Miss Doran* were missing.

By the next morning, a day and a half since the Dole Air Race commenced, it was clear the crews of *Golden Eagle* and *Miss Doran* were in trouble. Both planes would have certainly exhausted their fuel supplies by now, likely meaning their planes were atop or beneath the ocean. The navy ordered more than forty ships to search for the missing crews, and dozens of commercial watercraft joined in the hunt, too. Those looking for the missing aviators were reminded of the saga of Commander John Rodgers, who was rescued with his navy crew after sailing across the Pacific in his disabled flying boat for ten days. Certainly another miracle was possible.

Despite this slim hope, *Golden Eagle*'s and *Miss Doran*'s absence cast a pall over the celebrations planned in Honolulu for the winning racers. While the Dole fliers would be at the center of a parade in Honolulu and the honored guests of a luau at the home of James Dole in the coming days, these affairs were subdued, not nearly as spirited as the welcomes given the previous aviators who reached Hawaii earlier in the summer. A day after landing, Dole awarded his prizes to the first- and second-place winners during a ceremony at the Royal Hawaiian hotel. The two checks—for $25,000 and $10,000—each featured a hand-painted airplane on its face.

The men who received these checks were heartsick over their fellow fliers having gone missing. The morning before accepting his prize money, Martin

"Pineapple King" James Dole, center, sitting between the winning aviators of the Dole Air Race during the prize ceremony at the Royal Hawaiian hotel on Waikiki Beach. Navy lieutenant William V. Davis, navigator for the first-place *Woolaroc*, is seated at the far left, beside pilot Art Goebel. *Aloha* navigator Paul Schluter is seated at the far right, beside pilot Martin Jensen. *Courtesy of the Woolaroc Museum, Bartlesville, Oklahoma*

Jensen took *Aloha* up in the air with his wife, cruising out over the ocean in the hopes of spotting a downed plane. They saw nothing, but remained determined to continue assisting the search efforts. "I will not rest—I have no plans—there is only one thought in my mind, and that is to save my buddies," said Jensen, his eyes red from lack of sleep.

Art Goebel and Lieutenant Bill Davis volunteered their services, too, uncomfortable being praised while their fellow competitors were perhaps struggling to survive atop the waves. The pair had breakfasted with *Golden Eagle* pilot Jack Frost in California the morning of the flight, and had made plans to dine together again at the Royal Hawaiian the next day. As Goebel and Davis wrote together in a joint statement:

> In the light of what has happened, we forget the hero-worship that has been forced upon us. We forget the material gain that has come from our quest. . . . All that we can think of today is that we want to wind up our Whirlwind again, and if we can but be granted another triumph from the fates, go soar out from the scenes of our own little happiness, and give all—if necessary—that our less fortunate friends may be brought safely into port.

Yet the concern fellow aviators showed paled in comparison to the heartache the friends and family of the missing fliers suffered. On race day in Honolulu, *Miss Doran* sponsor William Malloska had sat despondently on the bleachers, hunched over with his elbows on his knees, as the hours passed and his friends aboard the red-white-and-blue biplane remained missing. The Michigan service station owner was so sick with worry that he refused every bit of food and drink offered his way, preferring to solemnly stare into his hands or the empty sky.

When it was clear *Miss Doran* faced some sort of hardship that delayed or prevented her arrival, Malloska spouted optimism, listing numerous reasons to believe the crew was alive and well. The airplane was designed to float, he said, thanks to a buoyant fuel tank and waterproof wings. Enough provisions were on board, he added, to feed the three-person crew for days. And they might not even be atop the water at all, but instead stranded on one of the other Hawaiian islands.

Malloska refused to believe the plane had engine trouble, reminding others he had traveled across the country to California with Mildred Doran and Auggy Pedlar before taking a steamship to Honolulu to wait on his flying friends. Yet the fact was *Miss Doran* had not arrived, and Malloska couldn't imagine any reason why. "I tell you it makes a man feel queer, a thing like this does," he said, his face unshaven and his eyes filling with tears. "Yesterday just knowing you'd see her come in with the rest—and now you're all up in the air. To think of Miss Doran just rarin' to go all the time. There was never another like her."

No matter the safety features of the plane, the chief reason Malloska held out hope for *Miss Doran* was because of the character and talents of those aboard. "I think we will pick them up. I have every faith in Pedlar and [Vilas] Knope," said the sponsor. "Pedlar has had as many hours in the air as any man in the United States. He started flying at 14 years of age. Lieutenant Knope, navy men tell me, is one of the best they have."

Even tougher was Doran, whom Malloska had known since she was a girl. When expressing hope for her safety, he removed crumpled telegrams from his pocket in which Doran had promised their reunion. "Everything all fixed up fine, see you Wednesday," said one cheerily. If anyone could survive a trial at sea, he believed it was the Flying Schoolma'am, a young woman who had endured hardship since losing her mother as a child. "There never was a girl like her for pluck and courage. She never had any father or mother since she was 14. Now she is 22 and raised two kids younger than herself," said Malloska. "She worked hard at her school teaching profession. Yes, Miss Doran could stand it. She's a regular little iron woman, strong as steel and a hard worker."

Also in agony over Doran's fate was her family back home in Flint, Michigan. Her two brothers and eleven-year-old sister listened to news reports until 2:00 AM at an aunt's house, finally going to sleep as the sun set in Hawaii. The day before, at the beginning of the Dole Air Race, the family had grown upset when *Miss Doran* returned to Oakland to make engine repairs. "It was terrible. I could not believe that all the preparation had gone for nothing," said twenty-four-year-old William Doran Jr. "But when we heard that Auggy had gotten off finally, the sun seemed to break through the clouds again."

The Dorans' excitement fizzled when their sister was late to Honolulu. After a restless night of worrying and little sleep, the Doran siblings woke at daybreak and headed to the offices of the *Flint Journal*. Weeks earlier Mildred had flipped a coin in the newsroom, with fortune deciding Auggy would become her pilot. Now the Dorans came to the *Journal* to learn of any updates on the flight that may have arrived by telegraph. Yet the telegraph machines yielded no answers. *Miss Doran* was still missing.

William Doran Jr. refused to let the absence of information get him down. "I have not given up hope and believe that all is safe and sound," he said. "Mildred will come through. She's too good to go that way." While the Doran children waited for good news in Flint, their father worked the oat fields at the family farm in nearby Otisville. He asked to be left alone until his daughter's fate was known. "I'll be glad when it's all over and Mildred is home," said William Sr. "I want to forget it all until some definite information is received."

More upbeat was the family of Gordon Scott, the young navigator aboard *Golden Eagle*. "My boy will turn up safe and sound—I just know it," said the navigator's mother, Sarah Stewart Scott. "Certainly he will, mother," agreed Gordon's seventeen-year-old sister, Sheila, who had returned to the family's home in Santa Monica, California, after watching her brother depart the Oakland airport. *Golden Eagle*, it was noted, was designed to float, containing inflatable pouches in its wingtips. And the plane's two-man crew could easily have been picked up by "some schooner without radio apparatus," said the family. Sister Kathleen Scott told her coworkers that "Gordon would come out all right. We expect any minute to get the news. Gordon's experience on the water between the mainland and the islands, and his knowledge of trade winds and ship lanes help strengthen our faith. We are following our daily routine."

As the hours passed, sightings of the planes were reported, most of them soon deemed false, each just another plane or a fishing boat that had been confused for the missing aircraft. Yet one report from Hawaii was briefly deemed legitimate, and news went out on the wire on the night of August 18—one day since the race concluded—that *Miss Doran*'s crew had been found safe on Maui.

William Doran Jr. heard this update in the newsroom of the *Flint Journal*, where he had been keeping constant vigil close to the telegraph machines. His mood brightened instantly. He soon sent a telegram to his sister rejoicing in her safe arrival to Hawaii: "Dear Mil: I experienced the greatest thrill of my life when I heard you had been found. God bless all of you." William then visited his aunt's house about midnight to spread the happy news. When he told his sister Helen that Mildred had been found, the young girl wrapped her arms around her oldest brother and exclaimed, "Oh Bill, that's the best news I ever heard in my life."

But Mildred Doran and her crewmates had not been found on Maui, or anywhere else. The news report from Hawaii was soon revealed as false.

Bill Erwin and Alvin Eichwaldt were heading to the Oakland airport—again. It had been three days since the start of the Dole Air Race, when their plane *Dallas Spirit* was forced to return to the airfield with a large tear in the fabric wrapping its fuselage. It had been two days since *Woolaroc* and *Aloha* landed in Hawaii, claiming the two prizes offered by Pineapple King James Dole. And yet Erwin and Eichwaldt were planning to retry their journey to the islands that morning, hoping to take off soon in their mended silver-and-green airplane.

On their way to Bay Farm Island, the pilot and navigator bumped into C. W. Saunders and H. E. MacConaughey, the two San Francisco executives (from the Matson Navigation Company and Hawaiian Pineapple Company, respectively) who had helped administer the race. The businessmen urged Erwin not to fly for Hawaii. There was no prize money left, they argued, and any chance of finding the missing fliers was slim. They warned that *Dallas Spirit*, too, could run into trouble.

The two airmen were unmoved by their appeals. They would fly to Hawaii. "It's very good of you to say that. I appreciate it. But I have five friends down in the ocean," said Erwin. "If I were down, I'm sure they would come out looking for me. I can't do less. Don't worry about me. I'll be all right." MacConaughey looked long and hard at Erwin before uttering a judgment: "Well, Captain Erwin, all I can say is that you are a man."

Erwin and Eichwaldt planned to take a zigzag course to Hawaii, searching areas of the ocean devoid of navy ships. If *Dallas Spirit* reached Hawaii and the missing aviators had been found, Erwin explained, he would then fly on to Tokyo and Hong Kong, hopeful of capturing the Easterwood Prize. But if the crews of *Golden Eagle* and *Miss Doran* were still missing when he reached Hawaii, then he said he'd fly back to California, scanning the seas again as he returned to the mainland and forfeited any potential prize.

Before leaving for Hawaii, Erwin penned a note to be shared with his loved ones and boosters. The flying ace, who had survived dogfights and being shot down during World War I, seemed to sense a flight to Hawaii could be as perilous as any combat mission:

> Tomorrow begins the great adventure. Flying personifies the spirit of man. Our bodies are bound to the earth; our spirits are bound by God alone, and it is my firm belief that God will guide the course of *Dallas Spirit* tomorrow over the shortest route from the Golden Gate to the Isle of Oahu. I want to thank each and every sponsor for the opportunity of doing this thing. If we succeed it will be glorious. Should we fail, it will not be in vain, for a worthy attempt could never result in a mean failure.
>
> I believe with my whole heart that we will make it. I believed in it when I first conceived it, and I believe it more strongly now. We will win because *Dallas Spirit* always wins.
>
> But if it be His will that we should not make it, and from the exploration of the Pacific we should suddenly be called upon to chart our course over the Great Ocean of Eternity, then be of good cheer. I hold life dear, but I do not fear death. It is the last and most wonderful adventure of life. If something should happen to me I know I don't have to ask you to look after Mrs. Erwin. It broke her heart that she could not accompany me. She is my life, gentlemen, and the sweetest, finest, truest girl the Almighty ever created.
>
> Knowing that she is safe gives me confidence and vigor for the trial. We will make it because we must, but whatever comes, I am the master of my fate, and, God willing, the captain of my soul.

Dallas Spirit took off from Oakland at 2:15 PM. Its fuel tanks carrying 480 gallons of gasoline, a supply that would ostensibly allow them to zig and zag their way to Hawaii. Also aboard was a radio salvaged from a wrecked competitor—*Pabco Pacific Flyer*. Navigator Eichwaldt made good use of the newly installed device, broadcasting a handful of messages each hour before night began to fall over the Pacific. Eichwaldt's reports indicated *Dallas Spirit* was flying across the ocean at close to one hundred miles per hour. The aviators enjoyed some sunshine and a high ceiling for a few hours before cloud cover forced them down in the evening to an altitude of five hundred feet or so. Eichwaldt was relaxed and playful. Not only did he broadcast updates of their position, but he also sent lighthearted messages such as "LOVE TO MA" and "ALL IS O.K. EXCEPT BILL JUST SNEEZED."

At 5:45 PM the aviators claimed they saw a rum runner on the seas below. "HAD A HELL OF A TIME KEEPING IKE IN," said a message facetiously attributed to Erwin. Twenty minutes later another message sarcastically complained of missing toothpicks in their supper. At 8:00 PM Eichwaldt reported that it was getting dark and that they had yet to see any downed airplanes or wreckage floating atop the waves. "WE APPARENTLY WILL NOT BE ABLE TO SEE MUCH UNTIL MORNING," wrote the navigator.

About this time *Dallas Spirit* encountered bumpy air and possibly a storm, as indicated by the fluctuating pitch of the radio waves sent from the plane when Eichwaldt broadcast messages. At 9:00 PM Eichwaldt confirmed they were having trouble when he transmitted an urgent call for help: "SOS, WE ARE IN A TAILSPIN." Moments later he continued his message, stating, "WE CAME OUT OF IT O.K., BUT WERE SURE SCARED. IT SURE WAS A CLOSE CALL. I THOUGHT IT WAS ALL OVER, BUT CAME OUT OF IT. THE LIGHT ON THE INSTRUMENT BOARD WENT OUT AND IT WAS SO DARK THAT BILL COU—"

The radio broadcast stopped abruptly in midsentence.

Moments passed. Then the navigator keyed a final, unfinished message: "WE'RE IN ANOTHER TAILSPIN—"

Eight airplanes smashed or gone missing. Ten vanished or dead aviators. Just two flying crews landed safely on the islands. The statistics of the Dole Air Race to Hawaii were abysmal.

In the wake of so much tragedy, the press, who for weeks had acted as boosters for the air race, promoting the personalities of the participants and publishing betting odds for the contest, turned a critical eye toward the proceedings. "Orgy of reckless sacrifice," claimed the *Philadelphia Inquirer*. "Death-dealing stunts," screamed the *St. Louis Star*. "Aviation asininity," cried the *Louisville Times*. "A gamble at long odds against suicide," said the *Syracuse Post-Standard*. "Will somebody please explain what good purpose has been served by this competitive flight?" asked the *Brooklyn Eagle*.

Down South, the Norfolk *Virginian-Pilot* was no less damning. That newspaper's editorial writer, however, did at least admit the complicity of the general public in encouraging aviators to attempt such a perilous challenge:

> The Dole Race has made this contribution to aeronautics—it has made it plain that transoceanic air races, unless guarded by the strictest preparation requirements, are criminally wasteful of human life. By this wisdom the country arrives, as usual, by hindsight. There is no room anywhere for self-righteousness. No warning voice was raised while there was yet time. For days the entries had been flocking to the Oakland airport. The ruling out of some entries as clearly unprepared, the fatal crashing of other entries, the mad scramble of others to make a sufficiently impressive showing to pass the minimum tests and get on the starting line—all of these signs pointed to impending tragedy, but everybody was silent on these signs of danger. The talk was all of the race—the money prizes—the glory to be won—the thrill of it all.

Even aviator Ernie Smith, honorary starter at the Dole Derby and a man whose own appetite for risk was substantial, as proved by his treetop landing on Molokai, decried the consequences of the air race. "It is stunt flying," said Smith. "And now there are six men and a girl out there somewhere, battling for their lives. All for $35,000. It isn't worth it."

Few rushed to defend the air race and its participants. An exception was the *New York Herald Tribune*, which lauded the adventurous instincts of the aviators who dared try to cross half the world's largest ocean in search of pinpoint islands:

> One automatically begins to exclaim that there ought to be a law, until one stops with the reflection that it would be a poorer world if a man were not allowed to hazard his life and every one were made a coward by legislative enactment. The motto "Better be safe than sorry," tho a sound workaday rule, is not a noble principle for extraordinary occasions. Anxious publics pray for the rescue of these aviators only because they took the risk of not being rescued. If they had not been permitted to take the risk, it would have mattered to few whether they lived or died. This is not cynicism. Were the emo-

tions and the risks of adventure to be eliminated, men and women would approach the status of automatons. The reckless way of man belongs with his finest side.

Though much of the criticism was sharp and accusatory, there was also tremendous public sympathy for those who lost their lives in the Dole Derby. Mildred Doran in particular was singled out as a brave innocent whose enthusiasm for flying cost her life. "If Mildred Doran is today a ghost, she is a ghost which regrets nothing," said the *Boston Daily Advertiser*. "Let her fellow-women be proud of her, but not pity her. Pity is rather to be accorded to those who have lived long and dully ambitious for nothing save food, shelter, and petty diversions."

In Doran's hometown of Flint, a pew at Lakeview Methodist Episcopal Church was kept empty in her honor during a service following her disappearance. "I believe that all pioneers have a great, pulsating desire to help others, not for popularity but for their benefit," said the Reverend R. H. Prouse. "Women of the nation ought to be proud of one who had daring and courage to blaze a trail."

One month after the Dole Air Race, on September 14, 1927, mourners gathered for a memorial service at Pier 30 along the San Francisco waterfront, where the Matson Navigation Company steam liner SS *Maui* was docked. Among the women dressed in black were *Dallas Spirit* navigator Alvin Eichwaldt's mother, along with the wife and young daughter of *Miss Doran*'s navigator, navy lieutenant Vilas Knope. The women sobbed and pressed handkerchiefs to their wet eyes as prayers were recited. Taps was played and a boys' choir sang. Then thousands of flowers were tossed to the water, along with two wreaths tossed by Knope's widow and daughter.

The ceremony ended as *Maui* departed for Honolulu, the longshoremen on the dock working with bared heads out of respect for the missing fliers. Two days later at sea, *Maui* pulled alongside fellow steam liner SS *Matsonia,* which was cruising in the opposite direction toward San Francisco. They hove to 750 miles off the California coast, at the spot where *Dallas Spirit* was believed to have crashed into the ocean. Another memorial service was held and plenty more flowers dumped into the sea, including a giant floral bible sent by the children of Caro, Michigan, where Doran had worked as a teacher.

"God Bless You Every One," said the children's gift, which featured a cork base so it could float.

While it is presumed, based on radio messages, that Eichwaldt and pilot Bill Erwin perished after *Dallas Spirit* spun into the Pacific, less certain are the fates of the crews aboard *Golden Eagle* and *Miss Doran*. Though race and plane sponsors James Dole, George Hearst, and Bill Malloska offered $40,000 in reward money, traces of the missing persons and planes were never found. It was not for a lack of trying.

In the case of *Golden Eagle*, some speculated that the lightning-quick plane overshot Hawaii entirely. If this was the case, some reasoned, then perhaps the aviators ran out of gas, landed at sea, and then drifted farther from the islands, possibly floating to remote Johnston Island, approximately 750 miles beyond Oahu. In October 1927 newspaper publisher William Randolph Hearst prevailed upon President Calvin Coolidge to order navy minesweeper USS *Whippoorwill* to Johnston Island to search for John Frost and Gordon Scott, as well as his son's missing plane. The navy found nothing.

A year later, Scott's brother, Denham, traveled to Hawaii's Big Island to search the long, broad slopes of Mauna Loa, the largest active volcano on Earth. The night *Golden Eagle* and *Miss Doran* had gone missing, a number of people had claimed seeing bright lights atop the volcano, possibly from flares. Denham Scott spent four months searching the slope of the volcano, forming a search party with pack mules and enlisting the help of the army and Dole Derby pilot Martin Jensen. The search party found nothing. In a letter to Frost's brother Ezra, Denham wrote of the "miles upon miles of tumbled lava masses, with boulders, cinder cones, ridges, ravines, lava tubes, raises, and ravines . . . the range of vision even in clear weather at all places very short." The search, Scott conceded, was "an impossible task . . . heartbreaking and hopeless."

Believing further investigation was warranted, Ezra Frost himself traveled to Hawaii a year later. There he persuaded the army, for whom he had formerly flown as a pilot, to conduct an aerial survey of the volcano. Soon eleven army airplanes carrying forty men passed over Mauna Loa again and again. Frost and the army found nothing.

Mildred Doran's brother William did not have any clues as to his sister's disappearance. He had remained at the *Flint Journal* for a day and a half after *Miss Doran* went missing before he was finally persuaded to give up his vigil beside the telegraph machines. He left the newsroom sobbing, heading off to grieve at a nearby lakeside cottage.

In the coming months and years a handful of bottles were found on the coasts of California and Hawaii containing notes supposedly signed by Mildred Doran. "Motor missing. All hope gone. We estimate it is 700 miles to Oahu. God bless you all. Mildred Doran," said one typical note, this one found within a bottle on the windward side of Oahu in 1932. None of these messages were considered credible.

Some people hypothesized that a recurrence of engine trouble doomed *Miss Doran*, and that the new spark plugs installed in its engine did not solve the plane's problems after it left the Oakland airport the second time. The plane could also have gotten lost, gone into a nighttime dive from which it did not recover, run out of fuel, caught on fire, suffered some other mechanical mishap, or encountered any other scenario one can dream up to explain its failed arrival. Similarly, one can only guess what happened to *Golden Eagle* as it shot across the Pacific. Ultimately, it is known only that both *Golden Eagle* and *Miss Doran* did not arrive as expected to Wheeler Field on Oahu after being seen passing the Farallon Islands. What happened to those planes and the five aviators they carried remains a mystery.

Less shrouded are the fates of the Dole Derby winners. Art Goebel gave up stunt flying after winning the derby and continued his aviation career by flying in cross-country races and working as a skywriter for Frank Phillips, his oilman friend in Oklahoma who helped sponsor, and later came to own, *Woolaroc*. While other pilots composed messages in block letters, Goebel was admired for skywriting in handsome script. In the 1930s he joined the Army Air Corps Reserve and then served as a pilot in the Pacific during World War II. In the 1940s the longtime bachelor was also married for six years to a cosmetics heiress before they divorced. Afterward Goebel traveled the world extensively and enjoyed a ranch in Texas for many years before dying in Los Angeles in 1973 at age seventy-eight.

Goebel's companion across the Pacific, Lieutenant William V. Davis Jr., returned to active duty with the navy in San Diego following his victory in the Dole Air Race. He soon became a pilot for the navy's first aerobatics team, the Three Sea Hawks. He would go on to enjoy a long and distinguished naval career in which he served prominently in the Pacific during World War II. He retired as a vice admiral and the deputy commander in chief of the Atlantic Fleet in 1960. Davis died in Mobile, Alabama, in 1981 at age seventy-nine.

The other winning derby navigator, Paul Schluter, left Hawaii disappointed. Though he had promised Martin Jensen he would fly to the islands for glory alone, he apparently changed his mind when he saw *Aloha*'s pilot accept a $10,000 check from James Dole. The navigator was supposedly only able to return to California after Dole bought his passage on a steam liner and dropped him off at the docks. Schluter died in 1962 at age seventy-two.

Jensen felt bad for the navigator but reiterated that nearly all his perceived winnings were in fact owed to the sponsors in Hawaii who enabled the purchase of *Aloha*. Jensen, who did ultimately give Schluter about $2,000 he had received from a newspaper for writing an account of their flight, claimed that he in fact suffered financially for flying the Dole Air Race, what with so many bills associated with buying, flying, fueling, and fixing an aircraft. "The expenses turned out to be a lot higher than the winnings," said the pilot. "But of course, the money wasn't the real reason we were in the race."

Just weeks after the race, and now a celebrity, Jensen returned to California to accept an offer from MGM Studios in Hollywood to fly its mascot—Leo the Lion—across the country to New York. He would be flying a Ryan Brougham airplane whose rear fuselage had been converted into a cage complete with milk containers and plate-glass windows, which allowed the observation of Leo, a lion whose real name was actually Jackie. On September 16, 1927, Jensen and Leo took off from San Diego and headed east across the desert.

The single-engine plane was carrying a heavy load. There were four hundred gallons of fuel aboard, a four-hundred-pound lion, a metal cage, and heavy panes of thick plate glass. As Jensen flew across Arizona, hills and mountains reached up toward the plane, which the pilot could coax to climb no higher than about 4,200 feet. Above the Tonto National Forest, he steered the plane into a canyon, hoping to discover a pass through the mountains. Instead the canyon ended suddenly against a mountainside, leaving Jensen no time or space to turn around. He braced himself for the unavoidable crash.

"It was a rough landing, but I managed to strike a treetop that stopped the plane, although it rolled over a couple of times after striking. I crawled out and looked to see what had happened to Leo. The cage had held tight and he wasn't scratched, although he did look disgusted, and I figured his opinion of me as a flyer is pretty low," Jensen later recalled. "It might not have been so bad," he continued, "if it hadn't been for all that plate glass. The crash shattered it into a million slivers. Leo was badly cut up. I had lots of gashes, too."

One month earlier to the day, Jensen had been lost above the Pacific with his navigator, with much of the world wondering where he was. Now he was lost in the Arizona desert with a lion, and again many people were wondering where he was. Bidding a temporary goodbye to Leo, the pilot started hiking. "When I asked him how he felt he licked his chops and settled himself as best as he could in the cage of the wrecked plane," he said. "Then I fixed him up with what milk we had left, divided my sandwiches with him and started down the canyon for help."

For three days and three nights Jensen trekked across treacherous desert terrain. The rocky landscape was punishing. His boots soon fell to tatters, the soles falling away entirely, leaving his feet swollen with blisters the size of silver dollars. The seat of his pants was also reduced to threads due to him sliding down so many rocks. At night he slept in trees or brush so as to protect himself from coyotes.

Finally, he reached a ranch, and soon after that, in Roosevelt, Arizona, he found a telephone. When he called up MGM to deliver the bad news, the movie studio had just one question: How's the lion? Jensen then led a rescue party back to the crash site. Leo was found alive, hauled out of the desert, and nursed back to health. "But I never flew him again," said Jensen. "In fact, that experience was enough to make me swear off flying lions for life."

Though he maintained a sense of humor, Jensen found little to laugh at in the months that followed the race. As he and Peg continued to struggle financially, Martin began to resent his wife and blame her for their money woes, alleging she had made poor business decisions while he was searching for an airplane. Complaining to a reporter in San Francisco, Jensen claimed he had four things to show from the Dole Air Race: a pin from the Hawaiian governor, a ukulele, a wristwatch from an oil company, and a bunch of unpaid bills. Speaking of his former airplane *Aloha*, he said, "I sometimes wish I had headed her nose into the water and let the troubles swim out."

Peg Jensen was in similar despair. Following a row with Martin and a brief separation, and while also mourning the deaths of a few aviator friends who perished in Hawaii, she allegedly tried to take her own life on at least two occasions, once by overdosing on sleeping pills and the other time with a gun that friends had to reportedly pry from her hands. Peg downplayed these stories as sensational, and the couple reconciled, though their marriage did not ultimately last.

Nearly three months after the Dole Air Race, Martin Jensen was conspicuously absent from a White House luncheon and a Washington dinner ceremony hosted by President Calvin Coolidge. The ceremonies on November 14, 1927, honored the handful of American transoceanic fliers who struck out successfully across the Atlantic or Pacific. Jensen, two months into his recovery from his crash in the desert, claimed his bandaged feet prevented him from making the trip to the nation's capital. Yet another time the pilot claimed he simply overlooked the president's invitation. Jensen, who stepped into *Aloha* in Oakland with a pocketful of unread telegrams, apparently had a habit of letting his mail accumulate for weeks or months at a time before taking the time to read through it.

His flying mate across the water, Schluter, and Dole Derby winner Goebel were present for the ceremonies, sharing the spotlight with Charles Lindbergh and enjoying the company of Orville Wright. *City of Oakland* fliers Ernie Smith and Emory Bronte were in attendance, too. After the Dole Derby, Bronte served as a naval aviator in World War II and eventually moved to Hawaii and worked as a business executive. He died in Honolulu in 1982 at age eighty. Smith became a Trans World Airline (TWA) pilot and executive after making his thrilling flight to Hawaii. He died in San Francisco in 1963 at age seventy. Both Smith and Bronte were awarded the US military's Distinguished Flying Cross for their pioneering civilian flight to Hawaii.

Also in attendance at the White House, and also recipients of the Distinguished Flying Cross for their flight to Hawaii, were US Army Air Corps lieutenants Lester Maitland and Albert Hegenberger. Following his own flight to Hawaii, Maitland continued his army service, eventually commanding an airfield in the Philippines at the outset of World War II and then flying bomber missions in Europe. After leaving the military, he became an Episcopal minister before dying in Scottsdale, Arizona, in 1990 at age ninety-one.

Hegenberger also enjoyed a long and decorated military career. In 1932 he was awarded a second Distinguished Flying Cross by President Franklin D. Roosevelt for making the first solo flight by instrument alone. Flying blind in a covered cockpit, Hegenberger took off from Patterson Field in Dayton,

Ohio, flew for ten miles, circled, and landed again. He completed the trip by using flying instruments he had helped develop himself, including those used on his pioneering flight to Hawaii. Later, after serving in World War II, he helped create a military system to detect nuclear blasts anyplace in the world. He retired from the US Air Force as a major general and died in Goldenrod, Florida, in 1983 at age eighty-seven.

As these assorted dates of death suggest, all those who participated in the pioneering flights to Hawaii have died. Gone, too, are nearly all the planes that carried these aviators across the Pacific. The exception is *Woolaroc,* which hangs from a ceiling at the Woolaroc Museum on Phillip's former ranch in Bartlesville, Oklahoma.

Many memorials have also not survived the nine decades since these first flights to Hawaii occurred. John Rodgers Field in Honolulu is now Daniel K. Inouye International Airport. Maitland Field once fronted Lake Michigan in downtown Milwaukee, but was eventually redeveloped into a waterside park bearing another gentleman's name. Maitland and Hegenberger also had streets named in their honor at the Oakland airport, and these at least remain today.

In Flint, Michigan, Bill Malloska built the Doran Tower in 1929 in honor of his lost friend. The windmill-shaped gas station featured a bronze plaque inscribed with the words of President Theodore Roosevelt: "Only those are fit to live who are not afraid to die." The tower was demolished in 1973. Yet in Ontario, Canada, lies Doran Lake, one of a number of bodies of water named for lost aviators.

In Wahiawa, Hawaii, the most obvious reminder of James Dole is the Dole Plantation tourist attraction. Promising "Hawaii's complete pineapple experience," the plantation and its pineapple garden maze exists on land close to Dole's original farm and welcomes more than a million visitors a year. The plantation's namesake fell on hard times, however, soon after sponsoring his 1927 air race. He was removed from the Hawaiian Pineapple Company's day-to-day leadership during the Depression as HAPCO faced cash shortages and had trouble paying its debts.

The Pineapple King did not retain happy memories from the Dole Derby. He was stung by charges that he had created a reckless contest. He regretted not having pushed for even stiffer safety standards, such as a requirement that every plane carry a two-way radio. Though he believed he had acted responsibly by turning administration of the race over to aviation experts, he also harbored bitterness over his association with so many fliers' deaths. "I had no idea that there were so many damned fools who were willing to risk their necks in old crates made of flour sacks and fishing poles," he once remarked dismissively. Dole died in Honolulu in 1958 at age eighty.

Though ten people lost their lives in the Dole Derby, the air race, as well as the flights of PN-9 No. 1, *Bird of Paradise*, and *City of Oakland*, did succeed in spurring air travel throughout the Pacific. In 1928, a year after the first flights to Hawaii, Australian pilot Charles Kingford Smith and three crewmates became the first aviators to cross the entire Pacific Ocean. Flying a trimotored Fokker named *Southern Cross*, the aviators left Oakland and made stops in Hawaii and Fiji before landing in Brisbane, Australia, ten days later.

In 1936 Pan American Airways began the first air passenger service to Hawaii, carrying about eight people at a time from San Francisco Bay to Hawaii aboard a Martin 130 Clipper. Jetliners started flying to Hawaii in the 1950s, and today the Honolulu airport hosts about twenty million passengers a year, a phenomenal increase from the days when the arrival of a single pilot and navigator was front-page news celebrated publicly for a week.

For a few hundred dollars, anyone can fly to Hawaii today. It's worth remembering the cost was once much steeper, with several intrepid aviators forfeiting their lives for the chance to blaze new air routes above the Pacific. To find those tiny islands within the world's mightiest ocean was an absolute triumph.

As pilot Ernie Smith said, "Anybody who thinks this ocean flying business is a cinch is all wet."

ACKNOWLEDGMENTS

MY INTRODUCTION TO THE first flights to Hawaii came courtesy of the wonderful museum exhibit *Hawaii by Air* created by David Romanowski, a writer and editor who's now retired from the Smithsonian National Air and Space Museum. David, whom I later had the pleasure of meeting in person, was successful in accomplishing the aims of any museum professional: to impart information and spark imagination. When I left the National Air and Space Museum in Washington, DC, one summer day in 2014, I could not stop thinking about the daring aviation pioneers who steered their airplanes toward Hawaii. I knew I had found the subject of my next book.

A few years later, as a bookend to my research for *Race to Hawaii*, I revisited the museum to make a final research sweep and review assorted odds and ends in the museum's archives. Again I had an excellent visit, able to view a few relevant relics from early aviation, including navigator Emory Bronte's leather flying helmet and the checkered starting flag for the Dole Air Race. For this trip, I very much appreciate the help provided by Roger Connor, Elizabeth Borja, and Mark Taylor.

Even better than the flying helmet and checkered flag was the chance to see a whole airplane from the 1920s. The sole surviving airplane to make an early flight to Hawaii is *Woolaroc*, the Travel Air 5000 that Art Goebel piloted to a first-place finish in the Dole Derby. *Woolaroc* is still in the air, albeit suspended by cables from the ceiling of the Woolaroc Museum in Bartlesville, Oklahoma. Shiloh Thurman at the museum was kind enough to allow me to hop on a scissors lift, rise twenty or so feet into the air, and inspect the hanging airplane. Perched atop the lift, I stuck my head into *Woolaroc*'s cramped cockpit and fuselage, the same spaces where Art Goebel and Bill Davis each sat, respectively, for more than twenty-four hours as they cruised to Oahu. Running my hand

273

gently across the painted fabric stretched tight across the fuselage, I marveled at the thinness of this sheathing, which resembled a drum skin. Was this really all that separated the Dole birds and others from the depths of the Pacific? Beyond being grateful to Shiloh at the Woolaroc Museum, I appreciate the help of Colin Dugan, David Baughn, and Linda Stone.

Many others facilitated my research, particularly Brett Stolle at the National Museum of the United States Air Force in Dayton, Ohio; Katherine Ets-Hokin at the San Francisco History Center in the San Francisco Public Library; the staff and volunteers at the National Naval Aviation Museum in Pensacola, Florida; Molly Marcusse at the American Heritage Center of the University of Wyoming; Brittany Phalen at the Sloan Longway Museum, Planetarium and Automotive Gallery in Flint, Michigan; Julie Takata at San Francisco's SFO Museum; Jennifer Bryan at the US Naval Academy; Jen Roger at the Hiller Aviation Museum in San Carlos, California; Kathleen Correia and Mike Dolgushkin at the California State Library in Sacramento; dmairfield.org; and friends Hannah Ashe, Jim Muir, and James Scott. Many thanks are due, as well, to literary agent Jessica Papin and editors Jerome Pohlen and Lindsey Schauer at Chicago Review Press, who provided crucial support and guidance for this story.

Outside St. Louis I was hosted by Liz Glaser, whose late father, Robert Scheppler, wrote his own fine account of the Dole Air Race. Liz graciously allowed me access to her father's files and even helped secure me a plane ride in a friend's vintage Stearman aircraft. Too bad I was too chicken to ever go up in the air. (Researching and writing about every which way people have perished in early airplanes has the effect of making one want to avoid a similar fate. Watching Susan Sarandon plummet to earth in *The Great Waldo Pepper* also didn't help.)

Finally, in Los Angeles I visited the Seaver Center for Western History Research at the Natural History Museum of Los Angeles County, benefiting from the help of John Cahoon and Betty Uyeda. There, too, I was assisted by the lovely Elizabeth Ryan, who dutifully helped me sift through countless old newspaper clippings. Moreover, Elizabeth's enthusiasm and encouragement, as well as the support of my family, was critical to this book's completion. To everyone mentioned I offer my sincere thanks and gratitude.

NOTES

Part I: The Navy's PN-9 No. 1

"leading a racehorse": *New York Times*, September 26, 1925.

"every success": *San Francisco Chronicle*, September 1, 1925.

"The proposed airplane flight": *Honolulu Advertiser*, August 21, 1925.

"Upon our arrival": *New York Times*, September 21, 1925.

"form a firmer roadbed": *San Francisco Chronicle*, September 21, 1925.

"bugaboo": Ibid.

"leviathan of air and sea": "Aircraft PN-9 Taxis in Water and Comes Up to the Seaplane Ramp HD Stock Footage," YouTube video, posted by CriticalPast, May 2, 2014, www.youtube.com/watch?v=Q1UgZv4ELj4.

"the best flying boat ever": *Washington Post*, December 1, 1925.

"The whole outfit was working": *San Francisco Chronicle*, September 21, 1925.

"During the past year": US Navy West Coast–Hawaii Flight Report, 1925, National Naval Aviation Museum, Pensacola, FL.

"No reason exists": Ibid.

"The chief concern": *San Francisco Chronicle*, September 22, 1925.

"He was to me": Thomas Hart Benton, *Thirty Years View; or, a History of the Working of the American Government for Thirty Years, from 1820 to 1850 [. . .]* (New York: D. Appleton, 1854), 2:144.

"gallantry . . . zeal and bravery": *Dictionary of American Biography*, 1936, s.v. "John Rodgers."

"Midshipman Rodgers gives promise": Student personnel file of John Rodgers, US Naval Academy, Annapolis, MD.

"human kite tail": Newspaper article, unknown origin and date, in vertical files at the San Francisco Public Library concerning aviation, the Dole Air Race, and assorted pilots (hereafter cited as SFPL).

"considerable surprise": John Rodgers, "My Acquaintance with the Wrights," *Slipstream*, January 1926, 18.

"I guess I will be": John Hammond Moore, "The Short, Eventful Life of Eugene B. Ely," *Proceedings Magazine*, January 1981, www.usni.org/magazines/proceedings/1981-01-short-eventful-life-eugene-b-ely.

"never showed good flying sense": George van Deurs, *Wings for the Fleet: A Narrative of Naval Aviation's Early Development. 1910–1916* (Annapolis, MD: Naval Institute Press, 2016), 48.

"The only fact": San Francisco Examiner, April 20, 1912.

"Tell you this": San Francisco Examiner, September 27, 1925.

I'll break this thing: San Francisco Chronicle, September 23, 1925.

"Running parallel with the shore": Honolulu Advertiser, September 1, 1925.

"mere silver butterflies": San Francisco Chronicle, September 1, 1925.

"SEE YOU TOMORROW": Honolulu Advertiser, unknown date.

"The boat came up": Albert Pierce Taylor, Under Hawaiian Skies (Honolulu: Advertiser, 1922), 235.

"deadheads": William J. Horvat, Above the Pacific (Fallbrook, CA: Aero, 1966), 25.

"I suppose we met": New York Times, July 15, 1911.

"entire city": Honolulu Advertiser, unknown date.

"Welcome": Honolulu Advertiser, unknown date.

"Ready to serve": Omaha (NE) Daily Bee, October 9, 1915.

"SAY HAVE YOU GOT ANY": Radio chatter featuring PN-9 No. 1, unless noted otherwise, is from transcripts within the US Navy West Coast–Hawaii Flight Report.

"feat of airmanship": Ibid.

"After each member": Ibid.

"Down we went": San Francisco Chronicle, September 3, 1925.

"giving the impression": San Francisco Bulletin, September 24, 1925.

When I tried my first: San Francisco Chronicle, September 23, 1925.

"He did this quite": New York Times, September 26, 1925.

"Every time I looked": Ibid.

"WE WILL CRACK UP": Honolulu Advertiser, September 2, 1925.

"dry as a powder house": New York Times, September 26, 1925.

"The messages were flying": Ibid.

"The Flight Is Doomed": Honolulu Advertiser, September 1, 1925.

"Rodgers knows what he is": Honolulu Advertiser, unknown date.

"We'll try again Thursday": Ibid.

"We are not worried yet": Honolulu Advertiser, September 2, 1925.

"If anybody can do it": Ibid.

"Shadows, grim and ghostly": Honolulu Advertiser, unknown date.

"shark feed": New York Times, September 26, 1925.

"perfect landing": Honolulu Advertiser, unknown date.

Here we had worked: San Francisco Chronicle, September 23, 1925.

"Captain, here's a little": New York Times, September 26, 1925.

It's better you took: Ibid.

"A great day for the fishes": Ibid.

"strong enough to knock one": San Francisco Chronicle, September 23, 1925.

"You'd better be saving that": New York Times, September 26, 1925.

"never could be put": Ibid.

"peaked under the gills": San Francisco Chronicle, September 25, 1925.

"It was a queer sensation": Honolulu Advertiser, unknown date.

"We were listening": Honolulu Advertiser, unknown date.

"How'd you happen": New York Times, September 26, 1925.

"They will find us": Ibid.

"I see smoke ahead": *San Francisco Chronicle*, September 23, 1925.

"search every drop of water": *Honolulu Advertiser*, unknown date.

"In spite of the recent": *Honolulu Advertiser*, unknown date.

"a parade of our navy" . . . *"The bodies of former companions"*: *Honolulu Advertiser*, September 6, 1925.

"CHEER UP JOHN": *New York Times*, September 24, 1925.

"Good morning, stranger": Ibid.

"Not today, mister, not today": *San Francisco Examiner*, July 8, 1937.

"big black fellows": *Honolulu Advertiser*, unknown date.

"You'll wait a long time": *San Francisco Chronicle*, September 24, 1925.

"Have a piece of toast": *San Francisco Chronicle*, September 25, 1925.

"It is like running": *New York Times*, September 24, 1925.

"You don't know how good": *New York Times*, September 13, 1925.

"It was tough": *San Francisco Examiner*, September 27, 1925.

"beautiful fish": *San Francisco Chronicle*, September 24, 1925.

"This remark was fully realized": *New York Times*, September 26, 1925.

"USE STARS AND TAP": *Honolulu Advertiser*, unknown date.

"Go easy on that hammer": *San Francisco Chronicle*, September 24, 1925.

"I don't think": *New York Times*, September 23, 1925.

"We managed to keep": *Honolulu Advertiser*, unknown date.

"At this rate": Byron J. Connell, "The Flight That Failed," *MIT Technology Review* 28, no. 1 (November 1925): 23.

"kiddies": *San Francisco Chronicle*, September 25, 1925.

"It's too bad": *Honolulu Advertiser*, unknown date.

"We'll be here all right": *Honolulu Advertiser*, September 7, 1925.

"TWENTY-ONE AVIATORS": Horvat, *Above the Pacific*, 57.

"We have virtually given up": *Washington Post*, September 8, 1925.

"Don't you think for a moment": *San Francisco Chronicle*, September 11, 1925.

"Whatever their fate": *Honolulu Advertiser*, unknown date.

"It made us damned mad": Newspaper article, unknown origin and date, SFPL.

"Only about a hundred miles": *San Francisco Chronicle*, September 24, 1925.

"Well, that is enough": *New York Times*, September 26, 1925.

"funny looks": *San Francisco Chronicle*, September 25, 1925.

"Pope kept looking back": *San Francisco Chronicle*, September 24, 1925.

"It was the best island": *Honolulu Advertiser*, September 11, 1925.

"I've had some pleasant experiences": *Honolulu Advertiser*, unknown date.

"slippery": *Honolulu Advertiser*, September 11, 1925.

"Fate seemed certainly against us,": *Honolulu Advertiser*, unknown date.

"That, I think": Ibid.

"bundle of pluck and courage": *San Francisco Examiner*, September 13, 1925.

"We knew our fate depended": *New York Times*, September 26, 1925.

"I knew I could not sleep": Ibid.

"There was Kauai": Horvat, *Above the Pacific*, 57.

"frowning cliffs": *Honolulu Advertiser*, unknown date.

"After sailing the plane 450 miles": *Honolulu Advertiser*, unknown date.

"We were confronted": *San Francisco Chronicle*, September 24, 1925.

"WHAT PLANE IS THAT": Horvat, *Above the Pacific*, 57.

"Do you want": John J. Geoghegan, "Nonstop to Hawaii by Air and Sea," *Aviation History*, March 2014, 52.

"All right, but give us": *New York Times*, September 15, 1925.

"Let them tow us in": Geoghegan, "Nonstop to Hawaii," 52.

"Give us some more": *Oakland (CA) Tribune*, July 15, 1927.

"Big boy, if you had": *Honolulu Advertiser*, September 10, 1925.

"I'm going to ride": *Honolulu Advertiser*, September 11, 1925.

"Another of his determinations": *Washington Post*, September 12, 1925.

"I don't want to go": *San Francisco Chronicle*, September 12, 1925.

"PLANE PN-9-1 LOCATED": *Honolulu Advertiser*, unknown date.

"Up to the wardroom": *Honolulu Advertiser*, unknown date.

"The indomitable spirit": *Honolulu Advertiser*, unknown date.

"thousands of persons shouting": *Honolulu Advertiser*, unknown date.

"Praise God from whom": *Honolulu Advertiser*, unknown date.

"Wait! Don't tell me": *Honolulu Advertiser*, unknown date.

"As the truth of the report": *Honolulu Advertiser*, unknown date.

"Few messages in all history": *Honolulu Advertiser*, unknown date.

Their son's name: *Honolulu Advertiser*, unknown date.

"We are delighted": *Honolulu Advertiser*, September 10, 1925.

"Will you please read that": Ibid.

"Oh thank God": Ibid.

"Oh . . . They've found my daddy": Ibid.

"tall, slender, blond": *San Francisco Chronicle*, September 12, 1925.

"I shouldn't talk about it": Ibid.

"Whether the beautiful Los Angeles girl": Ibid.

"Mathematical problems involving position": *Honolulu Advertiser*, September 11, 1925.

"That's easily explained": Ibid.

"He kidded us through": Ibid.

"always cheerful and worked": *Honolulu Advertiser*, unknown date.

"How are you old boy?": *Honolulu Advertiser*, unknown date.

"Good evening, governor": *San Francisco Chronicle*, September 12, 1925.

"Oh, John . . . John!": *Honolulu Advertiser*, unknown date.

"Feel fine": Ibid.

"They're going to shove us": Ibid.

"real Hawaiian aloha": Ibid.

"Now, let me correct": Ibid.

"This is not a land of cowards": Ibid.

"You newspaper men": Ibid.

"But I have nerves": Newspaper article, unknown origin, September 25, 1925, SFPL.

"endurance and heroism": *San Francisco Examiner*, September 25, 1925.

"Golden Gate, gee": Ibid.

"Aviation is a hazardous calling": *San Francisco Examiner*, August 28, 1926.

"If there are swivel": *San Francisco Examiner*, September 25, 1925.

"Go easy, boys": *Washington Post*, August 28, 1926.

Part II: The Army's *Bird of Paradise*

"I start[ed] to taxi": Charles A. Lindbergh, *The Spirit of St. Louis* (New York: Scribner, 1953), 492.

"You'd be like": Ibid., 44.

"Flyin' Fool": Ibid., 161.

"New York to Paris": Ibid., 14.

"The pioneering is over": *Battle Creek (MI) Enquirer*, September 13, 1927.

"IN VIEW LINDBERGHS ATLANTIC FLIGHT": Riley Allen and Joe Farrington to James D. Dole, telegram, 23 May 1927, Robert Scheppler Papers.

"lovely play ground": Richard Dole and Elizabeth Dole Porteus, *The Story of James Dole* (Aiea, HI: Island Heritage, 1990), 16.

"Jim did not": Ibid., 18.

"I got the notion": Ibid., 22.

"Don't take the business": Ibid., 15.

"Don't ask for pineapple alone": Ibid., 57.

"When I was growing up": Ibid., 8.

"We bought Lanai": Ibid., 72.

"square deal to every employee": Ibid., 78.

"I have been particularly interested": Ibid., 78.

"JAMES D. DOLE . . . BELIEVING THAT": James D. Dole to Riley Allen and Joe Farrington, telegram, 24 May 1927, Robert Scheppler Papers.

"NO PRECAUTION CAN BE": James D. Dole to Riley Allen and Joe Farrington, telegram, 25 May 1927, Robert Scheppler Papers.

"[go] mad about aviation": David McCullough, *The Wright Brothers* (New York: Simon & Schuster, 2015), 213.

"Every time we make": Ibid.

"To test a town": Don Dwiggins, *The Barnstormers: Flying Daredevils of the Roaring Twenties* (New York: Grosset & Dunlap, 1968), 43.

"The people who go": Ron Dick and Dan Patterson, *Aviation Century: The Golden Age* (Boston: Boston Mills, 2004), 197.

"The risk of starving": Dwiggins, *Barnstormers*, 46.

"Science, freedom, beauty, adventure": Lindbergh, *Spirit of St. Louis*, 261.

"Air racing may not be": Dick and Patterson, *Aviation Century*, 199.

"Why can't we just buy": Bob Dole, *Great Presidential Wit (. . . I Wish I Was in This Book)* (New York: Scribner, 2001), 68.

"to supply safe flying equipment": Maurer Maurer, *Aviation in the U.S. Army, 1919–1939* (Washington, DC: Office of Air Force History, US Air Force, 1987), 45.

"born flier": Justin Libby, "Lester Maitland and Albert Hegenberger; and the First Nonstop Flight to Hawaii," *American Aviation Historical Society Journal* (June 2010): 101.

"I went over": *Orange County (CA) Register*, January 1, 1986.

"I wrote a letter": Ibid.

"It is like flying": *San Francisco Examiner*, May 6, 1928.

"Blond, bumptious and a first": "Sky Pilot," *Time*, July 22, 1957.

"The front pages of newspapers": Lester J. Maitland, "Planes Across the Sea," *Liberty*, December 17, 1927, 13.

"I had a very fine chance": *Orange County (CA) Register*, January 1, 1986.

"I waited patiently": Lester J. Maitland, *Knights of the Air* (Garden City, NY: Doubleday, Doran, 1929), 318.

"I have the plane": *San Mateo (CA) Times*, June 23, 1927.

"The operation of present avigation": A. F. Hegenberger and Bradley Jones, "Oversea Navigation," *SAE Journal* 21, no. 6 (December 1927): 699.

"false sense of confidence": Albert Hegenberger, "The Importance of the Development of Aerial Navigation Instruments and Methods to the Air Service," September 1, 1923, unpublished article located in biographic and technical files of the Smithsonian National Air and Space Museum, 2.

"the science of directing": "Avigation," *American Speech*, August 1928.

"such an etymology is enough": "Avigation and Avigator," *American Speech*, October 1928.

"The time is not yet ripe": Libby, "Maitland and Hegenberger," 105.

"bored me to death": Ibid.

"I have regularly requested permission": Robert F. Hegenberger, "'The Bird of Paradise': The Significance of the Hawaiian Flight of 1927," *Air Power History*, Summer 1991, 7.

"Allow us to introduce": "A Real Hair Raising Affair (1926)," YouTube video, posted by British Pathé, April 13, 2014, www.youtube.com/watch?v=gNuZMD4zuLQ.

"No death is more horrible": Dick Grace, "Crashing Planes for the Movies," *Modern Mechanics and Inventions*, July 1930, 49.

"I've been called a fool": Ibid, 46.

"buying a new suit": Ibid., 48.

"The linen was all smooth": Ibid., 49.

"If I missed": Ibid., 182.

"It's the most popular topic": *Honolulu Advertiser*, July 13, 1927.

"I wouldn't be surprised": *New York Times*, June 8, 1927.

"That the newspapers have seen": H. E. MacConaughey to K. B. Barnes, 16 June 1927, Martin Jensen Papers (hereafter cited as MJP).

"We believe Mr. Dole's picture": MacConaughey to Barnes, 5 July 1927, MJP.

"Our ports will henceforth": *Honolulu Advertiser*, June 29, 1927.

"steps up to the plate": *Hawaii Hochi*, May 26, 1927, Bee Section.

"This is not too much": *Honolulu Star-Bulletin*, July 12, 1927.

"We are all afraid": R. F. Hegenberger, "'Bird of Paradise,'" 7.

"He is not only": Maitland, *Knights of the Air*, 318.

"Maitland's the high strung youngster": *San Francisco Chronicle*, June 29, 1927.

"Well, since everyone seems": *Bakersfield Californian*, June 22, 1927.

"From here the distance": Ibid.

"type of man": Maitland, *Knights of the Air*, 317.

"We believe that the hazard": *San Francisco Examiner*, June 22, 1927.

"There she is": *San Francisco Chronicle*, June 26, 1927.

"uncertain": Ibid.

"hard-living and utterly charming": "Ernest Smith," obituary, *San Francisco Chronicle*, March 27, 1963.

"Why don't you fellows": Ibid.

"bum sports," "crab the game": New Freedom (HI), June 18, 1927.

"suicide," "second hand": San Francisco Chronicle, June 23, 1927.

"Six men died in attempts": San Francisco Chronicle, June 24, 1927.

"Smith and Carter are going": San Francisco Chronicle, June 23, 1927.

"Those are the dirtiest tactics": Ibid.

"It seems to me that aviators": San Francisco Chronicle, June 24, 1927.

"I'll bet this against": San Francisco Chronicle, June 25, 1927.

"I am not questioning": San Francisco Chronicle, June 24, 1927.

"We have already spent": Ibid.

"boy," "First thing I knew": San Francisco Chronicle, June 27, 1927.

"at least for this trip": Ibid.

"I believe he'll make it": San Francisco Chronicle, June 28, 1927.

"I'll hop off Sunday night": San Francisco Chronicle, June 26, 1927.

"Both Maitland and I know": San Francisco Chronicle, June 24, 1927.

"electric highway": Maitland, Knights of the Air, 321.

"the faithful little jinni": Maitland, "Planes Across the Sea," 10.

"In a new instrument": San Francisco Chronicle, June 24, 1927.

"From here, those islands look": William J. Horvat, "Bird of Paradise: The First Non-Stop Flight to Hawaii," Aerospace Historian, June 1968, 27.

"It will be fine": San Francisco Chronicle, June 28, 1927.

"We don't want to talk": San Francisco Chronicle, June 26, 1927.

"I've never been up": San Francisco Chronicle, June 28, 1927.

"Smith himself was here": San Francisco Chronicle, June 27, 1927.

"Maitland and Hegenberger might fuel": Ibid.

"Let 'em": Ibid.

"two planes, their engines driven": Ibid.

"We can weather them": Ibid.

"They are watching each other": San Francisco Chronicle, June 26, 1927.

"this race will be": San Francisco Chronicle, June 28, 1927.

"I'm sorry": Ibid.

"As surely as the angel": Ibid.

"The ship's all right": Ibid.

"Give us a clear field": San Francisco Examiner, June 29, 1927.

"She wouldn't have missed": Ibid.

"With all the consideration": San Francisco Chronicle, July 9, 1927.

"not to worry": San Francisco Chronicle, June 29, 1927.

"We have every confidence": Ibid.

"boys": Berkeley (CA) Gazette, July 9, 1927.

"To the Mother of us": San Francisco in the 1930s: The WPA Guide to the City by the Bay, Federal Writers Project of the Works Progress Administration (Berkeley: University of California Press), 398.

"God bless you": Berkeley (CA) Gazette, July 9, 1927.

"Sorry I can't go myself": San Francisco Examiner, June 29, 1927.

"All heroes do not soar": Ibid.

"*God bless you, my boys*": *San Francisco Chronicle*, June 29, 1927.

"*General, you know we're going*": Ibid.

"*Goodbye, boys, we're off*": *Bakersfield Californian*, June 28, 1927.

"*Good luck*": *San Francisco Examiner*, June 29, 1927.

"*I may have a reputation*": Eugene J. Millikin, "Dick Grace and His Waterhouse Cruzair," *American Aviation Historical Society Journal* (Summer 1979): 134.

"*When I fly, my dog*": *Honolulu Advertiser*, July 10, 1927.

"*feeling of absolute safety*": Maitland, *Knights of the Air*, 320.

"*After all the years*": Ibid., 322.

"*I have seen many beautiful*": Ibid., 325.

"THE PLANE CAME UP LOW": *San Francisco Chronicle*, June 29, 1927.

"*It was a tremendous thrill*": *San Francisco Chronicle*, July 1, 1927.

"*We could clearly distinguish*": Ibid.

"*I forgot all about it*": *San Francisco Examiner*, July 1, 1927.

"*Yes, sir*": *San Francisco Chronicle*, June 29, 1927.

"*If Moffett doesn't leave*": Ibid.

"*Attaboy! Go get 'em, Ernie*": *San Francisco Examiner*, June 29, 1927.

"*Let's go anyway*": Ibid.

"*dropping a crate of eggs*": Ernie Smith, "I Was a Hero," transcribed by Paul Conant, *Popular Aviation*, October 1939, 65.

"*like jumping off a table*": Ernie Smith, "Ocean Flights Are the Bunk," *Popular Aviation*, January 1931, 23.

"*flying gas truck*": Ibid.

"*We'll make it yet*": *Bakersfield Californian*, June 28, 1927.

"*It was all simply unfortunate*": *San Francisco Examiner*, July 6, 1927.

"*It's too late now*": *San Francisco Examiner*, June 29, 1927.

"*I'm going home*": Ibid.

"*cold feet*": *San Francisco Examiner*, July 6, 1927.

"*If he wanted to proceed*": Ibid.

"*We're not going to quit*": *San Francisco Chronicle*, June 29, 1927.

"*I'll make a definite decision*": *San Francisco Examiner*, June 29, 1927.

"*Night flying over charted country*": Beryl Markham, *West with the Night* (Boston: Houghton Mifflin, 1942), 9.

"*You can't expect any news*": *San Francisco Examiner*, June 30, 1927.

"*Say, whoever named*": *San Francisco Examiner*, June 29, 1927.

"*That Ernie Smith has sand*": Ibid.

"*those pinpoint islands*": *San Francisco Chronicle*, June 30, 1927.

"*No alternative but death*": Lindbergh, *Spirit of St. Louis*, 355.

"*I've lost command*": Ibid., 354.

"*Wake up*": Libby, "Maitland and Hegenberger," 109.

"*We had plenty of gas*": *Orange County (CA) Register*, January 1, 1986.

"*The morning light struck*": *San Francisco Chronicle*, July 11, 1927.

"*We fully expected to find*": Ibid.

"*Hegenberger, old kid*": *San Francisco Chronicle*, June 30, 1927.

"*How about a cigarette*": *Bakersfield Californian*, June 29, 1927.

"I'm hungry": Oxnard (CA) Daily News, June 29, 1927.

"best navigator": Maitland, Knights of the Air, 323.

"Our dream of a lifetime": San Francisco Examiner, June 30, 1927.

"old-type compass": R. F. Hegenberger, "'Bird of Paradise,'" 16.

"Our compass is what": San Francisco Chronicle, June 30, 1927.

"Soldiers and civilians in tuxedos": San Francisco Chronicle, July 11, 1927.

"YOU HAVE ADDED": San Francisco Examiner, June 30, 1927.

"YOUR ACHIEVEMENT WILL GIVE CONFIDENCE": Honolulu Star-Bulletin, June 29, 1927.

"Please let's have some sleep": San Francisco Examiner, June 30, 1927.

"Tan I tum in": Ibid.

"They've arrived": Ibid.

"My boy's aid to science": San Francisco Chronicle, June 30, 1927.

"Gee—I bet those boys": Ibid.

"Oh! Isn't that wonderful": Bakersfield Californian, June 29, 1927.

"Long ago": San Francisco Chronicle, July 12, 1927.

"Well, mother, I guess we": San Francisco Chronicle, June 30, 1927.

"It was an awfully long night": Ibid.

"the happiest day": San Francisco Chronicle, July 1, 1927.

"unquestionably one of the greatest": Horvat, "Bird of Paradise," 31.

"the most perfectly organized": Maurer, Aviation, 260.

"If ranked in terms": Air Corps News 11, no. 9, Information Division, US Army Air Corps, Washington, DC.

"Grace seemed less concerned over": Millikin, "Dick Grace," 138.

"look as flat as yesterday's": San Francisco Examiner, July 13, 1927.

"I'm mighty glad you're back": San Francisco Chronicle, July 13, 1927.

"I'm glad you made it, Les": Ibid.

"Greetings to San Francisco": Ibid.

"Boats and trains": San Francisco Chronicle, July 11, 1927.

"Hello, Dad. Hello, Mother": San Francisco Chronicle, July 13, 1927.

"Not Penelope herself": Ibid.

"These boys are leaders": Ibid.

"They shook dice with death": Ibid.

"Your heroic flight": San Francisco Chronicle, July 16, 1927.

"In spite of the fact": San Francisco Chronicle, July 12, 1927.

"So there is a $35,000": Rose Anne Schalski to James Dole, 27 May 1927, MJP.

"I didn't know": Honolulu Advertiser, July 13, 1927.

"This is a free country": San Francisco Chronicle, June 27, 1927.

"I never wanted to race": Lindbergh, Spirit of St. Louis, 191.

"I still want to fly": Woodland (CA) Daily Democrat, July 1, 1927.

"As far as I'm concerned": Article, unknown origin and date, in scrapbooks celebrating flight to Hawaii by Ernest Smith and Emory Bronte, Steven F. Udvar-Hazy Center, Smithsonian National Air and Space Museum.

"I had looked the plane": Horvat, Above the Pacific, 71.

"I think Ernie": San Francisco Chronicle, July 15, 1927.

"friend, only": Oakland (CA) Tribune, July 14, 1927.

"*I'm not a bit afraid*": *San Francisco Chronicle*, July 15, 1927.

"*It'll help to keep*": Ibid.

"*Don't watch the instrument board*": Article, unknown origin and date, Smith and Bronte scrapbooks.

"*You fellows sure have been*": *San Francisco Chronicle*, July 15, 1927.

"*do anything rash*": *San Mateo (CA) Times*, July 14 1927.

"*lissome and trim*": *San Francisco Chronicle*, July 15, 1927.

"*Hold your breath*": *Oakland (CA) Tribune*, July 14, 1927.

"*You're not downhearted*": Ibid.

"*More fog*": City of Oakland flight log, July 14–15, 1927, SFO Museum.

"GOING STRONG": *San Francisco Chronicle*, July 15, 1927.

"*Looking ahead at the unbroken*": Lindbergh, *Spirit of St. Louis*, 197.

"*There was nothing to do*": Smith, "Ocean Flights," 24.

"*felt like I was hit*": Ibid.

"WE ARE GOING TO LAND": *San Francisco Chronicle*, July 16, 1927.

"*The way I worked*": Smith, "Ocean Flights," 24.

Thank God, it was all: Smith, "I Was a Hero," 42.

"*one of the old army*": Smith, "Ocean Flights," 58.

"*He couldn't speak any English*": *San Francisco Chronicle*, July 29, 1927.

"*Boy, doesn't that dust*": Margaret Shelgren, "Emory Bronte: Pioneer Pacific Navigator," *Air Line Pilot*, April 1979, 48.

"FORCED LANDING NEAR RADIO STATION": *San Francisco Chronicle*, July 16, 1927.

"*But it wasn't possible*": *Bakersfield Californian*, July 16, 1927.

"*We saw the kiawe*": Ibid.

"*We believed we faced*": Ibid.

"*I am a navigator*": Ibid.

"*There wasn't a drop*": *San Francisco Chronicle*, July 17, 1927.

"*Whether they went to Honolulu*": Ibid.

"*Darling: You have all*": *San Francisco Chronicle*, July 16, 1927.

"*Dearest: Hard trip*": *San Francisco Chronicle*, July 17, 1927.

"*That sounds just like Ernie*": Ibid.

"*Reached Hula land*": *San Francisco Call*, July 16, 1927.

"*Well, here we are*": *San Francisco Chronicle*, July 16, 1927.

"*We made the flight*": *San Francisco Chronicle*, July 17, 1927.

"*parades, banquets, dizzy offers*": Smith, "I Was a Hero," 43.

"*Not only are you aviators*": *San Francisco Chronicle*, July 30, 1927.

"*We may have been heavenly*": Ibid.

"*I'm a good loser*": *San Francisco Chronicle*, November 23, 1927.

"*All I can say is*": *San Francisco Chronicle*, July 29, 1927.

"*I want to go back*": Ibid.

Part III: The Dole Derby

"*The first time I saw*": *Valencia County (NM) News-Bulletin*, January 18, 2003.

"*do anything*": Art Goebel's 13 Black Cats business card, Arthur C. Goebel Papers.

"I cannot express the feelings": Art Goebel, *Art Goebel's Own Story: With an Introduction and Annotated Bibliography for the 21st Century Edition* (self-pub., 1929; repr. ed. G. W. Hyatt, self-pub., Davis-Monthan Field Register, 2007), 6, https://dmairfield .com/Goebel_Book_Free_Download.pdf.

"I had something now": Ibid., 7.

"Maybe it was without doors": Ibid., 9.

"In no other work": Ibid., 14.

"The next time": *Los Angeles Times*, August 18, 1927.

"The air is the only place": *Orlando Sentinel*, February 21, 2016.

"I've always wanted to fly": *San Francisco Chronicle*, June 23, 1927.

"Oh how I missed": *The Flying Schoolma'am and The Dole Birds* (San Francisco: Bulletin, 1927), 19.

"extremely attractive": *Flint (MI) Journal*, April 11, 1976.

"She wore short dresses": Ibid.

"Finally we went": *Flying Schoolma'am*, 24.

"After we began rushing": Richard DuRose, *Shooting Star: The First Attempt by a Woman to Reach Hawaii by Air* (self-pub., CreateSpace, 2011), 13.

"I told Mildred": *Honolulu Advertiser*, August 10, 1927.

"I have all the confidence": DuRose, *Shooting Star*, 36.

"I was so thrilled": *(Honolulu, HI) Nippu Jiji*, August 22, 1927.

"I would never have thought": *Flying Schoolma'am*, 17.

"I simply desire": *Flint (MI) Journal*, April 6, 1976.

"One by one the other fellows": Newspaper article, unknown origin and date, MJP.

"It was a thrill": Newspaper article, unknown origin and date, MJP.

"I had never considered flying": Martin Jensen to Herb Wetenkamp, 4 September 1977, MJP.

"until the island": *Maui News*, October, 27, 1965.

"I was carrying passengers": *Honolulu Advertiser*, August 18, 1967.

"When I am flying over": Martin Jensen, account of his flying activities in 1926 and 1927, MJP.

"I spent several sleepless nights": Martin Jensen, "Aloha: 1927 Air Races Across the Pacific, Oakland, Calif., to Honolulu, Hawaii," *Sport Aviation*, June 1967, 19.

"What kind of a ship": *San Francisco Examiner*, July 13, 1927.

"Down the runway": Ibid.

"Please keep out of airplanes": William Randolph Hearst Sr. to William Randolph Hearst Jr., telegram, 24 July 1927, Bancroft Library, University of California, Berkeley.

"We're going in to win": *San Francisco Chronicle*, July 16, 1927.

"Stack of Wheats": Al Stump, "The Great Airplane Massacre," *True*, December 1958, 122.

"While we were passing over": Newspaper article, unknown origin and date, MJP.

"We are going to do": Ted Dealey, "The Dallas Spirit: The Last Fool Flight," *Southwestern Historical Quarterly* (July 1959): 18.

"While I was plowing through": Ibid., 20.

"The worst part of the trip": Ibid.

"We were shaken about": DuRose, *Shooting Star*, 39.

"Auggie stepped on the gas": *Flint (MI) Journal*, April 6, 1976.

"We stayed in Mount Clemens": Ibid.

"We will be the first": DuRose, *Shooting Star*, 43.

"We are not going down": Ibid., 45.

"Everything is going fine": Ibid., 43.

"Although she photographs remarkably": Ibid., 48.

"We threw them off": Thomas Van Hare, "The Disaster Derby," *Historic Wings*, August 17, 2012, http://fly.historicwings.com/2012/08/the-disaster-derby/.

"She's a pretty girl": Du Rose, *Shooting Star*, 48.

"I'm going to leave": *Honolulu Advertiser*, June 16, 1927.

"It had no wheels": Martin Jensen, account of his flying activities in 1926 and 1927, MJP.

"God bless that darling wife": Newspaper, unknown origin, August 6, 1927, SFPL.

"boning up": Newspaper article, unknown origin and date, MJP.

"My wife is waiting now": Newspaper article, unknown origin and date, SFPL.

"I don't know—I'd like": Ibid.

"Wanted, Navigator to fly": Jensen, "Aloha," 19.

"Night and day": *San Jose (CA) Evening News*, August 15, 1927.

"This race should be": Newspaper article, unknown origin and date, MJP.

"Pacific Flyer, with 'Lone Eagle'": Ibid.

"Your number, Jack": Newspaper article, unknown origin and date, MJP.

"the fat boy from Texas": *San Jose (CA) Evening News*, August 15, 1927.

"Stands for In Addition": Ibid.

"If Auggy gets sleepy": Ibid.

"a bundle of optimism": Stump, "Great Airplane Massacre," 122.

"I have two advantages": Ibid.

"I admire Auggy": *Flying Schoolma'am*, 22.

"caught in a social whirl": *San Jose (CA) Evening News*, August 15, 1927.

"Miss Doran was a lady": *Flint (MI) Journal*, April 16, 1976.

"Why is it people": *Flying Schoolma'am*, 22.

"I'm not a bit worried": Newspaper article, unknown origin and date, MJP.

"They represent dead scalps": *Los Angeles Examiner*, August 17, 1927.

"get a firm grip": Jensen, "Aloha," 20.

"I will go for the glory": R. H. Scheppler, "Aloha," *Air Classics*, unknown month 1976, 51.

"Will you take me": Newspaper article, unknown origin and date, Arthur C. Goebel Papers.

"Girls and aviation": Ibid.

"We all wanted a crack": W. V. Davis Jr., "A Long Trail with No Dust," *Aerospace Historian*, December 1975, 181.

"Their price for the [plane]": Davis, "Long Trail," February 1928 draft, Woolaroc Museum, Bartlesville, OK.

"Hear you're flying to Honolulu": Ibid.

"entirely too dangerous": *San Francisco Examiner*, August 6, 1927.

"That old story that Lloyd's": Newspaper article, unknown origin and date, MJP.

"Their mishap comes": *San Francisco Chronicle*, unknown date, MJP.

"This flight is something different": *Flint (MI) Journal*, August 11, 1927.

"The planes and participants": Ibid.

"nothing short of suicide": Hugh A. Studdert Kennedy, "The Dole Air Race to Hawaii," *Outlook*, August 24, 1927, 534.

"*I am not writing much*": H. E. MacConaughey to James Dole, 10 August 1927, Robert Scheppler Papers.

"*He said if it were*": Ibid.

"*Let those who are ready*": *San Francisco Examiner*, August 12, 1927.

"*We may go anyway*": *Honolulu Star-Bulletin*, August 11, 1927.

"*It doesn't matter much*": *Honolulu Advertiser*, August 12, 1927.

"*preparation is part*": *San Francisco Chronicle*, August 12, 1927.

"*Did you say I can't*": *San Francisco Examiner*, August 12, 1927.

"*As a matter of fact*": Ibid.

"*In this way the responsibility*": *San Francisco Chronicle*, June 24, 1927.

"*With the usual oft-mentioned*": MacConaughey to Dole, August 10, 1927.

"*highly pleased with her appearance*": Davis, "Long Trail," 182.

"*in a blur of impressions*": Davis, "Long Trail," February 1928 draft.

"*The compass had to be*": Ibid.

"*I was finally forced*": Ibid.

"*I am glad that*": Ibid.

"*I could feel them slip*": *San Francisco Bulletin*, August 16, 1927.

"*And if you do*": Martin Jensen, account of his flying activities in 1926 and 1927, MJP.

"*I now christen you, Aloha*": Jensen, "Aloha," 20

"*Tell the people of Hawaii*": *Honolulu Star-Bulletin*, August 16, 1927.

"*My wife did it all*": Newspaper article, unknown origin, August 6, 1927, SFPL.

"*gay and nonchalant spirit*": Newspaper article, unknown origin and date, MJP.

"*When I get to Honolulu*": Newspaper article, unknown origin and date, MJP.

"*When we get over*": Ibid.

"*Please have the executives*": Ibid.

"*I expect to make this flight*": Ibid.

"*and having my life's ambition*": Ibid.

"*I don't know just how*": Ibid.

"*No, I won't keep*": *Honolulu Advertiser*, August 16, 1927.

"*My daughter is not yellow*": DuRose, *Shooting Star*, 37.

"*Scared? Sure*": Davis, "Long Trail," February 1928 draft.

"*The greatest race*": *Flying Schoolma'am*, 34.

"*All San Francisco*": *San Francisco Chronicle*, August 17, 1927.

"*The Department of Commerce*": *Los Angeles Evening Herald*, August 15, 1927.

"*I'm a homing pigeon*": *San Francisco Examiner*, August 18, 1927.

"*The biggest kick I got*": *Honolulu Advertiser*, August 22, 1927.

"*We finally wormed through*": Davis, "Long Trail," 182.

"*I just went to the president*": *San Francisco Examiner*, August 16, 1927.

"*Who could do such*": Ibid.

"*Anyone who interferes*": Newspaper article, unknown origin and date, MJP.

"*Afraid? Hmm, not a bit*": *Honolulu Star-Bulletin*, August 9, 1952.

"*feel a bit different*": *San Francisco Examiner*, August 18, 1927.

"*dancing lights*": Ibid.

"*scared to death*": Ibid.

"*I should say not*": *Los Angeles Examiner*, August 17, 1927.

"Why, of course, I'll doll": Ibid.

"I tried to sleep": San Francisco Examiner, August 18, 1927.

"What are your last words": San Francisco Bulletin, August 17, 1927.

"I really will be glad": Oakland (CA) Tribune, August 17, 1927.

"I'll be so glad": Ibid.

"I'm taking this with me": Ibid.

"I think I've received": Ibid.

"If we have to use": Flying Schoolma'am, 11.

"I'm tickled to death": Honolulu Star-Bulletin, August 9, 1952.

"Don't you wish": Newspaper article, unknown origin and date, MJP.

"beautiful, well-designed ships": Jack Northrop, interview in We Saw It Happen (United Technologies, 1953), documentary film, Steven F. Udvar-Hazy Center, Smithsonian National Air and Space Museum, Washington, DC.

"The excitement gradually heightened": Davis, "Long Trail," 182.

"I would rather have crashed": Los Angeles Times, August 17, 1927.

"I would like the Tribune": Oakland (CA) Tribune, August 17, 1927.

"It was an emotional day": Martin Jensen, account of his flying activities in 1926 and 1927, MJP.

"Dearest Old Big Boy": San Francisco Examiner, August 16, 1927.

"The Miss Doran, the Miss Doran": Los Angeles Times, August 17, 1927.

"Motor trouble": Ibid.

"It was a great thrill": San Francisco Examiner, August 18, 1927.

"Now don't let it": Ibid.

"I didn't want": San Francisco Bulletin, August 17, 1927.

"I hope we can get": San Francisco Examiner, August 18, 1927.

"No! No": San Francisco News, August 17, 1927.

"Scared—frightened?": Ibid.

"Please let me alone": Ibid.

"The damned ship was burning": Oakland (CA) Tribune, August 15, 1927.

"I guess we can go ahead": San Francisco Examiner, August 18, 1927.

"We can't": Dealey, "Dallas Spirit," 24.

"We'll be goddamned lucky": Ibid.

"Don't look Mr. Dealey": Ibid., 23.

"Well, by God": Ibid., 24.

"Now it's impossible for me": Newspaper article, unknown origin and date, MJP.

"We'll make it this time": San Francisco Examiner, August 18, 1927.

"There was plenty of time": Over Land and Sea: The Story of the Woolaroc, commemorative booklet held by (and likely produced by) the Woolaroc Museum, Bartlesville, OK, 1929, 10.

"SEVEN HOURS OUT": Newspaper article, unknown origin and date, Robert Scheppler Papers.

"the long hours of darkness": C. M. Daniels, "The Great Dole Derby," Wings, April 1983, 49.

"The sun went down": Over Land and Sea, 10.

"I prayed in my heart": Daniels, "Great Dole Derby," 49.

"I happened to have": Kansas City Star, October 16, 1977.

"crude affairs": Honolulu Advertiser, August 18, 1927.

"When [the oil] emptied": Los Angeles Illustrated Daily News, August 18, 1927.

"If we were in a spin": Dwiggins, Barnstormers, 76.

"I knew this instrument": Jensen, "Aloha," 21.

"Which way from here": Dwiggins, *Barnstormers*, 84.

"It was deadly": Ibid.

"All races in the territory": San Francisco Examiner, August 18, 1927.

"Kauai's boydom is what might": Honolulu Star-Bulletin, August 15, 1927.

"I'm confident Martin will be": Honolulu Star-Bulletin, August 17, 1927.

"I am glad the flight": Honolulu Advertiser, August 17, 1927.

"At first the stars": Los Angeles Times, October 23, 1927.

"I heard the noise": Honolulu Advertiser, August 18, 1927.

"It was only the suspense": Ibid.

"cold, dark and forbidding looking": Davis, "Long Trail," 183.

"I don't believe anyone": Davis, "Long Trail," 184.

"a bit pissed": Art Goebel, transcript of remarks presumably made at an aviation banquet in Kansas City, MO, 1964, Woolaroc Museum, Bartlesville, OK.

"Are you sure": Mike Stock, "Destination: Honolulu," *Foundation*, Fall 2012, 25.

"2 hours": Davis, "Long Trail," 184.

"We were in a funny": Honolulu Advertiser, August 18, 1927.

"I saw Molokai": Honolulu Star-Bulletin, August 18, 1927.

"A more beautiful sight": Davis, "Long Trail," 184.

"Here we are": Honolulu Star-Bulletin, August 22, 1927.

"Was I happy": Honolulu Advertiser, August 18, 1927.

"Honolulu looked deserted": Davis, "Long Trail," 184.

"I banged on the cowling": Stock, "Destination: Honolulu," 25.

"Say, folks, it certainly is": Honolulu Star-Bulletin, August 9, 1952.

"Honest, gosh, do you mean": Newspaper article, unknown origin and date, MJP.

"God bless you": Burl Burlingame, *Honolulu Star-Bulletin,* January 5, 2004, part of "The Pineapple King's Great Pacific Air Race," a three-part series, also published December 29, 2003, and January 12, 2004.

"Oh boy! We did it": San Francisco News, August 17, 1927.

"I'm mighty happy, boys": Newspaper article, unknown origin and date, MJP.

"We didn't have a bit": New York Times, August 18, 1927.

"I wanted to fly": Honolulu Advertiser, August 18, 1927.

"Why man, that wasn't": Davis, "Long Trail," 184.

"This was going to be": Jensen, "Aloha," 21.

"You can now sit down": Martin Jensen, account of his flying activities in 1926 and 1927, MJP.

"For God's sake don't do": Kansas City Star, October 16, 1977.

"Martin Jensen, where the hell": Kansas City Times, September 4, 1964.

"I'm sorry to keep you": San Francisco News, August 17, 1927.

"As [the] two greeted each": Honolulu Advertiser, August 18, 1927.

"I'm certainly glad to see": Los Angeles Illustrated Daily News, August 18, 1927.

"That's fine! Now for the other": New York Times, August 18, 1927.

"I will not rest": Honolulu Advertiser, August 19, 1927.

"In the light of what": San Francisco Examiner, August 19, 1927.

"I tell you it makes": Honolulu Star-Bulletin, August 18, 1927.

"I think we will pick": Ibid.

"Everything all fixed up fine": Ibid.

"There never was a girl": Ibid.

"It was terrible": *San Francisco News*, August 17, 1927.

"I have not given up": *Flint (MI) Journal*, August 18, 1927.

"I'll be glad when": Ibid.

"My boy will turn up": *Los Angeles Times*, August 19, 1927.

"some schooner without radio apparatus": Ibid.

"Gordon would come out": Ibid.

"Dear Mil: I experienced": *Flint (MI) Journal*, August 19, 1927.

"Oh Bill, that's the best": Ibid.

"It's very good of you": Dealey, "Dallas Spirit," 25.

"Well, Captain Erwin": Ibid.

"Tomorrow begins the great adventure": Dealey, "Dallas Spirit," 22.

"LOVE TO MA": Dealey, "Dallas Spirit," 26.

"Orgy of reckless sacrifice": Assorted editorials quoted in "Counting the Cost of Stunt Flying," *Literary Digest*, September 3, 1927, 10.

"It is stunt flying": Newspaper article, unknown origin and date, SFPL.

"One automatically begins to exclaim": "Counting the Cost," 10.

"If Mildred Doran is today": *Flint (MI) Journal*, September 18, 1927.

"I believe that all pioneers": *Flint (MI) Journal*, unknown date.

"God Bless You Every One": Untitled document regarding Dole Air Race, Woolaroc Museum, Bartlesville, OK.

"miles upon miles": Lesley N. Forden, "Part II: The Dole Race," *American Aviation Historical Society Journal* 20 (1975): 265.

"Motor missing. All hope gone": Newspaper article, unknown origin, March 9, 1932, SFPL.

"The expenses turned out": *Honolulu Advertiser*, October 28, 1965.

"It was a rough landing": *San Francisco Examiner*, September 20, 1927.

"When I asked him": Ibid.

"But I never flew him": *Honolulu Advertiser*, October 28, 1965.

"I sometimes wish": *San Francisco Bulletin*, December 8, 1927.

"Hawaii's complete pineapple experience": Dole Plantation (website), www.dole plantation.com.

"I had no idea": Dole and Dole Porteus, *Story of James Dole*, 89.

"Anybody who thinks": Smith, "Ocean Flights," 22.

BIBLIOGRAPHY

Books

American Council of Learned Societies. *Dictionary of American Biography*. New York: Scribner, 1936.

Benton, Thomas Hart. *Thirty Years View; or, A History of the Working of the American Government for Thirty Years, from 1820 to 1850 [. . .]*. Vol. 2. New York: D. Appleton, 1854.

Dick, Ron, and Dan Patterson. *Aviation Century: The Golden Age*. Boston: Boston Mills, 2004.

Dole, Richard, and Elizabeth Dole Porteus. *The Story of James Dole*. Aiea, HI: Island Heritage, 1990.

DuRose, Richard. *Shooting Star: The First Attempt by a Woman to Reach Hawaii by Air*. Self-published, CreateSpace, 2011.

Dwiggins, Don. *The Barnstormers: Flying Daredevils of the Roaring Twenties*. New York: Grosset & Dunlap, 1968.

The Flying Schoolma'am and The Dole Birds. San Francisco: Bulletin, 1927.

Forden, Lesley. *Glory Gamblers: The Story of the Dole Race*. Alameda, CA: Nottingham, 1986.

Goebel, Art. *Art Goebel's Own Story: With an Introduction and Annotated Bibliography for the 21st Century Edition*. Self-published, 1929. Reprint edition edited by G. W. Hyatt, self-published, Davis-Monthan Field Register, 2007. https://dmairfield.com/Goebel_Book_Free_Download.pdf.

Gwynn-Jones, Terry. *Wings Across the Pacific: The Courageous Aviators Who Challenged and Conquered the Greatest Ocean*. New York: Orion Books, 1991.

Horvat, William J. *Above the Pacific*. Fallbrook, CA: Aero, 1966.

Lindbergh, Charles A. *The Spirit of St. Louis*. New York: Scribner, 1953.

Maitland, Lester J. *Knights of the Air*. Garden City, NY: Doubleday, Doran, 1929.

Markham, Beryl. *West with the Night*. Boston: Houghton Mifflin, 1942.

Maurer, Maurer. *Aviation in the U.S. Army, 1919–1939*. Washington, DC: Office of Air Force History, US Air Force, 1987.

McCullough, David. *The Wright Brothers*. New York: Simon & Schuster, 2015.

Messimer, Dwight R. *No Margin for Error: The U.S. Navy's Transpacific Flight of 1925*. Annapolis, MD: Naval Institute Press, 1981.

Over Land and Sea: The Story of the Woolaroc. Commemorative booklet held by (and likely produced by) the Woolaroc Museum, Bartlesville, OK, 1929.

Phillips, Edward H. *Travel Air: Wings Over the Prairie*. Eagan, MN: Flying Books International, 1994.

San Francisco in the 1930s: The WPA Guide to the City by the Bay. Federal Writers Project of the Works Progress Administration. Berkeley: University of California Press, 2011.

Scheppler, Robert H. *Pacific Air Race*. Washington, DC: Smithsonian Institution Press, 1988.

Taylor, Albert Pierce. *Under Hawaiian Skies*. Honolulu: Advertiser, 1922.

Travel Air Manufacturing Co. *The Story of Travel Air: Makers of Biplanes and Monoplane*. Los Angeles: Periscope Film, 2013.

Van Deurs, George. *Wings for the Fleet: A Narrative of Naval Aviation's Early Development. 1910–1916*. Annapolis, MD: Naval Institute Press, 2016.

Wynne, H. Hugh. *The Motion Picture Stunt Pilots and Hollywood's Classic Aviation Movies*. Missoula, MT: Pictorial Histories, 1987.

Articles

"Avigation." *American Speech*, August 1928.

"Avigation and Avigator." *American Speech*, October 1928.

Connell, Byron J. "The Flight That Failed." *MIT Technology Review* 28, no. 1 (November 1925).

"Counting the Cost of Stunt Flying," *Literary Digest*, September 3, 1927.

Daniels, C. M. "The Great Dole Derby." *Wings*, April 1983.

Davis, W. V., Jr. "A Long Trail with No Dust." *Aerospace Historian*, December 1975.

Dealey, Ted. "The Dallas Spirit: The Last Fool Flight." *Southwestern Historical Quarterly*, July 1959.

Forden, Lesley N. "Part II: The Dole Race." *American Aviation Historical Society Journal* (Winter 1975).

Geoghegan, John J. "Nonstop to Hawaii by Air and Sea." *Aviation History*, March 2014.

Grace, Dick. "Crashing Planes for the Movies." *Modern Mechanics and Inventions*, July 1930.

Hegenberger, A. F., and Bradley Jones. "Oversea Navigation." *SAE Journal* 21, no. 6 (December 1927).

Hegenberger, Albert. "The Importance of the Development of Aerial Navigation Instruments and Methods to the Air Service." Unpublished article, September 1, 1923. Biographic and technical files, Smithsonian National Air and Space Museum, Washington, DC.

Hegenberger, Robert F. "'The Bird of Paradise': The Significance of the Hawaiian Flight of 1927." *Air Power History*, Summer 1991.

Horvat, William J. "Bird of Paradise: The First Non-Stop Flight to Hawaii." *Aerospace Historian*, June 1968.

Jensen, Martin. "Aloha: 1927 Air Races Across the Pacific, Oakland, Calif., to Honolulu, Hawaii." *Sport Aviation*, June 1967.

Kennedy, Hugh A. Studdert. "The Dole Air Race to Hawaii." *Outlook*, August 24, 1927.

Kurutz, Gary F. "Triumph and Tragedy over the Pacific: The 1927 Dole Air Race." California State Library Foundation bulletin, no. 93, 2009.

Libby, Justin. "Lester Maitland and Albert Hegenberger; and the First Nonstop Flight to Hawaii." *American Aviation Historical Society Journal* (June 2010).

Maitland, Lester. "Planes Across the Sea." *Liberty*, December 17, 1927.

Millikin, Eugene J. "Dick Grace and His Waterhouse Cruzair." *American Aviation Historical Society Journal* (Summer 1979).

Moore, John Hammond. "The Short, Eventful Life of Eugene B. Ely." *Proceedings Magazine*, January 1981.

Rodgers, John. "My Acquaintance with the Wrights." *Slipstream*, January 1926.

Shelgren, Margaret. "Emory Bronte: Pioneer Pacific Navigator." *Air Line Pilot*, April 1979.

"Sky Pilot." *Time*, July 22, 1957.

Smith, Ernie. "I Was a Hero." Transcribed by Paul Conant. *Popular Aviation*, October 1939.

Smith, Ernie. "Ocean Flights Are the Bunk." *Popular Aviation*, January 1931.

Stock, Mike. "Destination: Honolulu." *Foundation*, Fall 2012.

Stump, Al. "The Great Airplane Massacre." *True*, December 1958.

Van Hare, Thomas. "The Disaster Derby." *Historic Wings*, August 17, 2012. http://fly .historicwings.com/2012/08/the-disaster-derby/.

Newspapers

Bakersfield Californian

Battle Creek (MI) Enquirer

Berkeley (CA) Gazette

Flint (MI) Journal

Hawaii Hochi

Honolulu Advertiser

Honolulu Star-Bulletin

Kansas City Star

Kansas City Times

Los Angeles Evening Herald

Los Angeles Examiner

Los Angeles Illustrated Daily News

Los Angeles Times

Maui News

New Freedom (HI)

New York Times

(Honolulu, HI) Nippu Jiji

Oakland (CA) Tribune

Omaha (NE) Bee

Orange County (CA) Register

Orlando Sentinel

Oxnard (CA) Daily News

San Francisco Bulletin

San Francisco Call

San Francisco Chronicle

San Francisco Examiner

San Francisco News

San Jose (CA) Evening News

San Mateo (CA) Times
Valencia County (NM) News-Bulletin
Washington Post
Woodland (CA) Daily Democrat

Notable Museums, Archives, Libraries, Papers, and Collections

Arthur C. Goebel Papers. Seaver Center for Western History Research. Natural History Museum of Los Angeles County, Los Angeles.
Hiller Aviation Museum, San Carlos, CA.
Louis A. Turpen Aviation Museum and Gallery. SFO Museum, San Francisco.
Martin Jensen Papers. American Heritage Center. University of Wyoming, Laramie.
National Museum of the United States Air Force, Dayton, OH.
National Naval Aviation Museum, Pensacola, FL.
Robert Scheppler, private papers, Chesterfield, MO.
San Francisco Public Library
Sloan Museum, Flint, MI.
Smithsonian National Air and Space Museum, Washington, DC.
Woolaroc Museum, Bartlesville, OK

Government Reports and Publications

Air Corps News 11, no. 9. Information Division. US Army Air Corps, Washington, DC.
Student personnel file, John Rodgers. US Naval Academy, Annapolis, MD.
US Navy West Coast–Hawaii Flight Report. 1925. National Naval Aviation Museum, Pensacola, FL.

Newsreels

"Aircraft PN-9 Taxis in Water and Comes Up to the Seaplane Ramp HD Stock Footage." YouTube video. Filmed 1925. Posted by CriticalPast, May 2, 2014. www.youtube.com/watch?v=Q1UgZv4ELj4.
"A Real Hair Raising Affair (1926)." YouTube video. Posted by British Pathé, April 13, 2014. www.youtube.com/watch?v=gNuZMD4zuLQ.

Sources of Photographs

California History Room. California State Library, Sacramento.
Hawaii Department of Transportation, Honolulu, HI.
National Museum of the United States Air Force, Dayton, OH.
Naval History and Heritage Command, Washington, DC.
San Diego Air and Space Museum.
Woolaroc Museum, Bartlesville, OK.

INDEX